The Protest Hand

The Protest Handbook

Tom Wainwright
Barrister, Garden Court Chambers

Anna Morris
Barrister, Garden Court Chambers

Katherine Craig
Solicitor, Christian Khan

Owen Greenhall
Barrister

Bloomsbury Professional

Bloomsbury Professional Ltd, Maxwelton House, 41–43 Boltro Road, Haywards Heath, West Sussex, RH16 1BJ

© Bloomsbury Professional Ltd 2012
Bloomsbury Professional, an imprint of Bloomsbury Publishing plc

A CIP Catalogue record for this book is available from the British Library.

ISBN: 978 1 84766 981 0

Typeset by Columns Design XML Ltd, Reading
Printed and bound in Great Britain by Martins the Printers, Berwick upon Tweed

Foreword

Dissent is not disloyalty but a natural, noble and potentially powerful tradition. In this country it has played an important role in achieving social and political change – the extension of the franchise to all men and then to women, the establishment of the welfare state, the consolidation of union rights – and in resisting unjust laws – the poll tax being an obvious example. Abroad we have seen dictators toppled by the sheer force of numbers in the street.

Of course, it is rare for public demonstration alone to immediately or directly achieve its goals. The diversity of concerns people feel compelled to contest and the likelihood that, if some support a cause strongly enough to protest, it is almost certain that others will take an equally strong contrary view, make that unlikely.

At the very least however, is a vital pressure valve in any society. It allows those with keenly felt opinions on an issue – particularly, but not exclusively, those that are not promoted or prioritised by any of the mainstream political parties – to express them and in so doing to feel validated, vindicated or at least noticed. But one might argue that protest means even more. It is as important a part of our democratic system as the electoral process. Both are routes by which ideas can be promoted and debated. But while formal parliamentary politics is coordinated and constrained by party discipline and the search for the centre ground, protest is by its nature messy and disruptive. For this reason too many in authority can come to see it as an irritant in need of control.

The forms of even wholly non-violent protest are so wide and varied that those seeking to control it have at times resorted to creating quite specific offences to deal with a particular tactic. In 1994 Parliament created the offence of 'aggravated trespass' as a means of restraining hunt saboteurs. But an offence created in response to one type of protest can be used in other situations as well. So we have seen the same law used against UK Uncut protesters who staged a protest in Fortnum and Masons during the TUC's *March for the Alternative* in March 2011. Similarly, over-broad laws that were not created with protest especially in mind can have their original intent twisted for use against protesters. The Protection from Harassment Act 1997, designed to address the problem of stalking, has been employed by large companies to injunct those protesting against controversial developments.

But it is not all bad news. With the passage of the Human Rights Act 1998 a positive right to protest has for the first time been established in the United

Kingdom. Law, policy and action that unjustifiably interferes with the right to protest can be challenged as incompatible with the rights guaranteed by Articles 10, freedom of expression, and 11, freedom of assembly. At last we have a yardstick that those who would curtail protest can be measured against.

But the law remains a labyrinth both for those who organise and take part in demonstrations and for those who must advise them. It is therefore a pleasure to welcome a book such as this; one that compendiously sets out the law relevant to protest. It will no doubt become a standard resource for campaigners and their advisers. Those that are well-informed will be better able to challenge the actions of the police and others who overstep the mark and seek to suppress the hard-won democratic right to peaceful dissent.

Shami Chakrabarti and James Welch, Liberty
(the National Council for Civil Liberties)

March 2012

Preface

The idea of writing a book on the law of protest had been mooted for some years, but it was the wave of protests caused by the Conservative/Liberal Democrat Coalition policies which brought the issue to the fore. People who had never protested before took to the streets. Students, public sector workers, those who were incensed by government cuts and those who were outraged about the profligacy of the bankers. Frustration at broken promises, a lack of accountability and simple unfairness prompted a wide range of people to stand up and make their voices heard.

It was noticeable when writing this book that the same activists and legal representatives appeared in numerous cases over the years, more often perhaps than occurs in any other area of law. Whether or not one agrees with the particular cause being espoused at any given time, one must admire the determination of individuals who are willing to put themselves forward and challenge the boundaries of free expression and association time and again. Similarly, the dedication of the radical lawyers who doggedly fight such cases regularly, often for little or no remuneration, should be recognised.

In the recent wave of protests however, different names and faces appeared. People who were unfamiliar with the new reality of the policing of demonstrations and certainly unfamiliar with the court system. However, while many of those taking part were often new to protests, those policing them were not. The risks faced by protestors remain very real. Protestors who tirelessly campaign on a single issue are at risk of being labelled by the state as 'domestic extremists', and subject to invasive intelligence gathering. Public order policing tactics which were once rare are now used as a matter of routine. Demonstrators are filmed, contained and asked for personal details with little, if any, explanation of their legal rights. Where the two clash, the matters often end up in court where, thanks to the slashing of criminal legal aid, protestors often have to represent themselves. Even where legal assistance is available lawyers, who may be unfamiliar with this niche area of law, have to grapple with some of the most complex legal issues—encompassing police powers, human rights, criminal law and even elements of land law and the legality of administrative action—without a guide to see them through.

The aim of this book is to redress the balance. It is intended to promulgate the aspects of the law that those involved in protests will most commonly encounter and to share the expertise that we, as practitioners, have in the area. First, an understanding of police powers is essential, both for the protestor on the ground faced with a police demand and for the lawyer considering whether an officer has exceeded his powers. Second, given the cuts in availability of legal aid, an explanation of the court process is necessary for those who are arrested and must represent themselves. Third, the most common criminal offences faced by protestors are set out both so that demonstrators are able to identify that which is unlawful and regulate their actions accordingly and further, so that if matters do result in criminal proceedings, all the relevant authorities and arguments are gathered together in one easily accessible guide. Fourth, a guide on the law on 'occupations' is set out, again to advise and inform those who wish to register their protest in this way. Finally, the various methods of redress are explained so that when the State or their agents intrude into and impede the right to protest, steps can be taken to ensure that they do not do so again in the future.

The authors would like to thank the following:

- the clerks at Garden Court Chambers—particularly Colin Cook and Keith Poynter—for their patience;

- Henry Blaxland QC, Rajeev Thacker, Tim Baldwin, Liz Davies, Sarah Hemingway and David Renton for their input and advice on particular topics;

- the rest of Garden Court Chambers for the inspiration they provide, having fought a great number of the cases mentioned throughout the book: 'Do Right, Fear No-one!';

- all at Christian Khan for their ongoing commitment to representing individuals and communities against the state;

- Pippa Payne, Chris Jordan, Lauren Roth de Wolf and Gemma Hall for not being lawyers and for all their support and encouragement;

- special thanks must go to Thomas Stoate, Frances Trevena and Maha Sardar for all their research and hard work;

- Kiran Goss and all the staff at Bloomsbury Professional for all their hard work and enthusiasm for our ideas and for their flexibility with deadlines;

- finally, enormous thanks must go to those activists who have fought for the right to protest through the courts, often at great personal cost.

We have endeavoured to state the law as correct and up to date as of the 31st January 2012.

Regular updates will be provided at www.theprotesthandbook.com

Tom Wainwright
Anna Morris
Katherine Craig
Owen Greenhall
March 2012

Contents

Contents

Table of cases

Table of cases

E

F

G

H

I

J

K

Table of cases

S

T

U

W

Table of cases

Table of statutes

Table of statutory instruments

Table of statutory instruments

Chapter 1

Powers, rights and procedure

1.1 This chapter will set out what powers the police have prior to and during demonstrations and the criteria which must be fulfilled before those powers are exercised. As a result, it will also explain what protesters are and are not obliged to do: when they have to answer police questions; whether they are allowed to wear balaclavas or facial coverings; when the police can take their photograph and vice versa. If police officers exceed their powers this may give rise to actions for damages or other civil remedies and may provide a defence to some of the offences set out in Chapter 3. Finally, this chapter will set out the procedures which should take place at the police station if protesters are arrested. Often, decisions are made and steps are taken at this stage, which have a profound bearing on the likely success of any future proceedings.

POLICE POWERS AT PROTESTS

Power to ban, or impose conditions on protests

1.2 This part sets out the powers granted to police by legislation which are commonly used to control protests. For further common law powers see 'Power to take action short of arrest: 'kettling''[1].

1.3 Police powers in relation to protests sometimes differ depending upon which of two forms the protest takes. Unless specified otherwise:

- a 'public procession' means a body of persons moving along a route in a public place;

- a 'public assembly' means an assembly of two or more people in a public place which is wholly or partly open to the air.

---

1 Para **1.130** ff.

1.4 *Powers, rights and procedure*

1.4   A 'public place' for these purposes is any highway[2] or any place to which, at the material time:

- the public or any section of the public has access;

- on payment or otherwise;

- as of right or by virtue of express or implied permission.

Advance notice of protests

1.5   The first way in which State control can be exercised over a protest is by requiring notification under the Public Order Act 1986 (POA 1986), s 11. This legislation requires that written notice be given of any proposal to hold a public procession which is intended:

(a)   to demonstrate support for or opposition to the views or actions of any person or body of persons; or

(b)   to publicise a cause or campaign; or

(c)   to mark or commemorate an event.

1.6   The notice must specify:

- the date when it is intended to hold the procession;

- the time when it is intended to start;

- the proposed route;

- the name and address of the person (or one of the persons) proposing to organise it.

It must be delivered at least six clear days before the procession is due to start, to a police station in the police area in which it is proposed the procession will start. If done within this time period it may be sent by recorded delivery but will only count as being received from when it is actually delivered[3]. If notification within this time is not reasonably practicable, it should be delivered by hand as soon as is possible.

1.7   The European Court of Human Rights has found that requiring notice of protests will not automatically contravene the right to freedom of association[4]. Where the need to protest is so urgent that there is no time to provide notice, then it may be disproportionate for the police to break up a

---

2   See para **3.190**.
3   POA 1986, s 11(5).
4   European Convention on Human Rights, Article 11.

peaceful demonstration simply on the basis that no notice has been given[5]. However, what counts as 'urgent' has been viewed restrictively and it has been said that it covers only special cases, such as where any delay will render the protest obsolete[6]. Such cases will be very rare under the UK legislation as it would have to be necessary not only for the protest to take place immediately but also for it to take the form of a procession, as opposed to an assembly which does not require advance notice.

1.8 The organisers of a procession may commit an offence if the notice requirements are not satisfied or the date, start time or route differ from that in the notice[7].

1.9 The reasons set out at para **1.5** are broadly drawn and would seem to cover most, if not all, reasons for protesting. It would not cover, for example, a mass cycle ride held for the joy of cycling[8]. If disputed, a court would seek to infer from the nature of any chanting or placards etc what the purpose of the procession was.

1.10 Notice does not have to be given if either:

● it is not reasonably practicable to give any advance notice of the procession; or

● the procession is one commonly or customarily held in the police area (or areas) in which it is proposed to be held[9].

1.11 To be 'commonly or customarily' held, a procession must be the same procession as one or ones previously held. The fact that a procession follows a different route on each occasion will not prevent it being the same procession. Each case will turn on its own facts. The relevant factors which meant that the 'Critical Mass' bike rides in London were 'commonly held' were that on each occasion:

● it was made up of cyclists;

● it started at the same place on the same day and time each month;

● it took place in the Metropolitan Police Area;

● the participants shared a common intention;

● it was recognised and publicised by a single name: 'Critical Mass';

---

5   *Bukta v Hungary* [2007] ECHR 25691/04; *Aldemir v Turkey*, ECtHR, 18 December 2007.
6   *Molnar v Hungary*, ECtHR, 7 October 2008, para 38.
7   See para **3.131** ff.
8   *Kay v Commissioner of Police for the Metropolis* [2008] UKHL 69, [2008] 1 WLR 2723, [2009] 2 All ER 935, para 29.
9   POA 1986, s 11(2).

- it chose its route on a follow-my-leader basis[10].

As a result notice was not required.

1.12   Where there is no advance planning and/or no organisers, it is clearly not reasonably practicable to give advance notice. In those circumstances, the House of Lords observed that s 11 cannot apply[11]. Where the plan is for the protest to follow a spontaneous route, the law is not yet decided. The House of Lords expressed the view that either no notice needs to be given as it is not practicable to do so, or the notice needs to say that the route will be spontaneous[12].

Imposing conditions on protests

1.13   Conditions can be imposed on a protest if the 'senior police officer' reasonably believes that either:

(a)   it may result in serious public disorder, serious damage to property or serious disruption to the life of the community; or

(b)   the purpose of the persons organising it is the intimidation of others with a view to compelling them not to do an act they have a right to do, or to do an act they have a right not to do[13].

1.14   In relation to (a), it is not necessary that the protesters who are subjected to conditions have any intention or wish to cause these consequences, it may instead be the likely result of a counter-demonstration[14]. However, such cases should be very rare indeed[15].

1.15   Where the assembly or procession is being held, or people are assembling with a view to taking part in a procession, the 'senior police officer' who may impose the conditions is the most senior in rank of the police officers present at the scene and reasons for the order do not have to be given. Otherwise, the senior police officer is the chief officer of police, in which case the order must be in writing and the reasons outlined[16].

---

10   *Kay v Commissioner of Police for the Metropolis*, para 16.
11   *Kay v Commissioner of Police for the Metropolis*, paras 22, 69.
12   *Kay v Commissioner of Police for the Metropolis*, paras 25, 43, 52.
13   POA 1986, s 12 in relation to processions; s 14 in relation to assemblies.
14   *R (on the application of Brehony) v Chief Constable of Greater Manchester* [2005] EWHC 640 (Admin), para 16.
15   *Austin & Saxby v Commissioner of Police of the Metropolis* [2005] EWHC 480 (QB), [2005] HRLR 20, para 97.
16   *R (on the application of Brehony) v Chief Constable of Greater Manchester*, para 17.

1.16   The conditions which may be imposed on those organising or taking part in a *procession* under the POA 1986, s 12 include but are not limited to:

- conditions as to the route of the procession;

- prohibiting the procession from entering any public place specified in the directions.

1.17   The conditions which may be imposed on those organising or taking part in an *assembly* under the POA 1986, s 14 are limited to:

- conditions as to the place at which any assembly may be (or continue to be) held;

- the maximum duration of any assembly;

- the maximum number of persons who may constitute an assembly.

1.18   Conditions cannot be imposed under s 14 setting out the route to and from an assembly, although designated entrance and exit points for the assembly could be included[17]. Conditions could not be imposed under s 12 setting out the route to and from an assembly where the route in question was 800 yards from a disembarkation point to the assembly itself[18]. This will depend upon the circumstances, however, as it was clear in that case that the walk to the demonstration point was not itself part of the protest. In protests where there is a march followed by a static demonstration this may not be the case.

1.19   The officer must have regard to the time, place and circumstances of the protest and the route of any procession. Clearly, he must also have regard to the rights to freedom of expression and freedom of association of those taking part[19]. The conditions imposed must appear to the officer to be necessary to prevent the disorder, damage, disruption or intimidation which he foresaw. The officer will be allowed a margin of appreciation[20] but if his decision is unreasonable, and particularly if there is an unjustified interference with the protesters' rights under the European Convention on Human Rights, civil remedies may be available and any criminal proceedings arising from protesters breaching the order may be challenged.

---

17   *Director of Public Prosecutions v Jones* [2002] EWHC 110 (Admin).
18   *Director of Public Prosecutions v Jones* [2002] EWHC 110 (Admin).
19   European Convention on Human Rights, Articles 10 and 11.
20   *R v Ministry of Defence, ex p Smith* [1996] QB 517 at 554E.

> 'Conditions which are so demanding that they amount in effect
> to a ban are an improper use of the power and so are unlawful on
> ordinary public law principles'[21].

1.20   Therefore, although the power to impose conditions may be imposed to limit the duration of an assembly and so effectively bring it to an end, it would seem that it must be allowed to operate for a reasonable period beforehand.

1.21   The organisers of a protest and people who take part in a protest may commit an offence if they knowingly fail to comply with a condition imposed, as may someone who incites another to fail to comply with a condition[22].

Prohibiting protests

1.22   A protest can be banned if the chief officer of police[23] reasonably believes that:

- **in relation to processions**[24], because of particular circumstances existing in a particular area, the power to impose conditions will not be sufficient to prevent the holding of public processions in that area from resulting in serious public disorder;

- **in relation to assemblies**[25]:

    (a)   it is intended to hold an assembly of 20 or more people on land in the open air to which the public has no right of access (or only a limited right of access, ie only for a particular purpose); and

    (b)   the assembly is likely to be held without the permission of the occupier of the land **or** is likely to conduct itself in such a way as to exceed:

    —   the limits of any occupier's permission; or

    —   the limits of the public's right of access;

---

21   D Feldman, *Civil Liberties and Human Rights in England and Wales* (2nd edn, 2002) p 1063, cited with approval in *Austin & Saxby v Commissioner of Police of the Metropolis* [2005] EWHC 480 (QB), [2005] HRLR 20, para 92.

22   See para **3.131** ff.

23   In the City of London, the Commissioner of Police for the City of London. In the Metropolitan Police District, the Commissioner of Police of the Metropolis. In either case, the task can be delegated to an Assistant Commissioner of Police. Outside of London the powers can be delegated to an Assistant Chief Constable.

24   POA 1986, s 13.

25   POA 1986, s 14A.

and

(c)   the assembly may result in either:

— serious disruption to the life of the community; or

— significant damage to the land (or a building or monument on it) which is of historical, architectural, archaeological or scientific importance.

1.23   In those circumstances, the officer may apply to the District Council for the area in question, for an order prohibiting the holding of all (or a class of) public processions or 'trespassory assemblies' in the area concerned for a specified period[26]. The specified period cannot exceed three months for processions or four days for assemblies. The area concerned cannot exceed that of a circle with a five mile radius in relation to assemblies. The Secretary of State may then consent to the order being made by the council as requested or with amendments. Such an order must be made in writing or recorded in writing as soon as possible thereafter.

1.24   Obviously, the public body making the order must have regard to the rights to freedom of association and expression[27] of those who wish to take part in the protest. As well as the usual countervailing considerations of public order etc, in relation to 'trespassory assemblies' those rights will have to be weighed against the rights of land owners to a private life and peaceful enjoyment of possessions[28]. The officer or public body will be allowed a margin of appreciation but if the decision is arbitrary[29], and particularly if as a result there is an unjustified interference with the protesters' rights under the European Convention on Human Rights (ECHR), civil remedies may be available and any criminal proceedings arising from protesters breaching the order may be challenged.

1.25   A peaceful assembly on the highway which did not block the public's right of way did not exceed the limits of the public's right of access[30]. It could not, therefore, be covered by an order prohibiting trespassory assemblies.

1.26   The organisers of a protest and people who take part in a protest may commit an offence if they know it has been prohibited, as may someone who incites another to knowingly take part in a prohibited protest[31].

---

26   In the City of London or Metropolitan Police District the relevant officer may make the order himself with the Secretary of State's consent.
27   European Convention on Human Rights, Articles 10 and 11.
28   European Convention on Human Rights, Article 8 and Protocol 1 Article 1.
29   See for example, *Makhmudov v Russia* [2007] ECHR 35082/04.
30   *Director of Public Prosecutions v Jones* [1999] 2 AC 240.
31   See para **3.131** ff.

1.27   If an order has been made in relation to trespassory assemblies and a uniformed officer within the specified area reasonably believes that someone is on his way to a trespassory assembly, he may stop that person, and direct him not to proceed in the direction of the assembly[32]. It is an offence to fail to comply with such a direction, knowing it has been given. Note that the direction can be not to proceed 'in the direction of' the assembly and therefore a person could still commit the offence by continuing in the same direction, without intending to join, or actually joining, the group in question.

Demonstrations around Parliament Square, London

1.28   Different rules apply to static demonstrations in the area around the Houses of Parliament in London, which began in order to deal with the protest by Brian Haw in this area between 2001 and 2011. As of 30 March 2012, the previous regime set up under the Serious Organised Crime and Police Act 2005 (SOCPA 2005), ss 132–138 will have been completely repealed and replaced with the Police Reform and Social Responsibility Act 2011 (PRSRA 2011), ss 141–149 which started to have effect from 19 December 2011. Any challenge to the PRSRA 2011 should bear in mind that the restrictions imposed by the SOCPA 2005 system were found to be justified in *Rai & Evans v UK*[33]. This does not necessarily mean that prosecution and conviction for breaching the restrictions will always be justified.

1.29   Under the PRSRA 2011:

- the **controlled area** is the central garden in Parliament Square and the immediately adjoining footways;

- the **prohibited activities**[34] are:

    (a)   operating any amplified noise equipment (including loudspeakers and loudhailers)[35];

    (b)   erecting or keeping erected any tent or temporary residence[36];

    (c)   using any tent or other such structure for the purpose of sleeping or staying in that area;

---

32 POA 1986, s 14C.
33 Applications No's 26258/07 and 26255/07, 17 November 2009.
34 Unless done for police, fire and rescue authority or ambulance purposes, or by or on behalf of specified public bodies. Any byelaws which concern these activities in this area will no longer have effect.
35 Unless specifically authorised under PRSRA 2011, s 147.
36 Specifically 'any other structure that is designed, or adapted, (solely or mainly) for the purpose of facilitating sleeping or staying in a place for any period'.

(d)   placing, keeping in place or using any sleeping equipment[37] with a view to it being used for the purpose of sleeping overnight in that area (whether or not by the person placing it or keeping it in place).

1.30   A police officer or authorised officer[38] who has reasonable grounds for believing that a person is doing (or is about to do) a **prohibited activity** in the **controlled area** may direct them to stop (or not start) the activity[39]. Such a direction lasts for 90 days unless a shorter time is specified. It is an offence punishable by a £5,000 fine to not comply with such a direction without a reasonable excuse. It is immaterial whether a prohibited activity began before or after 19 December 2011 when the sections came into force.

1.31   A police officer[40] may seize and retain an item if it appears to that officer that the item is being, or has been, used in connection with the commission of such an offence and may use reasonable force in order to do so. Such an item must be returned within 28 days unless criminal proceedings have begun against someone within 28 days, in which case the item must be returned after the proceedings have concluded unless it is forfeited by the court.

1.32   Conditions can be imposed on assemblies in the area under the provisions of the POA 1986, s 14[41]. This includes assemblies which began or were being organised prior to 30 March 2012.

Dispersal directions

1.33   Another way in which the police can bring some demonstrations to an end is by making a dispersal direction under the Anti-social Behaviour Act 2003 (ASBA 2003), s 30.

1.34   If a superintendant or officer of higher rank has reasonable grounds for believing that:

- the presence or behaviour of groups of two or more people (including the behaviour of one member of a group);

- in any public place in that police officer's police area;

- has resulted in any members of the public being intimidated, harassed, alarmed or distressed; and

---

37   'Sleeping bag, mattress or similar': PRSRA 2011, s 143(7).
38   A person so authorised by the Greater London Authority or Westminster City Council.
39   A direction to stop includes a direction not to start again.
40   Or authorised officer if the item is within Parliament Square.
41   PRSRA 2011, s 141.

- that anti-social behaviour is a significant and persistent problem in that police area,

then the officer may give an authorisation under this section, to have effect for up to six months.

1.35 The authorisation must be in writing, must be signed by the relevant officer giving it, and must specify:

- the police area;

- the grounds on which the authorisation is given;

- the period for which the authorisation is to have effect.

An authorisation requires the consent of the local authority and must be publicised locally before it takes effect.

1.36 **If** an authorisation has been given and a constable in uniform or a PCSO has reasonable grounds for believing that:

- the presence or behaviour of a group of two or more persons (including the behaviour of one member of a group);

- in any public place in that police area;

- has resulted, or is likely to result, in any members of the public being intimidated, harassed, alarmed or distressed,

then he may give one or more of the following directions, namely:

(a) a direction requiring the people in the group to disperse (either immediately or by such time as he may specify and in such way as he may specify);

(b) a direction requiring any of those people whose place of residence is not within that police area to leave the police area or any part of the police area (either immediately or by such time as he may specify and in such way as he may specify);

(c) a direction prohibiting any of those people whose place of residence is not within the police area from returning to the police area or any part of the police area for such period (not exceeding 24 hours) from the giving of the direction as he may specify.

1.37 Such a direction cannot be given to those engaged in peaceful picketing in contemplation or furtherance of a trade dispute, where the place of business in question is nearby[42] or those who are taking part in a public procession as defined in the POA 1986, s 11[43] where either notice has been given or does not have to be given. Anyone who knowingly contravenes such a direction may commit an offence punishable by three months' imprisonment and/or a £2,500 fine.

1.38   In *R (on the application of Singh) v Chief Constable of the West Midlands*[44] it was confirmed that any authorisation or direction would have to be properly justified on an objective basis. It was also said that 'it is only when the behaviour of a group of people moves beyond legitimate protest and into the realms of behaviour that causes actual or likely intimidation, harassment, alarm and distress that an officer can use an authorisation to direct them to disperse'[45]. However, this fails to acknowledge that legitimate protest may cause intimidation, harassment, alarm and distress.

1.39   Police are entitled to use powers under a s 30 order against protesters even when the protest was not the original reason for the order being made[46].

Power to require removal of facial coverings

1.40   The police have the power[47] to require the removal of 'disguises' if either:

- a s 60 ('stop and search') authorisation[48] is in force in the area at the time; or

- a s 60AA authorisation has been given.

1.41   A s 60AA authorisation can only be given by an officer of the rank of inspector or higher, in relation to an area within that officer's police area and only if he reasonably believes that:

- activities may take place in that area; and

- those activities are likely (if they take place) to involve the commission of offences; and

- the authorisation is expedient, in order to prevent or control the activities.

---

42   See the Trade Union and Labour Relations (Consolidation) Act 1992, s 220.
43   See para **1.5**.
44   [2006] EWCA Civ 1118, [2006] 1 WLR 3374, [2007] 2 All ER 297.
45   At para 92.
46   *Singh v Chief Constable of the West Midlands* (ibid).
47   Criminal Justice and Public Order Act 1994, s 60AA, inserted by the Anti-terrorism, Crime and Security Act 2001, s 94(1).
48   See para **1.105**.

1.42   A s 60AA authorisation must be for a specified period not exceeding 24 hours. If offences have taken place during that time which have been (or are reasonably suspected to have been) committed in connection with the 'activities' for which the order was granted and it is expedient to do so, the order can be extended for a further 24 hours by a superintendant.

1.43   The authorisation must be in writing and signed by the officer giving it and must specify the grounds on which it is given, the locality in question and the specified time period. The area covered by the authorisation should not be wider than is necessary.

1.44   If such an order is in place a constable in uniform may require someone to remove an item if he reasonably believes that person is wearing an item wholly or mainly for the purpose of concealing his identity. Failing to remove such an item when required to do so may be a criminal offence[49].

1.45   An officer may seize an item if he reasonably believes a person is wearing it, or intends to wear it, wholly or mainly for the purpose of concealing his identity. There is no power to stop and search for disguises, but an officer may seize a disguise which happens to be discovered when exercising a power of search for something else.

1.46   The requirements under the Police and Criminal Evidence Act 1984 ('PACE 1984') Codes of Practice that govern searches do not apply to a request to remove a facial covering under s 60AA and therefore an officer making a request does not have to give his name, police station or his reasons for making the request[50]. The Notes for Guidance to the Codes state:

> 'Many people customarily cover their heads or faces for religious reasons—for example, Muslim women, Sikh men, Sikh or Hindu women, or Rastafarian men or women. A police officer cannot order the removal of a head or face covering except where there is reason to believe that the item is being worn by the individual wholly or mainly for the purpose of disguising identity, not simply because it disguises identity. Where there may be religious sensitivities about ordering the removal of such an item, the officer should permit the item to be removed out of public view. Where practicable, the item should be removed in the presence of an officer of the same sex as the person and out of sight of anyone of the opposite sex'[51].

---

49 See para **3.149** for defences.
50 *Director of Public Prosecutions v Avery* [2001] EWHC Admin 748, [2002] 1 Cr App Rep 31.
51 PACE 1984, Code of Practice A, Note for Guidance 4.

Power to take photographs

1.47 Police have the specific power to take photographs of individuals:

- arrested;

- detained by PCSOs;

- given a fixed penalty notice;

- given a direction to leave a locality under the Violent Crime Reduction Act 2006, s 27[52].

1.48 This can be done without the person's consent and using reasonable force if necessary. The officer can require the removal of an item or substance covering the whole or part of the head or face in order to take the photograph. The purpose and grounds for taking the photograph must be provided, together with an explanation of the purposes for which it may be used, disclosed or retained. A record must be made including this information[53].

1.49 The Notes for Guidance to the PACE Codes of Practice state:

'The use of reasonable force to take the photograph of a suspect elsewhere than at a police station must be carefully considered. In order to obtain a suspect's consent and cooperation to remove an item of religious headwear to take their photograph, a constable should consider whether in the circumstances of the situation the removal of the headwear and the taking of the photograph should be by an officer of the same sex as the person. It would be appropriate for these actions to be conducted out of public view'[54].

1.50 Other than in the above circumstances, the extent of the police power to take photographs is not entirely clear, yet a common sight at any major protest in the UK is the presence of 'Forward Intelligence Teams' (FITs) and/or Evidence Gathering Teams (EGTs). These are usually comprised of one or two photographers, acting under the direction of a police officer, filming and/or photographing protesters. The precise scope of their role and function is uncertain and in 2009 Her Majesty's Inspectorate of the Constabulary recommended that this should be clarified[55].

---

52 PACE 1984, s 64A. A complaint that the taking of photographs on and after arrest breached the right to a private life was deemed inadmissible by the Strasbourg Commission in *X v UK* (Application No 5877/72).
53 PACE 1984, Code of Practice D5.12–5.24.
54 PACE 1984, Code of Practice D, Note for Guidance 5F.
55 See 'Adapting to Protest—Nurturing the British Model of Policing' at pp 126–134.

1.51   What is clear is that there is no power to stop a person merely to record their image. There is no power to physically force someone to cooperate with being filmed except in the circumstances set out above. For example, there is no requirement to cooperate with filming whilst being detained in order to be searched.

1.52   There is no requirement therefore that protesters 'cooperate' with FIT filming. There is nothing to prevent a protester from covering their face in order to avoid being filmed, subject to any s 60AA (removal of disguises) authorisation[56] in force.

1.53   Protesters have been arrested for going further and physically blocking FIT cameras but there is no definitive authority on the question of whether or not this is unlawful. Such activists are sometimes charged with obstructing a police officer in the execution of their duty[57]. Whether the actions of FIT officers are lawful, or in the execution of their duty, in a given case will depend in part upon the reasons for and manner of filming and what happens to the images subsequently.

Reasons for filming

1.54   As a matter of common sense, the circumstances in which overt filming can take place should be defined by the objective pursued by such filming. In *Wood v Comr of Police for the Metropolis*[58], Laws LJ found that the police's power to take photographs was 'in accordance with the law' for the purpose of the ECHR on the basis that it derived from their common law powers to prevent and detect crime[59].

1.55   The Metropolitan Police's published policy headed 'The Use of Overt Filming/Photography' which was in place at the time of *Wood* and referred to in the judgment, elaborated further and stated that overt filming is:

> 'a particularly useful tactic to combat crime and gather intelligence and evidence relating to street crime, anti-social behaviour and public order. It may be used to record identifiable details of subjects suspected of being involved in crime or anti-sociable [sic] behaviour such as facial features, visible distinctive marks eg, tattoos, jewellery, clothing and associates for the purposes of preventing and detecting crime and to assist in the investigation for all alleged offences.

---

56 See para **1.40**.
57 See para **3.3** ff.
58 [2010] 1 WLR 123, [2009] 4 All ER 951.
59 At paras 50–55. However, Dyson LJ and Collins LJ do not come to a conclusion on this point and Dyson LJ expressed reservations about Laws LJ's analysis.

This tactic may also be used to record officers' actions in the following circumstances. Maintaining public confidence and to justify police tactics. During incidents where police face substantial levels of violence, immigration arrests, detention of mentally ill persons and actions taken during high profile or critical incidents'[60].

1.56 This policy document has now been replaced by a new policy entitled 'MPS Visual Evidence Policy'. The aims sought to be achieved by overt filming are not set out and there is simply a commitment to ensuring 'the correct authorisation and use of overt filming by police'.

Manner of filming

1.57 The previous Metropolitan Police Policy mentioned above states that:

'To demonstrate to the public that cameras are deployed overtly officers should clearly identify themselves as police officers or police staff and not hide the fact that they are filming. This can be achieved by:

- use of uniformed officers

- use of marked vehicles ...

When a pre-planned deployment is authorised officers must be able to clearly state the reasons for the filming or photography and provide a copy of an explanatory leaflet. These contain details of the purpose of the filming and provide guidance on how members of the public may obtain further information and access to their image'.

1.58 The new Visual Evidence Policy provides no guidance on this point and the Standard Operating Procedure (SOP)[61] associated with the new policy is not currently available under the Metropolitan Publication Scheme.

1.59 Taking photographs in an intrusive or violent manner which causes the subject to feel frightened and distressed is likely to 'grossly violate' the subject's right to a private life under Article 8 of the European Convention on Human Rights[62]. If this took place in the course of a protest then it is likely that the subject's rights to freedom of association and expression under Articles 10 and 11 would be similarly violated.

---

60 'Use of Overt Filming/Photography', Metropolitan Police, 6 April 2005.
61 Standard Operating Procedures support the published policies for the Metropolitan Police.
62 *Wood v Comr of Police for the Metropolis* [2009] EWCA Civ 414 at para 34.

1.60   Even where not done in this manner, the fact that photographs are being taken by the State can engage Article 8. In *Wood*, Article 8 was engaged when:

> 'the Metropolitan Police, visibly and with no obvious cause, chose to take and keep photographs of an individual going about his lawful business in the streets of London'[63].

1.61   Clearly, the circumstances in which the photograph is taken will be highly relevant. The fact that the subject in *Wood* was not protesting at the time his photograph was taken was particularly important. In an application before the European Commission on Human Rights, *Friedl v Austria*[64], it was decided that there was no breach of the right to privacy[65] when police took photographs at a demonstration, partly on the basis that the photographs related to a public incident in which the applicant was voluntarily taking part were solely taken for the purposes of recording the character and factual situation of the manifestation. However, the decisions in *Friedl* and *Wood* also both relied heavily on the State assurances as to what happened to the images subsequently.

What happens to the images subsequently

1.62   In *Friedl*, the Commission attached weight to the Austrian government's assurances that the individual persons on the photographs remained anonymous, the personal data recorded and photographs taken were not entered into a data processing system, and no action was taken to identify the persons photographed on that occasion by means of data processing.

1.63   According to the procedure disclosed in *Wood*, photographs taken by a FIT are stored on a disc at the SCD4(3) Forensic Science Service. They are catalogued by reference to the date and location of the protest. Copies also go to CO11 Public Order Branch where they are sifted for storage on a database. The storage is said to be secure and access restricted. The images are then reviewed on a regular basis to establish whether they have any significant ongoing intelligence value. Images may be placed on spotter cards for use at future demonstrations.

1.64   The previous criteria for retention of images was:

---

63   *Wood v Comr of Police for the Metropolis*, para 45.
64   (1995) 21 EHRR 83.
65   European Convention on Human Rights, Article 8.

'observed or suspected participation in unlawful activity at the event when the pictures were taken, or participation of such activity at an earlier time. Mere presence at a demonstration or other event is not enough'[66].

1.65   The question as to whether 'association' with known or suspected offenders is sufficient for inclusion in the database is a controversial one. A brief conversation with a protester known to have previous convictions was an insufficient justification in *Wood* for retaining the images.

1.66   The SOP was not disclosed to the court in *Wood* and therefore what was not considered was the fact that retention takes place in another form of *de facto* database. The SOP required that after overt filming takes place a Criminal Intelligence Report (CRIMINT) must be completed which includes details of any 'subjects' of the filming. It also notes that 'the details of all images recorded must be recorded on the CRIMINT to enable ... retrieval of images of people by name ...'.

1.67   The images must be reviewed every month to decide if it is appropriate to retain them. Images must always be retained whilst:

- a prosecution is pending or likely;

- they form useful intelligence about persons related to a specific police operation;

- notice of a complaint/civil action is likely.

Otherwise the images must be destroyed.

1.68   The final judgment in *Wood* was that in the circumstances retention beyond a few days was not proportionate as there was no evidence Mr Wood had committed an offence and no good reason to think he would. 'Nevertheless,' the court concluded, 'it is plain that the last word has yet to be said on the implications for civil liberties of the taking and retention of images in the modern surveillance society'[67].

Taking photographs of police officers

1.69   The Metropolitan Police make it clear: 'Members of the public and the media do not need a permit to film or photograph in public places and police

---

66 *Wood v Comr of Police for the Metropolis*, para 11.
67 *Wood v Comr of Police for the Metropolis*, para 100.

have no power to stop them filming or photographing incidents or police personnel'[68].

1.70   There have been reported incidences of the police invoking the Terrorism Act 2000 (TA 2000) to prevent members of the public filming at demonstrations. Officers only have the power to stop and search a person under the TA 2000, s 43 **if** they reasonably suspect that person to be a terrorist. Even then the power only extends to discovering whether that person has in their possession anything which may constitute evidence that they are a terrorist.

> 'Officers do not have the power to delete digital images or destroy film at any point during a search'[69].

1.71   It is an offence under the TA 2000, s 58 to collect or make a record of information of a kind likely to be useful to a person committing or preparing an act of terrorism, or to possess such a record without a reasonable excuse. 'Record' includes a photograph. The photograph would have to be 'designed to provide practical assistance to a person committing or preparing an act of terrorism'[70]. Documents in everyday use would not found an offence[71] and therefore it is unlikely that an arrest for taking photographs of police officers at a protest, without anything more, could be justified.

1.72   Section 58A of the TA 2000 covers the offence of 'eliciting, publishing or communicating information about members of the armed forces, intelligence services or police where the information is, by its very nature, *designed* to provide practical assistance to a person committing or preparing an act of terrorism' (emphasis added).

> 'It would ordinarily be unlawful to use s 58A to arrest people photographing police officers in the course of normal policing activities, including protests because there would not normally be grounds for suspecting that the photographs were being taken to provide assistance to a terrorist'[72].

---

68 www.met.police.uk/about/photography.htm.
69 www.met.police.uk/about/photography.htm.
70 *R v G* and *R v J* [2009] UKHL 13, [2009] 2 WLR 724, [2009] 2 Cr App Rep 4, para 43.
71 *R v Muhammed* [2010] EWCA Crim 227, [2010] 3 All ER 759, para 47.
72 www.met.police.uk/about/photography.htm.

Power to stop, search and seize items

1.73   The police have a wide range of powers to stop and search people deriving from a number of statutes. The most relevant of these provisions, and the conditions which allow the police to carry out a stop and search, are set out below. In addition to the legal requirements that need to be met for a search to be lawful, the PACE Codes of Practice set out guidelines about how searches must be conducted. PACE Code A is the most significant in relation to searches (discussed in more detail below), but there are others that may also be relevant. For example, PACE Code B sets out the guidance for searches of premises by police officers and the seizure of property, whilst Code C contains provisions regarding the conduct of searches at the police station.

1.74   If an officer fails to meet the conditions set out in statute the search will usually become unlawful, and may give rise to a claim against the police (see paras **5.157** and **5.172**). Conversely, a breach of the Codes will not necessarily make the search unlawful, although it may be of assistance in both defending criminal prosecutions or making complaints and bringing civil actions against the police.

Legal requirement for a search

Under PACE 1984, s 2 and PACE Code A3.8 an officer must provide certain information when carrying out most searches, if reasonably practicable to do so. This can be remembered by the acronym **GOWISELY**:

- **G**rounds for the search

- **O**bject of the search

- **W**arrant card must be produced if in plain clothes

- **I**dentify, the PC must inform the suspect of his name

- **S**tation, the police station at which the constable works

- **E**ntitlement to a copy of the search record

- **L**egal power being used for detention

- **'Y**ou are being detained for the purpose of search'

1.75   In criminal proceedings, evidence obtained in the course of an unlawful search is not automatically inadmissible. It will be a matter for the judge or magistrates to consider in the exercise of their discretion under PACE

1984, s 78[73] but an application to exclude such evidence is unlikely to succeed unless the searching officers acted in bad faith or in flagrant disregard of the PACE Codes or the reliability of the evidence has been undermined as a result[74].

1.76   The police cannot require a person to remove more than their outer clothing as part of a search in public. This is defined in PACE Code A3.5 as an outer coat, jacket or gloves. The exception to this is the power to remove facial coverings under the CJPO 1994, s 60AA (see para **1.40**).

1.77   PACE Code A3 sets out how searches must be conducted. All searches that do not result in an arrest should be recorded, electronically or on paper[75], and the person searched is entitled to a copy of such a record provided it is requested within three months from the date of the stop[76]. There are separate provisions for the execution of strip and intimate searches.

1.78   The powers to stop and search fall into two categories:

- those that require an officer to hold a reasonable suspicion that the person is in possession of an item listed in one of the Acts;

- those that do not require such reasonable belief.

1.79   The former category is often referred to as search under suspicion or 'sus' powers. What will, and will not, amount to reasonable suspicion will depend on the circumstances and is an objective test which will not be satisfied simply because an officer honestly (but unjustifiably) believed that the person searched was in possession of an item listed in one of the Acts.

1.80   Whether or not the belief was reasonably held will be judged on the basis of the information the officer had available to him or her at the time. PACE Code A2.2–2.12 contain some useful guidance on the issue, including that reasonable suspicion can never be supported on the basis of personal factors. For example, factors such as race or age are not grounds for suspicion unless these relate to the description of a suspect, and suspicions must rely on intelligence or information about, or some specific behaviour by, the person concerned[77].

---

73 See para **2.98**.
74 See *R v Khan, Sakkaravej and Pamarapa* [1997] Crim LR 508, CA.
75 See PACE Code A4 for details.
76 PACE 1984, s 3 (as amended by the Crime and Security Act 2010, s 1) and PACE Code A3.8(e).
77 Code A, paras 2.2 and 2.3.

1.81   In the context of protests, the latter category of searches, where no reasonable suspicion is required, has afforded the police a broad discretion to stop and search activists and has been the subject of considerable criticism and litigation.

Powers requiring reasonable suspicion: PACE 1984, s 1

1.82   The most commonly exercised power to stop and search in general terms is the power under PACE 1984, s 1, which states that a police officer may stop and search an individual (and their vehicle) for stolen or prohibited articles[78]. The police officer can detain the person for the purposes of the search. If, in the course of the search, the officer discovers an article which he has reasonable grounds for suspecting to be a stolen or prohibited article he may seize it[79].

1.83   A prohibited article is defined in s 1(7) as:

- an offensive weapon; or
- an article:

    (a)   made or adapted for use in the course of or in connection with an offence [listed in s 1(8)]; or

    (b)   intended by the person having it with him for such use by him or by some other person.

1.84   An offensive weapon is 'any article made or adapted for use for causing injury to the person, or intended by the person having it with him for such use or by someone else'[80].

1.85   The offences listed in PACE 1984, s 1(8) include burglary, theft, and—significantly for protest cases—offences under the Criminal Damage Act 1971, s 1 (destroying or damaging property)[81]. The legislation would therefore cover items such as spray paint cans and wire cutters but, as these items also have legitimate purposes, **only if** there is a reasonable suspicion that they are to be used for an offence. Importantly, a police officer will need an honestly held reasonable suspicion to make such a search lawful.

1.86   This power has been used against protesters, and indeed its application has been successfully challenged in the courts. *R (on the application of Morris,*

---

78 PACE 1984, s 1(2).
79 PACE 1984, s 1(6).
80 PACE Code C23.
81 See para **3.70**.

E and T) v Chief Constable of Kent Police[82] was a judicial review of the Kent police's decision to stop and search under PACE 1984, s 1 a number of activists taking part in the 'Climate Change Camp', a protest against the planned development of the Kingsnorth coal-fired power station in Kent. The police argued that they had received intelligence that some protesters were intent on causing damage to the power station, which resulted in the officer in charge of the policing operation issuing a document setting out the approach that the police would adopt to stop-and-searches:

> 'It is my intention therefore to instruct my officers to use the powers conferred by Section 1 of the Police and Criminal Evidence Act 1984 where they have reasonable grounds to suspect that prohibited articles are being carried by ... individuals or vehicles ... that may be used in offences of criminal damage. The intent is to remove these items to prevent unlawful activity'[83].

1.87   The notes for the internal police briefing prior to the event contained additional instructions that were read out to officers. These included the statement that:

> 'Intelligence and information received directly from protesters' website, in the lead up to Climate Camp, that they intend to break the law to attack the Power Station gives police the reasonable grounds'.

1.88   The three claimants successfully argued that in fact there was no reasonable suspicion to stop and search them and that there was a policy to stop and search those who wanted to pass through the police cordon and join the camp, which went beyond the legitimate bounds of a PACE 1984, s 1 stop-and-search[84]. The court found that the multiple stops and searches were unlawful, and amounted to a breach of protesters' Article 8, 10 and 11 rights under the European Convention on Human Rights. In addition to bringing a successful public law challenge in the form of a judicial review, the claimants settled a civil claim for damages.

1.89   By way of contrast, in *R (on the application of Howarth) v Commissioner of Police for the Metropolis*[85] it was held lawful and reasonable to search a train carriage of protesters on their way to a demonstration where officers had reasonable grounds to suspect that members of that group would be carrying items such as chalk intended for use in making marks at an oil refinery

---

82 [2009] EWHC 2264 (Admin).
83 *R (on the application of Morris, E and T) v Chief Constable of Kent Police* [2009] EWHC 2264 (Admin), para 41.
84 *R (on the application of Morris, E and T) v Chief Constable of Kent Police* [2009] EWHC 2264 (Admin), para 42.
85 [2011] EWHC 2818 (QB).

protest, and where criminal damage had taken place in the past, particularly where the level of search was said to be equivalent to that which took place at airports, sporting events and other private facilities. The court made some unhelpful comments for protesters seeking to challenge searches in this context, stating that there was

> 'a significant danger of the law becoming "over precious" ... about minimal intrusions into privacy and alleged indirect infringements of the rights of privacy, assembly and expression which are the price today of participation in numerous lawful activities conducted in large groups of people'.

1.90　　The court further stated that:

> 'Expression and assembly, like those other lawful activities, are nonetheless encouraged and fostered, rather than hindered, by sensible and good natured controls by the authorities and the sensible and good natured acceptance of such controls by members of the public'[86].

1.91　　The court therefore also held that there was no unlawful interference with the claimant's Human Rights under Articles 8, 10 and 11 of the ECHR.

Powers requiring reasonable suspicion: PACE 1984, s 32

1.92　　Section 32 of PACE 1984 confers upon the police the power to search a person after arrest if the constable has reasonable grounds for believing that the arrested person may present a danger to himself or others[87].

1.93　　A person may also be searched after arrest for anything which might:

● 　be used to assist him to escape from lawful custody; or

● 　be evidence relating to an offence[88].

1.94　　In circumstances where someone is arrested for an indictable offence[89], s 32 also confers a power to enter and search any premises in which that person was when arrested, or immediately before he was arrested, for evidence relating to the offence[90]. In those circumstances, the police will not

---

86　At para 41.
87　PACE 1984, s 32(1).
88　PACE 1984, s 32(2)(a).
89　See para **2.7**.
90　PACE 1984, s 32(2)(b).

require a warrant. However, there are limits as to which part of a property can be searched, especially in shared accommodation.

1.95   Searches under s 32 may only be lawfully exercised if the officer has reasonable grounds for believing that there may be concealed (on the person or the premises as appropriate) any item set out in paras **1.93** or **1.94**.

Powers requiring reasonable suspicion: PACE 1984, ss 54 and 55

1.96   Under PACE 1984, s 54 the police have a power to search someone at a police station once they have been arrested, or where they have been committed into custody by an order of a court. A record may be made of the outcome of the search, and this is usually done on the property sheet, which forms part of the custody record[91]. The custody officer is permitted to seize and retain items when someone is going into custody. This can include clothes and personal effects, but only where the custody officer believes that the person from whom they are seized may use them:

- to cause physical injury to himself or any other person;

- to damage property;

- to interfere with evidence;

- to assist him to escape; or

- where the custody officer has reasonable grounds for believing that they may be evidence relating to an offence[92].

1.97   The police can carry out a strip search and require the person searched to remove all their clothing in a police station if it is considered necessary to remove an article which a detainee would not be allowed to keep, and the officer reasonably considers the detainee might have concealed such an article.

1.98   There are specific guidelines set out at PACE Code C11 that regulate the conduct of a strip search. These include:

- a police officer carrying out a strip search must be the same sex as the detainee;

- the search shall take place in an area where the detainee cannot be seen by anyone who does not need to be present, nor by a member of the opposite

---

91 Section 54(2).
92 Section 54(4).

sex except an appropriate adult who has been specifically requested by the detainee;

- detainees who are searched shall not normally be required to remove all their clothes at the same time, eg a person should be allowed to remove clothing above the waist and redress before removing further clothing;

- a strip search shall be conducted as quickly as possible, and the detainee allowed to dress as soon as the procedure is complete.

1.99   An intimate search is defined as the physical examination of a person's body orifices other than the mouth. '[The] intrusive nature of such searches means the actual and potential risks associated with intimate searches must never be underestimated'[93]. The requirements for an intimate search are set out in PACE 1984, s 55. As these searches are unusual following protest-related arrests, the detailed legal requirements have not been set out here.

Powers requiring reasonable suspicion: Misuse of Drugs Act 1971, s 23

1.100   Section 23(2) of the Misuse of Drugs Act 1971 (MDA 1971) gives an officer the power to carry out a search if he has reasonable grounds to suspect that a person is in possession of a controlled drug. Under s 23(4) it is an offence to obstruct an officer in the exercise of his power under this section (similar to obstructing an officer under the Police Act 1996, s 89(2)[94] but with a maximum sentence of two years imprisonment).

Powers not requiring reasonable suspicion: TA 2000, ss 44 and 47A

1.101   Until March 2011, a senior officer could make an authorisation under the TA 2000, s 44 if he considered it 'expedient' for the prevention of acts of terrorism. Such an authorisation allowed the police to stop and search a person or vehicle for articles which could be used in connection with terrorism. The power did not require that the officer had formed any reasonable suspicion.

1.102   However, on 18 March 2011 the Home Secretary made a remedial order, which effectively revoked s 44[95], after a successful application by two protesters to the European Court of Human Rights[96]. The landmark case of *Gillan and Quinton v United Kingdom* ruled that the powers under s 44 were

---

93 PACE Code C, Annex A, para 1.
94 See para **3.3**.
95 Terrorism Act 2000 (Remedial) Order 2011, art 2.
96 *Gillan and Quinton v United Kingdom* (2010) 50 EHRR 45, (2010) 28 BHRC 420.

illegal and that Article 8 of the European Convention on Human Rights had been violated. Mr Gillan and Ms Quinton were stopped in 2003 outside the ExCeL convention centre in London, which at the time was hosting a military equipment exhibition. The court found the powers were 'not sufficiently circumscribed' and lacked 'adequate legal safeguards against abuse'.

1.103   The government has announced that it intends to replace the powers under s 44 with new powers in the Protection of Freedoms Bill, but in the interim they have been limited by the remedial order, providing what the government called 'a more targeted and proportionate power'[97]. The order introduces s 47A into the TA 2000, which sets out that an officer may conduct a stop and search of a vehicle or pedestrian where a senior officer has given an authorisation. The authorisation has to be on the basis that they:

- reasonably suspect that an act of terrorism will take place; and

- consider that:

    (a)   the authorisation is necessary to prevent such an act; and

    (b)   the specified area or place is no greater than is necessary to prevent such an act; and

    (c)   the duration of the authorisation is no longer than is necessary to prevent such an act.

1.104   There are additional specific provisions made for such searches in PACE Code A[98]. Following the decision in *Gillan* it is anticipated that the police are unlikely to use their powers under the Terrorism Act to target protesters, and the legal challenge (brought by campaigning human rights organisation Liberty) was a great victory for the right to protest. However, the reduction of the use of s 44 has seemingly given rise to an increased use of the Criminal Justice and Public Order Act 1994 (CJPO 1994), s 60 in the context of demonstrations.

Powers not requiring reasonable suspicion: CJPO 1994, s 60

1.105   Section 60 of the CJPO 1994 takes a similar format to TA 2000, s 44, in that it requires a prior authorisation by a senior officer, which then allows officers on the street to stop and search at will. The provision was primarily introduced to combat football hooliganism and gang-related violence, but it is increasingly used in the context of protests.

---

97 www.homeoffice.gov.uk/publications/counter-terrorism/terrorism-act-remedial-order/.
98 PACE Code A2.18A–2.26.

1.106   Under the CJPO 1994, s 60 a police officer can stop and search anyone for offensive weapons or dangerous instruments (effectively objects with blades or sharp points) in any area specified by an authorisation granted by an officer of the rank of inspector or above, who reasonably believes:

- that incidents involving serious violence may take place in any locality in his police area, and that it is expedient to give an authorisation under this section to prevent their occurrence; or

- that people are carrying dangerous instruments or offensive weapons in any locality in his police area without good reason.

The exercise of police officers' powers under s 60 is governed by PACE Code A, in particular paras 2.12–2.14A.

1.107   Although the order is originally only valid for 24 hours, it can be authorised on a rolling basis and in practice orders stay in place for much longer. The power has been very widely used, both in terms of its targets and its geographical application. Following the London riots in August 2011, orders were put in place across swathes of London. This was a controversial policing response, as numerous sources, including findings from The Guardian newspaper's 'Reading the Riots' project, indicate that police use of stop and search was a major contributory factor leading to that summer's unrest[99].

1.108   Criticism of the use of the CJPO 1994, s 60 is mounting well beyond the context of protests, as analysis of Home Office data by the London School of Economics and others established that black people are 30 times more likely than white people to be stopped and searched by police in England and Wales[100]. At the time of writing, legal challenges were under way seeking to review both the disproportionate targeting of black people under s 60 powers, and their blanket application in the context of protests.

Power to request information

1.109   The police can approach anybody in the street to seek information from them. There is no statutory provision prohibiting them from doing so, except in the context of arrests, where they must caution before asking questions. Excessive and/or unwarranted requests for information, especially where they are intimidating or repetitive, could amount to harassment and further infringe upon an individual's rights under Article 8 of the European

---

99   www.guardian.co.uk/uk/series/reading-the-riots.
100   www.guardian.co.uk/law/2012/jan/14/stop-search-racial-profiling-police.

Convention on Human Rights[101]. It could also amount to a breach of Articles 10 and/or 11 in the context of demonstrations, certainly where the questioning is prohibitive or acts as a deterrent to participating in legitimate protest.

Common law right to refuse to answer questions

1.110   There is no general duty to cooperate in those circumstances. In the case of *Rice v Connolly*[102] Mr Rice was charged with obstructing a police officer after he refused to answer questions when stopped by the police late at night. In that case, the judge stated that:

> 'It seems to me quite clear that though every citizen has a moral duty or, if you like, a social duty to assist the police, there is no legal duty to that effect, and indeed the whole basis of the common law is the right of the individual to refuse to answer questions put to him by persons in authority, and to refuse to accompany those in authority to any particular place; short, of course, of arrest'[103].

1.111   However, in *Rice v Connolly*, Mr Rice had displayed a 'sarcastic and unhelpful' manner. The judge considered whether the offence might be made out on the basis of the defendant's entire 'attitude and behaviour'. Whilst he saw difficulties in imposing liability on that basis, he stopped short of stating that displaying an uncooperative attitude could never amount to an obstruction.

1.112   The case of *Ricketts v Cox*[104] concerned two men who were approached by police officers who wanted to ask questions about their whereabouts. In this case, the court found that that 'the totality of their behaviour and attitude' amounted to an obstruction of the police officers[105]. However, the defendants' behaviour in this case was certainly considered by the court to be at the extreme end of the scale.

1.113   The court at first instance found that the police approached the men 'in a perfectly proper manner' after which the defendants were 'abusive, uncooperative and positively hostile towards the officers from the outset. They used obscene language, calculated to provoke and antagonise the officers, and ultimately made to walk away from the officers before the completion of their inquiries'.

---

101   See para **3.231**.
102   [1966] 2 QB 414.
103   Para 419.
104   (1982) 74 Cr App Rep 298.
105   Para 301.

1.114   It should also be noted that, in this case, one defendant punched an officer after the officer took hold of his arm. Therefore, whilst this case goes some way towards establishing that a hostile attitude can constitute an offence of obstructing a police officer in the execution of his duty, it cites quite extreme circumstances.

1.115   In *Sekfali v Director of Public Prosecutions*[106] the individuals approached by the police ran off in different directions *'with the intention of impeding their apprehension'* after officers identified themselves and produced a warrant card. This conduct was found to constitute a wilful obstruction, although the court also found that they:

> 'would have been entitled to remain silent and not answer any questions put to them. They could have refused, if they had not been arrested, to accompany the police to any particular place to which they might have been requested by the police to go. They could have said that they had no intention of answering questions and they could, no doubt, have said that as a result they were intent on going on their way and have done so without giving rise to a case which would entitle the court to conclude that in departing they were intending to impede the police officers and obstruct the police officers in the execution of their duty. Had they responded in that way, then it would have been for the police to have decided whether to arrest them …'[107].

1.116   A much clearer distinction can be drawn between exercising a common law right to refuse to answer questions asked by police officers, and intentionally providing them with false information[108]. The case law quite clearly states that providing false answers to questions is capable of amounting to an offence of obstructing a police officer[109].

1.117   Whilst in principle, therefore, a protester can (politely) refuse to engage with an officer and exercise his common law right to refuse to answer questions, there are certain circumstances, including where they display antagonistic behaviour and/or run away, that may result in an arrest for obstructing an officer in the execution of their duty.

---

106   [2006] EWHC 894 (Admin), (2006) 170 JP 393.
107   Para 10.
108   See for example *Rice v Connolly* [1966] 2 QB 414 at para 420.
109   *Dibble v Ingleton* [1972] 1 QB 480.

Common law duty to assist a constable dealing with a breach of the peace

1.118   There exists a slightly obscure common law obligation to assist a constable in dealing with a breach of the peace. It is an offence if:

- a constable saw a breach of the peace committed/anticipated an imminent breach of the peace; and

- there was a reasonable necessity for the constable to call upon the defendant for his assistance; and

- when specifically duly called upon, the defendant, without lawful excuse, refused to do so[110].

1.119   Whilst this power is rarely invoked (and it seems unlikely that the average police officer is aware of its requisite elements) it was raised by the police in the House of Lords in 2008 in *Austin v Commissioner of Police of the Metropolis*[111] which relates to the police's power to contain, or 'kettle', protesters[112]. In light of the fact that breach of the peace is a common issue raised by police in the context of protests it is possible that in future that this will increasingly become part of their repertoire to control protesters.

Police Reform Act 2002, s 50

1.120   Section 50 of the Police Reform Act 2002 (PRA 2002) was introduced in the context of the then government's crackdown on anti-social behaviour. It gives a police officer the power to request someone's name and address in certain circumstances, and make it a criminal offence to refuse to provide such information.

1.121   Section 50(1) of the PRA 2002 sets out that:

> 'If a constable in uniform has reason to believe that a person has been acting, or is acting, in an anti-social manner … he may require that person to give his name and address to the constable'.

1.122   'Anti-social behaviour' is defined in the Crime and Disorder Act 1998, s 1(1)(a) as acting:

---

110   *R v Brown* 174 ER 522, (1841) Car & M 314; *R (on the application of Laporte) v Chief Constable of Gloucestershire Constabulary* [2007] 2 AC 105.
111   [2009] UKHL 5, [2009] 1 AC 564.
112   See para **1.130**.

'in a manner that caused or was likely to cause harassment, alarm or distress to one or more persons not of the same household as himself'.

1.123   It is an offence under s 50(2) to fail to give a name and address when required to do so, or to give a false or inaccurate name or address in response to a requirement under that subsection. This is a summary only offence[113] and the maximum sentence is a fine not exceeding £1,000.

1.124   Leaving aside for one moment the various human rights implications of 'ASBO' legislation as a whole, the use of s 50 to gather intelligence in the context of protests is highly controversial, and increasingly prevalent.

1.125   One of the greatest concerns is that it seemingly equates protest (including peaceful protest) with anti-social behaviour. At the time of writing, a challenge by way of judicial review on the apparent use of s 50 to request details from protesters during a demonstration organised by public sector trade unions in London on 30 November 2011 had been lodged at the Administrative Court.

Stop and account

1.126   A police officer or Police Community Support Officer (PCSO) can stop an individual and ask them to account for themselves. For example, the police may ask someone what they are doing, why they are in an area, where they are going or what they are carrying.

1.127   The legal status of stop and account is ambiguous: it is not a defined power set out in primary legislation, yet its application is recognised by the Home Office, who describe it as 'an important part of on-street policing and constitutes the next step beyond the general conversations officers have with members of the public every day'[114].

1.128   Stop and account should be distinguished from general conversations with an officer which do not count as a stop, for example if they are looking for witnesses, ask a person for general information about an incident or are giving someone directions. There is no power of arrest attached to the failure to answer questions (as there is for the PRA 2002, s 50 above) but a refusal to cooperate may cause an officer to argue that this created reasonable grounds to suspect an individual of an offence, or of being in possession of a prohibited item. Furthermore, as set out above, in certain circumstances a police officer may not even need reasonable suspicion to stop and search an individual.

---

113 See para **2.7**.
114 www.homeoffice.gov.uk/police/powers/stop-and-search/.

1.129   Like with many of the policing tactics listed in this section, there are concerns about stop and account being used to disproportionately target particular sections of the population. At present, and following changes to PACE Code A in 2011 which mean it is no longer a national requirement for officers to record incidents of stop and account, these concerns focus around the use of stop and account in a racially discriminatory nature. The concerns about disproportionate targeting of black and Asian people in the context of stop and account are the subject of a legal challenge before the Administrative Court[115].

Power to take action short of arrest: 'kettling'

1.130   One of the most controversial police tactics in the context of protests is the containment or 'kettling' of protesters. Although not a novel practice (certainly, seasoned activists will talk of repeated containment during the Miners' Strike and Poll Tax demonstrations) its application, intensity and duration have significantly increased in recent years.

1.131   For those who have experienced containment in a police kettle, it is at best frustrating and at worst highly distressing and frightening. Kettles are often accompanied by extreme and coercive police enforcement, such as officers in riot gear equipped with batons and shields. Many protesters have questioned not only the legality of kettling, but also its efficacy, reporting that otherwise peaceful protesters have been aggressively confronted by police in the course of containment causing greater tension and, on occasion, violence.

1.132   Kettling has been considered by the courts in a number of cases, most recently in the Grand Chamber of the European Court of Human Rights (ECtHR)[116]. The courts have by and large favoured the police's position in the majority of cases brought. In doing so, they have afforded police forces a considerable discretion and power to contain protesters in a range of circumstances.

1.133   The courts have been particularly persuaded by the police's argument that they have very few alternatives to cope with (what they term) major disorder, and that of the alternatives that exist many are more invasive and objectionable, such as the use of rubber bullets or water cannons. In addition, the concept of kettling is not judged solely in the context of protests. The police have often cited other public order scenarios in which they would seek to rely on containment in order to convince the court that the tactic should remain available to them. The impact of the 2011 riots has reverberated through much of the legal system, and it is anticipated that large-scale events like this will have

---

115   *Diedrick v Chief Constable of Hampshire* CO/7567/2011.
116   *Austin v United Kingdom*, Application No 39692/09.

influenced (and will continue to influence) the courts' attitude towards public order policing. In short, courts have proven reluctant to altogether remove a tactic from the police arsenal which they consider may be usefully employed in limited circumstances.

1.134   The leading domestic authority on kettling is the House of Lords' decision in *Austin v Commissioner of Police for the Metropolis*[117]. This test case related to the decision of the Metropolitan Police to contain some 3,000 protesters in Oxford Circus for nearly seven hours during a May Day anti-globalisation demonstration in 2001. Protesters were held in the rain with no access to food, water or toilet facilities. The case before the House of Lords focused on two key questions. First, did the containment amount to a deprivation of liberty for the purposes of Article 5 of the European Convention on Human Rights. Second, if it did amount to a deprivation of liberty, could any interference with the right be justified under one of the six exceptions set out in Article 5(1)(a)–(f) of the Convention.

1.135   The court did not specifically address whether the containment was lawful at common law (ie whether it amounted to a false imprisonment), because it was common ground between the parties that the circumstances in which the containment would be lawful at common law were for practical purposes the same as the circumstances in which there would be no violation of Article 5. Therefore if Ms Austin's detention was an unlawful deprivation of liberty contrary to Article 5(1) of the Convention, the finding that this was a lawful exercise of breach of the peace powers[118] at common law could not stand, and vice versa.

1.136   Article 5(1) sets out that:

> 'Everyone has the right to liberty and security of person. No one shall be deprived of his liberty save in the following cases and in accordance with a procedure prescribed by law:

> (a)   the lawful detention of a person after conviction by a competent court;

> (b)   the lawful arrest or detention of a person for non-compliance with the lawful order of a court or in order to secure the fulfilment of any obligation prescribed by law;

> (c)   the lawful arrest or detention of a person effected for the purpose of bringing him before the competent legal authority of reasonable suspicion of having committed an offence or when it

---

117   [2009] UKHL 5.
118   See para **1.178**.

is reasonably considered necessary to prevent his committing an offence or fleeing after having done so;

(d)   the detention of a minor by lawful order for the purpose of educational supervision or his lawful detention for the purpose of bringing him before the competent legal authority;

(e)   the lawful detention of persons for the prevention of the spreading of infectious diseases, of persons of unsound mind, alcoholics or drug addicts, or vagrants;

(f)   the lawful arrest or detention of a person to prevent his effecting an unauthorized entry into the country or of a person against whom action is being taken with a view to deportation or extradition'.

1.137   The first question, namely whether Article 5 was engaged in the first place when the protesters in Oxford Circus were kettled, was answered by the House of Lords in the negative, and therefore they did not need to proceed to consider whether any of the exceptions under Article 5(1)(a)–(f) applied to this case[119].

1.138   Indeed, on a common sense and literal reading of the concept of a 'deprivation of liberty' one may be forgiven for believing that being contained for a period of seven hours, without the choice to leave, procure the bare necessities such as food or water, or access sanitary facilities seems a clear cut example of such a deprivation. Certainly there have been much less severe circumstances in which a deprivation of liberty was found to have taken place.

1.139   So how could the court find that these circumstances did not amount to a deprivation of liberty? The answer lies in Article 2 of the Fourth Protocol to the European Convention on Human Rights. Article 2 of the Fourth Protocol provides for a right to freely move within a country once lawfully there and for a right to leave any country. Article 2 Protocol 4 sets out that:

'1 Everyone lawfully within the territory of a State shall, within that territory, have the right to liberty of movement and freedom to choose his residence.

2 Everyone shall be free to leave any country including his own.

3 No restrictions shall be placed on the exercise of these rights other than such as are in accordance with law and are necessary in a

---

119 *Austin v Commissioner of Police for the Metropolis* [2009] UKHL 5, see Lord Hope (para 38) and Lord Neuberger (para 60).

democratic society in the interests of national security or public safety, for the maintenance of "ordre public", for the prevention of crime, for the protection of health or morals, or for the protection of the rights and freedoms of others.

4 The rights set forth in paragraph 1 may also be subject, in particular areas, to restrictions imposed in accordance with law and justified by the public interest in a democratic society'.

1.140   Ms Austin's containment was held to be a restriction on her freedom of movement, not a deprivation of her liberty. Crucially, Article 2 Protocol 4 has not been ratified by the United Kingdom, and therefore the government is neither bound nor legally answerable through the courts, for any breaches of this right.

1.141   In finding that there was no deprivation of liberty, the court started by examining the paradigm position on deprivation of liberty, confirming that in the circumstances of close confinement in a prison cell there is 'no room for argument'[120]. However, outside of that unambiguous example, the court stated that:

> 'the absolute nature of the right requires a more exacting examination of the relevant criteria. There is a threshold that must be crossed before this can be held to amount to a breach of Article 5(1). Whether it has been crossed must be measured by the degree or intensity of the restriction'[121].

1.142   The case often considered to have the clearest exposition of those relevant criteria is *Guzzardi v Italy*[122] which has been repeatedly cited and endorsed in subsequent cases:

> 'In order to determine whether someone has been "deprived of his liberty" within the meaning of Article 5, the starting point must be his concrete situation and account must be taken of a whole range of criteria such as the **type, duration, effects and manner of implementation** of the measure in question'[123] (emphasis added).

1.143   And further, that:

---

120   Para 18.
121   Ibid.
122   (1980) 3 EHRR 333.
123   Para 92.

'The difference between deprivation of and restriction upon liberty is nonetheless merely one of degree or intensity, and not one of nature or substance. Although the process of classification into one or other of these categories sometimes proves to be no easy task in that some borderline cases are a matter of pure opinion, the Court cannot avoid making the selection upon which the applicability or inapplicability of Article 5 depends'[124].

1.144   However, the claimant in *Austin* argued that the correct application of these criteria on her lengthy and absolute containment must lead to a conclusion that a deprivation of liberty had occurred. If this were the case, none of the exceptions specified at Article 5(1)(a)–(f), which must be narrowly construed, could be applicable[125].

1.145   The defendant police force in *Austin* sought to introduce a novel criteria (albeit one that the police argued was intrinsic in various other Strasbourg judgments and principles), namely that when determining the first question before the court, ie whether a deprivation of liberty had occurred in the first place, the court was entitled to take into consideration the purpose of a measure. The court agreed with the police and found that kettling would be lawful where the containment:

- had been resorted to in good faith[126];

- was proportionate to the situation which had made the measures necessary[127];

- was enforced for no longer than was reasonably necessary[128]; and

- was for a legitimate purpose, in this case to protect people and property from injury[129] and in broader terms to prevent serious public disorder and violence[130].

1.146   Following the House of Lords' judgment, Ms Austin made an application to the ECtHR, which was heard on 14 September 2011 before the Grand Chamber. The European Court, in its judgment dated 15 March 2012, accepted the government's argument that there was no deprivation of liberty in this case. It gave a clear, political rationale for its decision stating that:

---

124 Para 93.
125 See for example *Medvedyev v France* (2010) 51 EHRR 39 at paras 76–78 and *Haidn v Germany* (Application No 6587/04, 13 January 2011) para 88.
126 Para 37.
127 Para 34.
128 Para 37.
129 Para 57.
130 Para 60.

'Article 5 cannot be interpreted in such a way as to make it impracticable for the police to fulfil their duties of maintaining order and protecting the public, provided that they comply with the underlying principle of Article 5, which is to protect the individual from arbitrariness'[131].

The court found that whilst the starting point of an assessment of whether there has been a deprivation of liberty is the 'concrete situation'[132] of the person concerned, it is permissible 'to have regard to the specific context and circumstances surrounding types of restriction other that the paradigm of confinement in a police cell'[133]. The court considered various other examples of temporary restrictions placed on members of the public, including temporary police containment at a football match, and observed that those circumstances would not amount to a deprivation of liberty within the meaning of Article 5:

'so long as they are rendered unavoidable as a result of circumstances beyond the control of the authorities and are necessary to avert a real risk of serious injury or damage, and are kept to the minimum required for that purpose'[134].

In reaching its decision, the court was heavily influenced by a number of findings by the trial judge in the High Court, including that, in this particular case, the police were planning a controlled release within five minutes of the cordon being in place but that this, and repeated subsequent attempts, were thwarted by the violent behaviour of those within and outside the kettle[135].

The court explicitly limited its finding to the 'specific and exceptional facts of this case'[136], although the judgment does not contain a readily identifiable set of criteria that caused the court to reach its decision. Factors that appear to have influenced the court include that the police had 'no alternative but to impose an absolute cordon if they were to avert a real risk of serious injury or damage'[137] and that the containment was the 'least intrusive and most effective means to be applied'[138].

The court nevertheless concluded its judgment by stating that:

'It must be underlined that measures of crowd control should not be used by the national authorities directly or indirectly to stifle or

---

131 *Austin v United Kingdom*, para 56.
132 *Austin v United Kingdom*, para 57.
133 *Austin v United Kingdom*, para 59.
134 Ibid.
135 *Austin v United Kingdom*, para 67.
136 *Austin v United Kingdom*, para 68.
137 *Austin v United Kingdom*, para 66.
138 Ibid.

discourage protest, given the fundamental importance of freedom of expression and assembly in all democratic societies'[139].

1.147   The judgment contains a strong dissenting opinion of three judges who rejected the principle that the aim or intention of a restrictive measure may be taken into account when assessing if there has been a deprivation of liberty. The dissenting judgment adopts the argument put forward by Ms Austin, stating that:

> 'The court has always held that the aim or intention of a measure cannot be taken into account in assessing whether there has been a deprivation of liberty. These aspects are relevant only in assessing whether the deprivation of liberty was justified for the purposes listed in sub-paragraphs (a) to (f) of Article 5 § 1'[140].

And further:

> '(T)here is no reason to treat deprivations of liberty resulting from public order considerations any differently from other kinds of deprivation of liberty for which the provision is invoked. Otherwise, States would be able to "circumvent" the guarantees laid down in Article 5 § 1 (a) to (f), as long as they could show that the measure was necessary'[141].

On the facts of the case, the dissenting judges also took issue with the inability of the court to pinpoint a moment when, what started as a restriction of movement, became a deprivation of liberty. The dissenting opinion notes that 'in a situation of uncertainty, the presumption is normally in favour of respect for individual rights'[142] and expressed concern that the approach taken 'leaves the way open for *carte blanche* and sends out a bad message to police authorities'[143].

1.148   The case of *R (on the application of Laporte) v Chief Constable of Gloucestershire Constabulary*[144] is the main authority on the law surrounding breach of the peace. In this case, police intercepted a coach of protesters who were on their way to a demonstration and escorted them back to where they had come from, because it was believed that some of them were intent on causing a breach of the peace. Although no breach of the peace had actually occurred, the court confirmed that a reasonable apprehension of an imminent breach of the

---

139 *Austin v United Kingdom*, para 68.
140 *Austin v United Kingdom*, para 4 of dissenting opinion.
141 *Austin v United Kingdom*, para 5 of dissenting opinion.
142 *Austin v United Kingdom*, para 12 of dissenting opinion.
143 *Austin v United Kingdom*, para 7 of dissenting opinion.
144 [2007] 2 AC 105 discussed in more detail at para **1.181**.

peace could suffice to justify preventive action. The Court of Appeal in *Austin*[145] (whose decision was affirmed by the House of Lords) had similarly held that, where a breach of the peace was taking place or reasonably thought to be imminent, the police could interfere with or curtail the lawful exercise of rights of both protesters and bystanders, but only if they had taken all other possible steps to prevent the breach or imminent breach of the peace and to protect the rights of third parties, and only where they reasonably believed that there was no other means to prevent a breach or imminent breach of the peace[146].

1.149 The prevention of a breach of the peace may therefore be a legitimate purpose for the imposition of a kettle. However, for such a containment to be lawful the police must believe a breach of the peace is imminent[147], and in addition the kettle would still have to comply with the conditions set out at para **1.145**.

1.150 In summary therefore, kettling will be lawful in certain circumstances. However, recent reports from protesters suggest that the tactic is being used to gather intelligence about demonstrators, and to create a disincentive to protest. Such improper applications would almost certainly amount to a breach of Articles 5, 10 and 11 of the Convention.

1.151 The limitations placed on the legality of kettling by the *Austin* judgment in the House of Lords were tested in the context of the containment of protesters at the Climate Camp in London on 1 April 2009. This protest at Bishopsgate, alongside others such as those near the Royal Exchange and the Bank of England, was staged in opposition to the G20 summit due to take place the following day. Whilst police intelligence suggested that earlier environmental protest camps with a close nexus to the Bishopsgate Climate Camp had involved small numbers and had not become violent[148] the Royal Exchange demonstration was *'disorderly to the point of serious violence'*[149]. The Royal Exchange demonstration was kettled in the afternoon (a decision that was never challenged in the courts) and later progressively dispersed. The police argued that it was necessary for the Bishopsgate Climate Camp to be contained at the time of the dispersal of the Royal Exchange demonstration, causing some 4,000–5,000 protesters to be kettled.

---

145 [2007] EWCA Civ 989.

146 Paras 68 and 119.

147 *R (on the application of Laporte) v Chief Constable of Gloucestershire Constabulary* [2007] 2 AC 105, per Lord Carswell at para 102.

148 *R (on the application of McClure & Moos) v Commissioner of Police of the Metropolis* [2012] EWCA Civ 12, para 5.

149 *R (on the application of McClure & Moos) v Commissioner of Police of the Metropolis* [2012] EWCA Civ 12, para 7.

1.152 Ms McClure and Mr Moos were amongst those contained, and brought a challenge by way of judicial review against the use of kettling and the force used by police. At first instance, the Divisional Court found for the claimants, ruling that the containment was an unlawful policing operation and that the offensive 'shield strikes' used by police were unnecessary and unjustified.

1.153 The court held that:

> 'Containment of the Climate Camp was not justified by the behaviour and conduct of those at the Climate Camp alone. When the Royal Exchange protesters were dispersing … there was clearly a risk that some of them might head for the Climate Camp and the police were right to anticipate the risk and take appropriate steps to deal with it, if it materialised. But it was, we think, no more than a risk … '[150]

and further:

> 'There was … no reasonably apprehended breach of the peace, imminent or otherwise, within the Climate Camp itself sufficient to justify containment'[151].

1.154 However, the Commissioner of Police of the Metropolis successfully appealed the decision and, on 19 January 2012, the Court of Appeal overturned the decision. In doing so, it focused on two issues: first, whether the police's 'genuinely held apprehension that there was a breach of the peace at the Climate Camp imminent was a reasonable view' and second, whether their decision to contain the Climate Camp was 'unjustifiable' on the police's evidence[152].

1.155 The Court of Appeal held that the Divisional Court had applied the wrong test when assessing whether there was an imminent risk of breach of the peace in the Climate Camp[153]. The court should have determined whether, in the light of what the senior officer 'knew and perceived at the time' it was reasonable to fear an imminent breach of the peace. It was not for the court to 'form its own view as to imminence'[154].

---

150 *R on the application of (McClure & Moos) v Commissioner of Police of the Metropolis* [2011] EWHC 957 (Admin), para 58.
151 *R (on the application of McClure & Moos) v Commissioner of Police of the Metropolis* [2011] EWHC 957 (Admin), para 59.
152 *R (on the application of McClure & Moos) v Commissioner of Police of the Metropolis* [2012] EWCA Civ 12, para 65.
153 Para 76.
154 Para 68.

1.156   The Court of Appeal further found that the Divisional Court had erred in proceeding 'on the false basis that containment of the Climate Camp could only be justified by a risk emanating solely from the demonstrators within the Camp, rather than from a combination of some or all of those demonstrators with elements from the Royal Exchange demonstration'[155].

1.157   Whilst the Court of Appeal decision in *McClure* does not take away from the conditions in *Austin* and *Laporte*, it does contain various unhelpful comments which will no doubt be relied upon by the police in any future challenges. At para 96 the court stated:

> 'the Divisional Court also said that "[t]he test of necessity is met only in truly extreme and exceptional circumstances". This is no doubt true, but we doubt whether it gives any assistance over and above the requirements discussed in *Laporte* … Almost by definition, a decision to contain will only be made, or even considered, in extreme and exceptional circumstances: the Divisional Court made it clear that they thought the circumstances appertaining in the City of London on 1 April 2009 were extreme and exceptional … But an argument as to whether, in a particular case, the circumstances were extreme or exceptional enough, or "truly" extreme and exceptional, is scarcely likely to assist those deciding at the time whether to contain, or those subsequently deciding whether the containment was justified'.

The court thereby gave a clear indication that the test as set out in *Laporte* was not to be interpreted as placing too onerous a burden on the police.

1.158   Finally, consideration should be given to the use of kettling in the context of vulnerable protesters, and in particular children. It is possible that the courts will take a more stringent view on the application of requirements for a lawful kettle in these circumstances, although the law has not yet been decided on this issue. In the case of *R (on the application of Castle) v Commissioner of Police of the Metropolis*[156] the High Court ruled that the Metropolitan Police acted lawfully when they kettled three teenagers during the tuition fee protests in London on 24 November for about seven hours and that any interference that did take place with the teenagers' rights to liberty and to demonstrate 'was for a legitimate reason, in accordance with the law, and proportionate to the legitimate aim of preventing an imminent breach of the peace'[157].

1.159   The case is being appealed, but was stayed pending the outcome of the European Court's decision in *Austin*. The claimants are likely to argue that the

---

155   Para 83.
156   [2011] EWHC 2317 (Admin).
157   Para 72.

decision to kettle them was unlawful because the police were in breach of their duties to take account of the need to promote the welfare of children in accordance with the Children Act 2004.

FAQ: Is a kettle lawful?

Criteria include:

- Is there an alternative mechanism by which a breach of the peace, serious injury or damage can be prevented?

- Is a kettle the most effective means by which to do so?

- Is a kettle the least intrusive means by which to do so?

- Is the kettle imposed for no longer than is necessary?

- Is the necessity of the kettle kept under constant review and have the appropriate release efforts been made?

- Are there particularly vulnerable people contained in the kettle?

Power of arrest

What is an arrest?

1.160 What constitutes an arrest is not defined in PACE 1984. A classic definition of arrest was given by the Privy Council in *Shaaban bin Hussien v Chong Fook Kam*[158]:

> 'An arrest occurs when a police officer states in terms that he is arresting or when he uses force to restrain the individual concerned. It occurs also when by words or conduct he makes it clear that he will, if necessary, use force to prevent the individual from going where he may want to go'.

1.161 Whether particular use of words or contact constitutes an arrest is a matter of fact and degree. A police officer taking someone by the arm to draw their attention to what is being said to them will not constitute an arrest[159]. Any arrest effected by a police officer (or citizen) must be lawful or else it is likely to constitute an assault.

---

158 [1970] AC 942, [1970] 2 WLR 441.
159 *Mepstead v Director of Public Prosecutions* [1996] Crim LR 111, [1996] COD 13.

Arrest following the issue of a warrant

1.162   As the majority of arrests of protesters take place in the context of demonstrations and therefore without a warrant, this topic will be dealt with in brief.

1.163   Under the Magistrates' Courts Act 1980, s 1, following the laying of an information (a written charge) against an individual by a prosecutor, a magistrate can issue a warrant for that individual's arrest in order to secure his attendance before the court to answer the allegations contained within the information. The other alternative available to the court is the issue of a summons that requires a person to attend court at a particular date and time without the need for them to be arrested.

1.164   A warrant for a person's arrest means the potential loss of their liberty. Therefore, it can only be issued following the laying of a written information alleging that the individual has (or is suspected of having) committed a criminal offence that is either punishable with imprisonment or can be tried in the Crown Court, unless the individual's address is not sufficiently established for a summons to be served on him.

1.165   The warrant must state the person(s) to whom it gives the power of arrest (usually the police), the defendant against whom it was issued, the reasons for its issue, the court that issued it and the court officer who issued it.

1.166   See para **2.4** regarding the time limits in respect of laying of an information for summary only offences.

Arrest without warrant—statutory powers

1.167   PACE 1984, s 24 gives a police officer the power to arrest without a warrant:

- anyone who is about to commit an offence;

- anyone who is in the act of committing an offence;

- anyone whom he has reasonable grounds for suspecting to be about to commit an offence;

- anyone whom he has reasonable grounds for suspecting to be committing an offence.

1.168   An officer may also arrest without a warrant anyone he has reasonable grounds to suspect **has committed** an offence. There used to be a distinction between 'arrestable' and 'non-arrestable' offences and therefore these terms are mentioned a great deal in the relevant case law. However, since the enactment of the relevant provisions of the Serious Organised Crime and Police Act 2005 (SOCPA 2005), the distinction has been abolished.

1.169   There are three important criteria that must be fulfilled before an arrest by a police officer is lawful. These criteria were set out by the Court of Appeal in *Castorina v Chief Constable of Surrey*[160].

1.170   The first criteria to be satisfied for an arrest to be lawful is whether the officer does *actually* suspect that the person arrested has committed/is about to commit an offence and his suspicion must be genuine.

1.171   The second criteria is whether the arresting officer has 'reasonable grounds' for that suspicion. The question of whether his suspicion is reasonable is an objective test that requires 'the officer's grounds be examined objectively and that they be judged at the time that the power was exercised'[161]. What is regarded as reasonable depends on all the circumstances. A number of factors and sources of information may cumulatively amount to reasonable suspicion. The threshold is low and it is not necessary for the arresting officer to have admissible evidence that amounts to proof that there is a *prima facie* case for prosecuting the arrested person[162].

1.172   It is the reasonableness of the arresting officer's suspicions that is important, not the views of any other officers. The arresting officer cannot just follow orders, but he can rely on what he has been told by other officers, and information from other sources, including checks on the police national computer[163].

1.173   The third criteria that must be satisfied for a lawful arrest to take place is that he must reasonably believe that the arrest is necessary for any of the following reasons set out in PACE 1984, s 24(5):

(a)   to enable the name of the person in question to be ascertained (in the case where the constable does not know, and cannot readily ascertain, the person's name, or has reasonable grounds for doubting whether a name given by the person as his name is his real name);

(b)   as above, but as regards the person's address;

(c)   to prevent the person in question:

---

160   (1988) 138 NLJ Rep 180 CA confirmed by *Raissi v Commissioner of Police of the Metropolis* [2008] EWCA Civ 1237, [2009] QB 564, [2009] 2 WLR 1243, CA.
161   *O'Hara v Chief Constable of the Royal Ulster Constabulary* [1997] AC 286, [1997] 2 WLR 1, HL, per Lord Hope.
162   *Al Fayed v Commissioner of Police of the Metropolis* [2004] EWCA Civ 1579 at para 50, [2004] 1 Pol LR 370–389.
163   *O'Hara* ibid.

- causing physical injury to himself or any other person; or

- suffering physical injury; or

- causing loss of or damage to property; or

- committing an offence against public decency, or

- causing an unlawful obstruction of the highway;

(d) to protect a child or other vulnerable person from the person in question;

(e) to allow the prompt and effective investigation of the offence or of the conduct of the person in question;

(f) to prevent any prosecution for the offence from being hindered by the disappearance of the person in question.

1.174 The question of whether the arresting officer 'reasonably believes' that the arrest is necessary for one of the above reasons is, again, an objective assessment. What an officer has to consider in making this assessment was discussed by the Court of Appeal in *Hayes v Chief Constable of Merseyside*[164]. In *Hayes*, the court rejected any suggestion that the arresting officer has to actively consider every alternative to arrest (such as applying for a summons etc) but stated that 'the officer ought to apply his mind to alternatives short of arrest, and if he does not do so he is open to challenge'[165].

1.175 Whenever an officer does exercise his discretion to arrest, a court will subject that decision to the over-arching test of reasonableness set out in what is known as the '*Wednesbury*' test[166]. The '*Wednesbury*' test, in these circumstances, is an assessment as to whether the decision to arrest was so unreasonable, or capricious, or arbitrary that no reasonable police officer could have come to the conclusion that, in all the circumstances, he had a lawfully exercised power to make an arrest at that particular time.

1.176 If any of the above three criteria are not present during an arrest, then the arrest is unlawful. Although the fact the arrest is unlawful will not necessarily mean that person cannot be prosecuted, it may be the foundation for an argument at trial that the officer was not 'acting in the execution of his duty'[167] or found a criminal defence such as reasonableness[168] or a civil action in damages[169].

---

164 [2011] EWCA Civ 911, [2011] All ER (D) 286 (Jul).
165 At para 37 of the judgment.
166 *Associated Provincial Picture Houses v Wednesbury Corpn* [1948] 1 KB 223, [1947] 2 All ER 680, CA.
167 See para **2.32**.
168 See para **3.117**.
169 See Chapter 5.

1.177   It is also important to note that in effecting an arrest an officer can only use 'reasonable force', if necessary[170]. See para **3.37** for the effect of an officer using unreasonable force.

Arrest without warrant—common law powers (breach of the peace)

1.178   A breach of the peace is not a criminal offence, but both police officers and ordinary citizens have a common law duty to prevent and/or stop a breach of the peace[171]. This common law power is derived from what has been termed as a police constable's 'ultimate duty' to 'preserve the Queen's peace'[172]. For what constitutes a breach of the peace see para **3.171**.

1.179   The police may lawfully take a number of steps to prevent a breach of the peace, including detaining someone and using reasonable force if necessary, but only if they reasonably believe that person may commit a breach of the peace and only for as long as necessary to avoid the breach.

1.180   The common law gives both police officers and citizens a power of detention and arrest where:

(a)   a breach of the peace is committed in the presence of the person making the arrest; or

(b)   they reasonably believe that a breach of the peace will be committed by that person in the immediate future; or

(c)   where there has been a breach of the peace and it is reasonably believed that the breach will be repeated[173].

In order for a police officer to use his common law powers to prevent a breach of the peace, the breach must be **imminent**.

1.181   The question of what 'imminent' means was addressed by the House of Lords in *R (on the application of Laporte) v Chief Constable of*

---

170   PACE 1984, s 117.
171   The common law powers were expressly preserved by the Public Order Act 1986, s 40(4).
172   *R (on the application of Laporte) v Chief Constable of Gloucestershire Constabulary* [2007] 2 AC 105, HL.
173   *R v Howell* [1982] QB 416, CA.

Gloucestershire Constabulary[174]. In 2003, the claimant and others were travelling on a coach to RAF Fairford where they planned to take part in a demonstration against the war on Iraq. The police stopped the coach, believing it to contain 'hard-line' demonstrators who would use violence to enter the RAF base. It was accepted that Jane Laporte herself had purely peaceful intentions. The officer in charge noted that people on the coach were not to be arrested for a breach of the peace at that time, but the police went on to search everyone on the coach and then ordered the coaches to return London with a police escort.

1.182 The Lords confirmed that, before any preventative action could be taken by the police, a breach of the peace must be 'imminent' and that this was an objective test. On the facts of *Laporte*, the police could not show that such a breach of the peace by the individuals on the coach was 'imminent' therefore the police action was unlawful.

1.183 Lord Carswell stated that the imminence test 'can be properly applied with a degree of flexibility which recognises the circumstances of the case'[175]. Lord Rodger acknowledged that public order situations can change quickly, 'there is no need for the police officer to wait until the opposing group hoves into sight before taking action. That would be to turn every intervention into an exercise in crisis management'[176].

1.184 In the case of *R (on the application of McClure & Moos) v Commissioner of Police for the Metropolis*[177], the Court of Appeal upheld the decision of the police to detain or 'kettle' a group of demonstrators outside the Climate Exchange Building in Bishopsgate in order to prevent a breach of the peace, despite the fact that their behaviour was peaceful and did not of itself justify containment. The police justified the kettle on the basis that it was preventing infiltration of the peaceful group of demonstrators by what the police considered to be a group of more violent demonstrators, also contained, nearby. The Court of Appeal held that the decision to contain a substantial crowd of demonstrators, whose behaviour did not of itself justify containment, was justifiable on the ground that the containment was the least drastic way of preventing what the police officer responsible for the decision reasonably apprehended would otherwise be imminent and serious breaches of the peace.

1.185 Even where a police officer believes that a breach of the peace is imminent, that belief must be founded on reasonable grounds[178]. The test of

---

174 [2007] 2 AC, [2007] 2 WLR 46.
175 Ibid, para 102 of the judgment.
176 Ibid, para 69 of the judgment.
177 [2012] EWCA Civ 12.
178 *Foulkes v Chief Constable of Merseyside Police* [1998] 3 All ER 705.

reasonableness is an objective one and does not allow for the application of hindsight[179].

1.186   However, the power to take steps to prevent a breach of the peace, whether by detention or otherwise, may only be exercised for as long as the threat to the breach to the peace exists[180]. There must be a real (rather than fanciful) risk of another breach of the peace based on all the circumstances. The Court of Appeal in *Chief Constable of Cleveland Police v McGrogan*[181] noted that although a breach of the peace is not an 'offence' so that PACE 1984, s 34 applies[182], the courts have deemed it correct for the police to treat any person detained for a breach of the peace as if the PACE 1984 applied, in particular the need to regularly review whether continued detention is justified.

1.187   The courts have also been careful only to sanction the police taking such steps as are reasonable to prevent a breach of the peace. What is reasonable must be assessed in all the circumstances. Action short of detention may be taken, eg a warning which, if ignored, is followed by a threat of detention[183] or leading someone away from a breach of the peace in order to prevent their involvement in it[184]. See para **1.130** for the use of this power in 'kettling'.

Rights on arrest

1.188

> Upon arrest, unless the person detained is informed that they are under arrest as soon as practicable, the arrest is unlawful[185].

A person under arrest must also be:

(a)   told the grounds for the arrest as soon as practicable[186];

---

179   *Redmond-Bate v Director of Public Prosecutions* [1999] EWHC Admin 732.
180   *Albert v Lavin* [1982] AC 546, DC.
181   [2002] EWCA Civ 86, [2002] 1 FLR 707.
182   See para **1.200**.
183   *Howell*, ibid.
184   *King v Hodges* [1974] Crim LR 424, DC.
185   PACE 1984, s 28(1).
186   PACE 1984, s 28(3).

(b)   taken to the police station as soon as practicable[187] unless granted 'street bail'[188];

(c)   cautioned[189].

1.189   Upon arrest the police also have the right, under PACE 1984, s 32, to search the person detained for anything which he might use to assist him to escape from lawful custody or which might be evidence relating to an offence. Under s 32 the police also have the power to enter and search any premises that the arrested person was arrested in, or was present in before he was arrested, for evidence relating to the alleged offence.

Effect of breach of powers of arrest

1.190

FAQ: What happens if my arrest was unlawful?

An unlawful arrest *may* lead to:

- an argument that the officer was not acting in the execution of his duty for the purposes of a criminal prosecution under the Police Act 1996, s 89[190];

- a criminal defence of reasonableness or self-defence, where applicable[191];

- a civil action for damages[192];

- an argument to exclude evidence at a criminal trial under PACE 1984, s 78[193].

---

187 PACE 1984, s 30.
188 Released on the condition that they later attend the police station on a given date (PACE 1984, s 30A) See para **1.257** for more on 'street bail'.
189 PACE Code C10.4
190 See para **3.22**.
191 See para **3.117**.
192 See Chapter 5.
193 See para **2.98**.

AT THE POLICE STATION

Arrival at the police station

1.191   Once an individual under arrest arrives at the police station, their detention must be authorised by a custody officer. The custody officer (a designated police officer of at least the rank of sergeant) has a statutory responsibility[194] for ensuring that the detainee is treated in accordance with PACE 1984 and the PACE Codes[195]. These protect the detainee's rights and impose a number of duties upon the police in respect of their treatment.

1.192   The first duty of the custody officer is to ensure that the individual's detention is still necessary for one of the reasons in PACE 1984, s 24(5) (see para **1.173**). The most common reason given for authorising detention at the police station is 'to allow the prompt investigation of the offence alleged against the detained person', as the investigation can include interviewing the detainee on tape.

1.193   However, the custody officer has a duty to keep the grounds for detention under review[196] and must release a detainee if these grounds cease to exist.

1.194   The custody officer also has a responsibility to record anything that is required to be recorded by PACE 1984, or the PACE Codes, on the custody record. The custody record is an important document that can often help support (either by its inclusion or omission of key information) any complaints made in relation to mistreatment by police officers. It must be disclosed as of right to any defendant in criminal proceedings or claimant in civil proceedings[197].

1.195   Anyone detained in a police station is entitled to inspect a full copy of the PACE Codes at any time during their detention.

---

194   Under PACE 1984, s 39(1).
195   www.homeoffice.gov.uk/police/powers/pace-codes/.
196   PACE 1984, s 34. See para **1.200**.
197   PACE Code C2.4A.

Taking photographs, fingerprints and DNA

1.196   The police have the power to take the fingerprints[198], photographs[199] and non-intimate samples[200] (usually a mouth swab to establish DNA) of anyone arrested at the police station. They can do so by using reasonable force if necessary. DNA samples, profiles and fingerprints (also known as 'biometric data') can then be retained by police under PACE 1984, s 64(1A). At present the police have the discretion to retain this data indefinitely, although this has attracted much criticism from both the public and the courts. In particular the indefinite nature of the retention, and failure to distinguish between those merely arrested for an offence, those arrested, charged and acquitted and those arrested, charged and convicted has been found to be in breach of the European Convention on Human Rights (ECHR).

1.197   In 2008, the European Court in *S and Marper v United Kingdom*[201] departed from the then most recent UK domestic authority[202] in finding that the indefinite retention of the claimants' biometric data was an unjustified interference with their rights under Article 8 of the ECHR. This was subsequently confirmed by the Supreme Court in *R (on the application of GC) v Comr of the Police for the Metropolis*[203].

1.198   Individuals can apply to have their biometric data etc removed from the database. The mechanism by which to do this is to apply to the individual police force, who will usually allocate the request to a specific team. In the case of the Metropolitan Police, this is the Exceptional Cases Unit SCD12 (ECU). These teams are guided in their decision-making by a policy prepared by the Association of Chief Police Officers (ACPO) which allows retention of biometric data in all but the most exceptional circumstances. There is very little guidance about what may amount to exceptional circumstances. Although the ACPO policy does make reference to circumstances where it can be established that no offence took place, it fails to expand on this in any conclusive manner. Certainly simply being released without charge does not appear to be sufficient. The example provided suggests it may be possible to secure the deletion of DNA etc where an individual has been arrested as a result of a mistaken identity and the actual perpetrator has been caught. Additionally, if an arrest is unlawful, this could give rise to a challenge to the continuing retention of biometric data

---

198   PACE 1984, s 61.
199   PACE 1984, s 64A.
200   PACE 1984, s 63.
201   (2008) 48 EHRR 1169.
202   *R (on the application of S) v Chief Constable of South Yorkshire Police* [2004] UKHL 39, [2004] 1 WLR 2196.
203   [2011] UKSC 21, [2011] 1 WLR 1230.

seized during that arrest. If an application is unsuccessful, the only remedy is to seek a challenge of the decision by way of judicial review.

1.199 The ACPO policy remains in place despite *R (on the application of GC) v Comr of the Police for the Metropolis* determining its incompatibility with Article 8 of the ECHR. The Supreme Court has afforded the government some leeway in this matter allowing it a reasonable period of time in which to pass its proposed Protection of Freedoms Bill and/or introduce new guidelines. At the time of writing, the Bill had reached the report stage in the House of Lords. If the government fails to produce revised guidelines within a reasonable time, the *GC* case made it clear that the applicants in that case (and presumably therefore many others) would be able to bring a challenge by way of judicial review to the continuing retention of their data. What the courts consider to be a reasonable period of time remains to be seen.

Periods of detention

1.200

FAQ: How long can the police keep me at the police station?

- You can only be detained without charge at the police station for as long as the reasons for your detention under PACE 1984, s 24 exist (see below). Once they cease to exist, you must be released.

- If those reasons continue to exist, you can be detained at the police station initially for **24 hours** without charge.

- You can be detained at the police station for up to **36 hours** without charge *if authorised by a senior officer* (see para **1.201**).

- You can be detained at the police station for up to **96 hours** in total without charge *but only if your further detention is authorised by magistrates* (see para **1.202**).

Under PACE 1984, s 34 a suspect can only be detained at a police station for as long as the grounds for the initial detention continue to apply. If they cease to apply, that person must be released immediately. The custody officer has an ongoing duty to keep the grounds for detention under review.

1.201 The grounds for keeping an individual detained at the police station must be reviewed by either an inspector (in the case of someone who has not been charged) or a custody officer (in the case of someone who has been charged) at the following intervals:

(a)   not later than six hours after detention is first authorised;

(b)   nine hours after the first review;

(c)   subsequent reviews at intervals of not more than nine hours[204].

1.202   An individual can initially be detained for up to 24 hours without being charged[205]. Beyond the initial 24-hour period, detention can be authorised by an officer, of at least the rank of superintendent or above, for up to 36 hours if:

(a)   the individual is suspected of an *indictable* offence (ie one that can be tried at the Crown Court); and

(b)   there are reasonable grounds to believe that further detention is necessary to preserve evidence or obtain evidence by questioning[206].

The individual and/or their solicitor can make representations regarding their continued detention at this stage.

1.203   Before the expiration of the 36-hour period, the police can apply to the magistrates' court for a warrant of further detention to extend the period by another 36 hours, ie up to 72 hours[207]. The individual is entitled to be legally represented at any hearing of the application. If a warrant is granted, it can later be extended once again by an application to the magistrates up to a maximum period of 96 hours[208].

204 PACE 1984, s 40.
205 PACE 1984, s 41.
206 PACE 1984, s 42.
207 PACE 1984, s 43.
208 PACE 1984, s 44. There are separate and more onerous provisions in the Terrorism Act 2000, Sch 8, Pt II under which individuals suspected of committing offences under that Act can be detained with the approval of the court for up to 14 days without charge. However, these provisions will not be covered in depth in this text.

Forensic medical examiner and injuries

1.204

FAQ: What do I do if I have been injured or am feeling unwell at the police station?

- If you have been injured or are suffering from a physical or mental disorder you should be seen by a doctor at the police station. If you request to see a doctor, the police must arrange for one to see you (see below).

- The police can only interview you if it is determined you are fit to be interviewed.

- Ask the doctor to note all your injuries. Whether he does so or not, take *good quality* photographs of any injuries upon your release from the police station and again if, for example, bruising does not show up until a later stage.

If a detainee at the police station appears to have been injured, is suffering from a physical or mental disorder or for whatever reason requires clinical attention, it is the responsibility of the custody officer to ensure that they receive the appropriate attention. This responsibility is set out in PACE Code C9.5.

1.205 PACE Code C9.5 requires the custody officer to arrange clinical attention, normally in the form of a Forensic Medical Examiner (FME): a doctor who attends the police station, whether the detainee requests it or not. However, PACE Code C9.8 states that where a detainee does request to be seen by a doctor, an appropriate health care professional must be called as soon as possible.

1.206 An FME should conduct a clinical examination of a detainee in private and complete a record of his examination, which should then form part of the custody record. If a detainee has sustained any injuries, these should be clearly recorded. Some FME records contain a 'body map' where the doctor can mark on a body outline where injuries are present.

1.207 If an FME is called to see someone, under PACE Code C9.15 they must also give their opinion to the custody officer about the risk assessment of the person's continuing detention, taking into consideration their physical and mental health and that person's fitness to be interviewed.

1.208 The custody officer must record in the custody record any request from the detainee that an FME attend, any arrangements made for them to attend, any injuries or conditions that make attendance necessary and any clinical directions given to them by the FME.

Legal representation

1.209 Section 58 of PACE 1984 gives any person detained at the police station the right to speak to a solicitor, in private, if he requests to do so. Once the request is made, access to a solicitor either on the phone or in person should be provided as soon as practicable. The request should also be recorded in the custody record. The legal advice provided should be free and independent.

FAQ: How can I get legal advice at the police station?

- You should be told upon your arrival at the police station that you are entitled to legal advice and asked if you would like to speak to a solicitor.

  If you are arrested for a non-imprisonable offence (eg under the Public Order Act 1986, s 5) and the police do not intend to interview you, you may speak to a solicitor of your choice on the phone. The solicitor may charge you for any advice given over the phone, but most solicitors used to representing activists will not. Alternatively, you will be offered the opportunity to speak to a free legal adviser (not necessarily a qualified solicitor) at a call centre known as CDS direct. It is unlikely that call-centre advisers will have any specialist knowledge to advise activists.

  If you are arrested for a more serious, imprisonable, offence or one for which you are going to be interviewed, you are entitled free access a solicitor of your choice.

- If you are detained at a police station and do not have a named solicitor to represent you, request to speak to the duty solicitor. An accredited police station representative should then be contacted for you by the police, free of charge, via the Defence Solicitor Call Centre (DSCC). The call centre is open 24 hours a day, 365 days of the year.

- Via the DSCC, you should then be able to speak to an accredited representative either over the phone or in person and receive legal advice. Duty solicitors are required to attend the police station in certain circumstances including to attend interviews and where a client complains of serious maltreatment by the police.

All legal advice must be give to the detained person in private (or on the telephone) and the content of that advice is confidential between the detainee and their legal adviser and is protected by legal professional privilege.

1.210   In some circumstances a police officer of the rank of superintendent or above can authorise a delay in the provision of access to a solicitor for someone in detention charged with an indictable offence but only up to a period of 36 hours. These circumstances are where the officer has reasonable grounds to believe that having access to a solicitor will:

(a)   interfere with evidence in relation to the offence; or

(b)   cause personal injury to another person; or

(c)   alert other suspects not yet arrested about the offence.

1.211   PACE Code C6 sets out additional rights in relation to receiving free and independent legal advice at the police station. In particular, Code C6.4 states that no police officer shall say or do anything to dissuade a detainee from obtaining legal advice. Some detainees have reported that they felt pressured to be interviewed without receiving legal advice, by being told by police officers that it will take a long time for a solicitor to attend or for someone to advise on the phone. This is not true; duty solicitors should usually attend within a set period of time. If the detainee has requested a particular firm who are based a long distance from the police station, they can arrange for a local firm to act as their agent. Police investigators often take several hours until they are ready for interview and police officers should be able to notify solicitors in advance so that they arrive in good time for any interview.

1.212   Some detainees report officers telling them that they do not need a solicitor if they are innocent. Again, this is untrue. A solicitor's role at the police station is to uphold and protect all their client's basic and legal rights. They will ensure that the detainee's rights are being respected and can also record any welfare concerns or injuries observed. A solicitor can identify potential leads for the police to pursue before evidence is lost. They can also give advice to the detainee on gaps in the state of the prosecution evidence before the detainee is asked to answer questions in interview. For example, in a case where the defendant has acted in self-defence, the prosecution would first have to prove that the defendant hit the alleged victim. If the alleged victim was not willing to give evidence then a defendant putting forward self-defence in interview would, in the course of doing so, admit striking a blow that the prosecution could not otherwise prove. On the other hand, there are circumstances in which a solicitor may advise that a person should answer questions in order to avoid an adverse inference being drawn.

1.213 PACE Code C6.6 makes it clear that if an individual wants legal advice, he may not be interviewed until he has received that advice, unless access to that advice has been delayed for one of the reasons set out at the end of para **1.209** or unless he has refused to receive advice from the duty solicitors' scheme. The detainee is entitled to request that any solicitor he has consulted be present when he is interviewed under caution in relation to the allegation.

Interviews under caution

1.214 The Police and Criminal Evidence Act 1984 (Codes of Practice) (Code E) Order 2003[209] makes it mandatory for all interviews at a police station of persons suspected of the commission of indictable offences to be tape recorded. PACE Code C sets out further obligations on the police for the conduct of all police interviews.

1.215 An 'interview' is defined as the questioning of a person regarding their involvement or suspected involvement in a criminal offence[210]. An interview must be carried out under caution, the standard caution is:

> 'You do not have to say anything. But it may harm your defence if you do not mention when questioned something which you later rely on in court. Anything you do say may be given in evidence'.

1.216 Often individuals are asked questions by the police about an alleged offence which clearly relate to the individual's involvement in a criminal offence at the scene. For example, in the context of an allegation of criminal damage, 'did you break this window?'. These questions should not be asked unless the individual has been cautioned. Failure to do so may mean that there can be an application at trial to exclude questions and answers under PACE 1984, s 78[211].

1.217 Following an individual's arrest, a person must not be interviewed about an alleged offence except at a police station **unless** the delay would be likely to:

(a) interfere with or cause harm to evidence in the case;

(b) interfere with or cause physical harm to other people; or

(c) cause serious loss or damage to property[212].

---

209 SI 2003/705.
210 PACE Code C11.1A.
211 See para **2.98**.
212 PACE Code C11.1.

1.218 The above provisions mean that asking a detained person questions about an alleged offence whilst they are in the back of a police vehicle being conveyed to the police station following arrest would be a breach of the PACE Codes. Again, this may be form the basis of an application at trial to exclude the questions and answers under PACE 1984, s 78.

1.219 Once an interview has been commenced at the police station, the individual should be re-cautioned and reminded of their right to free legal advice. Any significant statement that the individual has made in the presence of any police officer before the start of the interview should be put to the individual in the interview, to allow them an opportunity to confirm or deny that it was said[213].

1.220 An accurate record must be made of any interview that takes place, even if it does not take place at a police station[214]. Any significant statement—whether or not in response to a question from an officer—should be recorded and the defendant given the opportunity to sign it as correct.

1.221 If an individual requires an interpreter, one must be obtained before the interview can commence, unless one or more of the conditions in para **1.217** justify a delay[215].

Vulnerable individuals

1.222 Before an individual is interviewed, the custody officer must consult with the officer in the case and any appropriate health care professional to determine whether that individual is fit to be interviewed[216]. This determination means an assessment of the risks to the individual's physical and mental health if the interview took place. The custody officer must also assess what safeguards are needed (if any) to protect the individual within the interview.

1.223 If an individual is deemed to be:

(a)   a juvenile (ie under the age of 17)[217]; or

(b)   suffering from a mental disorder; or

(c)   mentally vulnerable,

---

213   PACE Code C11.4.
214   PACE Code C11.7.
215   PACE Code C13.2.
216   PACE Code C12.3.
217   PACE Code C1.5.

they must not be interviewed in relation to their suspected involvement with an offence in the absence of an appropriate adult. An appropriate adult is defined by PACE Code C1.7. In the case of a juvenile this must be:

(a) a parent, guardian or someone authorised to care for that juvenile under the Children Act 1989;

(b) a social worker of a local authority;

(c) failing these, some other responsible adult aged 18 or over who is not a police officer or employed by the police.

1.224 In the case of a mentally disordered or mentally vulnerable person, the definition of an appropriate adult is the same, except for that instead of a social worker, an appropriate adult can be someone who is experienced in dealing with mentally disordered or mentally vulnerable people, as long as they are not a police officer or employed by the police.

1.225 However, a person should not be an appropriate adult if they are:

(a) suspected of involvement in the offence;

(b) a victim;

(c) a witness;

(d) involved in the investigation[218].

1.226 The above criteria therefore do not prevent a fellow activist from acting as an appropriate adult for a detained person, as long as they are themselves not a suspect or a witness to the alleged offence.

1.227 The purpose of an appropriate adult is to:

(a) advise the person being interviewed;

(b) observe whether the interview is being conducted properly and fairly;

(c) facilitate communication with the person being interviewed[219].

1.228 A juvenile or otherwise vulnerable person may not be interviewed without an appropriate adult unless an officer of superintendent rank or above considers that a delay in obtaining an appropriate adult will led to the consequences set out at para **1.217** and is satisfied that the conduct of the interview will not significantly harm the person's physical or mental state.

---

218 PACE Code C Notes for Guidance C1B.
219 PACE Code C15.

Charging decisions

1.229   PACE 1984, s 37 imposes a duty on a custody officer to determine, as soon as possible after an individual has arrived at the police station, whether there is sufficient evidence to justify a charge against that individual. If there is not sufficient evidence to charge, further detention can only be authorised if there are 'reasonable grounds for believing that his detention without charge is necessary to secure or preserve evidence relating to an offence for which he is under arrest or to obtain evidence by questioning him'. Any detention that is not 'necessary' for one of the above reasons may be unlawful.

1.230   Where the custody officer is satisfied that there is sufficient evidence to charge the detained individual with the offence for which he was arrested, the person can be:

(a)   charged;

(b)   subject to further detention in order for the CPS to be consulted in respect of charge;

(c)   released without charge and on police bail;

(d)   released without charge and not on bail.

1.231   Where the CPS are consulted on charge, they are obliged to follow the 'Code for Crown Prosecutors' and consider what is referred to as the 'Full Code Test'. The full code test is in two parts:

●   the evidential test; and

●   the public interest test.

1.232   The **evidential test** requires the CPS to assess whether there is sufficient evidence against the individual to provide a 'realistic prospect of conviction'. A realistic prospect of conviction is an objective test. It means that a jury, bench of magistrates, or judge hearing a case alone, properly directed and acting in accordance with the law, is more likely than not to find the case against the defendant proved beyond reasonable doubt. If the evidence passes the evidential test, the CPS must then consider the public interest test.

1.233   The **public interest test** requires the CPS to consider whether the prosecution is in the public interest. The CPS guidance suggests that a prosecution should take place:

'unless the prosecutor is sure that there are public interest factors tending against prosecution which outweigh those tending in favour, or unless the prosecutor is satisfied that the public interest may be properly served, in the first instance, by offering the offender the opportunity to have the matter dealt with by an out-of-court disposal'.

1.234 An important case in relation to charging decisions for protest cases is the High Court decision in *Dehal v Crown Prosecution Service*[220]. In *Dehal*, the applicant was charged with an offence contrary to the Public Order Act 1986, s 4A[221] for displaying a sign in a Sikh temple which was found by the Crown Court to be abusive and insulting, in that it called the president of the temple a hypocrite. On appeal, Dehal argued that the prosecution had constituted a violation of his right to freedom of expression as protected by Article 10 of the ECHR.

1.235 The High Court held that where Article 10 was engaged, the criminal law should not be invoked unless and until it was established that the conduct which was the subject of the charge amounted to such a threat to public order to require the involvement of the criminal law, and not merely the civil law.

1.236 The High Court found that in order to justify the interference with such a fundamental right as the right to freedom of expression, the prosecution had to demonstrate that the prosecution was being brought in pursuance of a legitimate aim and that the prosecution was the minimum necessary to achieve that aim, ie that criminal prosecution was a proportionate response to his conduct. On the facts of *Dehal*, the High Court ruled that the prosecution had not satisfied that requirement and therefore allowed the appeal against his conviction.

1.237 In the case of *Munim Abdul v DPP*[222] the High Court approved the approach in *Dehal*. Although on the facts of *Abdul*, the High Court upheld the conviction for Public Order Act 1986, s 5 offences where the defendants had chanted 'British soldiers burn in hell' at a homecoming parade, the court reiterated that the POA 1986, s 5 had to be read together with ECHR, Article 10. The starting point was the importance of the right to freedom of expression, but it was to be recognised that legitimate protest could be offensive at least to some and that the law could not simply protect those who held the majority view. The justification for invoking the criminal law had to be convincingly established and the restrictions to ECHR, Article 10 were to be construed narrowly.

Following *Abdul*, on the 6 March 2012, the Director of Public Prosecutions issued guidance to prosecutors in public protest cases. The guidance is available at www.cps.gov.uk/legal.p_to_r/public_protests/. The guidance states that in

---

220 [2005] EWHC 2154 (Admin), [2005] All ER (D) 152.
221 See para **2.98** ff.
222 [2011] EWHC 247 (Admin).

applying the public interest factors, a prosecution for offences committed during a public protest is more likely to be required where:

- violent acts were committed that caused injury or it is reasonably believed could have caused injury;

- the suspect took a leading role in and/or encouraged others to commit violent acts;

- the suspect took steps to conceal their identity;

- significant disruption was caused to the public and businesses;

- significant damage was caused to property;

- the suspect has a previous history of causing violence, damage or disruption of making threats at public protests;

- threats were made against an individual or business that caused or it is reasonable to believe they could have caused alarm, fear or distress.

The guidance states that a prosecution is less likely to be required where:

- the protest was essentially peaceful;

- the suspect had no more than a minor role;

- the suspect has no previous relevant history of offending a public protests or in general;

- the act committed was minor;

- the act committed was instinctive and in the heat of the moment.

Other forms of disposal

1.238   Where there is evidence that an individual has committed a criminal offence, the police and Crown Prosecutors have a number of options other than charging someone and initiating a criminal prosecution. These non-conviction disposals are discussed below. Those facing a charging decision should be aware that they (or their representatives) always have the option of making representations to the appropriate officer in respect of whether it is in the public interest to take any particular course.

Police cautions

1.239   Cautions are often used by police and prosecutors as an alternative to prosecutions. They are used for low-level offences, particularly where the individual has not been in trouble with the police before. Cautions are not a criminal conviction but do require a person to make a formal admission of guilt and are recorded on a person's criminal record. A caution can only be administered with the consent of the person it is being offered to.

1.240   Individuals under investigation should carefully consider whether to go down the route of accepting a caution if it is offered, as it does require a formal admission of guilt and the offer of a caution does not *always* negate the possibility of a prosecution once an admission has been made. Conversely, the decision to offer a caution can be challenged by judicial review if the appropriate criteria were not satisfied[223].

1.241   The decision to offer a simple caution to someone is made by the police alone and must always be considered as an alternative to charge under PACE 1984, s 37. A simple caution is normally administered by a custody officer or delegated to someone suitably authorised. The criteria for determining whether to offer a simple caution includes:

(a)   whether the individual has made a clear and reliable admission of the offence;

(b)   whether there is a 'realistic prospect of conviction' were the person to be prosecuted under the full code test set out in the Code for Crown Prosecutors[224];

(c)   whether it is in the public interest to use a simple caution as an appropriate means of disposal;

(d)   whether a caution is appropriate to the offence and the offender, having regard to the gravity of the offence[225].

1.242   If the individual has previously received a caution (including a conditional caution), then the police will not normally consider administering a further simple caution and may instead proceed to charge. However, representations can be made that if there has been a sufficient lapse of time (two years or more) which suggest that a previous caution has had a significant deterrent effect, then a simple caution can be administered.

1.243   A simple caution can also still be administered if the current offence is minor or unrelated to any previous offences, eg if the current offence is a minor public order offence and the individual has a previous caution for shoplifting.

1.244   A simple caution is not a criminal conviction but is recorded on the police national computer. If a caution is given to someone who is (or wishes to

---

223   *R v Commissioner of the Metropolitan Police, ex p Thompson* [1997] 1 WLR 1519.
224   See para **1.232**.
225   Home Office Circular 16/2008 *Simple Cautioning of Offenders*.

be) employed in a profession that requires notification by the police of any criminal convictions or cautions (eg those working with children, the disabled or other vulnerable people, or in roles that involve national security or the administration of justice)[226] then the police should disclose the caution to that person's employer.

Conditional cautions

1.245   A conditional caution is defined by the Criminal Justice Act 2003, s 22(2) as 'a caution which is given in respect of an offence committed by the offence which has conditions attached to it'. The decision to offer a conditional caution can only be made by a Crown Prosecutor and not the police.

1.246   A conditional caution may be offered for any summary only offence, eg:

- assaulting/obstructing a police officer: Police Act 1996, s 89;

- offences under the Public Order Act 1986, ss 4 and 5.

1.247   They may also be offered for some triable either way offences including criminal damage[227]. See para **2.6** for definition of 'summary' and 'triable either way' offences.

1.248   The criteria for imposing a conditional caution are set out in the CJA 2003, s 23 and include five requirements:

(a)   the authorised person has evidence that the offender has committed an offence;

(b)   a relevant prosecutor decides both that there is sufficient evidence to charge the offender with the offence and that a conditional caution should be given to the offender in respect of it;

(c)   the offender admits to the authorised person that he committed the offence;

(d)   the authorised person explains the effect of the conditional caution to the offender and warns him that failure to comply with any of the conditions attached to the caution may result in his being prosecuted for the offence; and

(e)   the offender signs a document which contains:

---

226 See Home Office Circular 6/2006, *The Notifiable Occupations Scheme: Revised Guidance for Police Forces.*
227 See the Director of Public Prosecution's *Guidance on Conditional Cautioning* Annex A for full list of offences.

- details of the offence;

- an admission by him that he committed the offence;

- his consent to being given the conditional caution;

- the conditions attached to the caution.

1.249   Any condition may be imposed upon the individual who has agreed to accept a conditional caution provided that it has one of the following purposes:

(a)   facilitating the rehabilitation of the offender;

(b)   ensuring the offender makes reparation;

(c)   punishing the offender.

1.250   For example, there may be a condition imposing a financial penalty[228] or requiring the individual to attend a course[229]. See the Criminal Justice Act 2003 (Conditional Cautioning Code of Practice) for more detail on the types of conditions which may be imposed[230]. Failure to comply with any of the conditions imposed renders a person liable for prosecution for the original offence[231] and any signed admission will be admissible in evidence to prove the charge[232]. A police officer can arrest, without a warrant, any person he has reasonable grounds to suspect has failed, without reasonable cause, to comply with any of the conditions of the caution[233].

Reprimands and warnings

1.251   In addition to the adult caution system, there is a similar but separate system of reprimands and warnings for those under 17. The criteria for the administration of a reprimand are similar to that set out at para **1.241** in relation to simple cautions. However, the administration of a reprimand is not dependant on the consent of the young person, or their parent or guardian but does require that the young person has no previous convictions. Both still require that the young person admits the offence.

---

228 Up to one quarter of that which could be imposed on summary conviction or £250, whichever the lower: CJA 2003, s 22(3A).
229 For up to 24 hours in total: CJA 2003, s 22(3A).
230 www.cps.gov.uk/publications/others/conditionalcautioning04.html.
231 CJA 2003, s 24(1).
232 CJA 2003, s 24(2).
233 CJA 2003, s 24A(1).

Fixed penalty notices

1.252   A police officer who suspects a person has committed a 'penalty offence' may issue that person with a penalty notice. The notice must be given at a police station or else by a constable in uniform[234] (although this can include Police Community Support Officers for certain offences)[235].

1.253   'Penalty offences' are defined by the Criminal Justice and Police Act 2001 and include[236]:

- offences under the Public Order Act 1986, s 5;

- trespassing on a railway;

- criminal damage (up to £300 worth of damage, or £500 if public property).

1.254   The penalty notice must comply with the following requirements under the Criminal Justice and Police Act 2001, s 3(3) in order for it to be valid. It must:

- be in the prescribed form[237];

- state the alleged offence;

- give such particulars of the circumstances alleged to constitute the offence as are necessary to provide reasonable information about it;

- specify the suspended enforcement period (21 days: see below) and explain its effect;

- state the amount of the penalty;

- state where the penalty might be paid; and

- inform the recipient of his right to ask to be tried for the alleged offence and explain how that right may be exercised.

1.255   The person given the notice can then pay the penalty and discharge their liability or dispute the matter and put the prosecution to proof in a normal criminal trial process. Anyone who receives a fixed penalty notice has 21 days

---

234 Criminal Justice and Police Act 2001, s 2(2).
235 Police Reform Act 2002, Sch 4.
236 Full   list   available   at   www.homeoffice.gov.uk/police/penalty-notices/penalty-notice-introduction11.
237 Ie comply with the regulations made by the Secretary of State; Criminal Justice and Police Act 2001.

to either pay the penalty or request a trial[238]. If the person does neither, he can be fined a sum equal to one and a half times the amount of the original penalty[239].

Bail after arrest

1.256   See para **2.16** for bail generally.

Street bail

1.257   After arrest, a police officer can grant the arrested person 'street bail' under PACE 1984, s 30A. If granted 'street bail' the individual is released on the condition that they attend the police station on a given date. There is no limit in PACE 1984 to the length of time between release and the time that the person must report.

1.258   When granting street bail, the police have the power to impose such bail conditions (except the imposition of sureties and securities) as appear to be necessary to ensure that the person:

- surrenders to custody; and/or

- does not commit offences on bail; and/or

- does not interfere with witnesses or otherwise obstruct the course of justice.

1.259   A person given street bail must be given a notice in writing[240] stating:

(a)   the offence(s) for which he has been arrested;

(b)   the ground(s) on which he has been arrested;

(c)   that he is required to attend a named police station at a given time; and

(d)   any bail conditions.

1.260   If someone breaches street bail, by either failing to attend the police station when required or by breaching one of the conditions of bail, then they can be arrested and taken to a police station[241].

---

238   Criminal Justice and Police Act 2001, s 5.
239   Criminal Justice and Police Act 2001, s 8.
240   PACE 1984, s 30B.
241   PACE 1984, s 30D.

1.261   Street bail conditions can be varied by a police officer at the police station where the individual is required to attend. Anyone subject to street bail can apply to the magistrates' court for a variation of the conditions imposed under PACE 1984, s 30CB.

Bail from the police station

1.262   From the police station, the police can release a detained person on bail, either before or after charge. The grant of bail by a custody officer is governed by PACE 1984, s 47. Bail can be granted for someone to return at an appointed date and time, to either:

- the police station (pre-charge); or

- a magistrates' court (post-charge).

1.263   If bail is granted, it is granted in accordance with the Bail Act 1976 (BA 1976), which means there is a duty on the individual to surrender on the specified date or else they face prosecution for an offence under the BA 1976, s 6. The individual can also be subject to bail conditions under BA 1976, s 3, the breach of which may result in their arrest and the withdrawal of bail.

1.264   Any decisions made by the police to either refuse bail or impose conditions on bail must be recorded and the reasons stated. See para **2.31** for duties to record bail decisions.

1.265   Conditions are often imposed by the police on those arrested at demonstrations or public assemblies that prevent them from returned to the site of the demonstration, if there is a belief that there will be further assemblies at that site, eg Whitehall, Trafalgar Square etc. Some protesters from outside London have even had conditions not to enter the M25.

1.266   If the conditions imposed effectively mean that the individual is prevented from taking part in peaceful and lawful demonstrations, then the conditions are arguably a disproportionate breach of Articles 10 and 11 of the ECHR and should be challenged. Anyone granted bail by the police who has not yet appeared before a court can apply to the magistrates' court to vary any conditions imposed[242].

1.267   It is a criminal offence for someone bailed from the police station to fail to re-attend the police station at the appointed date and time[243]. If someone bailed from the police station fails to return to the police station at the appointed

---

242   PACE 1984, s 47(1E) and the Magistrates' Courts Act 1980, s 43B.
243   Bail Act 1976, s 6.

time the police have the power to arrest him. They can also arrest someone they reasonably suspect will fail to attend the police station[244]. On arrest, he must then be taken to the police station as soon as practicable. From the police station, the individual may be granted bail again, with the same or different conditions[245] or the matter may proceed to charge and a fresh decision made on whether to grant or refuse bail[246].

1.268   It is also a criminal offence for someone bailed from the police station to attend court to fail without 'reasonable cause' to attend court at the appointed date and time[247]. Even if someone has 'reasonable cause' not to attend at the appointed date and time it is a further offence not to attend court 'as soon after the appointed time as is reasonably practicable'[248].

1.269   Where the police have reasonable grounds to believe that someone has not attended court, or will not attend court, they have the power to arrest him without a warrant and bring him before the court[249]. Once at court, the individual will face a hearing in relation to the breach, conducted by the magistrates.

1.270   At the hearing, the individual can put forward that he had reasonable cause for not attending court at the appointed time. The question of what is 'reasonable cause' is a matter of fact for the magistrates to determine and will normally require documentary proof (eg medical documentation) if available.

1.271   If the court determines that the individual has breached bail, he can face a sentence of up to three months' imprisonment and/or a fine[250]. The magistrates will also have to consider the issue of bail for the remainder of the criminal proceedings, and the fact that the person has been found guilty of failing to surrender may justify the imposition of more onerous bail conditions or even the refusal of bail.

1.272   It is not a criminal offence to breach the conditions of bail granted by police or magistrates. However, if a police officer has reasonable grounds to suspect that a person has or will breach the conditions imposed, he has the power to arrest that individual and bring him to either the police station or produce him before the court, depending on where he was bailed to next attend. Once in the custody of either the police or the court, and if the police or the court consider that the individual did break or is likely to break any of the conditions,

---

244 PACE 1984, s 46A.
245 PACE 1984, s 37C.
246 Under PACE 1984, s 38.
247 Bail Act 1976, s 7.
248 Bail Act 1976, s 6(2).
249 Bail Act 1976, s 7(3) and (4).
250 Not exceeding Level 5.

the question of whether the individual should be granted bail with the same or more onerous conditions, or remanded into custody will be considered.

Chapter 2

Criminal court procedural issues

2.1   The following is intended only as an outline to criminal court procedure for adults, including particular issues relating to protest cases. There are separate and distinct provisions in relation to children and young people under the age of 18. This section also focuses predominantly on the procedure for summary trials (cases that are tried in the magistrates' court) as the majority of protest cases are dealt with in this way. See Annex A for Summary Trial Case Management Flowchart and Summary Trial Flowchart.

FIRST APPEARANCE AT THE MAGISTRATES' COURT

Timing

2.2   If an individual has been charged with a criminal offence at the police station and released on police bail, he will be bailed to attend the nearest magistrates' court on a particular date. If not granted bail after charge, the detained person must be produced before the magistrates' court as soon as possible, preferably at the next sitting of that court[1].

2.3   Where someone has been issued a summons to attend the magistrates' court to answer an information (written charge) laid against them under the Magistrates' Courts Act 1980 (MCA 1980), s 1, this summons will normally state the date and time the accused is required to attend.

2.4   It is important to note that in relation to summary only offences (ie offences that can only be tried in the magistrates' court) including aggravated trespass, assaulting/obstructing a police officer in the execution of his duty and offences under the Public Order Act 1986 (POA 1986), s 5, an information **must** be laid at the magistrates' court, or the person **must** be formally charged at the police station, within six months of the date of the

---

1   PACE 1984, s 46.

alleged offence. If it is not laid within the six-month time limit, the information is invalid and cannot be proceeded with[2].

2.5 It is only usually at the first appearance before the magistrates' court that a defendant will receive 'advance information' which sets out the basics of the prosecution case against him.

Mode of trial

2.6 There are three categories of criminal offence:

(a) summary only;

(b) triable either way offences;

(c) indictable only.

2.7 Summary only offences can only be tried at the magistrates' court. Offences that can be tried only on indictment have to be tried at the Crown Court before a jury. Triable either way offences can be tried at either the magistrates' court or the Crown Court. Because triable either way offences *can* be tried in the Crown Court they can be referred to as **indictable** offences, but they are not **indictable only** offences.

2.8 The majority of prosecutions arising from protests are for summary only offences such as aggravated trespass, criminal damage (below £5,000), offences under the POA 1986, s 5, obstruction of the highway etc. However, it is worth noting that high value criminal damage (ie damage over £5,000) is a triable either way offence and therefore gives a defendant the right to elect Crown Court trial (see para **2.12** for the right to elect Crown Court trial). In addition, a number of cases in recent years, eg *R v Jones*[3] (RAF Fairford), the 'Ratcliffe-on-Soar' case (Nottingham Crown Court) and the 'EDO Decommissioners' case (Lewes Crown Court) etc, have been charged as a conspiracy to commit criminal damage or a conspiracy to commit aggravated trespass. A criminal conspiracy is an indictable only offence, contrary to the Criminal Law Act 1977, s 1[4], and can only be tried at the Crown Court, before a jury.

2.9 For summary only offences, defendants will normally be expected to formally enter a plea (ie guilty/not guilty) at the first appearance. For either way offences they will be asked simply to indicate a plea. A guilty plea at the first opportunity will entitle a defendant to a one third reduction on their sentence.

---

2   MCA 1980, s 127.

3   *R v Jones (Margaret), Ayliffe and Swain* [2006] UKHL 16, [2007] 1 AC 136.

4   See 'Some basic terms' following para **3.1** for the elements of a conspiracy.

2.10   For triable either way offences where the defendant pleads not guilty or gives no indication as to plea at the first appearance, the magistrates have to address the question of whether the trial will be held in the magistrates' court or the Crown Court. This is known as determining mode of trial. The consideration of which mode of trial is governed by the MCA 1980, ss 19 and 20, and essentially depends on two things:

(a)   the view the magistrates take of the seriousness of the case; and

(b)   whether the defendant elects trial in the Crown Court.

2.11   In order to determine whether summary trial is appropriate under the MCA 1980, s 19 the magistrates usually ask to hear a summary of the allegations from the Crown Prosecution Service (CPS). They then determine whether, in the event of a conviction, their maximum sentencing powers of six months' imprisonment[5] would be sufficient to meet the seriousness of the allegation and whether there are any other reasons why Crown Court trial is more suitable. If they determine that their powers would be sufficient, they will accept jurisdiction over the case. See also the Criminal Procedure Rules 2011 Case Management Extract for more guidance[6].

2.12   If the magistrates accept jurisdiction, the defendant is then asked whether he consents to summary trial or wishes to elect Crown Court trial[7]. If the defendant elects Crown Court trial then, irrespective of whether the magistrates were content to deal with the matter by way of summary trial, the case must go for trial at the Crown Court. If the magistrates decline jurisdiction on the grounds that their sentencing powers are insufficient, then the issue of the defendant's election is irrelevant. The end result is that whilst a defendant in an either way offence will always be able to choose a Crown Court trial, they will not be able to insist on a magistrates' court trial against the magistrates' wishes.

2.13   There are a number of advantages and disadvantages to each mode of trial. The magistrates' court has a much higher conviction rate, but trials are quicker and lower costs may be imposed if a defendant is convicted. The Crown Court has a lower conviction rate but trials often take longer to be heard and costs imposed may be higher.

2.14   If the defendant faces an either way charge which it is determined will be tried at the Crown Court and also faces any **specified** summary only charges including:

---

5   Twelve months for two either way offences and twelve months from a date to be appointed: Criminal Justice Act 2003, s 154.
6   www.justice.gov.uk/guidance/courts-and-tribunals/courts/procedure-rules/criminal/.
7   MCA 1980, s 20(3).

- common assault; or

- low-value criminal damage,

then the summary only offence may also be tried alongside it at the Crown Court on the same indictment if the two (or more) charges are:

(a)   founded on the same facts; or

(b)   part of a series of offences of the same or similar character.

This procedure is set out in the Criminal Justice Act 1988 (CJA 1988), s 40.

2.15   There is a separate procedure under the CJA 1988, s 41, which applies where any person due for trial at the Crown Court also faces any other linked summary only offence not listed within the CJA 1988, s 40. Under s 41, the summary only offence is also transferred to the Crown Court but effectively adjourned until the conclusion of the trial of the indictable matter. Only at that stage is a plea taken from the defendant in relation to the summary only matter. If he pleads guilty then the Crown Court can proceed to sentence but only within the sentencing powers of the magistrates' court. If he pleads not guilty then the Crown Court can try the summary only matter, but if convicted may only sentence within the magistrates' maximum sentencing powers of six months' imprisonment.

Bail

2.16   Another issue that the magistrates will consider at a first appearance is the issue of bail. If the defendant appears before the court in custody, then that person or his representative can make a bail application. The grant of bail in criminal proceedings is governed by the Bail Act 1976 (BA 1976). See para **1.262** for bail granted by the police before the first appearance in the magistrates' court.

2.17   There is a presumption in favour of granting a defendant bail under the BA 1976, s 4, but bail can be withheld if the court is satisfied that there are substantial grounds for believing that the defendant if granted bail would:

(a)   fail to surrender to custody; or

(b)   commit an offence whilst on bail; or

(c)   interfere with witnesses or otherwise obstruct the court of justice[8].

---

8   BA 1976, Sch 1, Pt 1, para 2.

2.18   Bail can also be withheld if the court is satisfied that the defendant should be kept in custody for his own protection[9].

2.19   A defendant who is granted bail is under a duty to surrender to the custody of the court. This means surrendering himself into the custody of the court at the time and place for the time being appointed for him to do so[10]. Any failure to surrender on this given date without reasonable cause amounts to a separate criminal offence under the BA 1976, s 6.

Grant of conditional bail

2.20   Bail may also be granted subject to conditions. The imposition of bail conditions is subject to the BA 1976, s 3, which stipulates that conditions can be imposed by the court if they appear to be necessary:

(a)   to secure that he surrenders to custody;

(b)   to secure that he does not commit an offence on bail;

(c)   to secure that he does not interfere with witnesses or otherwise obstruct the course of justice;

(d)   for his own protection;

(e)   to ensure he makes himself available for the purposes of a report being prepared;

(f)   to ensure that he attends an interview with his lawyer.

2.21   Common bail conditions imposed by courts in protest cases include:

•   to live and sleep each night at a given address;

•   not to contact directly or indirectly prosecution witnesses;

•   not to contact directly or indirectly co-defendants;

•   not to attend a given location.

2.22   There are a number of more onerous conditions that may be imposed, such as requiring the defendant to sign on at the police station at a given date and time and the imposition of a curfew, with or without an electronic tag[11].

2.23   The court also has the power under the BA 1976, s 3 to require the provision of a financial surety (ie someone who promises an amount of money

---

9   BA 1976, Sch 1, Pt 1, para 3.
10   BA 1976, s 2(2).
11   BA 1976, ss 3AB, 3AC.

to the court if the defendant fails to attend court) or security (ie money paid into court that is surrendered if the defendant fails to attend court) before releasing the defendant on bail.

Bail in protest cases

2.24   There have been instances in protest cases where bail has been granted with conditions that prevent the individual from attending a particular demonstration, or a particular location where demonstrations frequently take place. It is not unknown for conditions to be imposed preventing protesters from going to a broad geographical location, eg not to enter the London Borough of Westminster.

2.25   Any bail conditions imposed by the magistrates can only be justified on one of the statutory criteria set out above at para **2.20**. The most frequent justification by the prosecution for the imposition of conditions preventing attendance at a particular location is to prevent the commission of further offences.

2.26   First, although each case is fact specific, it is difficult to see how a broad prohibition from a large area or a particular location could ever be said to be justifiable without evidence that a particular individual had a proven history of offences committed in that borough or at that particular location. Second, any conditions imposed must be proportionate and not constitute an unjustified interference with the defendant's rights under the European Convention on Human Rights (ECHR), Articles 10 and 11.

Variations of bail

2.27   As set out in paras **1.261** and **1.266**, the magistrates can hear and decide applications to vary bail conditions from those on 'street bail' and on police bail who have yet to formally appear before the magistrates (either because they are pre-charge or the date for their first appearance before the magistrates is listed in the future).

2.28   Where an individual has been granted bail by the magistrates' court, both the prosecution and the defence can make an application to the court to vary any conditions imposed[12].

2.29   In *R (on the application of Fergus) v Southampton Crown Court*[13], the High Court reiterated that any change of bail status must be 'necessary' in all

---

12   BA 1976, s 3(8)(a) and (b).
13   [2008] EWHC 3273 (Admin).

the circumstances, bearing in mind the presumption in favour of bail and the fact that a decision in respect of bail engages ECHR, Article 5.

2.30   *Fergus* involved a decision of a Crown Court judge to withdraw bail despite the fact that there had not been a change of circumstances since the grant of bail. However, it is submitted that it also supports the proposition that conditions should not be imposed or varied in respect of bail where there has not been a change of circumstances since the last bail decision.

Duty to give reasons

2.31   If someone is refused bail or has conditions imposed upon his bail by the court (or the police) then the decision-maker must make a record of the decision and the reasons for it and provide a copy of that record to that person[14].

Renewed applications for bail

2.32   If an individual is refused bail by the magistrates under the BA 1976, s 4(1) he can make a renewed application at the first hearing after the hearing where bail was refused. In this renewed application he may put forward any arguments, even if they were argued before in the first bail application.

2.33   If bail is refused for a second time, although the magistrates must consider the issue of bail at each and every subsequent hearing, they are not obliged to hear any arguments that have been advanced on previous occasions. Therefore, in reality, detained persons only have two full applications for bail in the magistrates' court, unless they are able to persuade the court that there has been a material change in circumstances or circumstances that have not been brought to the court's attention which justify a fresh application for bail.

Appeal to Crown Court against bail decisions

2.34   A person refused bail by the magistrates also has a right of appeal to the Crown Court against the refusal of bail[15]. The appeal can only be made if the magistrates issue a certificate of full argument[16] confirming that they have fully considered the issue of bail after hearing full representations from either the detained person or his legal representative.

---

14   See PACE 1984, s 30B (street bail), s 38(3) (post-charge bail decisions); BA 1976, s 5 (police bail) and s 5A (court decisions on bail).
15   Senior Courts Act 1981, s 81(1)(g).
16   BA 1976, s 5(6A).

2.35 An individual granted conditional bail by the magistrates can appeal against the imposition of certain bail conditions to the Crown Court at particular stages of the magistrates' court proceedings. The conditions that may be appealed and the circumstances in which an appeal may be made are set out in the CJA 2003, s 16.

2.36 See the Ministry of Justice website for the relevant forms for making applications to the Crown Court against the refusal or imposition of conditions on bail[17].

2.37

FAQ: How do I instruct a solicitor?

- Many of those arrested at protests already have the contact details of recommended solicitors either through 'bust cards' which provide advice on what to do if arrested, or through websites offering information in advance of the demonstration. Otherwise, if there is the opportunity to do so, it is worthwhile researching firms online prior to the first appearance.

- At the magistrates' court on any given day there will be a duty solicitor who is available to give advice and representation to those eligible for Legal Aid. The duty solicitor will belong to a private firm of solicitors who form part of the duty solicitor scheme or rota. They are not connected to the police or the courts. If you do not already have a firm of solicitors who you wish to act for you by the time of your first court appearance you should approach the duty solicitor if you wish to be represented.

- Even when Legal Aid is available, some protesters prefer to represent themselves at court. Whilst this is certainly better than being poorly represented, it often puts the protester at a disadvantage in relation to their knowledge of the law and the rules of evidence and procedure, compared to those who deal with such matters everyday. The court and prosecuting advocate are under a duty to assist to a degree, but not to the same level as a defence advocate. It is therefore worth considering firms that are highly recommended where the option is available.

---

17 www.justice.gov.uk/guidance/courts-and-tribunals/courts/procedure-rules/criminal/ formspage.htm.

FAQ: How do I get Legal Aid?

- The provision of Legal Aid is means tested at the magistrates' court. In recent years this has meant that a large number of protesters facing summary trial have found themselves without legal representation and having to represent themselves. The threshold for eligibility at the time of writing was an annual income of in excess of £20,000, however there are exceptions to this.

- For more detail see the Legal Services Commission website: www.legalservices.gov.uk/criminal/getting_legal_aid/means_ testing_magistrates_court.asp#who and the eligibility calculator: www.legalservices.gov.uk/criminal/getting_legal_aid/eligibility_ calculator.asp.

- In order to apply for Legal Aid, the person you instruct to represent you will have to complete a number of forms on your behalf. In order to complete the application you will also need to provide proof of any income such as wage slips, bank statements etc.

- Some firms have the capacity to advise and represent *pro bono*, particularly where there is a trial of more than one defendant and the firm already represents one of the others. However, it is hoped that the following overview of how a criminal case proceeds from the first appearance in the magistrates' court will assist those who represent themselves.

- Legal Aid at the Crown Court is currently not means tested but you are still required to provide proof of income and may be required to make a contribution towards the case costs in certain circumstances.

- You should bear in mind that once Legal Aid is granted to a particular solicitors' firm, the courts are very reluctant to allow it to be transferred to another firm if you are dissatisfied. You should therefore make sure you are happy with your choice before signing the form.

Case progression

2.38   If the matter is to be tried in the Crown Court, the matter is either sent straightaway (for indictable only offences) or committed after a further hearing to the Crown Court (for triable either way offences).

2.39   If there is to be a trial in the magistrates' court (which is the case in the majority of protest cases) then the date for that trial will usually be given at the first appearance. See Annex A for Summary Trial Case Management Flowchart.

2.40   The magistrates will then engage in the process of case management and may give a number of directions for the prosecution and defence to follow. Part 3 of the Criminal Procedure Rules[18] sets out the steps the magistrates should follow in pursuit of effective case management.

2.41   The defendant (or his representative) will be expected at the first appearance to indicate:

- what the issues are in the case, (eg whether the defendant was trespassing, whether the officers were acting in the lawful execution of their duty: see Chapter 3 for potential issues);

- any defence he seeks to rely on (see Chapter 3);

- what he wishes to challenge, normally by way of cross-examination of prosecution witnesses;

- what prosecution evidence (if any) he is prepared to accept;

- any defence witnesses he intends to call[19];

- any expert evidence he intends to call[20].

2.42   In respect of defence witnesses, the defendant is now required to notify the court of any witnesses other than himself that he intends to call to give evidence[21]. Notice is required to be given 14 days after initial prosecution disclosure. A pro forma defence witness notice is available on the Ministry of Justice website[22].

2.43   In complex cases, the court may indicate the need for a Pre-Trial Review (PTR) on a given date to deal with issues such as disclosure, witness availability and legal arguments.

2.44   If the defence is putting forward any complex legal arguments, for example on abuse of process, then it is likely the magistrates will also order the service of written 'skeleton' arguments and any relevant case law in advance of the trial.

---

18 www.justice.gov.uk/guidance/courts-and-tribunals/courts/procedure-rules/criminal/index.htm#.
19 Criminal Procedure and Investigations Act 1996, s 6C.
20 CPIA 1996, s 6D.
21 CPIA 1996, s 6C.
22 www.justice.gov.uk/guidance/courts-and-tribunals/courts/procedure-rules/criminal/formspage.htm.

DISCLOSURE

2.45 'Disclosure' is the term used for the process during which the prosecution (and in certain circumstances the defence) are required to give the other party/parties material under their obligation to assist in the progress of a fair trial. The proper and just conduct of the disclosure processes by the prosecution is fundamental to the right to a fair trial, as protected by Article 6 of the ECHR which requires that the defence and the prosecution must enjoy an equality of arms.

2.46 In reality, there is a huge disparity between the resources available to the police and the prosecuting authorities as state agencies and an individual defendant in criminal proceedings. The police frequently gather a mass of material and information in the course of criminal investigations, only some of which will be deemed relevant by them at trial. However, some of this material held by the police may, in fact, assist the defence. It is therefore in the interests of fairness and equality of arms that there is an obligation on the prosecution to also disclose this material, as otherwise the defence would be unable to access it.

2.47 In the case of *Jespers v Belgium*[23] the European Commission on Human Rights decided that the 'equality of arms' principle imposed on prosecuting and investigating authorities an obligation to disclose any material in their possession or to which they could gain access, which may assist the accused in exonerating himself. In order to address this disparity and to ensure a fair trial, the statutory disclosure regime set out in the Criminal Procedure and Investigations Act 1996 (CPIA 1996) (see below) should be rigorously adhered to by prosecutors and police.

2.48 Disclosure is often a major issue in protest trials. The framework for disclosure by the prosecution to the defence is governed by the Criminal Procedure and Investigations Act 1996, the Codes of Practice issued under the Criminal Procedure and Investigations Act 1996, Part II and Part 22 of the Criminal Procedure Rules 2011[24]. Also of importance are the Attorney General's 2005 Guidelines on Disclosure and the CPS Disclosure Manual[25].

Principles of disclosure

2.49 In the first stage of 'disclosure', the prosecution must serve their case on the defence in advance of the trial. This should include any material that the

---

23 (1983) 5 EHRR CD305.
24 SI 2011/1709.
25 www.attorneygeneral.gov.uk/Publications/Pages/AttorneyGeneralsGuidelines.aspx.

prosecution intends to rely on at trial, although material may be served later if it has only then become available or relevant. The prosecution evidence at this preliminary stage will normally include:

- witness statements and notebooks of any witnesses it proposes to call to give evidence;

- any CCTV footage it intends to play;

- any photographs it proposes to show;

- any forensic evidence (fingerprints/DNA evidence) it intends to rely upon;

- a transcript and/or tape of the defendant's interview under caution at the police station, if relied upon.

2.50   However, the evidence that the prosecution will rely on at trial is often only part of the evidence that has been collected as part of the criminal investigation. The police are under a duty to retain any material that comes into their possession that may be relevant to the investigation[26].

2.51   Any material that is retained as part of an investigation should be logged by the police disclosure officer on form MG6C, otherwise known as the 'Non-Sensitive Schedule of Unused Material'. Each item should be listed with a brief description of what the item is, where it is held and whether it has been disclosed. See the CPS Disclosure Manual for guidance: www.cps.gov.uk/legal/d_to_g/disclosure_manual/annex_c_disclosure_manual/#a08.

2.52   Under CPIA 1996, s 3, the prosecution has an overarching duty to disclose to the defence any prosecution material (including material that appears on the 'unused' schedule) which has not previously been disclosed to the accused and which might reasonably be considered capable of:

- undermining the case for the prosecution against the accused; or

- assisting the case for the accused.

2.53   What this means in practice is that once the police have prepared the schedule of unused material, the disclosure officer and/or the prosecuting lawyer should review the material on the schedule and consider whether any of the material on it falls within the criteria of the CPIA 1996, s 3. The decision made in relation to each item on the schedule should be marked next to it. Usual markings include 'E' for evidence, 'D' for disclose, and 'CND' for clearly not disclosable.

---

26 See AG Guidelines on Disclosure at para 28.

2.54   If there is unused material that the prosecution claim should not be disclosed as it is subject to Public Interest Immunity (PII)[27] then it should be listed separately on a 'Sensitive Schedule of Unused Material'. The contents of this schedule may not be disclosed to the defence but the defence must be informed if such a schedule exists. See para **2.81** for public interest immunity applications.

2.55   Under the CPIA 1996, s 3 if a decision is made not to disclose some or all or the material on the schedule then the prosecution must produce a written statement (normally in the form of a letter) informing the defendant that undisclosed material does not meet the statutory test for disclosure.

2.56   In determining the question of whether material is capable of assisting the case for the accused, the Attorney General's Guidelines on Disclosure[28] make it clear that what can assist includes material that not only could be used to explain the accused's actions, support his case, or provide material for cross-examination of prosecution witnesses, but also where it might support submissions that could lead to the exclusion of evidence, a stay or proceedings, or a finding that any public authority (including the police) had acted in a way that was incompatible with the accused's rights under the ECHR.

2.57   For example, if there was evidence in the prosecution's possession that showed that the defendant's arrest might have been unlawful then this should be disclosed, even if the conduct of the arrest is not a central issue in the case. The credibility of the arresting officer as a witness may be called into question by the defence, in light of the evidence and it may be used to establish a broader point for the defence in relation to the conduct of the policing on that given day.

2.58   The House of Lords made it clear in the case of *R v H, R v C*[29] that the question of disclosure should be looked at widely:

> 'Fairness ordinarily requires that any material held by the prosecution which weakens its case or strengthens that of the defendant, if not relied on as part of its formal case against the defendant, should be disclosed to the defence. Bitter experience has shown that miscarriages of justice may occur where such material is withheld from disclosure. The golden rule is that full disclosure of such material should be made'.

2.59   The disclosure obligation on the Crown is to disclose material that assists the defence by allowing a defendant to put forward 'a tenable case in the

---

27 See para **2.80**.
28 At paras 10–14.
29 *R v H; R v C* [2004] 1 All ER 1269.

best possible light' or material that assists the defence to make further enquiries which might assist in showing the defendant's innocence or in avoiding a miscarriage of justice[30].

2.60 Examples of material which have been found to be disclosable at this stage include:

- the identity of potential witnesses[31];

- details of the reward to be paid to a prosecution witness[32];

- the information provided to a prosecution expert and his working papers[33];

- all notes and statements from eye-witnesses[34].

2.61 As stated above (at para **2.41**) at the first appearance for summary trials, defendants are required to indicate any issues they take with the prosecution case and any defences that they will rely upon for trial. One of the supposed advantages of doing so is that this should enable the prosecution to consider the issue of disclosure knowing what the outline of the defendant's case is, and therefore they are better able to determine what material in their possession may assist the defendant.

Defence statements

2.62 Despite its name, a defence statement is not a witness statement made by the defendant and served on the court and the prosecution. It is a (usually short) document that sets out in simple terms the key issues in the case and the key facts that the defendant relies upon in his defence.

In some cases before the magistrates, it may be to the defendant's advantage to go further than simply indicating the issues in the case, and serve a defence statement that complies with the CPIA 1996, ss 5 and 6A. The service of defence statements is not mandatory for cases being tried in the magistrates' court but, if it is to be done, should be served within 14 days of the prosecution

---

30 *R v Makin* [2004] EWCA Crim 1607.
31 *R v Heggart* [2001] 4 Archbold News 2, CA.
32 *R v Allan* [2004] EWCA Crim 2236, [2005] Crim LR 716.
33 *R v Olu, Wilson and Brooks* [2010] EWCA Crim 2975, [2011] Cr App Rep 33.
34 Ibid.

serving their s 3 CPIA letter, otherwise an adverse inference can be drawn. A pro forma defence statement can be downloaded from the Ministry of Justice website[35].

2.63   A defence statement, if served, must set out:

(a)   the nature of the accused's defence and any particular defences upon which he will rely;

(b)   the matters of fact on which he takes issue with the prosecution, and why;

(c)   the particulars of fact on which he intends to rely at trial;

(d)   any point of law which he wishes to rely on and any legal authorities that support it;

(e)   details of any alibi (if applicable);

(f)   details of any alibi witnesses (if applicable).

2.64   The advantage of serving a defence statement is that it can prompt further disclosure from the prosecution. It can also form the basis of an application for disclosure of specific material that is believed to be in the hands of the police.

2.65   If further disclosure is sought then it is usual to set out in a defence statement why it is argued that a particular item on the unused schedule should be disclosed. A defence statement is also an opportunity to request items that are not on the schedule if it is believed that:

(a)   the item exists; and

(b)   it would undermine the prosecution or assist the defence.

2.66   For example, where the lawfulness of the deployment of Public Order Act powers against a defendant is central to a defence, there may be evidence which assists the defence in the police briefing documentations or the commanding officer's record sheets. These may set out or summarise discussions in relation to the imposition of restrictions on the protest and show whether due regard was given to ECHR, Articles 10 and 11. See para **2.76** for examples of other relevant disclosure requests in protest cases.

2.67   In some cases, there may be material held in the hands of third parties that the defendant believes may be of assistance to his defence. There is guidance to be found in respect of third party material in the AG Guidelines on

---

35   www.justice.gov.uk/guidance/courts-and-tribunals/courts/procedure-rules/criminal/formspage.htm.

Disclosure[36]. Therefore, if the police believe that a government department or other Crown body has information relevant to an issue in the case then 'reasonable steps' should be taken to obtain it, although what is 'reasonable' will vary from case to case.

2.68 There may be cases where the police believe that a third party (such as a school, local authority, social services department, hospital, doctor or provider of forensic services) has information which might be relevant to a prosecution and it may be capable of undermining the prosecution case or assisting the defence. In those circumstances the police should take such steps as they regard appropriate to obtain that information.

It is also arguable that where the police have been in liaison with a private body (such as a company, business or retail premises) in advance of a public order policing operation, then any material generated through that liaison, such as notes from meetings, emails etc, could be disclosable if relevant.

2.69 Even if the police do obtain such material, however, it does not mean that it will be disclosed. The disclosure officer must still consider the material in line with the CPIA 1996, s 3 criteria.

CPIA 1996, section 8 applications for further disclosure

2.70 Once the prosecution has considered any defence statement and any disclosure requests contained within it, they should respond confirming whether they consider any further items are disclosable and if so, they should be disclosed[37].

2.71 If at any time after the service of his defence statement, the defendant has reason to believe that the prosecution has failed to comply with its disclosure obligations and that there is further prosecution material that should be disclosed, he can apply to the court for an order requiring its disclosure under the CPIA 1996, s 8. A pro forma s 8 CPIA application can be downloaded from the Ministry of Justice website[38].

2.72 No CPIA 1996, s 8 application can be made unless a defence statement has been served and the procedure for the application is set out in the Criminal Procedure Rules 2011, r 22.5. A defendant is still entitled to disclosure, even if the defence statement was served late[39].

---

36 At paras 47–54.
37 CPIA 1996, s 7.
38 www.justice.gov.uk/guidance/courts-and-tribunals/courts/procedure-rules/criminal/formspage.htm.
39 *DPP v Wood; DPP v McGillicuddy* [2006] EWHC 32 (Admin), (2006) Times, 8 February.

2.73 Any CPIA 1996, s 8 application must:

(a) be in writing;

(b) describe the material that the defendant wants the prosecution to disclose;

(c) explain why the defendant has reasonable cause to believe that:

- the prosecutor has that material, and

- it is material that the CPIA 1996, s 3 requires the prosecution to disclose;

(d) indicate whether an oral court hearing is required.

2.74 If a CPIA 1996, s 8 hearing takes place, the court will consider first whether the requested material is currently in the prosecution's possession and whether it reasonably ought to be disclosed (see AG Guidelines on Disclosure paras 47–48). The court can direct that the police obtain the material if it deems it to be relevant and potentially disclosable.

2.75 If the material is already in the prosecution's possession and available, then the court must, after hearing submissions on disclosure from the prosecution and defence, rule on whether the material does meet the statutory criteria in CPIA 1996, s 3 and therefore should be disclosed to the defence.

What to request

2.76 It is impossible to compile a list of material that should be requested in every case, as each case depends on its individual facts. However, it is hoped that the following non-exhaustive list may provide some relevant suggestions for the types of material that the prosecution may hold which may be of relevance to the facts of a particular case:

- unedited CCTV footage;

- interview transcripts/tapes;

- briefing notes/slides;

- details of civilian witnesses;

- details of other officers present;

- communications between police and protest site;

- details of covert operations/surveillance;

- previous convictions, complaints against officers.

2.77 The following may also be useful and should be considered:

(a) Police Officer's Pocket Notebooks: These may contain the officer's notes made at the scene, any details of potential witnesses, any other enquiries made at the time and the time the notes were made;

(b)   Police Officer's Incident Report Books/Draft Witness Statements: The original accounts of police officers and witnesses should be disclosed so that any inconsistencies between their accounts can be identified. Other police officers present at the scene may have made notes even if they are not relied on as witnesses;

(c)   Plans/maps: Helpful if there is an issue of trespass and the Crown have to prove that the defendant was in fact on private land;

(d)   Crime Reports: Crime Reports vary in detail but they are essentially computer reports generated by the police into which they enter names and details of all witnesses spoken to, information received, decisions made etc;

(e)   Computer Aided Dispatch records (CADs): Usually record the making of a 999 call, the details relayed to and the response from the police;

(f)   Use of force forms: Every officer who uses force against any civilian during a police operation should complete one of these forms and set out his justification for the use of force. Can be useful to compare against anything later stated in statements or oral evidence;

(g)   Police Evidence Gathering Team (EGT) footage: Police are increasingly using EGT filming at protests and demonstrators often know whether their interaction with the police was/should have been captured on that footage;

(h)   Audio recordings/transcripts: EGT officers often have audio recorders on their person;

(i)   Records of decisions made by commanding officers: In advance of a public order policing operation, the 'Gold' and 'Silver' command often record core decisions made in the deployment of particular powers and/or resources; eg a record of when/if a s 14 Public Order Act direction was given;

(j)   Briefing notes and intelligence material: Before most major policing operations, the officers involved may be briefed on the information the police have about what is to take place, the tactics to be used and individuals to look out for. This material may be relevant to what was in an officer's mind at any given time and may show whether proper consideration was given to the necessity of any particular strategy;

(k)   Whether any undercover officers were involved: The use of such officers may give rise to arguments in relation to entrapment[40]. Even if not, such officers may be able to provide evidence which supports the defence case;

---

40   See para **2.94**.

(1)   Custody records: Custody officers should record any incidents that take place in custody as well as any injuries on the defendant and any complaints made by him about his treatment in custody.

2.78   What the higher courts have made clear time and time again is that what is to be avoided in defence disclosure requests is a 'fishing expedition'. That is asking for material which may be of interest to them but has no direct relevance to the issues for trial. It is important to argue in relation to each item that is requested in either a defence statement or CPIA 1996, s 8 application, the direct relevance and why it is said that it may either undermine the prosecution case or assist the defence.

2.79   The phrase 'fishing expedition' is often misunderstood, however, and is used as a 'catch-all' response to defence requests for disclosure. A 'fishing expedition' **does not mean** asking for material not knowing whether or not it assists. The defence will not usually **know** if material assists or not. When putting forward a defence of self-defence, for instance the defendant will often not know if the person they say attacked them has previous convictions for violence. However, if they do, the defence are undoubtedly entitled to disclosure of this material. Similarly, asking if there are any witnesses known to the police but not relied upon by them, is not 'fishing' for material. The relevance is obvious even though the defence do not know the answer. If the defence knew the answer, there would often be no reason to ask for disclosure of the material.

Non-disclosure and abuse of process

2.80   In limited circumstances the prosecution's failure to disclose evidence due to its non-availability, destruction or even due to a refusal or failure by the prosecution to do so when ordered, may result in a successful application by the defence to stay the proceedings as an abuse of process. See para **2.86** for abuse of process.

Public Interest Immunity

2.81   CPIA 1996, s 3(6) states that material must not be disclosed if the court, on an application by the prosecution, concludes that it is not in the public interest to disclose it and therefore orders that it not be disclosed. Public Interest Immunity, or PII can only be claimed over material that should otherwise be disclosed under the CPIA 1996, s 3.

2.82   The prosecution may claim PII over a range of material, from information that would reveal the existence of covert or intelligence operations, to records of strategic decisions that they claim, if disclosed, would compromise effective policing or national security.

2.83   In an application for PII it is for the court to determine whether in fact the disclosure of the material is not in the public interest. See the Criminal Procedure Rules 2011, rr 22.3 and 22.6 and Chapter 13 of the CPS Disclosure Manual for the full procedure that should be followed in an application for PII. The usual procedure is for the court to be provided with a copy of the material in question, without a copy being provided to the defence. The defence will normally be told the category of material unless this would in itself give away that which was sought to be withheld. The defence are then entitled to make submissions (although they are somewhat 'blind') and the court will then rule on the issue of disclosure. If disclosure is not ordered, the material will not be seen by the defence. If disclosure is ordered, then it must be disclosed to the defence immediately.

2.84

Disclosure checklist

- Has the prosecution disclosed all the evidence it will rely upon at trial? (see para **2.49**)

- Has the prosecution served a 'Schedule of Unused Material'? (see para **2.51**)

- Is there anything on the schedule that has not been disclosed that ought to have been? (see para **2.56**)

- Should a defence statement be served (see para **2.62**ff)

- Has the prosecution responded to the defence statement?

- Is there anything not on the schedule that the defence believe exists and should be dislosed?

- Does the defence need to make a s 8 CPIA application? (see para **2.70**ff)

- Has the prosecution prepared a 'Schedule of Sensitive Material'?

- Will the prosecution be making a PII application? (see para **2.81**)

SUMMARY TRIAL PROCEDURE

2.85   See Annex A.2 for Summary Trial Procedure.

ABUSE OF PROCESS

General

2.86   The courts have an inherent power to protect their processes from being used as an abuse either against a particular defendant or against the common principles of justice and fairness. The court can therefore stop or 'stay' any proceedings it rules to be an abuse of its process.

2.87   The power to stay can be used in many different ways but the classic definition of where the power should be exercised was set out by the Court of Appeal in *R v Beckford*[41] namely:

(a)   where the defendant would not receive a fair trial; and/or

(b)   where it would be unfair to try the defendant.

2.88   This power should not be used where a court considers a prosecution unwise or ill-advised. The question as to whether to prosecute a defendant or not is always at the discretion of the prosecutor, not the court[42].

2.89   The magistrates' court has the power to stay proceedings as an abuse of process but the Court of Appeal has made clear that the power should be used very sparingly by magistrates and 'very strictly confined' to:

● matters which will have a direct effect on the fairness of the trial that the magistrates themselves are dealing with; and

● should only be employed if there is no other course[43].

2.90   This restrictive approach is attributed to the fact that in triable either way cases of any significant complexity, the magistrates can decline jurisdiction. There is also a high degree of supervision that can be exercised over the magistrates' court decisions by the High Court by way of applications for judicial review or appeals by way of case stated (see para **2.116** ff). These are seen to offer an additional layer of protection for defendants and fair trial procedure.

Examples

2.91   There are a number of situations in which an application to stay proceedings as an abuse of process may be appropriate. What follows is not an

---

41   [1996] Cr App Rep 94, [1995] RTR 251.
42   See *DPP v Humphrys* [1977] 1 AC 1, HL.
43   *R v Horseferry Road Magistrates' Court, ex p Bennett* [1994] 1 AC 42, [1993] 3 WLR 90, HL.

exhaustive list of scenarios, as there are numerous cases all of which turn on their individual facts. The following is also not intended to be a definitive analysis of the law as there are full specialist texts dedicated to the subject. It is hoped that it can be a helpful indicator of areas where concerns may arise.

Prosecution going back on a promise

2.92   Where an individual has been led to believe that he will not be prosecuted, but then is, this is capable of founding an application to stay as abuse of process. However, the Court of Appeal decision in *R v Abu Hamza*[44] has made it difficult to succeed in any application unless there is evidence:

- of an unequivocal representation by those with the conduct of an investigation or the prosecution that the defendant will not be prosecuted; and

- that the defendant has acted on that promise to his detriment.

2.93   One example may be where an individual at the police station is given an unequivocal promise that he will be given a caution if he admits guilt. That individual then makes a false admission of guilt in order to avoid a prosecution and the risk of a conviction. However, even if there has been an unequivocal representation and reliance, the prosecution may be justified if additional facts come to light that were not known at the time.

Entrapment

2.94   For example, where a police officer (usually an undercover officer) induces an individual to commit a criminal offence and then prosecutes them for it[45].

Undue delay in bringing a case to court

2.95   This will normally only amount to an abuse if the defendant has been prejudiced by the delay. The delay would normally need to be significant and without good reason.

---

44 [2006] EWCA Crim 2918, [2007] QB 659, [2007] 2 WLR 226.
45 See *R v Looseley; Attorney General's Reference (No 3 of 2000)* [2001] UKHL 53, [2001] 1 WLR 2060, [2001] 4 All ER 897.

Manipulation or misuse of the court process

2.96   For example, where a prosecutor, without reaching a final decision as to whether to prosecute, lays an information before magistrates just within the time limit in order to 'keep his options open'[46].

Loss or destruction of evidence

2.97   If there has been a breach by the police and/or prosecution of their obligation to obtain and retain relevant material from the investigation (see para **2.49** in relation to disclosure obligations) then the court will have to decide whether the defence can show, on the balance of probabilities, that the non-availability of that evidence would cause serious prejudice to the defendant so that he could not have a fair trial[47]. However, the courts have been reluctant to approve stays on this basis in the absence of clear bad faith or at least some serious fault on the part of the prosecuting authorities, instead encouraging the trial process itself to seek to remedy any unfairness, for example, through the exclusion of evidence. (See below on the exclusionary power under PACE 1984, s 78.)

Excluding evidence under PACE 1984, s 78

2.98   PACE 1984, s 78 gives a criminal court the power to refuse to allow the prosecution to rely on certain evidence if it appears to the court that:

(a)   having regard to all the circumstances

(b)   including the circumstances in which the evidence was obtained

(c)   that the admission of the evidence against the defendant would have such an adverse effect of the fairness of the proceedings that

(d)   the court ought not to admit it.

2.99   Section 78 of PACE 1984 is arguably the most important protection for a defendant in a criminal trial. It gives a judge or magistrates a broad discretion to exclude evidence that makes proceedings unfair and is therefore an important tool for the courts to use to uphold the defendant's right to a fair trial under the ECHR, Article 6.

2.100   There is no guidance set out in PACE 1984 itself as to how and when the discretion in s 78 should be exercised. Each case will depend on its facts.

---

46 *R v Brentford Justices, ex p Wong* (1981) 73 Cr App Rep 65, DC.
47 *R (on the application of Ebrahim) v Feltham Magistrates' Court; Mouat v DPP* [2001] EWHC Admin 130, [2001] 1 WLR 1293, [2001] 1 All ER 831.

There is a large amount of case law on the topic, which will not be repeated here for the sake of brevity. However, the most common area for s 78 applications to arise in, is where there is an allegation that the police have breached the provisions of PACE 1984 or the PACE Codes in their conduct of the investigation, including the defendant's arrest and any searches that take place.

Significant and substantial breaches of PACE 1984

2.101   From the cases that have been decided in relation to the use of the power under PACE 1984, s 78 it has been suggested in three key cases that a 'significant and substantial' breach of PACE or its Codes should trigger the exercise of the discretion to exclude[48].

2.102   There is no requirement for police officers to have acted in bad faith in respect of the defendant before evidence is excluded. However, evidence of bad faith will strengthen any application to exclude. The presence of bad faith may make a breach of PACE or its Codes 'significant and substantial' where it otherwise may not have been considered to be so.

The following are some examples of where evidence may be excluded under PACE 1984, s 78.

2.103   **Unlawful searches.** The simple fact that prosecution evidence is discovered as the result of an unlawful search does not automatically render that evidence inadmissible or automatically liable to exclusion under PACE 1984, s 78[49]. In a case involving an unlawful search, the judge or magistrates have a discretion to exclude evidence of what was found and must consider all the circumstances, whether any of the breaches of PACE or the Codes were deliberate and/or done in bad faith.

2.104   **Failure to comply with the requirements of PACE Code C.** PACE Code C deals with detention, treatment and questioning of detained persons (see para **1.191** for more details). It contains a number of key protections for those detained by police officers. Breaches of PACE Code C may be 'significant and substantial' and lead to the exclusion of evidence under PACE 1984, s 78.

2.105   For example, a detained person should only be asked questions regarding their involvement in an offence after they have been given the full caution by a police officer[50]. Failure to caution where it should have been given

---

48   *R v Keenan* [1990] 2 QB 54; *R v Absolam* (1989) 88 Cr App Rep 332 and *R v Walsh* (1990) 91 Cr App Rep 161.
49   *R v Khan, Sakkaravej and Pamarapa* [1997] Crim LR 508, considered and approved by the House of Lords in *R v P* [2002] 1 AC 146.
50   PACE Code C10.1.

will usually amount to a significant and substantial breach of the PACE Code and may lead to the exclusion of any interviews, or comments attributed to the defendant, that should have been carried out under caution[51].

2.106 Similarly, there are detailed provisions within PACE Code C11 in respect of the recording of interviews and the ability of a detainee to check any records for accuracy. These provisions apply whether the person is interviewed at or outside the police station. They are commonly known as the 'anti-verballing' provisions and their importance has been repeatedly underlined by the Court of Appeal. It has been repeatedly noted that if there is a significant and substantial breach of them then evidence obtained should be excluded[52].

PACE 1984, s 78: procedure

2.107 The following procedural matters are important to note for the purposes of magistrates' court trials.

2.108 An application to exclude evidence can be considered by the magistrates as the evidence arises or the magistrates may leave the decision to the end of the evidence.

2.109 There is no 'burden of proof' as such on the defendant to prove that there has been a breach and that the evidence should be excluded. It is the court's own power to control the fairness of proceedings that is being invoked in an application under PACE 1984, s 78 and therefore it is for the court to address the issue of whether the inclusion of the evidence would be unfair.

2.110 Any refusal to exclude evidence under PACE 1984, s 78 can be challenged in the High Court by way of case stated or judicial review (see paras **2.116** and **2.120**).

APPEALS

2.111 See Annex A for Appeals Flowchart.

---

51 *R v Pall* [1992] Crim LR 126, CA.
52 See *R v Keenan* [1990] 2 QB 54, [1989] 3 WLR 1193, CA; *R v Delaney* [1988] 88 Cr App Rep 338, CA; *R v Ward* [1993] 1 WLR 619, [1993] 2 All ER 577.

Appeals from the magistrates' court to the Crown Court

2.112   There is an automatic right of appeal against conviction and sentence by the magistrates to the Crown Court[53]. An appeal against conviction takes the form of a fresh trial before a Crown Court judge and two lay magistrates, but not a jury. The Crown Court will hear the evidence and submissions and come to their own conclusions on the facts and the law. The Crown Court can then dismiss the appeal (upholding the conviction), quash the conviction or remit the case back to the magistrates' court for a re-hearing[54].

2.113   An appeal against sentence can be heard alongside an appeal against conviction or on its own. The Crown Court can substitute the sentence passed with any sentence it feels appropriate on the facts of the case, including one that is higher than that passed by the magistrates[55].

2.114   The procedure governing appeals to the Crown Court is contained within Part 63 of the Criminal Procedure Rules 2011. The Rules and pro forma appeal forms can be found on the Ministry of Justice website[56]. Any appeal from the magistrates' court must be lodged with the Crown Court within 21 days of the sentence in the lower court[57].

2.115   The magistrates may grant bail pending appeal[58] and any person refused bail pending appeal may appeal to the Crown Court[59]. As discussed in para **2.34**, the Crown Court can also hear appeals against the refusal of bail by magistrates at the pre-trial stage.

Appeal by way of case stated from the magistrates' court (and Crown Court) to the High Court

2.116   Section 111(1) of the Magistrates' Courts Act 1980 states that:

> 'Any person who was a party to any proceeding before a magistrates' court or is aggrieved by the conviction, order, determination or other proceeding of the court may question the proceeding on the ground that it is wrong in law or is in excess of jurisdiction by applying to the

---

53 Magistrates' Courts Act 1980, s 108(1)(b).
54 Senior Courts Act 1981, s 48.
55 Senior Courts Act 1981, s 48(4).
56 www.justice.gov.uk/guidance/courts-and-tribunals/courts/procedure-rules/criminal/formspage.htm.
57 Criminal Procedure Rules 2011, r 63.2.
58 Magistrates' Courts Act 1980, s 113.
59 Senior Courts Act 1981, s 81(1).

justices composing the court to state a case for the opinion of the High Court on the question of law or jurisdiction involved'.

2.117   Therefore, the appeal to the High Court[60] by way of 'case stated' is a legal review in relation to errors of law or jurisdiction (ie where the magistrates have done something they had no power to do). The High Court will not review any findings of fact made by the magistrates, unless so unreasonable that no magistrates properly directed on the law could have made that finding.

2.118   In practice, either the prosecution or defence can ask the magistrates to 'state a case'. They do so by submitting a written application within 21 days of the decision they wish the High Court to review[61]. The magistrates then draft a question of law upon which the opinion of the High Court is sought. The High Court can 'reverse, affirm or amend' the magistrates' decision or send the case back to the magistrates with its opinion[62].

2.119   The procedure for stating a case is set out in Part 64 of the Criminal Procedure Rules 2011. The Rules, along with pro forma application forms, can be found on the Ministry of Justice website[63].

Applications for judicial review

2.120   Applications for judicial review are heard by the High Court[64] and are a method of challenging the decision of the magistrates (and other public bodies and tribunals). The principal grounds for review are:

- errors of law;

- errors in the exercise of a discretion (eg whether to exclude evidence under PACE 1984, s 78);

- excess of jurisdiction (ie going beyond the powers given to the court by statute or common law);

- breaches of natural justice (eg bias);

- that a decision was so unreasonable or irrational that no reasonable tribunal which properly directed itself could reach such a decision as a matter of law.

---

60   Applications to state a case are heard by the Divisional Court section of the High Court.
61   Magistrates' Courts Act 1980, s 111(2).
62   Senior Courts Act 1981, s 28A.
63   www.justice.gov.uk/guidance/courts-and-tribunals/courts/procedure-rules/criminal/formspage.htm.
64   Applications for judicial review are heard by the Administrative Court section of the High Court.

2.121 On application for judicial review, the High Court can:

(a) quash or nullify a decision or order made (known as a 'quashing order');

(b) compel the magistrates to comply with its obligations (known as a 'mandatory order');

(c) prohibit the magistrates from acting in excess of its jurisdiction (known as a 'prohibiting order')[65].

2.122 The full scope of judicial review principles are outside the scope of this handbook. The procedure to be followed for an application for judicial review is found in Part 54 of the Civil Procedure Rules[66]. The time limit for submitting an application for judicial review is three months from the date of the decision challenged but, in order to succeed, it must be promptly made.

Which appeal route?

2.123 There is a large degree of overlap between the appellate jurisdiction of the High Court's judicial review and case stated routes as well as the Crown Court's own jurisdiction. The normal route of appeal for errors of law should be the case stated route but judicial review might be appropriate where there is an allegation of unfairness or bias[67]. Issues in respect of any sentence passed should normally be dealt with by the Crown Court, unless the challenge is that the court did not have the power to pass such a sentence.

2.124 Where a person wishes to challenge the version of the facts found by the magistrates, it is very rare that the High Court will find that magistrates were unreasonable in coming to their conclusion. The most realistic option, therefore, is to appeal to the Crown Court who will hear the matter afresh, although there may be the risk of a higher sentence being imposed. It is also important to bear in mind that even when the main appeal is based on a question of law, the chances of success may depend upon a particular version of the facts being accepted.

---

65 Senior Courts Act 1981, s 31.

66 SI 1998/3132, which can be found at www.justice.gov.uk/guidance/courts-and-tribunals/courts/procedure-rules/civil/index.htm.

67 As stated by Mr Justice Collins in the case of *R (on the application of P) v Liverpool City Magistrates* [2006] EWHC 887 (Admin), (2006) 170 JPN 453.

Chapter 3

Common offences and defences

3.1   This chapter will set out the most common charges brought against protesters. It will identify what the prosecution must prove and, as a result, what potential challenges and legal arguments may be run at trial depending on the circumstances. This chapter will then look at specific defences which only apply to particular offences, before considering general defences which may apply to a number of different offences. Finally, an overview of the Human Rights Act 1998 and the European Convention on Human Rights (ECHR) will be provided in order to set out the framework for making such arguments in criminal proceedings. The issues that are raised in this chapter will also inform the requests for disclosure which should be made to the prosecution before trial.

Some basic terms

Beyond reasonable doubt: Standard to which prosecution must prove their case.

Maximum penalty: Maximum sentence which can be imposed. Very rarely imposed.

Guidelines: Guidelines published by the Sentencing Council and available at http://sentencingcouncil.judiciary.gov.uk/.

Conspiracy: An agreement to commit a particular offence. Only triable in the Crown Court.

Joint enterprise: Acting together to commit a criminal offence, eg assisting a bank robbery by driving the getaway car, knowing or foreseeing that sort of offence would take place.

ASSAULTING/RESISTING/OBSTRUCTING A POLICE OFFICER IN THE EXECUTION OF THEIR DUTY

3.2

Legislation	Police Act 1996, s 89
Maximum penalty	6 months' imprisonment and/or £5,000 fine for assaulting; 1 month imprisonment and/or £1,000 fine for resisting/obstructing
Guidelines	Sentencing Council Guidelines on Assault and Magistrates Court Guidelines
Venue for trial	Magistrates' court only

3.3   These are possibly the most common offences faced by protesters following incidents taking place at demonstrations, but the use of these charges is not without controversy. They are sometimes used even when the level of injury caused to police officers, according to the prosecution case, would support a charge of assault occasioning actual bodily harm under the Offences against the Person Act 1861 (OAPA 1861), s 47. Alternatively, the facts of the offence may be sufficient to make out an allegation of assault with intent to resist arrest contrary to the OAPA 1861, s 38. However, both these offences would give defendants the option of being tried in the Crown Court before a jury. Assaulting, resisting or obstructing a police officer can only be tried in the magistrates' court where the conviction rate is significantly higher[1].

3.4   The slight advantage to the defendant in being charged with these offences is that the prosecution have to prove that the officer was acting 'within the execution of his duty'. If he was not then the offence cannot be proved, even if the assault on the officer was serious. Whilst for minor injuries an alternative count of common assault could be charged, the effect of this would be for the prosecution to undermine their own witness from the start. This is because it would allow the defence to argue that the prosecution themselves had doubts about whether the officer was acting in the course of his duty.

3.5   The prosecution must prove that a person:

(a)   assaulted or resisted or wilfully obstructed

---

1   In 2009 the statistics were 98% in the magistrates' court, compared to 81% in the Crown Court (www.matrixknowledge.com/evidence/wp-content/uploads/2011/03/Matrix-Evidence-crime-facts-booklet2.pdf).

(b)   a police officer

(c)   in the execution of his duty.

3.6   Identical offences relating to Police Community Support Officers are set out in the Police Reform Act 2002, s 46.

What is an assault?

3.7   When used in the offence of assaulting a police officer, 'assault' means:

(a)   intentionally or recklessly

(b)   causing a person to apprehend or sustain

(c)   immediate

(d)   unlawful

(e)   violence.

3.8   The slightest touch will technically amount to an assault and no injury needs to be caused. However, such touching is not an offence when it occurs in the ordinary, expected course of everyday life. For example, bumping into someone in a crowd is not a crime nor is patting a person on the back in greeting as it is reasonable and expected. Neither protesters nor police officers will commit an assault if they tap the other on the shoulder to attract their attention, unless they go beyond what is reasonable, for instance perhaps doing so for a long period of time.

3.9   The following examples could amount to an assault:

- drawing a weapon[2];

- throwing something at someone[3];

- spitting at someone[4];

- striking a horse causing the rider to fall[5];

- the use of words alone[6];

- cutting a person's hair[7].

---

2   *Martin v Shoppe* (1837) 3 C&P 373.
3   *Martin v Shoppe* (1837) 3 C&P 373.
4   *R v Lynsey* [1995] 3 All ER 654, [1995] 2 Cr App Rep 667.
5   *Dodwell v Burford* (1669) 1 Mod Rep 24.
6   *R v Ireland; R v Burstow* [1998] AC 147, [1997] 3 WLR 534, HL.
7   *Director of Public Prosecutions v Smith* [2006] EWHC 94 (Admin), [2006] 1 WLR 1571, [2006] 2 All ER 16.

What is resisting?

3.10 The Oxford English Dictionary (OED) definition states that 'resist' means *'to withstand, strive against, oppose'* which would suggest physical action is required. If this is correct, refusing to move when asked to do so will not amount to the offence. It may not always be clear. For example, a person may be asked to bring their hands out from behind their back so that handcuffs can be applied. If they simply do nothing this would not be physical action. If they then tensed their muscles so that the officer cannot bring their hands out, would this be physical action? If they were already tensed when they were asked, would this amount to physical action?

3.11 The necessary mental element is not spelled out as it is with 'wilful obstruction' below, and the authorities do not make the position clear. The OED definition above implies a settled decision to do something and it is likely that the mental element is similar to that required for wilful obstruction, and, therefore, it may be argued that the resistance must be deliberate.

What is wilful obstruction?

3.12 A person wilfully obstructs a police officer if he makes it more difficult for that officer to carry out his duty[8]. For this offence, 'wilful' means the obstruction must be deliberate, with the intention of obstructing the police and without lawful excuse.

3.13 Amongst other things, the following **will** amount to wilful obstruction:

- deliberately delaying police entry to premises[9];

- preventing an officer from lawfully arresting the wrong person[10];

- giving false information[11].

3.14 The following **will not** amount to wilful obstruction:

- doing something with the intention of assisting the police which in fact obstructs them[12];

---

8 *Hinchcliffe v Sheldon* [1955] 1 WLR 1207, [1955] 3 All ER 406; *Rice v Connelly* [1966] 2 QB 414, [1966] 3 WLR 17.
9 *Hinchcliffe v Sheldon* [1955] 1 WLR 1207, [1955] 3 All ER 406.
10 *Hills v Ellis* [1983] QB 680, [1983] 2 WLR 234. It will still be an offence even if obstructing the police is not the sole intention or the motives are laudable.
11 *Rice v Connelly* [1966] 2 QB 414, [1966] 3 WLR 17.
12 *Willmott v Atack* [1977] QB 498, [1976] 3 WLR 753.

- doing something with the intention of preventing offences being committed[13];

- preventing an unlawful arrest[14];

- taking proper steps to identify defence witnesses[15];

- refusing to answer police questions **subject to the provisos below**;

- advising another person not to answer police questions unless done in such a way as to prevent the officer from otherwise carrying out their duty[16].

3.15   It was decided in *Rice v Connelly*[17] that refusing to answer questions put by a police officer will not amount to wilful obstruction as 'the whole basis of the common law is that right of the individual to refuse to answer questions put to him by persons in authority, and a refusal to accompany those in authority to any particular place, short, of course, of arrest'[18].

3.16   This is a particularly important principle but it is important that this dictum is not misunderstood. In the circumstances of the incident in *Rice* where this point was decided, the officer was entitled to ask questions but there was no legal obligation to answer those questions. There are now certain circumstances in which there is an obligation to answer questions. For example, it is now an offence for someone to refuse to provide their name and address when asked by a police officer who has reason to believe they are acting in an anti-social manner[19]. Police officers also have some powers to require citizens to move from their location without arresting them, for example, giving dispersal directions under the Anti-social Behaviour Act 2003, s 30.

3.17   Furthermore, although there is no obligation to accompany police if not arrested, in *Sekfali v Director of Public Prosecutions*[20] the court found that running away from police when approached for questioning **could** amount to wilful obstruction. However, this was only on the basis that the court found that Mr Sekfali and the other defendants had run away *with the intention of avoiding apprehension*. The case is perhaps close to the borderline between non-cooperation and obstruction, but the factual conclusion is possibly best

---

13 *Bastable v Little* [1907] 1 KB 59; *Green v Moore* [1982] QB 1044, [1982] 2 WLR 671.
14 *Cumberbatch v Crown Prosecution Service* [2009] EWHC 3353 (Admin), (2010) 174 JP 149; *Christie v Leachinsky* [1947] AC 573, [1947] 1 All ER 567.
15 *Connolly v Dale* [1996] QB 120, [1995] 3 WLR 786. Even when those steps involved showing the potential witnesses a photograph of the suspect and thereby contaminating a proposed identification procedure.
16 *Green v Director of Public Prosecutions* [1991] Crim LR 782, (1991) 155 JP 816.
17 [1966] 2 QB 414, [1966] 3 WLR 17.
18 1966] 2 QB 414 at 419, per Lord Parker CJ.
19 Police Reform Act 2002, s 50.
20 [2006] EWHC 894 (Admin), (2006) 170 JP 393.

explained on the basis that one of the defendants was found to have incriminating articles on him when finally arrested. Therefore, running away from the police should be lawful if the intention was to get to one's destination quicker, or where the police presence is obstructing one's right to protest, or if, for innocent reasons, one simply wants to be somewhere the police are not.

3.18 Subject to the above provisos, the reasoning in *Rice* that simple non-cooperation does not amount to obstruction, may be extended to other circumstances. For example, in the same way there is no obligation to answer questions, there is no obligation when not under arrest to cooperate with overt filming by Forward Intelligence Teams. The police have no greater power to take photographs than citizens do. Therefore, subject to any requirement to remove facial coverings under the Criminal Justice and Public Order Act 1994 (CJPO 1994), s 60AA, it should not amount to obstructing a police officer to cover one's face when such filming is taken place, even if other people's faces were unintentionally blocked from the camera's view as a result. On a practical note, covering one's face upon spotting the police may well attract police attention as a result.

3.19 A more difficult question would be whether one could go further and deliberately cover other people's faces or block the cameras completely. There is no authority on the question, and doing either may well lead to arrest, but it could be argued that covering other people's faces, where they are not committing and have not committed any offence, is protecting their common law rights[21]. Blocking the cameras completely could be argued on the one hand to be going beyond what is reasonable, and on the other to be enforcing and protecting the rights of the protesters, not all of whom are practically able to prevent themselves being filmed against their wishes. It may also amount to a separate protest in itself against the use of such filming.

Who counts as a police officer?

3.20 The offences apply either to a police officer or a person assisting a police officer. The police officer can be of any rank and need not be in uniform.

3.21 If a defendant does not know or believe that a person is a police officer this will not provide a defence[22]. However, if they do not believe that someone is a police officer and assault them, mistakenly believing it necessary to do so in

---

21 *Green v Director of Public Prosecutions* [1991] Crim LR 782, (1991) 155 JP 816.
22 *R v Forbes and Webb* (1865) 10 Cox CC 362.

order to defend themselves, the usual rules on self-defence should apply and, so long as the response was reasonable, the defendant should be acquitted[23].

When is an officer acting in the execution of their duty?

3.22   An officer being 'on duty' is not the same as being 'in the execution of their duty'.

3.23   There is no definitive list of the circumstances in which an officer will or will not be acting in the execution of his duty. The following guidance has been given:

> '… it would be difficult … to reduce within specific limits the general terms in which the duties of police constables have been expressed. In most cases it is probably more convenient to consider what the police constable was actually doing and in particular whether such conduct was prima facie an unlawful interference with a person's liberty or property. If so, it is then relevant to consider whether (a) such conduct falls within the general scope of any duty imposed by statute or recognised at common law and (b) whether such conduct, albeit within the general scope of such a duty, involved an unjustifiable use of powers associated with the duty'[24].

Did the police officer unlawfully interfere with a person's liberty?

3.24   Any assault, battery, unlawful arrest or trespass to property by a police officer will interfere with a person's liberty and, unless justified, take an officer outside the execution of his duty[25]. Not every physical contact with a person will amount to an assault and there are a large number of cases which concern police officers touching someone without arresting them. If such contact goes beyond what one would expect in everyday life from another citizen, it will amount to an assault and, therefore, be outside the officer's duty unless it can be justified by reference to a specific power[26].

3.25   The following physical conduct has been found to be generally acceptable (based upon the specific facts in question at the time) and therefore in the course of an officer's duty:

---

23 *Kenlin v Gardner* [1967] 2 QB 510, [1967] 2 WLR 129; *Blackburn v Bowering* [1994] 1 WLR 1324.
24 *R v Waterfield* [1964] 1 QB 164, [1963] 3 WLR 946.
25 *Davis v Lisle* [1936] 2 KB 434.
26 *Collins v Wilcock* [1984] 1 WLR 1172, [1984] 3 All ER 374.

- tapping someone on the shoulder to engage their attention unless persisted with beyond generally acceptable standards[27];

- tapping someone on the shoulder and following them[28];

- holding out an arm and requesting that someone stop but not making contact[29];

- escorting a drunk person down a steep set of steps[30].

3.26   The following have been said to be beyond what is generally acceptable and therefore outside the officer's duty:

- taking hold of someone by the arm to restrain them simply in order to put questions to them[31];

- taking hold of someone by the arm to detain them while they discovered if they were the person the police were seeking[32].

Was the interference within the scope of a statutory or common law duty?

3.27   It is not possible to list all of the police's powers and duties. The most important and most relevant so far as protesters are concerned are set out in Chapter 1. If police are entitled to use reasonable force in exercising a statutory power it is set out in the relevant legislation. For example, the Police and Criminal Evidence Act 1984 (PACE 1984), s 117 provides that:

'Where any provision of this Act:

(a)   confers a power on a constable; and

(b)   does not provide that the power may only be exercised with the consent of some person, other than a police officer,

the officer may use reasonable force, if necessary, in the exercise of the power'.

---

27   *Wiffin v Kincard* (1807) 2 Bos & PNR 471.
28   *Donnelly v Jackman* [1970] 1 WLR 562, [1970] 1 All ER 987.
29   *D v Director of Public Prosecutions* [2010] EWHC 3400 (Admin), [2011] 1 WLR 882.
30   *McMillan v Crown Prosecution Service* [2008] EWHC 1457 (Admin), (2008) 172 JP 485.
31   *Collins v Wilcock* [1984] 1 WLR 1172, [1984] 3 All ER 374.
32   *Wood v Director of Public Prosecutions* [2008] EWHC 1056 (Admin).

3.28   Therefore, when police officers were using their powers under PACE 1984, s 17 to enter premises in order to 'save life and limb', they were entitled to move a person out of the way in order to do so[33].

3.29   The scope of the common law powers of a police officer are not spelled out as clearly, but certainly:

> '… it is part of the obligations and duties of a police constable to take all steps which appear to him necessary for keeping the peace, for preventing crime or for protecting property from criminal injury. There is no exhaustive definition of the powers and obligations of the police, but they are at least those, and they would further include the duty to detect crime and to bring an offender to justice'[34].

3.30   In addition, the Criminal Law Act 1967, s 3 provides:

> '(1) A person may use such force as is reasonable in the circumstances in the prevention of crime, or in effecting or assisting in the lawful arrest of offenders or suspected offenders or of persons unlawfully at large'.

3.31   Therefore in *Albert v Lavin*[35] an off-duty police officer was entitled to use reasonable force to detain someone who jumped the queue at a bus stop, in order to prevent the other passengers assaulting him and a breach of the peace occurring.

3.32   In *Johnson v Phillips* an officer was found to be acting in the execution of his common law duty when directing someone to disobey traffic regulations in order to protect life or property[36]. The extent to which an officer can direct a person to disobey the law has not been tested and is not made clear from the judgment in that case.

3.33   It will make no difference that the officer is acting at another's behest[37]. Therefore an officer assisting another officer who is making an unlawful arrest will also be outside the execution of his duty. Furthermore, if the person unlawfully arrested resists the first officer, the second officer cannot justify his own actions on the basis that he was seeking to prevent a breach of the peace. The breach was only brought about because of the first officer's

---

33 *Smith v Director of Public Prosecutions* [2001] EWHC 55 (Admin), [2001] Crim LR 735.
34 *Rice v Connelly* [1966] 2 QB 414, [1966] 3 WLR 17.
35 [1982] AC 546, [1981] 3 WLR 955.
36 *Johnson v Phillips* [1976] 1 WLR 65, [1975] 3 All ER 682.
37 *Bentley v Brudzinski* [1982] Crim LR 825, (1982) 75 Cr App Rep 217.

unlawful actions, and the detainee would be acting reasonably. If the detainee used excessive force to resist then arrest would be justified[38].

3.34   So, for example:

- PC A unlawfully arrests B

  PC A is not in the execution of his duty and B is entitled to resist him

  If B uses excessive force to resist PC A: He may be guilty of common assault

- PC C then assists PC A

  PC C is not in the execution of his duty, B is entitled to resist him

  If B uses excessive force to do resist PC C: He may be guilty of common assault

  If B was using excessive force to resist PC A and this is why PC C became involved:

  PC C may be in the execution of his duty in arresting B and any assault on PC C could amount to assaulting a police officer in the execution of their duty.

- D intervenes to prevent PC C assisting PC A in carrying out an unlawful arrest

  PCs A and C are acting unlawfully and D is entitled to assist B resisting them.

3.35   How far this principle extends has not been tested before the courts. For example, if officers were acting in pursuance of a stop and search policy which was subsequently deemed to have been unlawful, would they have been acting in the execution of their duty? Each case will turn on its own facts, and the degree of remoteness between the officer and the unlawful act and the reason it was found to have been unlawful will be material factors.

Was the use of the powers unjustifiable within the general scope of the duty?

3.36   Where powers are exercised arbitrarily and without justification then they cannot be within the scope of an officer's duty. This imports a level of objective scrutiny and requires that the officer's actions are reasonable. In many cases, this adds little as most powers can only be exercised if there is a 'reasonable suspicion' or 'reasonable belief'.

---

38 *Cumberbatch v Crown Prosecution Service* [2009] EWHC 3353 (Admin), (2010) 174 JP 149.

3.37   A common difficulty in this regard is an officer using excessive force in carrying out an arrest. In *Simpson v Chief Constable of South Yorkshire*[39] it was held that excessive force will not render an otherwise lawful arrest unlawful. On the other hand, the use of excessive force by an officer will amount to an assault and an assault cannot be in the course of an officer's duty. It is important to note that *Simpson* was a civil claim for false imprisonment which argued that as a result of the force used at the time of the defendant's otherwise lawful arrest, his entire time in detention at the police station amounted to false imprisonment. Therefore, the solution may be that *whilst using excessive force* the officer is outside the course of his duty as he is committing an assault, otherwise he is within his duty. The defendant may then still be entitled to rely on self-defence, even after the assault by the officer is over, if he fears further imminent attack.

Specific defences

Self-defence/defence of others

3.38   This defence is considered in general terms at para **3.202** but there are specific factors which apply when it is asserted in this context. The defence would only fall to be considered here if it was found that the officer was acting in the course of their duty, otherwise the offence will not have been proved and there would be no need to consider any defences. The difficulty will therefore be in proving to the court that it was necessary to defend oneself against a police officer acting in the execution of his duty.

3.39   In *R v Browne*[40] it was said that:

> 'Where a police officer is acting lawfully and only using such force as is reasonable in the circumstances in the prevention of crime or in effecting the lawful arrest of offenders or suspected offenders, self-defence against him is not an available defence'.

3.40   This is perhaps too general. The basic principle remains that if a person honestly believes that they need to use force to defend themselves, then the normal rules on self-defence apply, even if the threat or perceived threat is derived from the actions of a police officer.

3.41   **Level of force used:** If the officer's use of force was excessive then, whilst this will not render an otherwise lawful arrest unlawful, it may amount to an assault and would assist a defendant in establishing that they felt it necessary

---

39   (1991) 135 SJ 383, (1991) Times, 7 March.
40   [1973] NI 96, at 10.

to defend themselves and thereby lay the basis for self-defence[41]. It may also be the case that, even if the police officer's use of force was not excessive, if a person honestly believed that it was excessive he would be entitled to rely upon self-defence[42]. Whether the force used was excessive must be a question of fact and a person is entitled to rely upon honest mistakes of fact.

A person would not be entitled to rely on self-defence simply because they believed that an arrest was unlawful.

3.42 A belief that an arrest was unlawful is a mistake in relation to the law as opposed to a mistake in relation to the relevant facts and will not provide a defence.

3.43 **Belief that the attacker is not a police officer:** It is not a defence simply to assert that the defendant did not know that the victim was a police officer. The case the prosecution have to prove is that:

(a)   the defendant carried out an assault; and

(b)   the person assaulted was a police officer; and

(c)   the police officer was in the execution of their duty.

They do not have to prove that:

(a)   the defendant carried out an assault; and

(b)   *knew* the person assaulted was a police officer; and

(c)   *knew that* the police officer was in the execution of his duty.

3.44 However, where a person honestly believes that the person detaining him is not a police officer and that therefore it is necessary to use force to defend himself, he is able to rely upon self-defence[43]. For example, a plain clothes police officer using powers *which he only has by virtue of being a police officer* and not making his authority known, may appear to the outside world to be a thug or a vandal.

---

41   See *R v McKoy* [2002] EWCA Crim 1628.
42   Criminal Justice and Immigration Act 2008, s 76(4).
43   *Blackburn v Bowering* [1994] 1 WLR 1324.

AGGRAVATED TRESPASS

3.45

Legislation	Criminal Justice and Public Order Act (CJPO) 1994, s 68
Maximum penalty	3 months' imprisonment and/or £2,500 fine
Venue for trial	Magistrates' court only

For other offences relating to trespassing on land see para **4.2ff.**

3.46   For aggravated trespass the prosecution must prove:

(a)   a person trespassed on land;

(b)   where people were engaging in, or were about to engage in, lawful activity;

(c)   and did something (distinct from the trespass itself)[44] with the intention of:

- intimidating those people or any of them so as to deter them from engaging in that activity; or

- obstructing that activity; or

- disrupting that activity.

3.47   The senior police officer present at the scene has the power under CJPO 1994, s 69 to direct that people leave particular land if he believes that they have committed, are committing or are about to commit aggravated trespass. If such a direction has been given, breach of it is an offence with the same penalties as for CJPO 1994, s 68. The prosecution would have to prove that:

(a)   the defendant knew that a s 69 direction had been given; and

(b)   the defendant knew that the direction applied to him; and

(c)   he failed to leave the land as soon as practicable; or

(d)   having left, he entered the land again as a trespasser within three months of the direction.

---

44   *Director of Public Prosecutions v Barnard* [2000] Crim LR 371.

What amounts to trespassing on land?

3.48   'Trespass' is not defined in CJPO 1994. Applying the principles of statutory construction it can be presumed that the draftsman who wrote the legislation intended the meaning to be the same as in the offence of burglary, which requires that someone enters or has entered 'as a trespasser'.

3.49   In relation to burglary, 'trespass' is defined as entering or remaining on land without express or implied permission. A person must know he is trespassing or be reckless as to whether he is trespassing[45].

3.50   Entry may only be for a limited purpose. In relation to an offence of burglary, it was implied that a son had a general permission to enter his father's house but not to steal items from inside the house, therefore when he did so he was trespassing[46]. Importantly, however, he had to enter:

> 'knowing that he is entering in excess of the permission that has been given to him, or being reckless as to whether he is entering in excess of the permission that has been given to him to enter, providing the facts are known to the accused which enable him to realise that he is acting in excess of the permission given or that he is acting recklessly as to whether he exceeds that permission'[47].

3.51   In some cases, it will be obvious that permission has been granted for specific purposes only. In other cases, it may not be clear. Certainly, if the general public is allowed access it should not automatically be implied that access did not extend to anyone intending to carry out a peaceful protest.

3.52   Permission to enter or remain does not have to be given by the owner, tenant or occupier[48]. The crucial question may be whether the defendant believes that the person inviting them in had the authority to do so. If he honestly believed they did, he would not be intentionally trespassing. The reverse position—who is entitled to refuse entry—is not clear. In most circumstances, a request to leave will put someone on notice of a risk that they are trespassing and they would therefore be reckless if they remained.

3.53   'Entering' land does not have to mean that a person's whole body is on the land. There simply has to be an 'effective' entry[49], therefore leaning into a building through a window may be sufficient. It may be argued that the crucial

---

45   *R v Collins* [1973] QB 100, [1972] 3 WLR 243.
46   *R v Smith and Jones* [1976] 1 WLR 672, [1976] 3 All ER 54.
47   [1976] 1 WLR 672 at 675.
48   *R v Collins* [1973] QB 100, [1972] 3 WLR 243.
49   *R v Brown* [1985] Crim LR 212.

point is whether the entry allows the person to commit the prohibited act. So, if reaching in through a window allows a person to switch off computers or if leaning across a fence allows a person to block someone's free passage, thereby disrupting a lawful activity, the entry will be effective. Conversely, a person would not be trespassing if they chained themselves to railings but remained outside the land itself. Therefore, it should not matter if part of their body strayed across the boundary as the effect is the same.

3.54   A person entering land honestly not realising it to be private may become a trespasser when informed of the fact. For some protesters, it may then be impossible to leave if they have in the meantime attached themselves to the fixtures. It may be argued in such circumstances that remaining on land thereafter is not intentional or reckless.

3.55   'Land' for the purposes of the CJPO 1994, s 68 does not include a highway or a footpath at the side of the road[50]. It does include:

(a)   a footpath not at the side of the road;

(b)   a highway to which the public have right of way only by foot or on horse (a bridleway) or which is mainly used for that purpose;

(c)   a highway to which the public have right of way only by foot, horse or non-mechanically propelled vehicle;

(d)   a cycle track;

(e)   buildings[51].

> In ordinary terms, a person cannot commit aggravated trespass if they are on a public road or on the pavement[52].

3.56   It is often worthwhile challenging whether the prosecution are able to prove that protesters did in fact trespass on land, as precise boundaries may be unclear, ownership may not be obvious and the legal status of the land may not be proved. Often the prosecution will rely on a witness statement of the occupier or landlord to evince the fact of trespass but defendants should consider requesting disclosure of Land Registry documents, lease agreements and/or Land Registry approved maps to ensure clarity on the issue of trespass.

---

50   Criminal Justice and Public Order Act (CJPO) 1994, s 68(5).
51   *Director of Public Prosecutions v Chivers* [2010] EWHC 1814 (Admin), [2011] 1 WLR 2324.
52   See, however, the offence of obstructing the highway at para **3.187**.

3.57   Even if land is technically private, this will not always be obvious and the mental element of intention or recklessness may not be made out.

What is lawful activity?

3.58   If the prosecution can prove trespass on land, they then have to prove that a 'lawful activity' was being undertaken on that land. A person who could be intimidated, obstructed or disrupted has to be present for there to be an 'activity'. In *Director of Public Prosecutions v Tilly*[53], protesters entered land and damaged GM crops but the farmer who owned the land was not present at the time, and therefore no offence was committed.

3.59   An activity is 'lawful' for a particular person or group of people if they may engage in it on that occasion without committing an offence or trespassing[54]. Difficulties may arise where a particular activity is partly lawful and partly unlawful.

3.60   In *Hibberd v Muddle*[55], Mr Hibberd had climbed a tree intending to prevent it being felled to make way for the Newbury bypass. The chainsaw operator who approached his tree was not wearing a visor or gloves. Mr Hibberd argued that this was in breach of the Health and Safety at Work etc Act 1974 and therefore the activity of cutting down trees was not a 'lawful activity'. The High Court decided that the 'fundamental' activity in question was the clearing of the land by the contractors and not the actions of the individual chainsaw operative. It was the former that Mr Hibberd had intended to obstruct and therefore they ruled that he was properly convicted.

3.61   It is important to view this decision on its particular facts: the High Court were very likely influenced by the tenuous nature of the argument and the fact that the offence allegedly being committed by the chainsaw operative was vague. Certainly, it should not found a general principle in the terms summarised by Staughton LJ that 'one should define the activity as the task to be carried out and not the way it is to be done'. The distinction between the task itself and how it is done is not always clear. The two may be inextricably linked. For example, if one defines the task as 'having a bonfire' and the way it is done as 'using tyres', the activity itself would be lawful. If one defines the task as 'burning tyres' then the activity would not be a 'lawful activity' for the purposes of CJPO 1994, s 68.

---

53   [2001] EWHC (Admin) 821, [2002] Crim LR 128.
54   CJPO 1994, s 68(2).
55   [1997] CLY 1251 Also known as *Hibberd v Director of Public Prosecutions*.

3.62 In *Nelder v DPP*[56] a fox hunt (at the time lawful) was taking place over land which included some land upon which the hunt was unintentionally trespassing. The hunt was disrupted by saboteurs, both whilst the hunt was trespassing and whilst it was not. Again the High Court held that the protesters were properly convicted, predominantly as the disruption had continued some time after the hunt had finished trespassing. It was held in *Nelder*, however, that if the disruption had been confined to the period in which a significant proportion of the hunt had been trespassing, no offence would have been committed.

3.63 It was also said that if the hunt's 'central objective' had been to hunt over land where they were trespassing, the fact that some lawful hunting also took place would not make the activity lawful as a whole. If the reference to the hunt's 'objective' is interpreted as meaning that the intentions of the people who are disrupted should be taken into account, this would cause real difficulties. For example, whether or not a person should be entitled to prevent their neighbour from burning tyres in their back garden should not depend upon whether the neighbour knew they were committing an offence.

3.64 Any assessment of whether an activity was unlawful would also have to take into account the fact that the legislation asks whether the person *'may'* engage in it without committing an offence. It is submitted that it would be no answer to say that the person on the land *'may'* not commit an offence because the activity could be carried out in a different way to the method actually being used. The legislation also refers to carrying out the activity *'on that occasion'*. Returning to the example of the neighbour burning tyres, the activity of having a bonfire *may* be carried out using wood instead of tyres and burning wood would be lawful. However, the activity *on that occasion* was not burning wood, it was burning tyres. The definition of the activity should reflect what was actually taking place.

3.65 What is clear from these examples is that, where it is possible to distinguish lawful activity from unlawful activity, any disruption should be focused on the element of the activity which is unlawful.

3.66 The 'offence' taking place on the land must be a crime contrary to common law or statute. It does not include crimes only recognised in international law such as the crime of aggression. Therefore, military bases supporting the war in Iraq, which has been argued to be a crime of aggression, were not carrying out unlawful activities for the purposes of CJPO 1994, s 68. As a result, in *R v Jones*, protesters who trespassed on to the bases and disrupted

---

56 *Nelder v DPP* (1998) Times, 11 June.

their activities were properly convicted of aggravated trespass[57]. See para **3.205** for further consideration of this case.

Intention to intimidate/obstruct/disrupt

3.67   Actual intimidation, obstruction or disruption is not required[58].

Specific defences

3.68   There are no specific defences in the legislation but it is often argued that there is no public interest in prosecuting offences of aggravated trespass when protesters were exercising their rights under the ECHR, Article 10 (see para **3.121**). The general defences of self-defence or necessity may apply depending upon the circumstances.

CRIMINAL DAMAGE

3.69

Legislation	Criminal Damage Act 1971, s 1
Maximum penalty	10 years' imprisonment where value is more than £5,000
	Three months' imprisonment and/or £2,500 fine where value is £5,000 or less
Guidelines	(When dealt with in the Magistrates Court) Sentencing Council Magistrates Court Sentencing Guidelines
Venue for trial	Crown Court or magistrates' court where value is more than £5,000
	Magistrates' court only where value is £5,000 or less

---

57 *R v Jones; Swain v Director of Public Prosecutions; Ayliffe v Director of Public Prosecutions; R v Richards; R v Pritchard; R v Olditch; R v Milling* [2006] UKHL 16, [2007] 1 AC 136.
58 *Winder v Director of Public Prosecutions* (1996) 160 JP 713.

3.70 The offence of criminal damage, which can apply to a wide range of behaviour, is often alleged in the context of protests, for example, when protesters have written slogans on pavements or buildings, superglued themselves to fixtures and fittings or damaged machinery at industrial plants.

3.71 There are a number of related offences, which include:

(a) criminal damage with intent to endanger life (maximum sentence: life imprisonment);

(b) criminal damage being reckless as to whether life is endangered (maximum sentence: life imprisonment);

(c) arson (causing criminal damage by fire) (maximum sentence: life imprisonment);

(d) threatening to destroy or damage property (maximum sentence: 10 years' imprisonment);

(e) possessing an article with intent to damage or destroy property (maximum sentence: 10 years' imprisonment).

3.72 For the basic criminal damage offence, the prosecution have to prove that someone:

(a) destroyed or damaged property;

(b) belonging to another;

(c) intending to destroy or damage such property or being reckless as to whether such property would be destroyed or damaged;

(d) without lawful excuse.

3.73 For the most part the elements of the offence are self-explanatory. In considering whether there is a 'lawful excuse', specific defences are considered at para **3.81** ff and for self defence and prevention of crime see para **3.202**.

What amounts to 'damage'?

3.74 What amounts to damage is not limited to an act that has permanent effect. Temporarily impairing an item's 'value' or usefulness can be enough[59]. Whether something does amount to damage has been said to be 'a matter of fact and degree, applying common sense'[60]. Each case depends on its own facts but 'common sense' does not seem to have provided much of a restraint on what the courts have found amounts to criminal damage.

---

59 *R v Whiteley* (1991) 93 Cr App Rep 25.
60 *Roe v Kingerlee* [1986] Crim LR 735.

3.75   Less obvious examples of actions that the courts have found can amount to damage, which may be relevant in the context of protests, include:

- removing or displacing parts of a machine so the whole machine is made temporarily useless[61];

- applying water-soluble paints to the pavement[62];

- altering the magnetic particles on computer discs (thereby changing data held in a computer system, which was the actual intended purpose)[63].

3.76   The last of these would not still be charged as criminal damage as a section subsequently inserted into the Criminal Damage Act 1971 states that 'a modification of the contents of a computer shall not be regarded as damaging any computer or computer storage medium unless its effect on that computer or computer storage medium impairs its physical condition'[64]. Although altering or deleting data requires a physical change on some level it will not normally amount to an impairment. The intention of the above change would seem to be that such 'hacking' type offences would instead be dealt with in other ways, for instance as an offence under the Computer Misuse Act 1990. *R v Whiteley* is still important, as it makes the point that even if the alteration is invisible to the naked eye it can still amount to 'damage'. However, in the case in question, it was not simply one magnetic particle which was altered but a great number and the effect of the changes made was significant. This undoubtedly influenced the court's decision. In other cases, there may still be scope for 'common sense' where the impairment is minimal.

What is property?

3.77   For the purposes of the Criminal Damage Act 1971 (CDA 1971), 'property' means only tangible (ie physical) property, and includes[65]:

- land;

- money;

- wild creatures which have been tamed or are ordinarily kept in captivity;

- other wild creatures or their carcasses **if** 'they have been reduced into possession which has not been lost or abandoned or are in the course of being reduced into possession'. For example, a pheasant or rabbit in the butcher's window would legally count as property.

---

61 *R v Fisher* (1865) LR 1 CCR 7; *R v Tacey* (1821) 168 ER 893, (1821) Russ & Ry 452.
62 *Hardman v Chief Constable of Somerset* [1986] Crim LR 330.
63 *R v Whiteley* (1991) 93 Cr App Rep 25.
64 Criminal Damage Act 1971, s 10(5).
65 CDA 1971, s 10(1).

3.78   Property does not include[66]:

- any mushroom or fungus growing wild on any land;
- flowers, fruit or foliage of a plant, shrub or tree growing wild on any land.

When does property belong to another?

3.79   Property belongs to another if:

(a)   they have custody or control of it; or

(b)   they have any proprietary right or interest in it (other than an equitable interest which has only arisen from an agreement to transfer or grant an interest); or

(c)   they have a charge on it;

(d)   the property is subject to a trust, and they have the right to enforce the trust;

3.80   The other person can include a 'corporation sole' (this usually means a religious position such as Archbishop of Canterbury) and property can still belong to a corporation even if there is a vacancy in the corporation.

Specific defences

3.81   There are special defences available in the case of criminal damage which are set out in the CDA 1971, s 5. They do not apply to threatening to damage one's own property knowing that the damage would endanger life. Nor do they apply to possessing an item with the intent to cause criminal damage knowing that the damage would endanger life.

3.82   CDA 1971, s 5 provides that it is a lawful excuse for committing criminal damage if, at the time of the act in question, either:

(a)(i)   the defendant believed that the person who would be entitled to consent to the property being damaged had consented, or would have done if he had known of the circumstances; or

(a)(ii) he acted in order to protect property, or a right or interest in property, belonging to himself or another;

        and

---

66   CDA 1971, s 10(1).

(b)   he believed that the property, right or interest was in immediate need of protection; and

(c)   he believed that the means of protection were reasonable in all the circumstances.

3.83   In relation to (b) and (c), an honest belief that the property was in immediate need of protection or that the actions taken were reasonable does not have to be an objectively justified belief[67]. Therefore, defendants are not precluded from arguing that particular action was necessary simply because the threat to property involves questions of international law and the actions do not have to be reasonable on an objective view. This may be contrasted with the position in relation to the general law on prevention of crime, for which see para **3.205** and para 74 of *R v Jones*[68].

3.84   The courts will take a strict view on whether it was possible for the effect of the damage to have protected people's property and whether that property was in immediate need of protection. If the defendant believed that property might have been saved as a result of his actions but it was not, or where the defendant mistakenly thought there was an immediate need to protect it when there was not, this will cause no problem as it is the defendant's honest belief which provides him with a defence. Where, even on the defendant's own account, there is no or little link between the damage and the property to be protected, the defence will not be made out.

3.85   For example, when a Mr Kelleher knocked the head off a statue of Margaret Thatcher due to 'concerns about materialistic values and the influence of major corporations on seemingly democratic governments' he failed to identify any property which he believed would be saved as a result and certainly not any in *immediate* need of protection[69]. Therefore, his justification could not amount to a defence in law.

3.86   Similarly, cutting a link in the fence of an American airbase, in order to persuade others to do the same and thereby persuade the Americans to close down the base and thereby protect local property from being a target for immediate attack from anti-American forces, was too remote to amount to the defence[70].

3.87   However, in *R v McCann*[71] the Northern Ireland Court of Appeal considered the identical legislation in effect in Northern Ireland. They

---

67   CDA 1971, s 5(3).
68   *R v Jones; Swain v Director of Public Prosecutions; Ayliffe v Director of Public Prosecutions; R v Richards; R v Pritchard; R v Olditch; R v Milling* [2006] UKHL 16, [2007] 1 AC 136.
69   *R v Kelleher* [2003] EWCA Crim 3525, (2003) 147 SJLB 1395.
70   *R v Hill; R v Hall* (1989) 89 Cr App Rep 74.
71   [2008] NICA 25.

confirmed that defendants could run a defence based on their assertion that they had destroyed property at Raytheon Systems Limited in order to prevent them supplying missiles to the Israeli Defence Force, thereby protecting Lebanese homes from being bombed in the military action ongoing at that time. An important question was whether or not the defendants' actions were actually done for this purpose, as opposed to generating publicity or simply being a spontaneous outburst of violence for example, and this was a matter for the jury to decide. A number of factors were highlighted which, the court suggested, the jury may think pointed away from the defendants' assertion that the criminal damage was being done to protect property. These included the fact that the relevant property was only destroyed some time after entry had been gained and that the premises remained occupied by the protesters for some time after the damage took place. In the event, these factors do not seem to have weighed heavily with the jury as, when the matter returned to the Crown Court for the trial to continue, the defendants were acquitted.

3.88   The wording of the judgment in *McCann* suggests that the protection of property must be the only purpose behind causing the criminal damage. If that is correct, someone damaging vehicles, predominantly to prevent them being used to transport illegal weapons, but also to draw attention to the fact that this is what they were being used for, would not be able to rely on this defence. While this is one meaning of the phrase 'acted in order to protect property' it is perhaps unduly narrow as it may not be unreasonable to try to kill two birds with one stone. Outside of the protest context, a person plugging a leak with a piece of clothing should not be committing an offence simply because they took the opportunity to use the item they most hated in their partner's wardrobe to do so.

'PUBLIC ORDER' OFFENCES

Riot/violent disorder/affray

3.89

Legislation	Public Order Act (POA) 1986, ss 1–3
Maximum penalty	10 years' imprisonment and/or a fine for riot
	Five years' imprisonment and/or a fine for violent disorder
	Three years' imprisonment and/or a fine for affray

121

Venue for trial:	Crown Court only for riot
	Crown Court or magistrates' court for violent disorder or affray

3.90   The prosecution must first prove that:

(a)   for riot (POA 1986, s 1):

- a person used unlawful violence;

- intending to use violence or being aware that his conduct may be violent;

- whilst present together with another 11 or more people;

- who were using or threatening unlawful violence for a common purpose.

(b)   for violent disorder (POA 1986, s 2):

- a person used or threatened unlawful violence;

- intending to use or threaten violence or being aware that his conduct may be violent or threaten violence;

- while present together with another two or more people;

- who are using or threatening unlawful violence.

(c)   for affray (POA 1986, s 3):

- a person used or threatened unlawful violence;

- intending to use or threaten violence or being aware that his conduct may be violent or threaten violence;

- towards another person (who must be present at the scene)[72];

- other than by words alone.

(d)   and for riot, violent disorder or affray:

- the conduct of all those present taken together would cause a person of reasonable firmness present at the scene to fear for their own personal safety.

All three offences can be committed in private as well as in public places.

---

72 *I v Director of Public Prosecutions; M v Director of Public Prosecutions; H v Director of Public Prosecutions* [2001] UKHL 10.

What counts as violence?

3.91   'Violence' for the purposes of the POA 1986 means any violent conduct and so (except for offences of affray) includes violent conduct towards property as well as violent conduct towards persons[73].

3.92   Violence is not restricted to conduct causing or intended to cause injury or damage but includes any other violent conduct (for example, throwing at or towards a person a missile of a kind capable of causing injury which does not hit or falls short).

Person of reasonable firmness

3.93   None of the offences require a person 'of reasonable firmness' to actually be present, or be likely to be present[74], but the fact that the behaviour in question could cause such a person to fear for their own personal safety is an important factor for the prosecution to prove.

3.94   It was confirmed in *R v Sanchez*[75] that for the offence of affray the hypothetical 'person of reasonable firmness' cannot be the same person to whom violence is used or threatened. The Court of Appeal approved Professor John Smith's commentary on the earlier case of *R v Davison*[76] in which he stated that the offence 'is designed for the protection of the bystander. It is a public order offence. There are other offences for the protection of persons at whom the violence is aimed'[77].

3.95   The importance of this point is that it means that violence focused against an individual victim and not directed at, or threatened towards, anyone else should not cause a reasonable bystander to fear for their own safety, particularly if the assault takes place out in the open[78]. Therefore, a fight in public does not automatically amount to an affray. Whether it does or not is predominantly a question for the jury.

3.96   Whether the same reasoning and conclusion apply to offences of riot and violent disorder has not yet been considered by the Appeal Courts. On the one hand, these offences do not require that the violence is directed 'towards another'. On the other hand, Professor Smith's comments apply with equal

---

73 POA 1986, s 8.
74 POA 1986, ss 1(4), 2(3), 3(4).
75 [1996] Crim LR 572, (1996) 160 JP 321.
76 [1992] Crim LR 31.
77 *R v Sanchez* [1996] Crim LR 572, (1996) Times, 6 March.
78 *R v Plavecz* [2002] EWCA Crim 1802, [2002] Crim LR 837; *R (Leeson) v Director of Public Prosecutions* [2010] EWHC 994 (Admin), (2010) 174 JP 367.

force. If there is a victim towards whom the violence is directed, for that person also to be the 'reasonable person present at the scene' would turn all assaults in public into public order offences, which cannot have been the intention. The fact that for these offences, a large number of people must be threatening violence may of course make it more likely that the reasonable bystander would fear for their safety, even when the assault is focused on an individual.

Fear of violence/harassment, alarm or distress

3.97

Legislation	POA 1986, ss 4, 4A, 5
Maximum penalty	Six months' imprisonment and/or a £5,000 fine for s 4 and s 4A
	£1,000 fine for s 5
Guidelines	Sentencing Council Magistrates Court Guidelines
Venue for trial	Magistrates' court only

3.98   First, the prosecution must prove that the defendant did one of the following:

s 4	Used towards another person threatening, abusive or insulting behaviour; or	Displayed to any other person any writing, sign or other visible representation which was threatening, abusive or insulting	
s 4A	Uses threatening, abusive or insulting words or behaviour; or	Displays any writing, sign or other visible representation which is threatening, abusive or insulting, or	Used disorderly behaviour.

s 5	Uses threatening, abusive or insulting words or behaviour, or disorderly behaviour, or	Displays any writing, sign or other visible representation which is threatening, abusive or insulting, or	Used disorderly behaviour.

3.99   Second, the prosecution must prove that the defendant:

s 4	Intended his words or behaviour, or the writing, sign or other visible representation, to be threatening, abusive or insulting; or	Was aware that it may be threatening, abusive or insulting	
s 4A			
s 5	Intended his words or behaviour, or the writing, sign or other visible representation, to be threatening, abusive or insulting; or	Was aware that it may be threatening, abusive or insulting	If charged with 'disorderly behaviour': intended his behaviour to be disorderly; or If charged with 'disorderly behaviour': was aware that his behaviour was disorderly

125

3.100   Third, the prosecution must prove one of the following:

s 4	He intended to cause that person to believe that immediate unlawful violence would be used against him or another person; or	The behaviour was likely to cause a person to believe that immediate unlawful violence would be used against him or another person; or	He intended to provoke immediate unlawful violence by that person or another; or	The behaviour was likely to provoke immediate unlawful violence
s 4A	He intended to cause, and did cause, harassment, alarm or distress			
s 5	The behaviour was within the sight or hearing of a person likely to be caused harassment, alarm or distress			

Definitions

3.101   'Threatening', 'abusive' and 'insulting' are ordinary English words and it will be for the court to decide if what was said or done satisfies this section. In a protest case, the court should consider this question in light of the presumption in favour of freedom of expression under the ECHR, Article 10[79].

> 'Behaviour causing resentment, protest or annoyance may not amount to threats, abuse or insults'[80].

---

79 *Abdul v Director Public Prosecutions* [2011] EWHC 247 (Admin), [2011] HRLR 16.
80 *Brutus v Cozens* [1973] AC 854, [1972] 3 WLR 521.

3.102 'Disorderly behaviour' is also an ordinary English phrase and it will be for the court to decide if what was said or done satisfies this section. It is intended to cover conduct which is not necessarily threatening, abusive or insulting and there need not be any element of violence present or threatened[81].

3.103 'Violence' for the purposes of the POA 1986 means any violent conduct and so includes violent conduct towards property as well as violent conduct towards persons[82].

3.104 Violence is not restricted to conduct causing or intended to cause injury or damage but includes any other violent conduct (for example, throwing at or towards a person a missile of a kind capable of causing injury which does not hit or falls short).

3.105 'Harassment' does not require emotional disturbance and although the impact does not have to be grave, it should not be trivial[83]. It does not require that a person fears for their own safety[84]. 'Distress' requires real emotional disturbance or upset. Again, although this does not need to be grave it should not be trivial[85]. Harassment, alarm and distress are all 'relatively strong words befitting an offence which may carry imprisonment or a substantial fine'[86].

Evidence from alleged victims

3.106 In *Atkin v Director of Public Prosecutions*[87] it was decided that though behaviour had to be 'used towards' another person for the purposes of POA 1986, s 4, it had to be used 'in the presence of and in the direction of another person directly'. Therefore, where the threat was passed on by a third party this was insufficient. The headnote to the case suggests that the threat has to actually be perceived by the person to whom it is directed. This, however, is not in the judgment itself, where it was only required that the person be 'within earshot'[88]. For different reasons, it was held in *Swanston v Director of Public Prosecutions*[89] that it was not necessary for the prosecution to call the alleged victim in order to show that he 'perceived' the conduct in question. In that case the victim was face to face with the defendant when the threats were issued and

---

81 *Chambers v Director of Public Prosecutions, Edwards v Director of Public Prosecutions* [1995] Crim LR 896.
82 POA 1986, s 8.
83 *Southard v Director of Public Prosecutions* [2006] EWHC 3449 (Admin), [2007] ACD 53.
84 *Chambers v Director of Public Prosecutions; Edwards v Director of Public Prosecutions* [1995] Crim LR 896.
85 *R (R) v Director of Public Prosecutions* [2006] EWHC 1375 (Admin), (2006) 170 JP 661.
86 *R (R) v Director of Public Prosecutions* [2006] EWHC 1375 (Admin), (2006) 170 JP 661.
87 [1989] Crim LR 581, (1989) 89 Cr App Rep 199.
88 (1989) 89 Cr App Rep 199 at 205.
89 (1997) 161 JP 203.

so there was little doubt that he heard the threat. In other cases, it may be difficult for a court to be sure whether or not someone was within earshot.

3.107   The victim's evidence is less important in cases of POA 1986, s 4 because their reaction to the threatening behaviour is not part of the offence. Depending on the wording of the charge, the POA 1986, s 4 could be proved if a defendant displays a threatening sign intending a person to fear violence, but the intended victim is made of sterner stuff and is unaffected. Alternatively, it may be proved if the behaviour is used towards one person and another person is provoked to violence.

3.108   However, for POA 1986, s 4A someone must have perceived the behaviour, as otherwise they could not have been caused harassment, alarm or distress by it. It is important not to take for granted the requirement that the prosecution prove that the behaviour did in fact cause harassment, alarm or distress. In *R v Jahnke*[90], a protester threw his shoe at the Chinese Prime Minister whilst he was giving a speech, in protest at China's human rights record. He was charged with an offence contrary to POA 1986, s 4A but the prosecution failed to prove that anyone was harassed, alarmed or distressed and he was acquitted.

3.109   If a witness *is* called and gives evidence, and does not say that they were harassed, alarmed or distressed, it is not open to the court to infer that they were[91]. Clearly, they do not necessarily need to use the precise words 'harassment', 'alarm' or 'distress'. Although this was decided in a case only concerning POA 1986, s 5, it is submitted that the same argument applies to the other sections above. Each case will depend upon its own facts, and simply because one witness was not distressed does not mean others were not or were not likely to have been.

3.110   Police officers can be caused harassment, alarm or distress. However, it has been noted that '[very] frequently, words and behaviour with which police officers will be wearily familiar will have little emotional impact on them save that of boredom'[92] and police officers are 'undoubtedly expected to be stoical'[93].

3.111   In *Harvey v Director of Public Prosecutions*[94] it was said that it was not possible to infer that a group of young bystanders in a block of flats would

---

90   (2009) Cambridge Magistrates' Court. See www.guardian.co.uk/education/2009/jun/02/china-shoe-protest-jibao.
91   *Harvey v Director of Public Prosecutions* (17 November 2001, unreported), QBD (Admin).
92   *Director of Public Prosecutions v Orum* [1989] 1 WLR 88, [1988] 3 All ER 449.
93   *Southard v Director of Public Prosecutions* [2006] EWHC 3449 (Admin), [2007] ACD 53.
94   *Harvey v Director of Public Prosecutions* (17 November 2001, unreported), QBD (Admin).

have been harassed, alarmed or distressed by the use of 'rather commonplace swearwords'.

Specific defences

3.112   All three offences 'may be committed in a public or a private place, except that no offence is committed where the words or behaviour are used, or the writing, sign or other visible representation is displayed, by a person inside a dwelling and the other person is also inside that or another dwelling'[95]. This is an element of the offence and is therefore for the prosecution to prove beyond reasonable doubt that it does not apply.

3.113   For POA 1986, ss 4A or 5 it is a defence to prove that the defendant 'was inside a dwelling and had no reason to believe that the words or behaviour used, or the writing, sign or other visible representation displayed, would be heard or seen by a person outside that or any other dwelling'[96]. This is for the defence to prove on the balance of probabilities.

3.114   A dwelling means 'any structure or part of a structure occupied as a person's home or as other living accommodation (whether the occupation is separate or shared with others)' but does not include any part of the structure not occupied as a person's home or as other living accommodation[97]. It does not include a police cell[98], but in other cases, for instance, a student halls, a hotel room, it will be a question of fact and degree.

3.115   A structure includes:

- a tent;
- a caravan;
- a vehicle;
- a vessel;
- a temporary or movable structure.

3.116   For POA 1986, s 5 it is a defence to prove that the defendant 'had no reason to believe that there was any person within hearing or sight who was likely to be caused harassment, alarm or distress'. This is for the defence to prove on the balance of probabilities.

---

95 POA 1986, ss 4, 4A, 5.
96 POA 1986, ss 4A, 5.
97 POA 1986, s 8.
98 *R v CF* [2006] EWCA Crim 3323, [2007] 1 WLR 1021.

3.117   It is also a defence to POA 1986, s 4A or s 5 for a defendant to prove that his behaviour was 'reasonable' in the circumstances. This too is for the defence to prove on the balance of probabilities.

3.118   Ordinarily, whether behaviour is reasonable will simply be a question of fact for the court. There are some helpful comments, however, in the case of *Kwasi-Poku v Director of Public Prosecutions*[99]. The facts themselves have nothing to do with protests but are necessary to explain the ruling. Police officers told an unlicensed ice-cream vendor that they had the power to seize his van when in fact they did not. The High Court decided that 'if law enforcement officers, in relation to a valuable item such as a van, threaten to exercise confiscatory powers, in excess of those which they possess it is, in my judgment, only to be expected that the person threatened will protest, perhaps in vehement terms, and in those circumstances his conduct cannot necessarily be described as unreasonable'[100].

3.119   The same argument can be deployed in a protest context. If police officers exceed their powers, a vociferous response may be expected. For a similar result in relation to assaulting a police officer see *Cumberbatch v CPS* at para **3.33**. Where state action is subsequently deemed unlawful, this may add weight to an argument that colourfully expressed objection to that action was reasonable.

3.120   It may be more difficult to establish this defence in relation to a charge under the POA 1986, s 4A. The court in *Norwood v Director of Public Prosecutions*[101] had difficulty envisaging circumstances in which behaviour could be intentionally insulting and could cause alarm or distress and yet could still be reasonable. Depending on the circumstances, stand-up comedy and 'justified anger' as outlined above may be two possibilities.

Human rights

3.121   Although not, strictly speaking, a defence in itself, it is necessary to give particular consideration to the protections of the ECHR in relation to the 'lower end' Public Order Act offences. Although the arguments below also apply to any criminal offence, it is around this area that difficult questions have arisen, as to the extent to which the right to protest should be allowed to impinge on the rights of others. The courts have had to consider where the boundaries of the right to freedom of expression under Article 10 of the ECHR should be drawn.

---

99   [1993] Crim LR 705, (1993) Times, 19 January.
100   [1993] Crim LR 705 at 706.
101   [2003] EWHC 1564 (Admin), [2003] Crim LR 888.

3.122   Article 10 provides that:

'1 Everyone has the right to freedom of expression. This right shall include freedom to hold opinions and to receive and impart information and ideas without interference by public authority and regardless of frontiers. This Article shall not prevent States from requiring the licensing of broadcasting, television or cinema enterprises.

2 The exercise of these freedoms, since it carries with it duties and responsibilities, may be subject to such formalities, conditions, restrictions or penalties as are prescribed by law and are necessary in a democratic society, in the interests of national security, territorial integrity or public safety, for the prevention of disorder or crime, for the protection of public health or morals, for the protection of the reputation or rights of others, for preventing the disclosure of information received in confidence, or for the maintaining the authority and impartiality of the judiciary'.

3.123   Participation in a political protest or demonstration constitutes an act of expression which attracts the protection of Article 10. This includes protest activity that others find shocking, offensive or disturbing[102]. Any restriction on this right must be 'narrowly constrained and convincingly established'[103].

3.124   For further detail on how the ECHR relates to criminal proceedings in general see para **3.217**. For the purposes of POA 1986, Article 10 may be relevant to proceedings in a number of ways. When deciding whether to uphold a submission by the defence that there is no case to answer[104], the offence in question must be 'read together with' Article 10[105]. In other words, the court must, for example, consider whether it is possible for particular words to be threatening, abusive or insulting in light of an individual's freedom of expression. The same consideration must also be borne in mind at the conclusion of the case when deciding whether the prosecution have proved their case. In cases involving POA 1986, s 4A or s 5 it may be necessary to consider Article 10 in deciding whether the defence of 'reasonableness' has been made out.

3.125   Even if all of these elements are made out it is still necessary to then go on and consider whether a prosecution is necessary and proportionate in the circumstances. This is because the prosecution and conviction of a person for

---

102 *Handyside v UK* (1979) 1 EHRR 737.
103 *Sunday Times v UK (No 2)* (1992) 14 EHRR 229.
104 See Trial Flowchart at Annex A.
105 *Abdul v Director of Public Prosecutions* [2011] EWHC 247 (Admin), [2011] HRLR 16.

offences arising out of a protest interferes with their rights of freedom of expression and assembly and therefore must be justified by the State[106].

3.126   Therefore the prosecution must demonstrate that the proceedings are:

'being brought in pursuit of a legitimate aim, namely the protection of society against violence and that a criminal prosecution is the only method necessary to achieve that aim. The court must carefully consider those considerations and set out their findings as to why they have reached their conclusion ... the criminal law should not be invoked unless and until it is established that the conduct which is the subject of the charge amounts to such a threat to public disorder as to require the invocation of the criminal as opposed to the civil law'[107].

3.127   The application of this principle can be seen in *Abdul v Director of Public Prosecutions*[108] which concerned a protest against UK military action in Afghanistan and Iraq that took place during a parade for returning soldiers. Arguments were put forward by both sides on the question of whether a prosecution was necessary and proportionate, and a number of relevant factors were suggested, including:

- whether protesters entered into a dialogue with the police beforehand;

- whether arrests took place on the day or some time later;

- whether protesters had cooperated with the police;

- whether warnings to the protesters about their actions had been disregarded;

- the level of harassment, alarm or distress caused;

- the likelihood of further similar protests.

3.128   Ultimately, in that case, the court found that the district judge was entitled to conclude that a prosecution was proportionate and was not much swayed by the fact that arrests did not take place until some time later. However, each case will depend upon its own facts and, as the High Court found, 'context is of the first importance'.

3.129   In *Percy v Director of Public Prosecutions*[109], by comparison, the court was not convinced that a prosecution was a proportionate response. The defendant was charged under the POA 1986, s 5, having stood on the American

---

106   *Ezelin v France* (1992) 14 EHRR 362.
107   *Dehal v Crown Prosecution Service* [2005] EWHC 2154 (Admin), (2005) 169 JP 581.
108   [2011] EWHC 247 (Admin), [2011] HRLR 16.
109   [2001] EWHC 1125 (Admin), [2002] Crim LR 835.

flag in front of American servicemen in what was, the magistrates' court found, an act intended to insult but which arose out of a protest against American military policy. Relevant factors to be weighed in the balance in deciding whether it was reasonable and proportionate to prosecute included:

- whether the behaviour went beyond legitimate protest;

- whether the behaviour had not formed part of an open expression of opinion on a matter of public interest, but had become disproportionate and unreasonable;

- whether the defendant knew the likely effect of his conduct upon witnesses;

- whether the accused deliberately chose to desecrate a symbol of very considerable importance to many;

- whether the defendant was aware of the likely effect of his conduct;

- whether the method of protest had anything to do with conveying a message or expressing an opinion or was simply a gratuitous and calculated insult.

FAILING TO COMPLY WITH ORDERS

Failing to comply with the requirements of notice for a public procession

3.130

Legislation	POA 1986, s 11
Maximum penalty	£1,000 fine
Venue for trial	Magistrates' court only

3.131   The prosecution must prove that[110]:

(a)   a public procession was held; and

(b)   the defendant was one of the people organising it; and either

---

110   POA 1986, s 11.

- the notice requirements were not satisfied[111]; or

- the date when it is held or the time when it starts or its route differs from that specified in the notice.

Specific defences

3.132 Two specific defences are provided for within the section itself, both of which have to be proved by the defendant on the balance of probabilities.

3.133 The first is that the defendant:

(a) did not know of; and

(b) neither suspected nor had reason to suspect either:

- the failure to satisfy the requirements or (depending upon the allegation);

- the difference of date, time or route[112].

An example of how this defence may arise would be where one organiser completing the notice gave the name or address of another nominated organiser incorrectly but in good faith.

3.134 The second is that where an allegation turns upon a defendant taking part in a march at a different date, time or route to that which was authorised, it is a defence for the defendant to prove that the difference arose:

(a) from circumstances beyond their control; or

(b) from something done with the agreement of a police officer; or

(c) from something done by a police officer's direction[113].

Examples may be where a route has to be changed due to unexpected road closures or where it is not possible to start when intended, due to last-minute delays.

3.135 It may be argued that 'differs' should be taken to mean 'significantly differs'. Otherwise, minor deviations within the organisers' control, such as starting a few minutes late, while unlikely to lead to charges would technically lead to offences being committed. At the other end of the spectrum, there may come a point at which a difference in date, time or route beyond the defendant's

---

111 See para **1.5** for requirements
112 POA 1986, s 11(8).
113 POA 1986, s 11(9).

control means that it is possible to argue that the procession cannot be said to be the same procession for which notice was given. This has the benefit of returning the burden of proof to the prosecution to prove that the defendant was the 'organiser' of the breakaway procession.

Failing to comply with requirements imposed on a public procession or assembly

3.136

Legislation	POA 1986, s 12 or s 14
Maximum penalty	Three months' imprisonment and/or £2,500 fine for organisers
	£1,000 fine for participants
	Three months' imprisonment and/or £2,500 fine for inciting participants
Venue for trial	Magistrates' court only

3.137   The prosecution must prove that:

(a)(i)   a person organised a public procession or public assembly; or

(a)(ii)   a person took part in a public procession or public assembly; and

(b)   knowingly failed to comply with a condition which had been imposed.

3.138   It is also an offence to incite someone taking part in a public procession or assembly to knowingly fail to comply with a condition imposed.

Specific defences

3.139   It is a defence for an organiser or a participant to prove that the failure arose from circumstances beyond his control. No such defence is available for a person inciting someone to knowingly fail to comply with a condition. This seems odd, as someone taking a different route on a procession due to road closures would have a defence, while someone directing others to do the same may not. It may be possible to raise a defence of prevention of crime or necessity in some circumstances. Alternatively, it may be possible to construe the statute to mean that if the incited person would have a defence, they have not committed an offence and therefore the incitor is not guilty.

135

3.140   It should also be noted that, on one reading of the law, a person inciting others to breach conditions only commits an offence if those incited *know* they are breaching conditions. Therefore, deliberately misdirecting innocent protesters would not be an offence.

Taking part in a prohibited procession or trespassory assembly

3.141

Legislation	POA 1986, s 13 or s 14B
Maximum penalty	Three months' imprisonment and/or £2,500 fine for organisers
	£1,000 fine for participants
	Three months' imprisonment and/or £2,500 fine for inciting participants
Venue for trial	Magistrates' court only

3.142   The offences mirror those for failing to comply with conditions under POA 1986, s 12 or s 14. The prosecution must prove that:

(a)(i) a person organised a prohibited procession or prohibited trespassory assembly; or

(a)(ii) a person took part in a prohibited procession or prohibited trespassory assembly; and

(b)   they knew that the procession or trespassory assembly was prohibited.

3.143   Similarly, it is also an offence to incite someone to take part in a prohibited procession or trespassory assembly.

Specific defences

3.144   No specific defences are provided for in the legislation. Therefore, if the prosecution can prove the elements of the case beyond reasonable doubt, the only possibilities would be the general defence for failing to comply with orders[114] or the general defences of prevention of crime, necessity etc[115].

Failing to stop and failing to remove an item of clothing

3.145

Legislation	CJPO 1994, s 60 and s 60AA
Maximum penalty	One month imprisonment and/or a £1,000 fine
Venue for trial	Magistrates' court only

3.146   The prosecution must prove that:

(a)   an order was in force under CJPO 1994, s 60 or s 60AA[116];

(b)   a constable, in the exercise of his powers under the relevant section, required the defendant to:

- stop (s 60); and/or

- remove an item of clothing (s 60 or s 60AA);

and

(c)   he failed to do so.

3.147   On a narrow reading of the offence no mental element (mens rea) is required. However, this could mean that the offence would be committed even if:

(a)   the defendant did not hear the request; or

(b)   the defendant did not understand the request due to language difficulties; or

(c)   the defendant was unable to remove a facial covering, for example because they were handcuffed.

3.148   However, 'strict liability' offences are rare and it is 'firmly established by a host of authorities that mens rea is an essential ingredient of every offence

---

114 See para **3.151**.
115 See para **3.202**.
116 See para **1.40**.

unless some reason can be found for holding that that is not necessary'[117]. It can be argued, therefore, either that to 'require' someone to do something is interpreted to mean that the requirement is expressed to them and they are aware of it, or that 'failed to do so' should be read as 'intentionally failed to do so'.

Specific defences

3.149   No specific defences are provided for by the statute. Therefore, if the prosecution can prove the elements of the case beyond reasonable doubt, the only possibilities would be the general defences for failing to comply with orders[118] or the general defences of prevention of crime, necessity etc[119].

3.150   It is not a defence to argue that a facial covering was not being worn to conceal one's identity. The offence only requires that the officer making the request **reasonably believes** that a person is wearing an item, wholly or mainly, for the purpose of concealing his identity.

General defences for failing to comply with orders

3.151   A defendant in a criminal case may wish to challenge the lawfulness or the validity of the order made under POA 1986, CJPO 1994 or other legislation, the breach of which led to his arrest. There is no authority which considers the question directly but strong support can be found in the case of *Boddington v British Transport Police*[120]. In that case, Mr Boddington was charged with an offence of smoking in a train carriage. Railway byelaws prohibited smoking in a carriage where a non-smoking sign was displayed. The train company, upon whose train Mr Boddington was travelling, had put non-smoking signs up in every carriage, in response to which Mr Boddington smoked a cigarette in one of the carriages.

3.152   Mr Boddington sought to argue that the byelaws were invalid. He also sought to argue that the **administrative action** of the train company in putting up signs in every carriage was unreasonable, and therefore invalid, and as a result he should be acquitted. The House of Lords were agreed that, even though the byelaw and the administrative action could have been challenged in other ways, Mr Boddington was entitled to raise its validity as a defence in criminal proceedings.

---

117   *Sweet v Parsley* [1970] AC 132, per Lord Reid at 149.
118   See para **3.151**.
119   See para **3.202**.
120   [1999] 2 AC 143, [1998] 2 WLR 639.

3.153   Two useful authorities relied on were *Director of Public Prosecutions v Head:*

> 'Is a man to be sent to prison on the basis that an order is a good order when the court knows it would be set aside if proper proceedings were taken? I doubt it'[121],

and *R v Wicks*[122], in which it was held that 'the proper starting point' must be a presumption that 'an accused should be able to challenge, on any ground, the lawfulness of an order the breach of which constitutes his alleged criminal offence'[123].

3.154   This will not always be the case and whether a particular order can be challenged in the course of criminal proceedings depends on the wording of the statute granting the power to make the order[124]. Parliament may specifically prevent a particular order from being challenged in any way other than a prescribed route.

3.155   Furthermore, the same rule does not apply to court orders, which are valid until set aside, for example on appeal. Therefore, the validity of an anti-social behaviour order (ASBO) cannot be challenged in the course of criminal proceedings for breaching that order[125].

3.156   Orders under the POA 1986 and CJPO 1994 are likely to be considered **administrative action** in the same way that the actions of the train company were in *Boddington* and therefore open to challenge. Furthermore, an officer making a request to someone to stop and/or remove clothing under CJPO 1994, s 60 or s 60AA is also likely to be open to challenge for the same reason.

3.157   *Boddington* also confirmed that not only could a defendant challenge an order on the basis that it was unlawful *in substance* but also on *procedural* grounds. A detailed review of procedural challenges to public law decisions is outside the scope of this book, but such challenges can include arguments that the decision was carried out in breach of statutory procedures or that the decision-maker was biased.

---

121   [1959] AC 83, per Somervell of Harrow LJ at 104.
122   [1998] AC 92.
123   At 106.
124   *Boddington v British Transport Police* [1999] 2 AC 143 at 160, [1998] 2 WLR 639 at 651.
125   *Director of Public Prosecutions v T* [2006] EWHC 728 (Admin), [2007] 1 WLR 209.

3.158   Such challenges may not always be available depending on the particular order made but, if properly founded, such an argument would necessitate substantial disclosure of the decision making process by the officer in question.

3.159   It is not open to a defendant to sit back and then claim that the prosecution have not proved that the order is valid. It is for the defence to prove that the order is unlawful on the balance of probabilities[126].

Human rights

3.160   Orders must comply with the provisions of the ECHR. Otherwise, the police officer making the order is not acting in accordance with the ECHR and a court upholding the order by convicting would not be acting in accordance with the ECHR. Both are impermissible under the Human Rights Act 1998, s 6[127]. For example, if conditions imposed upon the location of a public assembly under POA 1986, s 14 mean that the defendants could not see or be seen by the target of their protest, it could be argued that their Article 10 and 11 rights had been breached and the order was therefore unlawful.

3.161   In reviewing such decisions the court's approach will be that they:

'may not interfere with the exercise of an administrative discretion on substantive grounds save where the court is satisfied that the decision is unreasonable in the sense that it is beyond the range of responses open to a reasonable decision-maker. But in judging whether the decision-maker has exceeded this margin of appreciation the human rights context is important. The more substantial the interference with human rights, the more the court will require by way of justification before it is satisfied that the decision is reasonable in the sense outlined above'.

On the other hand, while 'the court must properly defer to the expertise of responsible decision-makers, it must not shrink from its fundamental duty to "do right to all manner of people ..." '[128].

3.162   An example arising out of criminal proceedings relates to the use of the power to require removal of facial coverings under CJPO 1994, ss 60 or

---

126   *Boddington v British Transport Police* [1999] 2 AC 143 at 155, [1998] 2 WLR 639 at 647.
127   See para **3.221**.
128   *R v Ministry of Defence, ex p Smith* [1996] QB 517, per Sir Thomas Bingham MR at 554E and 556E. Applied in *R (Brehony) v Chief Constable of Greater Manchester* [2005] EWHC 640 (Admin).

60AA. In *Director of Public Prosecutions v Avery*[129] it was held that the power to make such a request 'creates a significant power to interfere with the liberty of the subject, which it is appropriate to subject to scrutiny not only in accordance with the common law but also having regard to the Human Rights Act 1998'.

3.163 In the circumstances of *Avery* the power itself was found to be lawful, partly on the basis that CJPO 1994, s 60 orders could only be made in anticipation of violence, and that the wearing of masks to conceal identity helped an 'offender' to impede arrest and impeded control of 'troublemakers'. Presumably it was the ECHR, Article 8 which was being considered, the right to respect for private and family life, although this is not set out in the judgment. Each case will need to be considered on its own facts, and the justification for the interference identified within the exceptions under ECHR, Article 8(2). In some cases there may also be interference with Articles 10 and 11 which will need to be justified. The assumption that anyone wearing a mask is an 'offender' or a 'troublemaker' may not always survive scrutiny.

3.164 Even if the principle is correct, the court in *Avery* seems to have only considered the lawfulness of the legislation, not the individual acts. The court relied very heavily on the assumption that the proper procedure was followed both for the CJPO 1994, s 60 order being given and for the particular request being made. Therefore, there is still scope to argue that if the inspector's belief which led to him giving the order is not reasonable, the request may amount to an unjustified interference with a person's rights.

Partially invalid orders

3.165 If some of the conditions imposed are invalid this does not necessarily mean that the whole notice is invalid, *so long as* those conditions can be struck out without affecting the remainder, either textually or substantially[130]. For example, a condition that only people over six feet tall may take part in an assembly is clearly unlawful. A notice which imposed the following conditions:

- only people over six feet tall may take part in the assembly;

- no more than 30 people may take part in the assembly;

could have the first condition struck through, while the second would still make sense and be unaffected in substance. Therefore the second condition would still be valid.

---

129 [2001] EWHC (Admin) 748, [2002] 1 Cr App Rep 31.
130 *Director of Public Prosecutions v Jones* [2002] EWHC 110 (Admin), [2002] Po LR 4.

3.166 Conversely, a notice which said:

> 'no more than 30 people over six foot tall may take part in the assembly'

could not be rescued by striking out the words 'over six foot tall' as this fundamentally changes the meaning of the condition. Therefore, the whole condition could be argued to be invalid.

BREACH OF THE PEACE

3.167

Legislation	None: common law
Maximum penalty	Binding over to keep the peace
Venue for trial	Magistrates' court

3.168 Breach of the peace is a common law offence which until relatively recently was vaguely and inconsistently defined. Technically, it is not a criminal offence, as one does not get charged, convicted and sentenced for breach of the peace[131]. The only punishment is being bound over to keep the peace which does not count as a criminal conviction. However, it does count as an 'offence' for the purposes of the European Convention on Human Rights and therefore the safeguards of the Convention apply[132].

3.169 Breach of the peace rarely gives rise to court proceedings in and of itself. It is usually mentioned in reported case law because it was the purported reason for an arrest, or action short of arrest, which has led to a civil action against the police or an argument that the police officer was not acting 'in the execution of his duty' for the purposes of the Police Act 1996, s 89[133].

3.170 The main importance so far as protesters are concerned is in the wide-ranging power that it gives the police (or any other citizen) to take action.

---

131 *R v County of London Quarter Sessions Appeals Committee, ex p Metropolitan Police Commissioner* [1948] 1 KB 670, 673 and 676.
132 *Steel v UK* (1999) 28 EHRR 603.
133 See para **3.22**.

'[Every] citizen in whose presence a breach of the peace is being, or reasonably appears to be about to be, committed has the right to take reasonable steps to make the person who is breaking or threatening to break the peace refrain from doing so; and those reasonable steps in appropriate cases will include detaining him against his will' [134].

For more on breach of the peace and police powers see para **1.179** and for an example of the power being used see para **1.131** in relation to 'kettling'.

This section is concerned with the offence itself and any consequent proceedings.

What amounts to a breach of the peace?

3.171   The definition of breach of the peace now approved is that set out in *R v Howell* [135]:

'There is a breach of the peace whenever harm is actually done or is likely to be done to a person or in his presence to his property or a person is in fear of being so harmed through an assault, an affray, a riot, unlawful assembly or other disturbance' [136].

3.172   This was summarised in *R (Laporte) v Chief Constable of Gloucestershire Constabulary* [137] as meaning that the essence of breach of the peace was 'violence or threatened violence' [138]. Whilst a pithy abstract, if *Howell* is accurate, 'violence' would have to include damage to property, and it would have to be noted that any 'threatened violence' does not have to emanate from the defendant.

3.173   Examples of behaviour which **did not** amount to breach of the peace include:

(a)   where hunt saboteurs had blown horns and 'hallooed' in order to disrupt a fox hunt, but there was no violence or threat of violence, there was no breach of the peace [139];

(b)   being abusive and refusing to get out of a police car did not amount to an actual breach of the peace, but the particular circumstances could have

---

134   *Albert v Lavin* [1982] AC 546, [1981] 3 WLR 955.
135   [1982] QB 416, per Watkins LJ at 427.
136   Approved in *Steel v UK* [1999] 28 EHRR 603 and *R (Laporte) v Chief Constable Gloucester Constabulary* [2006] UKHL 55, [2007] 2 AC 105.
137   [2006] UKHL 55, [2007] 2 AC 105.
138   [2007] 2 AC 105 at 123.
139   *Hashman & Harrup v UK* (2000) 30 EHRR 241.

caused officers to anticipate a breach of the peace and did amount to obstructing police[140];

(c) 'agitated' or 'excited' behaviour where there was no injury or threat of injury was not a breach of the peace[141].

3.174 Where harm is actually done the behaviour will usually amount to a criminal offence, for example, common assault, criminal damage or a Public Order Act offence[142]. Threats to cause harm may also amount to an offence, for example, threatening to damage someone's property contrary to the CDA 1971, s 2.

3.175 One remaining role for breach of the peace *as an offence in its own right* may be where harm is likely but the defendant's behaviour is lawful. In these circumstances the power of arrest is exceptional and should be exercised by the police officer 'only in the clearest of circumstances, and when he is satisfied on reasonable grounds that a breach of the peace is imminent'[143]. The most difficult cases have arisen when the defendant's actions were lawful but were thought likely to provoke others to violence.

3.176 The criteria to consider in deciding whether an arrest for breach of the peace is justified in these circumstances have been set out as follows[144]:

(a) there must be 'the clearest of circumstances and a sufficiently real and present threat to the peace';

(b) the threat to the peace must be coming from the person who is to be arrested;

(c) the conduct of the person to be arrested must clearly interfere with the rights of others;

(d) the natural consequence of that conduct must be violence from a third party;

(e) the violence from a third party must not be wholly unreasonable;

(f) the conduct of the person to be arrested must be unreasonable.

3.177 There is an obvious overlap between these principles. For example, in order to decide where the threat is 'coming from', the court will look at the

---

140 *R (Hawkes) v Director of Public Prosecutions* [2005] EWHC 3046 (Admin), (2005) Times, 29 November.
141 *Jarrett v Chief Constable of West Midlands Police* [2003] EWCA Civ 397, (2003) Times, 28 February.
142 See observations of Brown LJ in *R (Laporte) v Chief Constable Gloucester Constabulary* [2007] 2 AC 105 at 150.
143 *Foulkes v Chief Constable of Merseyside Police* [1998] 3 All ER 705.
144 *Bibby v Chief Constable of Essex Police* (2000) 164 JP 297.

question of who was acting reasonably. The question of reasonableness will require particular care in protest cases as the right to freedom of expression under the ECHR, Article 10 may cover conduct which could reasonably provoke others to violence. This would not necessarily mean that the person exercising their right to protest is acting unreasonably[145].

3.178   Applying these criteria retrospectively to two examples, in *Beatty v Gilbanks*[146] a lawful Salvation Army march attracted disorderly opposition and led to a breach of the peace. The Salvation Army could not be bound over to keep the peace as violence towards them was not the natural consequence of their march. In *Wise v Dunning*[147] a Protestant preacher was liable to be bound over to keep the peace as he habitually accompanied his public speeches with behaviour 'calculated to insult Roman Catholics'. His behaviour was unreasonable and resulting violence from others was a natural and not unreasonable consequence.

3.179   A breach of the peace may take place on private land[148].

Procedure

3.180   Where someone is arrested for breach of the peace and is detained at a police station, the provisions of PACE 1984 and the Codes of Practice thereunder do not strictly apply. However, 'the practice of the police in treating any person so detained as if PACE applied to the detention … is plainly correct'[149].

3.181   Where a person is detained for breach of the peace, there is no power to grant that person bail to appear before the magistrates' court. Either the arrested person must be brought from the police station to the magistrates' court as soon as reasonably practicable[150], or, if at any point there is no longer a real danger that, if released, the detained person will commit or repeat his breach of the peace within a short time, then they must be released[151]. If released, then proceedings for breach of the peace can be commenced by way of summons[152].

---

145   See *Redmond-Bate v Director of Public Prosecutions* [2000] HRLR 249.
146   (1882) 9 QBD 308.
147   [1902] 1 KB 167.
148   *McConnell v Chief Constable of Greater Manchester* [1990] 1 WLR 364.
149   *Chief Constable of Cleveland Police v McGrogan* [2002] EWCA Civ 86, [2002] Po LR 31.
150   *John Lewis & Co v Tims* [1952] AC 676 at 691–2.
151   *Williamson v Chief Constable of West Midlands Police* [2003] EWCA Civ 337, [2004] 1 WLR 14.
152   Magistrates' Courts Act 1980, s 51.

3.182   Where proceedings are launched they are begun by 'complaint' to the magistrates and the procedure is set out in the Magistrates' Courts Act 1980 (MCA 1980), ss 51–57. The procedure largely matches that of ordinary criminal proceedings and the standard of proof is the criminal standard[153]. If the magistrates' court finds that a person breached the peace this may be appealed to the Crown Court[154], or to the High Court by way of case stated on a point of law[155].

Binding over to keep the peace

3.183   This is undertaking not to breach the peace or to be 'of good behaviour' for a set period of time, otherwise payment of a set amount of money, or 'recognisance', will be made to the court. The Consolidated Criminal Practice Direction[156] provides that:

> 'courts should no longer bind an individual over "to be of good behaviour". Rather than binding an individual over to "keep the peace" in general terms, the court should identify the specific conduct or activity from which the individual must refrain'[157].

3.184   Where the proceedings have taken place by way of complaint under the MCA 1980 as set out above, the power to bind over is provided for in MCA 1980, s 115. There are also a number of other common law and statutory powers which allow the magistrates to bind someone over in other criminal proceedings, including the power to do so of their own motion[158]. These powers can even be exercised against an acquitted defendant or a witness who has given evidence, although the former will rarely be appropriate[159]. When it is proposed that a witness be bound over they should be given the opportunity to be heard on the matter, and before binding over a complainant justices have a clear duty to warn him that they are contemplating doing so[160]. Under whichever power is being exercised the standard of proof is 'beyond reasonable doubt'[161].

---

153   *Percy v Director of Public Prosecutions* [1995] 1 WLR 1382; Consolidated Criminal Practice Direction III.31.5.
154   Magistrates' Courts (Appeals from Binding Over Orders) Act 1956, s 1.
155   *Percy v Director of Public Prosecutions* [1995] 1 WLR 1382.
156   www.justice.gov.uk/guidance/courts-and-tribunals/courts/procedure-rules/criminal/pd_consolidated.htm.
157   At III.31.3.
158   Under common law, Justices of the Peace Act 1361, Justices of the Peace Act 1968, Magistrates' Courts Act 1980.
159   *R v Middlesex Crown Court, ex p Khan* (1997) 161 JP 240.
160   *R v Hendon Justices, ex p Gorchein* [1973] 1 WLR 1502, [1974] 1 All ER 168.
161   *Percy v Director of Public Prosecutions* [1995] 1 WLR 1382.

3.185   There is no limit on the amount of recognisance which may be set by a court in support of a bind over, but it must be reasonable and proportionate and, when it is more than a trivial amount, an enquiry should take place into the person's means or an opportunity given to that person to make representations on the size of the recognisance[162]. There is also no limit on the time period which may be set, but generally speaking they should not exceed 12 months[163].

3.186   If a person refuses to consent to the order, the court may commit him to prison for up to six months or 'until he sooner complies with the order' in the case of an order made under the MCA 1980. Where the court is using its powers, other than under the MCA 1980, the person may be committed to prison for an unlimited period.

OBSTRUCTION OF THE HIGHWAY

3.187

Legislation	Highways Act 1980, s 137
Maximum penalty	£1,000 fine
Venue for trial	Magistrates' court

3.188   The prosecution have to prove that a person:

(a)   wilfully

(b)   obstructed the free passage along the highway

(c)   without lawful authority or excuse.

3.189   If a person is convicted, the obstruction is still continuing and it is in that person's power to remove it, he may be ordered to take steps within a reasonable time to do so by the court. Failure to do so is punishable by a £5,000 fine, and failure to do so after *that* conviction is punishable by a fine of £250 for every day thereafter that the failure continues. If a highway authority removes

---

162 *R v Central Criminal Court, ex p Boulding* [1984] QB 813, [1984] 2 WLR 321.
163 Consolidated Criminal Practice Direction (above) III.31.4.

the obstruction they can recover the costs of doing so from a convicted defendant[164].

Obstructed the free passage along the highway

3.190

> The highway is 'anywhere that the public has a right to pass and repass, either on foot or with animals or in vehicles, as the case may be'[165].

The highway has been held to include:

- a grass verge at the side of a carriageway[166];

- the pavement outside Parliament, which was 11 feet wide[167];

- a cul-de-sac[168];

- a footpath[169];

- an industrial estate[170];

- parts of the churchyard of St Paul's Cathedral, London[171].

3.191 '[Any] occupation of part of a road, thus interfering with people having the use of the whole of the road, is an obstruction'[172] and 'any stopping on the highway, whether it be on the carriageway or on the footway, is prima facie an obstruction'[173]. If the stopping or the resulting impediment is particularly minimal it will not amount to an obstruction[174].

---

164 Highways Act 1980, s 137ZA.
165 *Lang v Hindhaugh* [1986] RTR 271.
166 *Worth v Brooks* [1959] Crim LR 855.
167 *Westminster City Council v Haw* [2002] EWHC 2073 (QB), (2002) 146 SJLB 221.
168 *Putnam v Colvin* [1984] RTR 150.
169 *R (Ashbrook) v East Sussex County Council* [2002] EWCA Civ 1701, [2003] 1 PLR 66.
170 *Scott v Mid-South Essex Justices* [2004] EWHC 1001 (Admin).
171 *City of London v Samede* [2012] EWHC 34 (QB), (2012) Times, 27 January.
172 *Nagy v Weston* [1965] 1 WLR 280, [1965] 1 All ER 78.
173 *Hirst v Chief Constable of West Yorkshire* (1987) 85 Cr App Rep 143, per Glidewell LJ at 151.
174 *Putnam v Colvin* [1984] RTR 150.

Wilfully

3.192 The stopping has to be intentional. It is clear that stopping in the street because there is no choice, for example because someone is in the way, would not be sufficient as it was not intentional[175].

3.193 There is conflicting authority on whether preventing others passing along the highway must also be intentional[176]. Stopping in the street to look in a shop window is done intentionally. It may in fact obstruct others but that is not the intention. In many protest cases the purpose is not to block the highway but it is a necessary consequence of having to carry out a protest in a particular place or in front of a particular building.

Without lawful authority or excuse

3.194 Lawful authority for obstructing the highway includes things such as permits and licenses for market traders and people collecting for charity[177].

3.195 Lawful excuse requires that the activity is:

- lawful in itself; and
- reasonable.

3.196 So, for example, people may lawfully use the highway for a number of reasons. It is not limited to simply going from one place to another. Otherwise 'ordinary and usual activities as making a sketch, taking a photograph, handing out leaflets, collecting money for charity, singing carols, playing in a Salvation Army band, children playing a game on the pavement, having a picnic, or reading a book' would be technically unlawful[178].

3.197 Even if a person is conducting a lawful activity on the highway, it must also be reasonable. What is reasonable takes into account all the circumstances 'including the length of time the obstruction continues, the place where it occurs, the purpose for which it is done, and of course whether it does in fact cause an actual obstruction as opposed to a potential obstruction'[179].

3.198 Therefore, pausing to take a photograph in Oxford Street in London will not amount to an obstruction. Spending hours setting up photographic

---

175 *Hirst v Chief Constable of West Yorkshire* [1987] Crim LR 330, (1987) 85 Cr App Rep 143.
176 *Hirst v Chief Constable of West Yorkshire* [1987] Crim LR 330, (1987) 85 Cr App Rep 143; cf *Eaton v Cobb* [1950] 1 All ER 1016.
177 *Hirst v Chief Constable of West Yorkshire* [1987] Crim LR 330, (1987) 85 Cr App Rep 143.
178 *Director of Public Prosecutions v Jones* [1999] 2 AC 240, per Lord Irvine of Lairg LC at 254.
179 *Nagy v Weston* [1965] 1 WLR 280, per Lord Parker CJ at 284.

equipment in a narrow road and preventing pedestrians from passing whilst this is done will almost certainly amount to an obstruction.

3.199   What is reasonable in the circumstances of a protest which is obstructing the highway must take into account Articles 10 and 11 of the European Convention on Human Rights (ECHR). In *Westminster City Council v Haw*[180], Brian Haw's protest in Parliament Square was found not to be an obstruction of the highway as it was reasonable, bearing in mind his right to protest.

3.200   By way of contrast, in *Birch v Director of Public Prosecutions*[181], protesters lay in the road in front of vehicles trying to enter a factory. It was held that lying in the road was not a lawful activity and therefore could not amount to a lawful excuse. However, the case was decided before the coming into force of the Human Rights Act 1998 and there is no mention of the ECHR in the judgment. The case may now be considered differently and, in any event, each case will turn on its own facts.

MISCELLANEOUS OFFENCES

3.201   There are a huge number of other offences which may be relevant in the context of protests and it is not possible to analyse them all in this text. The most common offences are those set out above but others which may be relevant in specific circumstance include:

- interfering with contractual relations so as to harm an animal research organisation[182];

- intimidating people connected with an animal research organisation[183];

- intimidation or annoyance by violence or otherwise[184];

- harassment[185];

- harassment of a person in their own home[186];

- trespass to Protected Sites[187];

- local byelaws.

---

180   [2002] EWHC 2073 (QB), (2002) 146 SJLB 221.
181   [2000] Crim LR 301.
182   Serious Organised Crime and Police Act 2005, s 145.
183   Serious Organised Crime and Police Act 2005, s 146.
184   Trade Union and Labour Relations (Consolidation) Act 1992, s 241.
185   Protection from Harassment Act 1997, ss 2 and 4.
186   Criminal Justice and Police Act 2001, s 42A.
187   Serious Organised Crime and Police Act 2005, ss 128–131.

GENERAL DEFENCES

Self-defence/defence of property and other people

For what purpose can force be lawfully used?

3.202   Force can be used by either police or civilians:

(a)   in self-defence[188];

(b)   in defence of other people[189];

(c)   in defending property under Criminal Law Act 1967 (CLA 1967), s 3;

(d)   in the prevention of crime, under CLA 1967, s 3;

(e)   'in effecting or assisting in the lawful arrest of offenders or suspected offenders or of persons unlawfully at large' under CLA 1967, s 3.

3.203   Once raised by the defence, it is for the prosecution to disprove the defence beyond reasonable doubt.

3.204   The scope of defence of other people is not clear. It was originally only available in specific relationships such as a parent protecting a child or a wife protecting a husband[190] but has since been greatly extended and has been said to apply to 'any person present'[191]. It has been recommended that it be available whenever one person believes it necessary to act in defence of another[192]. This will not usually be a problem as most attacks on other people will be crimes and therefore defending other people will be acting to prevent crime under CLA 1967, s 3.

3.205   The scope of prevention of crime was considered in *R v Jones*[193]. It was decided that, for the CLA 1967, s 3, 'crime' does not include crimes which are only recognised in international law such as the crime of aggression. Therefore, it was not possible to argue that the use of force against military bases supporting the war in Iraq, which has been argued to be a crime of aggression, was done to prevent 'crime'. It would be possible to rely on 'defence of others' in many such circumstances, however *Jones* placed a different hurdle in the way of this, as will be set out below.

---

188   Under common law, see *Palmer v R* [1971] AC 814.
189   Under common law, see *Hale's Pleas of the Crown* Vol 1 p 484.
190   *Hale's Pleas of the Crown* Vol 1 p 484.
191   *R v Chisam* [1963] 47 Cr App Rep 130.
192   Criminal Law Revision Committee (14th Report).
193   *R v Jones; Swain v Director of Public Prosecutions; Ayliffe v Director of Public Prosecutions; R v Richards; R v Pritchard; R v Olditch; R v Milling* [2006] UKHL 16, [2007] 1 AC 136.

In what circumstances can force be lawfully used?

3.206   Self-defence must be 'reasonably necessary'[194] and the use of force in the prevention of crime under CLA 1967, s 3 must be 'reasonable in the circumstances'.

3.207   The question of whether it was reasonable to use force must be judged based on the circumstances as the defendant believed them to be. This applies even if the defendant's belief in the circumstances was mistaken and/or unreasonable[195] unless that mistake was due to intoxication[196]. A court could take into account how unreasonable the belief was in deciding whether the defendant was telling the truth about whether he believed it or not.

3.208   A person does not have to wait to be struck and can strike first. In these circumstances, it has been held in a Northern Irish case that the anticipated attack must be 'imminent'[197]. The leading Privy Council case[198] does not refer to imminence but simply states that 'circumstances may justify' a pre-emptive strike. The House of Lords in *Jones* refers to imminence, but it may be argued that the question really comes down to reasonableness. If an attack is not imminent, then other options are usually available (retreat, contacting the authorities) and using force is not reasonable.

3.209   In deciding what is reasonable, Lord Hoffmann in *Jones* asked whether the question of what was reasonable should be judged as if the defendant:

> 'was the sheriff in a Western, the only lawman in town, or whether it should be judged in its actual social setting, in a democratic society with its own appointed agents for the enforcement of the law'[199].

He concluded that the:

> 'rule of law requires that disputes over whether action is lawful should be resolved by the courts. If the citizen is dissatisfied with the law as laid down by the courts, he must campaign for Parliament to change it'[200].

---

194 *Palmer v R* [1971] AC 814.
195 CJIA 2008, s 76(4).
196 CJIA 2008, s 76(5).
197 *Devlin v Armstrong* [1971] NI 13.
198 *Beckford* [1987] 3 All ER 425.
199 At para 74.
200 At para 84.

Although arguably not technically binding, this observation presents a significant obstacle to anyone seeking to rely on 'defence of others' arguing that force was reasonable to protect those others from war crimes. Of course in the Crown Court, whilst they may be directed in these terms the final arbiter of what is reasonable will be the jury.

How much force can be used?

3.210 A defendant can only use such force as is reasonable in the circumstances. Force is not reasonable if it disproportionate[201]. Having established what the defendant believed the circumstances to be, the level of force which may be used has to be assessed objectively. So:

- **A** goes to punch **B**. **B** thinks it reasonable to punch **A** first to defend himself. The court may find that this was reasonable and acquit;

- **A** goes to punch **B**. **B** thinks it reasonable to stab **A** first to defend himself. The court are likely to find this was disproportionate and convict;

- **A** goes to punch **B**. **B** *honestly believes that A is about to stab him and so* thinks it reasonable to stab **A** first to defend himself. The court may find this was reasonable and acquit.

3.211 In deciding what is within the range of reasonable responses a court has to take into account:

'(a) that a person acting for a legitimate purpose may not be able to weigh to a nicety the exact measure of any necessary action; and

(b) that evidence of a person's having only done what the person honestly and instinctively thought was necessary for a legitimate purpose constitutes strong evidence that only reasonable action was taken by that person for that purpose'[202].

Necessity and duress of circumstances

3.212 The terms 'necessity' and 'duress of circumstances' are sometimes used interchangeably. However, duress would not appear to be available to offences of murder, attempted murder and treason involving the sovereign's death. Conversely, in wholly exceptional circumstances, necessity may provide a defence to murder. The case in which this was suggested was the well-known

---

201 CJIA 2008, s 76(6).
202 CJIA 2008, s 76(7).

of case of *Re A (children) (conjoined twins: medical treatment) (No 1)*[203] in which, in order to save the life of one conjoined twin, surgeons would have to perform an operation which hastened the death of the other. This indicates just how exceptional circumstances would need to be for the defence to be available and indicates that it could not be used to justify killing one healthy person in order to save others.

3.213   However it is termed, they are defences which will only succeed in extreme circumstances and are, as a result, only considered by the appeal courts in particularly difficult cases. Perhaps because of this, the scope and relevant principles may seem to vary depending on the particular facts of the case before the court. The following criteria appear to be relevant:

(a)   the defendant (reasonably) believed it was necessary to commit the offence in question

(b)   in order to prevent death or serious injury to himself or another;

(c)   the commission of the offence was reasonable in the circumstances.

The defendant (reasonably) believed it was necessary to commit the offence in question

3.214   The binding authority is currently *R v Martin*[204] which requires that the defendant's belief was reasonable. This is inconsistent with the general law on mistake of fact which simply require that a belief was honest.

In order to prevent death or serious injury to himself or another

3.215   Necessity did not justify trespass to prevent homelessness[205].

The commission of the offence was reasonable in the circumstances

3.216   This will be a matter for the jury or magistrates to decide on an objective basis. This will include consideration of whether it was possible to avoid the threat by other means, for example, retreating or summoning the authorities.

---

203   [2001] Fam 147.
204   (1989) 88 Cr App Rep 343.
205   *London Borough of Southwark v Williams* [1971] 2 All ER 175.

EUROPEAN CONVENTION ON HUMAN RIGHTS

Human Rights Act 1998

3.217   Some, but not all, of the Articles of the ECHR were incorporated into UK law by the Human Rights Act 1998 (HRA 1998).

3.218   There are a number of ways in which criminal courts may have to consider the ECHR. First, under the HRA 1998, s 3:

'So far as it is possible to do so, primary legislation and subordinate legislation must be read and given effect in a way which is compatible with the Convention rights'.

3.219   As a result, where legislation requires a defendant to 'prove' a certain fact in order to establish a particular defence, the court will **in some circumstances** find that this is not compatible with the presumption of innocence under the ECHR, Article 6. They can then use the HRA 1998, s 3 to interpret 'prove' to mean that the defence only have to produce some evidence of that fact and once that is done, the prosecution must disprove it beyond reasonable doubt[206].

3.220   If it is not possible to interpret legislation so that it is compatible with the ECHR, the Supreme Court, Court of Appeal or High Court can make a 'declaration of incompatibility' under the HRA 1998, s 4. Therefore, for criminal proceedings it will generally only be available on appeal. It is only a remedy of last resort and does not in any event invalidate the law in question. It simply identifies the incompatibility to Parliament who may then legislate to amend it.

3.221   Perhaps most importantly for criminal proceedings, the HRA 1998, s 6 provides that 'It is unlawful for a public authority to act in a way which is incompatible with a Convention right.' Courts and tribunals are public authorities[207], as are the police and the Crown Prosecution Service. Where a defendant is tried for activities done in the course of exercising their rights under the European Convention both the prosecution and any conviction are interferences with those rights. If the interference cannot be justified it will be unlawful[208]. For examples of this being applied in practice see para **3.124**.

---

206 *Attorney-General's Reference (No 4 of 2002); Sheldrake v Director of Public Prosecutions* [2004] UKHL 43, [2005] 1 AC 264, [2004] 3 WLR 976.
207 HRA 1998, s 6(3)(a).
208 *Dehal v Crown Prosecution Service* [2005] EWHC 2154 (Admin), (2005) 169 JP 581 at para 12.

3.222   In deciding the meaning and scope of Convention Rights the court has to take into account any judgment, decision, declaration or advisory opinion of the European Court of Human Rights. It must also take into account any opinion or decision of the European Commission of Human Rights and any decision of the Committee of Ministers[209]. Where these rulings conflict with binding rulings made in the United Kingdom courts, then the magistrates' court or Crown Court should follow the UK precedent[210].

Rights under the European Convention

3.223   The rights under the ECHR are of different types. The right to life and the prohibition of torture under Articles 2 and 3 respectively are **Absolute Rights**. They cannot be derogated from under any circumstances.

3.224   Other rights such as the right to liberty and security under Article 5 and the right to a fair trial under Article 6 are **Limited Rights**. They can only be interfered with in specific circumstances. For example, Article 5(1)(a) provides that a person can be deprived of their liberty 'after conviction by a competent court'.

3.225   Articles 8–11 are **Qualified Rights** and these are the rights which are most relevant in a protest context. Each follows the same pattern, in that it can only be interfered with if the interference is:

(a)   in accordance with the law;

(b)   necessary in a democratic society;

(c)   in pursuit of a legitimate aim;

(d)   proportionate.

3.226   An interference is 'in accordance with the law' if set out and sufficiently accessible in the domestic law[211].

3.227   'Necessary in a democratic society' indicates that interference can only take place if it is in pursuit of a pressing social need[212].

3.228   The 'legitimate aims' that may justify interference are set out in the second paragraph of each Article.

---

209   HRA 1998, s 2.
210   *Kay v Lambeth Borough Council* [2006] UKHL 10, [2006] 2 AC 465.
211   *Sunday Times v UK* (1979) 2 EHRR 245.
212   *Sunday Times v UK* (1979) 2 EHRR 245.

3.229 'Proportionality' is a key concept of the ECHR and requires that the interference is no more than necessary to accomplish the objective[213].

3.230 Each of the key Articles 8–11 is set out below with some elaboration of the important points. Their practical application is addressed where they arise elsewhere in this book.

Article 8: Right to respect for private and family life

3.231 Article 8 provides that:

'(1) Everyone has the right to respect for his private and family life, his home and correspondence.

(2) There shall be no interference by a public authority with the exercise of this right except such as in accordance with the law and is necessary in a democratic society in the interests of national security, public safety or the economic well-being of the country, for the prevention of disorder or crime, for the protection of health or morals, or for the protection of the rights and freedoms of others'.

3.232 Intrusive surveillance[214], searches[215] and photographing suspects[216] can interfere with Article 8. The extent of the interference and whether it can be justified will vary according to the circumstances.

Article 9: Freedom of thought, conscience and religion

3.233 Article 9 sets out that:

'1 Everyone has the right to freedom of thought, conscience and religion; this right includes freedom to change his religion or belief and freedom, either alone or in community with others and in public or private, to manifest his religion or belief, in worship, teaching, practice and observance.

2 Freedom to manifest one's religion or beliefs shall be subject only to such limitations as are prescribed by law and are necessary in a democratic society in the interests of public safety, for the protection of public order, health or morals, or for the protection of the rights and freedoms of others'.

---

213 *R v A (No 2)* [2001] UKHL 25, [2002] 1 AC 45.
214 *Klass v Germany* (1979–80) 2 EHRR 214.
215 *Gillan and Quinton v UK* (2010) 50 EHRR 45.
216 *Murray v UK* (1994) 19 EHRR 193.

3.234 *Common offences and defences*

3.234 Article 9 is not simply limited to religious beliefs but can only extend to beliefs comparable to religious beliefs. It has therefore been held to extend to pacifism[217], atheism[218], agnosticism[219] and veganism[220].

3.235 The HRA 1998, s 13 specifically provides that:

> 'If a court's determination of any question arising under this Act might affect the exercise by a religious organisation (itself or its members collectively) of the Convention right to freedom of thought, conscience and religion, it must have particular regard to the importance of that right'.

Article 10: Freedom of expression

3.236 Article 10 provides that:

> '(1) Everyone has the right to freedom of expression. This right shall include freedom to hold opinions and to receive and impart information and ideas without interference by public authority and regardless of frontiers. This article shall not prevent States from requiring the licensing of broadcasting, television or cinema enterprises.
>
> (2) The exercise of these freedoms, since it carries with it duties and responsibilities, may be subject to such formalities, conditions, restrictions or penalties as are prescribed by law and are necessary in a democratic society, in the interests of national security, territorial integrity or public safety, for the prevention of disorder or crime, for the protection of health or morals, for the protection of the reputation or rights of others, for preventing the disclosure of information received in confidence, or for maintaining the authority and impartiality of the judiciary.'

Participation in a protest or demonstration constitutes an act of expression which attracts the protection of Article 10[221].

---

217 *Arrowsmith v UK* (1978) 19 DR 5.
218 *Kokkinakis v Greece* (1994) 17 EHRR 397.
219 *Kokkinakis v Greece* (1994) 17 EHRR 397.
220 *UK Application No* 00018187/91 (1993, unreported).
221 *Steel v UK* (1999) 28 EHRR 603.

3.237   Where rights under the ECHR, Article 10 are engaged, restrictions on that right must be 'narrowly construed' and the justification for any criminal sanction must be 'convincingly established'[222].

3.238   Article 10 extends to protest activity that others find shocking, offensive or disturbing. 'Such are the demands of that pluralism, tolerance and broad-mindedness without which there is no democratic society'[223]:

'Free speech includes not only the inoffensive but the irritating, the contentious, the eccentric, the heretical, the unwelcome and the provocative provided it does not tend to provoke violence. Freedom only to speak inoffensively is not worth having'[224].

3.239   Article 10 can cover not only the substance of what is expressed but also the means of expressing it. Therefore in *Tabernacle v Secretary of State for the Defence*[225], a byelaw prohibiting camping near a nuclear weapons site was held to unjustly interfere with the Article 10 (and 11) rights being exercised at a longstanding 'peace camp', despite the fact that there were other ways of carrying out the protest.

3.240   Practically speaking, the State should recognise that 'any demonstration in a public place may cause a certain level of disruption to ordinary life and encounter hostility'[226]. Furthermore, the extent to which the State is obliged to protect the rights of demonstrators under Article 10 can extend to taking reasonable steps to protect them from counter-demonstrators[227].

3.241   The HRA 1998, s 12(4) specifically provides that:

'The court must have particular regard to the importance of the Convention right to freedom of expression and, where the proceedings relate to material which the respondent claims, or which appears to the court, to be journalistic, literary or artistic material (or to conduct connected with such material), to:

(a)   the extent to which:

(i)   the material has, or is about to, become available to the public; or

---

222   *Sunday Times v UK (No 2)* 14 EHRR 229.
223   *Handyside v UK* (1979) 1 EHRR 373.
224   *Redmond-Bate v Director of Public Prosecutions* (2000) HRLR 249, [1999] Crim LR 998.
225   [2009] EWCA Civ 23.
226   *Aldemir v Turkey*, Application No 32124/02 (2007) 18 December, unreported.
227   *Plattform 'Artze fur das Leben'* (1991) 13 EHRR 204.

> (ii) it is, or would be, in the public interest for the material to
> be published;

(b) any relevant privacy code.'

Article 11: Freedom of association

3.242 Article 11 of the ECHR states:

'(1) Everyone has the right to freedom of peaceful assembly and to
freedom of association with others, including the right to form and to
join trade unions for the protection of his interests.

(2) No restrictions shall be placed on the exercise of these rights other
than such as are prescribed by law and are necessary in a democratic
society in the interests of national security or public safety, for the
prevention of disorder or crime, for the protection of health or morals
or for the protection of the rights and freedoms of others. This article
shall not prevent the imposition of lawful restrictions on the exercise
of these rights by members of the armed forces, of the police or of the
administration of the State'.

3.243 This Article does not create a general right to associate, for example
for recreational purposes. It covers the freedom to associate in order to share
information and ideas and to voice them collectively[228].

---

228 *R (on the application of Countryside Alliance) v A-G* [2007] UKHL 52, [2007] 3 WLR 922,
[2008] 2 All ER 95, per Baroness Hale at para 118.

Chapter 4

Occupations

4.1   Occupations have constituted an influential and popular form of
protest around the world. Early examples include sit-down strikes in the US
during the Great Depression and later Civil Rights movement sit-ins at
segregated businesses. The 1960s gave rise to several notable cases, from the
1968 French student and Columbia University occupations, to the occupation
of Alcatraz by Native Americans in 1969. In the following decade, four
Indigenous Australians established the Aboriginal Tent Embassy on the lawns
of Old Parliament House, Canberra in 1972. The 1980s saw large-scale
occupations by Brazil's Landless Workers Movement, Movimento dos
Trabalhadores Rurais Sem Terra, and the iconic images of Tiananmen Square.
Recent occupations include those in Tahrir Square in Egypt and the Occupy
Wall Street demonstration which spawned sister-protests around the world,
including OccupyLSX at St Paul's Cathedral, London.

4.2   This chapter covers some of the most common legal issues that arise in
both civil and criminal proceedings. There is inevitably a focus on longer term
occupations, particularly in civil proceedings, since these are more likely to be
resolved through the courts.

WHAT IS AN OCCUPATION?

4.3   There are as many forms of occupation as there are places to occupy,
from large camps in public squares[1] to small groups of protesters living in trees[2]
and lone protesters camped out on the pavement[3]. However, the common theme
to occupations is the use of physical presence in a space to mark a protest[4]. This
presence need not be continuous[5] and can be of short, long or indefinite
duration. The occupation may completely take over an area or it may allow

---

1   *City of London v Samede* [2012] EWHC 34 (QB).
2   *Manchester Airport v Dutton* (2000) 79 P & CR 541.
3   *Westminster City Council v Haw* [2002] EWHC 2073 (QB).
4   The word 'occupation' is here used to refer to a type of protest and not in any legal sense.
5   *Tabernacle v Secretary of State for Defence* [2008] EWHC 416 (Admin).

others to continue to use the area occupied in certain ways. The occupation may be formed by the same people throughout or those taking part may change over time. Given the variety of forms of occupation, the legal issues that can arise are similarly multifarious.

CRIMINAL LAW

4.4   There are a range of criminal offences for which those participating in an occupation may be liable to prosecution. The majority of these are dealt with elsewhere in this book, but they are also listed here for ease of reference:

- where those occupying are trespassers and by occupying they intend to intimidate, obstruct or disrupt lawful activity, they may commit aggravated trespass[6];

- where an occupation consists of more than 20 people and is on land in the open air then, provided other relevant conditions are met, it may constitute a trespassory assembly that may be banned under the Public Order Act 1986 (POA 1986), s 14A[7] leading to criminal sanctions under ss 14B and 14C[8];

- an occupation may be subject to the police's public order powers under the POA 1986, s 14[9];

- occupations which take place on a public highway risk constituting an unlawful obstruction contrary to the Highways Act 1980, s 137[10];

- occupations may also raise liabilities for general public order offences, in particular causing (intentional) harassment, alarm or distress under the POA 1986, ss 4A and 5[11].

4.5   There are, however, a number of criminal offences that are of specific relevance to occupations. These are covered below.

---

6 See para **3.46**.
7 See para **1.22**.
8 See para **3.142**.
9 See para **1.13**.
10 See para **3.189**.
11 See para **3.98**.

Section 61: Direction to leave

4.6

Legislation	Criminal Justice and Public Order Act 1994, s 61
Maximum penalty	3 months' imprisonment and/or £2,500 fine
Venue for trial	Magistrates' court

4.7   One offence of direct relevance to occupations relates to trespassers intending to reside on land under the Criminal Justice and Public Order Act 1994 (CJPOA 1994), s 61.

4.8   If the senior police officer present at the scene reasonably believes that:

(a)   two or more persons are trespassing on land; and

(b)   are present there with the common purpose of residing there for any period; and

(c)   reasonable steps have been taken by or on behalf of the occupier to ask them to leave; and

(d)(i)   any of those persons has caused damage to the land or to property on the land or used threatening, abusive or insulting words or behaviour towards the occupier, a member of his family or an employee or agent of his; or

(d)(ii)   those persons have between them six or more vehicles on the land,

he may direct those persons, or any of them, to leave the land and to remove any vehicles or other property they have with them on the land.

4.9   Whilst the direction must be made by the senior officer at the scene, it can be communicated by any constable[12]. A direction may not be given to leave buildings (other than agricultural buildings or scheduled monuments)[13]. Nor may a direction be given to leave land forming part of a road or highway unless it is a footpath, cyclepath, bridleway or byway[14].

---

12 CJPOA 1994, s 61(3).
13 CJPOA 1994, s 61(9)(a).
14 See s 61(9) and references therein for a detailed definition of these exceptions.

4.10 *Occupations*

4.10   Anyone who knows that a direction under s 61 applying to him has been made commits an offence if he either refuses to leave the land or, having left, returns within three months[15]. The offence of returning within three months is committed regardless of the purpose for which the person returns.

4.11   A direction may be given both to those who enter the land as trespassers and those who later become trespassers by exceeding the limits of any permission granted to them[16]. It may only be given to the latter where the conditions in para **4.8**(b)–(d) above were satisfied after they became trespassers.

4.12   A direction may only be lawfully given after trespassers have refused to comply with a clear request to leave by the occupier[17]. A valid direction by the police under s 61 must be a direction to leave immediately rather than at some future time[18].

4.13   It is a defence to a charge under s 61 that the person charged was either not trespassing on the land or that he had a 'reasonable excuse' for failing to leave the land as soon as reasonably practicable or for entering again as a trespasser[19].

4.14   On its face, a person commits an offence under s 61 by returning to land no matter what purpose they return to the land for. The offence would appear to be made out if the trespasser returned to the land without the purpose of residing there, but simply to hold a temporary demonstration. The point is yet to be decided, but it is arguable that the 'reasonable excuse' provisions should be read in a way so as to prevent disproportionate interference with a person's rights to freedom of expression and freedom of association under the European Convention on Human Rights (ECHR)[20].

4.15   In order to comply with the requirements of Article 6 of the ECHR and the presumption of innocence, it may be argued that the accused is only under an evidential burden to raise the 'reasonable excuse' defence. Once some

---

15 CJPOA 1994, s 61(4).
16 CJPOA 1994, s 61(2). Specific provisions are made in the statute for trespass on common land to include exceeding the limits of commoners' rights (s 69(7)).
17 *R (on the application of Fuller) v Chief Constable of Dorset Police* [2001] EWHC 1057 (Admin), [2003] QB 480 at para 43. The 'occupier' need only have a right to possession of the land and does not need to actually be in physical occupation (s 61(9)).
18 *R (on the application of Fuller) v Chief Constable of Dorset Police* [2001] EWHC 1057 (Admin), [2003] QB 480 at para 47.
19 CJPOA 1994, s 61(6).
20 See D Mead, *The New Law of Peaceful Protest* (2010), p 402 for similar concerns over SOCPA 2005, s 42. See also *Director of Public Prosecutions v Jones* [1999] 2 AC 240 and *Westminster City Council v Haw* [2002] EWHC 2073 (QB) for a similar approach to 'reasonableness' provisions in pre- and post- Human Rights Act cases respectively.

evidence has been provided by the accused to support the defence, it must then be disproved by the prosecution beyond reasonable doubt. However, the point has not been definitively decided in the case law[21].

Removal of vehicles

4.16   In addition to the offence under s 61, the police have powers to seize vehicles that a person to whom a s 61 direction has been given has failed to remove from the land concerned or which have been used to re-enter the land within three months of the direction. The definition of 'vehicle' is widely drawn, it does not need to be in a fit state for use on roads and includes caravans and 'any chassis or body, with or without wheels, appearing to have formed part of such a vehicle, and any load carried by, and anything attached to, such a vehicle'[22].

4.17   A similar power to remove trespassers with caravans is contained in ss 62A–62E of the CJPOA 1994 (as amended by the Anti-social Behaviour Act 2003). Section 77 of the CJPOA 1994 provides local authorities with powers to direct the removal of those residing in vehicles on the highway, unoccupied land or occupied land without the occupier's consent. Whilst typically used against travellers, the definition of vehicle is similarly widely drawn as in s 61.

Violence for securing entry: 'The Squatter's Shield'

4.18

Legislation	Criminal Law Act 1977, s 6
Maximum penalty	6 months' imprisonment and/or £5,000 fine
Venue for trial	Magistrates' court

4.19   In the context of occupations, this offence is notable because it may be committed both by activists seeking to occupy a space and by those who wish to get them out.

---

21 See *Sheldrake v Director of Public Prosecutions* [2004] UKHL 43 and *R v Lambert* [2001] UKHL 37 for discussion of this issue.
22 CJPOA 1994, s 61(9).

4.20 *Occupations*

4.20   Section 6 of the Criminal Law Act 1977 creates an offence of using violence to secure entry. It provides that any person who, without lawful authority, uses or threatens violence for the purpose of securing entry into any premises for himself or for any other person, is guilty of an offence, provided that:

(a)   there is someone present on those premises at the time who is opposed to the entry which the violence is intended to secure; and

(b)   the person using or threatening the violence knows that that is the case.

4.21   Obviously, activists who use or threaten violence for the purpose of gaining entry into a property may be liable under s 6 if there are other people present in the premises at the time. This is so whether the violence is used against people or property[23] and s 6 is therefore an additional offence to that of criminal damage which may be committed if locks or other items are broken to enter a building.

4.22   Section 6 only applies to 'premises'. However, the definition of this term is wide, including[24]:

- any building;
- any part of a building under separate occupation;
- any land ancillary to a building;
- the site comprising any building or buildings together with any land ancillary thereto.

4.23   Land is 'ancillary to a building' if it is adjacent to it and used (or intended for use) in connection with the occupation of that building or any part of it[25]. 'Building' includes structures (moveable or not) and vehicles or vessels, 'designed or adapted for use for residential purposes'[26].

4.24   An offence under s 6 may also be committed by those seeking to remove activists, because it is explicitly provided that:

'the fact that a person has any interest in or right to possession or occupation of any premises shall not ... constitute lawful authority for the use or threat of violence by him or anyone else for the purpose of securing his entry into those premises'.

---

23   CLA 1977, s 6(4).
24   CLA 1977, s 12(1)(a).
25   CLA 1977, s 12(2)(a).
26   CLA 1977, s 12(2).

There is a specific defence for displaced residential occupiers or protected intending occupiers (see below) or those acting on their behalf[27]. However, this defence does not apply to non-residential properties.

4.25   Section 6 is one reason why those seeking to remove an occupation are likely to use the civil courts rather than attempting to force people out themselves. A valid warrant/writ for possession does constitute 'lawful authority' for the purposes of s 6. If someone attempting to remove an occupation is unaware of the terms of s 6 it can be worth informing them by putting a notice up outside the occupation. Suitable notices can be downloaded from several sources on the internet, including the website of the Advisory Service for Squatters: www.squatter.org.uk.

Adverse occupation of residential premises

4.26

Legislation	Criminal Law Act 1977, s 7
Maximum penalty	6 months' imprisonment and/or £5,000 fine
Venue for trial	Magistrates' court

Section 7 of the Criminal Law Act 1977[28] makes it an offence to fail to leave residential premises once requested to do so by a displaced residential occupier or protected intending occupier. This reinforces the protection given to these groups in s 6 and underscores the law's opposition to those who seek to occupy another person's home.

4.27   The offence covers failure to leave both residential premises and 'access' to those premises[29]. Access to premises includes 'any part of any site or building within which those premises are situated which constitutes an ordinary means of access to those premises (whether or not that is its sole or primary use)'[30].

4.28   A displaced residential occupier (DRO) is someone who 'was occupying any premises as a residence immediately before being excluded

---

27   Sections 12 and 12A, and see para **4.26** ff.
28   As amended by the CJPOA 1994.
29   CLA 1977, s 7(4).
30   CLA 1977, s 12(1)(b).

from occupation by anyone who entered those premises, or any access to those premises, as a trespasser'[31].

4.29 The definition of a protected intending occupier (PIO) is someone who intends to live in the premises themselves, who is excluded from doing so by someone who entered the premises as a trespasser and:

(a) who owns either the freehold title to the premises or a leasehold with at least two years left to run; or

(b) who has been granted a tenancy or licence to occupy a property as a residence (see below for the definition of a licence) from someone that either owns either the freehold or a leasehold with two years left to run; or

(c) who has been granted a tenancy or licence to occupy a property as a residence by a local authority or housing association.

4.30 A PIO must also possess a sworn statement confirming his intention to occupy the premises as his own residence and confirming:

(a) his intention to live in the premises as his own residence; and

(b) the nature of his interest in the land as set out above[32].

4.31 It is a defence to a charge under s 7 to show that the premises are used mainly for non-residential purposes and that the person charged was not on any part of the premises used for residential purposes[33]. This limits the scope of the offence somewhat in relation to large mixed-use buildings.

4.32

DRO (Displaced residential occupier)	PIO (Protected intending occupier)
A person, D, is a DRO if:	A person, P, is a PIO if:
(a) D was occupying any premises as a residence immediately before being excluded from occupation; **and**	(a) P intends to live in the premises themselves and has a sworn statement to this effect; **and**
(b) D was not himself occupying the premises as a trespasser immediately before being excluded.	(b) P is excluded from doing so by someone who entered the premises as a trespasser, **and**

---

31 CLA 1977, s 12(3). The definition of DRO is drawn in such a way as to prevent activists from themselves relying on this clause if they are evicted (s 12(4)).

32 A PIO relying on limb (c) of the definition above may rely on a written certificate from the local authority rather than a sworn statement.

33 CLA 1977, s 7(3).

	(c) P has one of the following interests in the property:
	P owns either the freehold title to the premises or a leasehold with at least two years left to run and has a sworn statement to this effect; **or**
	P has been granted a tenancy or licence to occupy a property as a residence from someone that either owns either the freehold or a leasehold with two years left to run and has a sworn statement to this effect; **or**
	P has been granted a tenancy or licence to occupy a property as a residence by a local authority or housing association and has a written certificate to this effect.

Resisting an officer of the court (bailiff)

4.33

Legislation	Criminal Law Act 1977, s 10
Maximum penalty	6 months' imprisonment and/or £5,000 fine
Venue for trial	Magistrates' court

4.34   A final offence of specific relevance to occupations is obstructing officers of the court under the CLA 1977, s 10. This makes it an offence if someone 'resists or intentionally obstructs' a bailiff or High Court Enforcement Officer executing a warrant or writ of possession[34]. The phrase 'resists or intentionally obstructs' is similar to that in the offence of obstructing a police officer[35] and hence similar considerations will apply.

---

34   For details on warrants/writs of possession see the section on civil proceedings below.
35   See para **3.3**.

4.35   The offence under s 10 only applies where the premises are solely occupied by trespassers[36]. The person resisting or obstructing also has a defence if he can show that he believed that the person resisted or obstructed was not an officer of the court[37].

Further offences

4.36   There are a range of further offences that may be relevant to occupations in certain locations. These include trespass on a protected site contrary to the Serious and Organised Crime and Police Act 2005, s 128. 'Protected sites' are made up of 'nuclear sites' and 'designated sites'. The former include nuclear power stations. The latter are designated by statutory instrument and include some military bases (such as RAF Fairford and RAF Brize Norton), some Royal Palaces (such as Buckingham Palace and St James's Palace) and other significant buildings (such as 10 Downing Street, Chequers and the Palace of Westminster)[38]. As set out in Chapter 1, the Police Reform and Social Responsibility Act 2011 (PRSRA 2011) contains a range of restrictions on tents, sleeping equipment and noise amplification equipment in Parliament Square[39].

4.37   Local byelaws are another source of legislation that may be used to prevent occupations. However, where a byelaw is incompatible with the European Convention on Human Rights, including Articles 10 and 11, its legality may be challenged in the courts[40]. Recently, local authorities have created byelaws that extend the restrictions on tents and other sleeping equipment around Parliament Square under the PRSRA 2011 to other areas[41]. As with the PRSRA 2011, ss 142–149, these byelaws allow constables and other 'authorised officers' of the local authority to make directions to stop prohibited activities within specified areas. Prohibited activities include erecting or sleeping in tents and operating noise amplification equipment.

---

36 CLA 1977, s 10(2).
37 CLA 1977, s 10(3). In common with the approach to s 61 offences outlined above, the defendant ought only to be under an evidential burden to raise this defence.
38 See SI 2005/3447, SI 2007/1387 and SI 2007/930. Additional limitations on protest around Parliament are covered in the chapter on criminal offences.
39 The provisions are contained in PRSRA 2011, ss 142–149. See paras **1.28–1.31** for discussion.
40 See, for example, *Tabernacle v Secretary of State for Defence* [2009] EWCA Civ 23.
41 Examples include the City of Westminster Byelaws to Regulate Tents and Other Structures [2012] and the draft Trafalgar Square Byelaws [2012]. The power to create such byelaws is found in the Local Government Act 1972, s 235, which permits a local authority to create byelaws for 'good rule and government' and for the 'prevention and suppression of nuisances'. The Greater London Authority Act 1999, s 385 and the Parks Regulation (Amendment) Act 1926, s 2 confer similar powers. The PRSRA 2011, s 150 permits a power of seizure to be added to byelaws created under these Acts.

Prohibited items, including tents or sleeping equipment, can also be seized. Breach of such byelaws may result in a fine and/or forfeiture of items seized.

4.38   Other offences that can apply to occupations include trespass on a railway[42], harassment of a person in his home[43] and harassment intended to deter lawful activity[44]. Beyond this brief list, it is not possible to cover the panoply of offences that might arise in the context of occupations.

4.39   The Legal Aid, Sentencing and Punishment of Offenders Bill 2010–12 (LASPO Bill), which is before Parliament at the time of writing, contains a new offence of squatting in a residential building[45]. The offence criminalises trespass in a residential building for the purposes of living in the building for any period. There is a specific exception for those who were previously tenants in the building[46]. Whilst the offence will only criminalise acts of trespass that occur after it has come into effect, the fact that a trespasser entered a building before the section is in force will not be a defence[47]. The proposed offence may clearly be modified or abandoned during the Parliamentary process.

CIVIL LAW

4.40   As well as criminal matters, occupations may bring activists into civil litigation, primarily as defendants in possession proceedings. This section outlines the basic aspects of possession claims and injunctions that may be brought against occupiers.

Trespass

4.41   Trespass is the unlawful encroachment on land by persons or things; classically this consists in being present on land without a legal right to be there[48]. There are several different ways through which a person can have a right to be present on land:

(a)   someone who owns land will own either a freehold or leasehold title. A

---

42 Railway Regulation Act 1840, s 16; Regulation of the Railways Act 1868, s 23 and British Transport Commission Act 1949, s 55.
43 Criminal Justice and Police Act 2001, s 42A, as amended by SOCPA 2005.
44 Protection from Harassment Act 1997, s 1(1A), as amended by SOCPA 2005.
45 LASPO Bill, cl 130.
46 LASPO Bill, cl 130(2).
47 LASPO Bill, cl 130(7).
48 The merest encroachment by a person on another's land is trespass (*Ellis v The Loftus Iron Company* (1874–75) LR 10 CP 10). Trespass may also arise in other ways, for example failing to prevent animals from entering land (*see League against Cruel Sports v Scott* [1986] QB 240).

freehold is equivalent to permanent ownership of the land, a leasehold is ownership for a limited period. Ownership of land confers a right of possession, unless such right is given up by granting a lease to someone else. A tenancy, for example to rent a flat for a year, is a type of lease;

(b)   someone who does not own either a freehold or leasehold but who has permission from the owner to use land has a licence. A licence can be either expressly granted, possibly written into a contract, or it can be impliedly given. For example, customers in a shop typically have an implied licence to be on the premises to purchase items or browse. In its simplest form a licence is just permission to occupy land or use it for particular purposes;

(c)   finally, a right to use land may arise from the existence of a right of way or other legal right over the land.

4.42   Someone who is on land without one of the above rights is a trespasser. Someone who enters land under a legal right which is later withdrawn becomes a trespasser if he remains on the land. Someone who only has a licence to use land for limited purposes and exceeds those limits is a trespasser[49]. Where someone enters land intending to breach the limited permission in the licence granted, they will be treated as if they were a trespasser from the point of entry[50]. In the remainder of this chapter it will be assumed, unless otherwise stated, that those taking part in an occupation are trespassers. However, activists should be mindful of situations in which they may have a legal right of occupation through a licence.

4.43   The vast majority of land in England and Wales is registered, which means that details of the freehold or leasehold title are held by the Land Registry[51]. Anyone may get the details of registered land from the Land Registry by paying a small fee. This can be done online at www.landreg.gov.uk. This is a way to check both whether land is owned by a public body and whether a person seeking to remove trespassers has a right to possession, factors which are relevant to defending possession proceedings.

---

49 Technically, a licensee becomes a trespasser by exceeding the terms of the licence only when breach of those terms has the legal effect of terminating the contract or otherwise revoking the permission to occupy land.

50 This applies whether the licence is granted by law (*Six Carpenters' Case* 77 ER 695, (1610) 8 Co Rep 146a) or by the express or implied consent of the landowner (*R v Jones and Smith* [1976] 1 WLR 672). The position where someone enters land with a number of purposes in mind only some of which exceed the licence granted is more complex (see *Byrne v Kinematograph Renters Society Ltd* [1958] 1 WLR 762).

51 What unregistered land remains is mainly in rural areas. It should be noted that only freeholds and leases of more than seven years' duration can be registered as individual *titles* in the registry. A shorter lease, can, but need not be, included in the registry as a notice or restriction on the superior title.

4.44 Trespass is a 'tort', ie a civil law wrong. In certain circumstances, it is lawful for the owner of land to use reasonable force to remove a trespasser. However such 'self-help' is only appropriate in an emergency or other situation of urgency[52]. Any unjustified force would constitute an assault (both in criminal and civil terms) and the owner may also be committing an offence under the Criminal Law Act 1977, s 6 (see para **4.19**)[53].

4.45 For these reasons, landowners almost always use the civil courts to remove trespassers[54]. The most common mechanism by which to seek to remove trespassers is to bring possession proceedings. This is a two-stage process: first the owner applies for a **possession order**, after this is granted they can apply for a **warrant** or **writ of possession** which enables bailiffs to physically remove trespassers. To regain possession more quickly, an **interim possession order** (IPO) may also be sought. This is a temporary order granting possession to the claimant before the hearing for the full possession order. The other means that may be used to prevent or remove an occupation is an injunction.

Civil procedure

4.46 It is not possible here to give anything approaching a comprehensive treatment of civil procedure. The aim is to cover enough so that those who face possession proceedings are able to orientate themselves and know what to expect, particularly in the early stages of proceedings. Protesters facing possession orders and other civil proceedings are advised to contact a solicitor with experience of housing and/or human rights law and, ideally, also demonstration cases. It should, however, be noted that it is very unlikely that Legal Aid will be available for these cases. Whilst activists may well find a sympathetic solicitor who is prepared to act *pro bono*, there can be severe cost consequences to defending possession proceedings if the case is unsuccessful.

4.47 Civil litigation in both the county court and the High Court is regulated by the Civil Procedure Rules 1998 (CPR 1998)[55]. These rules specify how to start a claim, how much notice each side must have of a hearing and other

---

52 See *Burton v Winters* [1993] 1 WLR 1077 and *Macnab v Richardson* [2008] EWCA Civ 1631.

53 In addition to this, where a person has previously had a tenancy or licence to live in a dwelling that has come to an end but they continue to reside in the premises the Protection from Eviction Act 1977, s 3 specifically prevents the owner from obtaining possession without using the courts. There are specific exclusions for former tenants who share a home with the owner and also for some protected tenancies (see ss 3 and 3A of the Act).

54 There are some bailiff companies that offer to carry out 'common law evictions', ie evictions without a court order.

55 SI 1998/3132. The rules are available online at: www.justice.gov.uk/guidance/courts-and-tribunals/courts/procedure-rules/index.htm.

procedural matters. Judges have a considerable amount of power to vary the rules to fit the needs of a specific case. For example, they can either extend or shorten the amount of time a person must be given to prepare for a hearing and can dispense with certain procedural requirements. However, the overriding objective in the CPR 1998 is to deal with cases justly. This includes, so far as is practicable:

(a) ensuring that the parties are on an equal footing;

(b) saving expense;

(c) dealing with the case in ways which are proportionate:

(i) to the amount of money involved;

(ii) to the importance of the case;

(iii) to the complexity of the issues;

(iv) to the financial position of each party;

(d) ensuring that it is dealt with expeditiously and fairly; and

(e) allotting to it an appropriate share of the court's resources, while taking into account the need to allot resources to other cases.

4.48 Activists who are representing themselves should, when necessary, try to use these requirements to argue for modifications of court procedure to assist them. For example, a request for greater time to deal with legal documents might be made on the basis that the court must ensure that the parties are on an equal footing and that matters are dealt with proportionately to both the importance of the case and the complexity of the issues. Activists should expect that those seeking possession of land will attempt to use the provisions regarding saving expense and ensuring the cases are dealt with expeditiously to secure the swift return of their land.

Strategy and negotiation

4.49 Whilst civil litigation can on occasion move very rapidly, it can often take some time. Either way, if lawyers are involved it may get very expensive and the danger of costs should not be underestimated. For these reasons it is important for occupiers to have clearly defined aims before civil proceedings begin. In particular, the proposed length of the occupation should be considered: whether it is to be for a defined time, until a specific event or for as long as possible. Other factors that are relevant include the size and extent of the occupation and whether occupiers are prepared to alter the form of the occupation to lessen disruption for particular groups or not. Clearly, where there are large numbers of people in the occupation there is a strong need for mechanisms to ensure clarity and consensus in decision making.

4.50   Cost is often an issue for those seeking to remove occupiers and the factors above should all be borne in mind when considering the possibility of negotiating a settlement which avoids the need for any civil litigation at all. The benefit of negotiation to a landowner will be heightened when there is a danger of adverse publicity or there is likely to be an ongoing relationship between the parties after the occupation has ended.

4.51   Typically, a negotiated settlement will consist in an agreement to leave by a certain date, and perhaps also to allow access for certain things and not to damage the property. It is advisable to ensure that any agreement is put in writing, to prevent misunderstanding and in case those in occupation later need to rely on it. If litigation has started then such an agreement may be framed as a 'consent order' and given judicial authority by the court. Alternatively, it may be framed as an undertaking to the court by those in occupation to leave by a certain date.

4.52   If a settlement is reached then those in occupation will have a licence to remain until the agreed time for leaving, provided that all other conditions are adhered to. The courts are likely to take a dim view of a landowner who seeks to back out of a previously agreed settlement without good reason. Similarly, they will not be sympathetic to an occupier who seeks to stay beyond the terms of an agreement[56].

4.53   Even if negotiations fail and possession proceedings are brought, the fact that genuine attempts to reach a settlement were made are also one way to minimise the risks of costs orders being made against occupiers. These practical considerations should therefore be given due weight alongside any reluctance to negotiate with the subject of a demonstration.

Possession orders

4.54   A possession order is a court order requiring that possession of the land to which the order relates is given to the claimant by the date specified (which may be 'forthwith'). Having 'possession' of land means exercising an appropriate degree of exclusive physical control over it. What is sufficient to constitute an appropriate degree of control will depend on the nature of the land and the circumstances[57]. Giving possession of land therefore means giving control to the owner by leaving the land.

---

56   Breach of an undertaking is considered equivalent to breach of a court order (*Birmingham Railway Co v Grand Junction Canal Co* (1835) 1 Ry Ca 224) and both constitute contempt of court (see below).
57   See *J A Pye (Oxford) Ltd v Graham* [2002] UKHL 30 [2003] 1 AC 419 and *Powell v McFarlane* (1979) 38 P & CR 452 for discussion of the legal requirements for 'possession'.

4.55   The procedure for obtaining a possession order is set out in the CPR 1998, Part 55. Proceedings may be brought either as a standard possession claim or as a 'possession claim against trespassers'[58]. It is the latter that is of relevance here. A 'possession claim against trespassers' means a claim for the recovery of land (including buildings or parts of buildings) which the claimant alleges is occupied only by a person or persons who entered or remained on the land without the consent of a person entitled to possession of that land. A claim against trespassers does not include a claim against a tenant or sub-tenant whether his tenancy has been terminated or not[59].

Who can bring a claim?

4.56   A claim may be brought by anyone who has a right to immediate possession or control of the land. This will usually be the freeholder or leaseholder, but it may also be a licensee. In the protest case of *Manchester Airport plc v Dutton*[60] the land was owned by the National Trust, the airport company did not have a lease, but did have a licence to occupy the land to cut trees in order to build a new runway. This was held to be a sufficient interest to bring a possession claim against activists who had set up camp in the trees to disrupt the development. However, a mere contractual right of entry which does not confer a right of control of the land is insufficient to bring a possession claim[61].

4.57   Where an occupation takes place on a highway maintainable at public expense, the highway authority, which for most roads will be the local authority, may bring a possession claim. The authority will, however, need to demonstrate to the court that it does in fact have sufficient right to bring proceedings. Under s 1 and s 263 of the Highways Act 1980 (HA 1980), the freehold title of a highway maintainable at public expense vests in the highway authority and this provides a basis on which they may seek possession[62]. The local authority must keep an up to date list of all streets that are maintainable at public expense[63] and could reasonably be expected to produce such a list to demonstrate their right to seek possession.

4.58   A local authority may also bring a claim for possession of other public spaces if this right is implicit in management powers granted by statute[64].

---

58 CPR 55.2(1).
59 CPR 55.1(b).
60 [2000] QB 133.
61 As another protest case shows: *Countryside Residential (North Thames) Ltd v Tugwell* (2001) 81 P & CR 2.
62 See *Wiltshire County Council v Frazer* (1984) 47 P & CR 69.
63 HA 1980, s 36(6).
64 See *Mayor of London v Hall* [2011] 1 WLR 504 at 517.

What land can a possession order cover?

4.59   A possession claim may cover all land solely occupied by trespassers. The claim may also cover a larger area than that which is currently occupied, providing the wider area is not separated from the area currently occupied and is not otherwise distinct land. A possession order therefore need not simply cover the only room that is currently occupied in a building, but may include the rest of the property. Similarly, it need not be limited to a small corner of a wood where trespassers are currently camped. However, the order should not be overly broad and certainly should not cover separate parcels of land that are not yet occupied by the defendants.

4.60   In *Secretary of State for the Environment, Food and Rural Affairs v Meier*[65] new age travellers had set up camp in an area within Hethfelton Wood in Dorset, a wood managed by the Forestry Commission. Some of the travellers had previously been camped on other areas of Forestry Commission land within Dorset. The Forestry Commission sought a possession order for the whole of Hethfelton Wood and also fifty other parcels of land in separate areas. The Supreme Court upheld the order for possession of the whole of Hethfelton Wood, but it struck down the possession order for the separate parcels of land and indicated that an injunction was the appropriate remedy. However, in *University of Essex v Djemal*[66] a possession order was granted to cover an entire university campus when only particular buildings had been occupied by student protesters. The order was made following the granting of a more limited possession order after which the students had simply moved on to another part of the campus. Concerns over the order in *Djemal* were raised by Lord Neuberger MR in *Meier*[67] though these are strictly obiter.

Who can a claim be brought against?

4.61   A claim against trespassers may be brought either against individual named defendants or 'persons unknown'[68] or both. Where identified individuals are known to be in occupation they should be named on the claim form[69]. In demonstration cases, it is common for a claim to name any known defendants, but to also include 'persons unknown' as a catch-all. Anyone who is not specifically named on the claim form, but who wishes to defend the claim will need to apply to the court to be named as a defendant. This should be done at the first hearing of the claim or sooner if time allows.

---

65 [2009] UKSC 11, [2010] 1 All ER 855.
66 [1980] 1 WLR 1301.
67 Para 70.
68 'Persons in occupation' is another formulation that is essentially equivalent.
69 This requirement is implicit in the provision that only allows 'persons unknown' to be used when the name of a defendant is not known (CPR 55.3(4)).

4.62   There are both advantages and disadvantages to being a named defendant. Someone whose name was listed as a defendant on the claim form by the claimant has no choice in the matter, but the decision to add someone, particularly if there is no named defendant, is likely to be the most significant decision in the early litigation process. The main advantage of having at least one named defendant is that it will allow someone to present a defence to the possession action in court. Even if the defence is ultimately unsuccessful it may delay matters, either for a few days for several weeks. The court process can also generate publicity providing an opportunity to communicate to a wider audience. However, the courts may be slow to permit discussion of the underlying reasons for the occupation in court[70].

4.63   The major disadvantage of being a named defendant is that named defendants are at risk of paying the costs of both sides if, as is likely, the case is ultimately lost. The costs, even in relatively simple proceedings can run to tens of thousands of pounds. Further, each individual who is a named defendant can be held both joint and severally liable for the full costs of the proceedings. Whilst the landowner may not insist on recovering their costs, the risk is a significant inhibitor to many people who would otherwise take part in proceedings[71].

4.64   There are some sensible steps that can be taken to minimise the risks of a costs order being made:

- one named defendant can usually present the same argument on behalf of others in the occupation. The court can formally rule that one person is to act as a representative defendant for a particular group under CPR 19.6(1) if it is clear that all those in the group 'have the same interest in the claim' (ie that they are all have the same defence and want the same outcome)[72];

- in the very unlikely event that a named defendant is able to obtain Legal Aid then this will provide them with some protection against costs;

- whilst the normal rule is that the losing party pays the costs of both sides, the court ultimately has discretion to award costs as it sees fit. When a losing party is seen as having unnecessarily wasted the court's time by presenting spurious defences or otherwise disrupting proceedings, then

---

70 See generally defences at para **4.96**.
71 Factors that might prevent a landowner from seeking costs include the adverse publicity that may be generated, for example for a university seeking costs against students or a local authority that wishes to avoid further fuss. However, it must be emphasised that there is no guarantee that adverse publicity will prevent costs being recovered.
72 The court is more likely to make such a ruling if the parties agree. Since using a representative reduces costs for the landowner, this is a factor that may be used to negotiate an agreement to waive or limit costs before the hearing.

any chance they may have of avoiding a costs order is much reduced. In other words, it can pay to be polite and efficient;

- the ability of a defendant to pay costs may sway a sympathetic court to reduce the amount, as will the argument that the named defendant was not occupying the land or property for his or her personal benefit. However, this is a matter for the judge's discretion, and some judges may be entirely unconvinced by such submissions.

Issuing, service and notice

4.65   A possession claim is issued by completing form N5, taking it to the court and paying the issue fee. The claim will then be stamped (sealed) by the court. A possession claim should usually be issued in the county court in the district where the land is situated. However, it may be brought in the High Court if the matter is particularly complex in either legal or factual terms, or there is a 'substantial risk of public disturbance or of serious harm to persons or property which properly require immediate determination'[73]. In 2010 two separate possession orders relating to occupations were applied for in short succession by the University of London's School of Oriental and African Studies and University College London. The first application was made before the High Court; the latter was issued in the county court. Yet both cases argued similar points arising out of similar circumstances. Landowners may believe that starting a claim in the High Court will make matters move more swiftly, but it is more expensive. High profile demonstration cases are often either started in, or transferred to, the High Court but they need not be.

4.66   The particulars of claim, which set out the detailed basis for the claim, should accompany the claim form on form N121 (or may be attached on a separate sheet). The particulars must:

(a)   identify the land to which the claim relates;

(b)   state if it is residential property;

(c)   give the ground on which possession is sought (ie trespass); and

(d)   give details of every person who, to the best of the claimant's knowledge, is in possession of the property[74].

4.67   The particulars must also state the claimant's interest in the land, or the basis of his right to claim possession, and the circumstances in which it has

---

73   CPR 55, PD 1.3.
74   CPR 55, PD 1.4.

been occupied without licence or consent[75]. If a claimant is aware that the property is occupied as part of a demonstration then this fact should be set out in the particulars.

4.68   When the claim form is issued, the court will fix a date for the initial hearing. This initial hearing may turn out to be the final hearing or it may be used to give case management directions. Once the claim is issued, the defendant must be served with the following documents:

(a)   the claim form;

(b)   particulars of claim; and

(c)   all witness statements on which the claimant intends to rely[76].

4.69   Serving a claim means delivering it to the other parties in the case[77]. For a claim relating to residential land, these documents must be served on the defendants at least five clear days before the hearing. For non-residential land, the time limit is shortened to two clear days[78]. There are specific provisions for shortening these time limits or otherwise determining the case 'as quickly as reasonably practicable' when there is evidence that the defendants have used, or threatened to use, violence against the claimant, their staff or other residents in the locality. Similarly, if the defendant, or a person for whom he is responsible, has caused or threatened to cause serious damage to the property. The court may also use its general case management powers to abridge time for service[79].

4.70   Where a claim is brought against 'persons unknown', the documents referred to in (a)–(c) above must be served by attaching copies to the main door of the property or some other part of land 'so that they are clearly visible' and, if practicable, by inserting copies in a sealed transparent envelope addressed to 'the occupiers' through the letter box. Alternatively, the documents may be served by placing stakes in the land in places where they are clearly visible and

---

75   CPR 55, PD 2.6.

76   CPR 55.8(5).

77   See the CPR, Part 6.

78   CPR 55.5(2). For possession claims not brought against trespassers, the standard notice period is not less than 21 days, with at least 28 clear days between issuing and the hearing date (CPR 55.5(3)). Proceedings against trespassers are hence significantly expedited even without the provisions relating to interim possession orders (see below).

79   Where a court does abridge time for service, the means used must nonetheless be adequate to allow those in occupation to participate in proceedings should they wish to do so. In *Sun Street Property Ltd v Persons Unknown* [2011] EWHC 3432 (Ch), (2012), Times, 16 January, notice of the final hearing in a possession claim was reduced by the court from 2 days to 45 minutes, with the final hearing to be heard by telephone at 10pm. Details of this hearing were buried within 100 pages of documents delivered to the defendants at 9:10pm. The out of hours phone number provided for the court was incorrectly stated and the number given would not have been answered after 5pm. This attempt by the claimants to provide notice was described by Roth J as 'profoundly unsatisfactory' and 'grossly inadequate' (para 22).

attaching copies of the documents in sealed transparent envelopes addressed to 'the occupiers'[80]. There is no requirement for a defendant to formally acknowledge service.

4.71   Contrary to some common misunderstandings, providing the documents have been served in one of these ways, it will not matter if those in occupation do not actually read the documents. However, if a person with a substantive defence to the claim is not aware, through no fault of their own, that it has been issued, this may form grounds for an application to adjourn proceedings.

4.72   Even when proceedings have been issued, this does not mean that negotiations with landowners must stop. Whilst much will depend on the particular circumstances, it may be beneficial to negotiate at the same time as preparing a defence. This chimes with the spirit of the overriding objective of the CPR 1998 and can be a means to limit the risk of costs.

Hearings

4.73   The initial hearing for a possession claim is usually very brief, particularly when the claim has been issued in the county court. Most county courts will list a large number of initial hearings in possession claims during a morning or afternoon session ('the possession list'). Each individual claim is allocated very little court time for these hearings, sometimes no more than ten minutes per claim. The court will begin by checking that the basic procedural requirements for the claim have been met. Where documents have been served by the claimant, he must produce a certificate of service at the initial hearing[81]. The court should also check that the claimant has sufficient interest in the land to bring a possession claim (usually by checking that a title from the Land Registry has been provided).

4.74   If nobody turns up at court to defend the claim, then, providing these basic requirements have been met, the court will issue a possession order. It is therefore important that activists commencing an occupation consider carefully, and in advance, how they will be dealing with an application for possession, as time may be very limited.

4.75   If someone does wish to defend the claim, then there will be some other procedural matters to deal with. Importantly, if any parties wish to be added as named defendants, an application should be made to do this at the first

---

80   CPR 55.6.
81   CPR 55.8(6).

hearing. It will obviously be essential to add a defendant if the claim has been issued solely against 'persons unknown' and those in occupation wish to contest it[82].

4.76   Those wanting to defend a claim should 'wherever possible' file a defence which includes all evidence that they wish to rely on and should be verified by a statement of truth[83]. The form on which to set out a defence is N11, it is available from the court offices or online[84]. If time allows, the defence and all witness statements should be filed two days before the hearing, otherwise it may be submitted at court on the day of the initial hearing[85]. Ultimately, however, there is no requirement for a defence to be served in a claim against trespassers.

4.77   Given both the short period of time from issuing the claim to the initial hearing and the short duration of the first hearing itself, it will clearly be difficult for those involved to present a full defence there and then. Those who wish to contest the possession claim will therefore usually want an adjournment in order to have more time to prepare and present their defence. Delay in itself is also usually valuable to those staging an occupation. At the initial hearing, or any adjournment of it, the court can either determine the claim or adjourn and make directions for a later hearing. The courts have a wide power to adjourn cases where that is necessary to deal with cases justly: for example, to allow parties to prepare their cases, gather evidence, arrange legal representation or continue negotiations[86]. Where a party wants further time to complete a step, a judge may wish to see evidence that efforts have been made to progress the case.

4.78   A court is unlikely to grant an adjournment if there is no possibility whatsoever that those in occupation have a defence, but if there is some chance that a defence may exist then an adjournment is possible. A brief adjournment

---

82 Defendants may use an application notice (form N244) if they have time to set out their application in advance. Otherwise they can make the application orally at the hearing.

83 CPR 55 PD 5.1. The ordinary mandatory requirement in civil litigation that a defendant who wishes to contest the claim must complete a written defence that should be filed at court and served on the other parties to the case within 14 days of service of the claim does not apply to possession claims against trespassers (CPR 55.7(2)).

84 See hmctscourtfinder.justice.gov.uk/HMCTS/FormFinder.do.

85 The claimant should have included all witness statements they intend to rely on with the documents initially served with the claim (CPR 55.8(5)). However, if new matters arise following service of the claim form the claimant may seek to update the material in front of the court.

86 The power to adjourn in the county court is under the County Courts Act 1984, s 3(2). It is supplemented by CPR 3.1(2)(b) which gives a general power to adjourn that should be exercised in line with the overriding objective of dealing with cases justly (CPR 1.1(1)). See *North British Housing Association v Matthews* [2001] EWCA Civ 1736, [2005] 1 WLR 3133 for discussion on adjournments in possession claims.

may simply result in the case being relisted in the possession list a few days or a week later. However, if the claim 'is genuinely disputed on grounds which appear to be substantial', the court must refuse to decide the claim summarily and instead make more substantial case management directions to prepare the case for a full hearing[87]. Whilst more details of the defence may be provided later, enough detail should be given at the first hearing and any adjournment to meet the 'genuinely disputed' test. If the case proceeds to a trial then the timetable will depend on the urgency of the issue and how busy the particular court is.

4.79   A case which is scheduled too quickly could breach the defendants' right to a fair trial protected under the ECHR, Article 6. It is accepted that defendants who are not legally represented may require more time to prepare their case than professional lawyers. In the 'Democracy Village' case where protesters occupied Parliament Square, 18 days from the date of issue to the first day of the trial was held not to breach Article 6[88]. However, it is important to note that several, though not all, of the defendants were legally represented. In the OccupyLSX case, a large occupation at the foot of the steps to St Paul's Cathedral, there were 30 days from the date of issue to the first day of the trial[89].

4.80   Clearly, it is in the defendants' interest to ensure they have sufficient time to prepare a defence, and consideration should be given to what arguments may persuade the court to grant a lengthy adjournment. The court will have to balance this against the interests of the claimant. Therefore, activists should make submissions to the court about the type of evidence they intend to submit in broad terms, eg witness statements, photographs etc, why this evidence is relevant and important, and how long it will take to obtain. Assurances may also be given in the interim that certain terms will be abided by, for example that health and safety requirements will be complied with. The advantage of such assurances is that they may defeat arguments by the claimant that a lengthy adjournment would be hazardous or too inconvenient. An adjournment would of course enable activists to extend the occupation for the duration of the adjournment. However, activists should be cautious about the format and terms of the assurance.

4.81   Like other civil proceedings, evidence in possession claims is primarily given in written form through witness statements. The written evidence will be read in advance by the judge and the party for whom the witness appears should only ask oral questions relating to points of clarification

---

87 See CPR 55.8(2). Directions made when a case is 'genuinely disputed' include allocating the case to a 'track' which will reflect the importance and complexity of the issues (see CPR 55.9). Activists are recommended to seek legal advice if their claim reaches this stage.
88 *Mayor of London v Hall* [2010] EWCA Civ 817.
89 *City of London v Samede* [2012] EWHC 34 (QB).

or updating. Oral cross-examination then follows by the other party to the claim. The parties should, where possible, indicate in advance of the hearing which witnesses they wish to question. If one party disputes evidence that is in a witness statement and the maker of the statement does not attend court, and the evidence is material to the claim, then the court ought to adjourn the case so that oral evidence can be given[90]. However, a landowner may be able to persuade the court not to follow this requirement if the claim based only on undisputed evidence is strong.

Interim possession orders

4.82   An addition to the standard possession claim against trespassers is the 'interim possession order' (IPO) which imposes criminal sanctions on those who remain in occupation before the main possession hearing. Whilst an IPO is technically a limited order that only gives the landowner a right to possession until the main hearing, granting an IPO often causes trespassers to leave effectively bringing an end to proceedings.

4.83   An IPO may only be granted when:

- the landowner is claiming possession of premises solely occupied by trespassers[91];

- the occupiers both entered and remained on the property as trespassers (ie they were not given consent to enter by someone who had a right to immediate possession of the land, nor did such a person at any point whilst the occupiers were on the land give them permission to remain for any length of time)[92];

- the claim is made within 28 days of when the landowner knew, or ought reasonably to have known that the defendants were in occupation[93];

- the landowner has an immediate right to possession and had such a right throughout the period of occupation[94];

- the landowner is claiming possession only and no other remedy such as damages or an injunction[95].

---

90 CPR 55 PD 5.4. The case of *Benesco Charity Ltd v Kanj* [2011] EWHC 3415 (Ch) is authority that: 'a witness statement should be not rejected at a summary stage unless the evidence is incredible' (para 21).

91 CPR 55.21(1)(a) 'Premises' is defined as in the Criminal Law Act 1977, s 12 (CPR 55.20(3)), see para **4.22**.

92 CPR 55.21(2).

93 CPR 55.20(1)(c).

94 CPR 55.20(1)(b).

95 CPR 55.21(1)(a).

4.84   In practice therefore, an IPO is unlikely to be successful where an occupier had a licence to enter a property since they will not have entered as a trespasser (though if they entered intending to breach the licence they will be treated as trespassers from the start). An IPO is also unavailable if the claimant ought to have known about the occupation for at least 28 days. These points are clearly relevant to occupations in buildings that have wide or public access or where the claimant has delayed bringing possession proceedings.

4.85   If the landowner seeks an IPO, the application should be filed with the court at the same time as the possession claim is issued. The claim should therefore consist of:

(a)   a standard possession claim on form N5; and

(b)   an application for an IPO on form N130; and

(c)   written evidence.

4.86   The written evidence supporting the IPO application must be given by the claimant personally, with a signed statement of truth. A solicitor or agent cannot sign the statement. Where the claimant is a corporate body the statement should be signed by a 'duly authorised officer'.

4.87   When the court issues the claim and IPO application, it will set a date for a hearing of the application 'not less than three days after the date of issue'[96]. Within 24 hours of the court issuing the claim, the claimant must serve the defendants with form N130 together with N5 and all written statements and a blank form for the defendant's witness statement (form N133)[97]. Where the claim is brought against 'persons unknown' the practicalities of service consist of attaching it to the property and posting through the letterbox as with a standard possession claim[98].

4.88   The IPO application will be dealt with at the date specified on the issued application. If an occupier wishes to fight the IPO, he should complete and file at court a witness statement in reply setting out his defences before the hearing. If this is not done then there is a risk that the court will refuse to allow defendants to even be present at the hearing. Neither party has to attend the hearing, but if one party is absent they will usually lose.

4.89   At the hearing the court will consider whether the landowner agrees to give any undertakings towards the court, which may benefit the defendant,

---

96   CPR 55.22(6). Note that Saturdays, Sundays and Bank Holidays do not count (CPR 2.8).
97   CPR 55.23(1).
98   CPR 55.23(2) and CPR 55.6(a).

including not to dispose of or damage any of the defendant's property left on the land in the event an IPO is granted[99]. The court will make an IPO if[100]:

(a)   the claimant has proved that he has complied with the requirements of service including filing a certificate of service; and

(b)   the basic requirements for using the IPO procedure set out above are met; and

(c)   the undertakings given by the claimant are 'adequate'.

4.90   If an IPO is issued, the court will also set a date for the hearing of the substantive possession claim within seven days. If an IPO is not made the court will make other directions for dealing with the substantive possession claim, including setting a date for the hearing.

4.91   The IPO itself is issued on form N134. To be effective, it has to be served on the defendants within 48 hours of being sealed by the court[101]. The IPO must be served together with copies of the claim form and written evidence.

Trespass during currency of an interim possession order

4.92

Legislation	Criminal Law Act 1977, s 10
Maximum penalty	6 months' imprisonment and/or £5,000 fine
Venue for trial	Magistrates' court

4.93   Once an IPO is granted and served, it is a criminal offence to be present on the premises specified in the order as a trespasser. There is, however, a statutory amnesty allowing 24 hours from service of the order in which to leave[102]. Anyone present on the premises when the IPO was served will

---

99   CPR 55.25(1). Other relevant undertakings include the claimant agreeing to reinstate the defendant if the IPO should not have been granted and not to grant a right of occupation to anyone else until the final possession hearing.
100 CPR 55.25(2).
101 CPR 55.26(1).
102 CJPOA 1994, s 76.

automatically be a trespasser whether or not they were part of the initial occupation[103].

4.94   The IPO will lapse on the date set for the hearing of the possession claim[104]; however, those who were present on the premises when the IPO was served will remain liable under s 76 if they re-enter, or attempt to do so, for an entire year from the date the IPO was issued[105]. Because of these criminal sanctions it is imperative that IPOs are only issued when the court is fully satisfied that all formal requirements are met, so those fighting an IPO should highlight any procedural flaws there may be.

4.95   It is possible to apply to have an IPO set aside, but a defendant can only do this if they have already left the premises[106]. Any application to have the IPO set aside should be supported by a witness statement. It is not possible to apply to set aside an IPO simply on the basis that the defendant did not attend the initial hearing[107]. Once an application to set aside is made, the court will decide the date for dealing with it and the amount of notice that should be given to the claimant.

Defences to possession claims

4.96   In order to bring a possession claim against trespassers the landowner only has to prove his title and intention to regain possession. This is typically done by providing a copy of the title to land and a witness statement. The burden of proving any grounds for resisting the claim lies on the occupier. There are four categories of defences:

(a)   that the occupier is not a trespasser;

(b)   that the claimant lacks an immediate right to possession;

(c)   procedural failures;

(d)   public law/Human Rights Act defences.

The occupier is not a trespasser

4.97   Whilst in most demonstration cases this will not be a live issue, in cases where the land ownership is complex and some parties involved support

---

103   CJPOA 1994, s 76(6).
104   CPR 55.27(2).
105   CJPOA 1994, s 76(4).
106   CPR 55.28(1).
107   CPR 55.28(4).

the presence of the demonstration, or where activists can rely on some right to be on the land, it may form the basis of a defence.

4.98 It is unlikely that an occupier will successfully argue that they were not a trespasser because of the need to carry out direct action. The courts have examined the scope of necessity and public interest defences to trespass and they are extremely limited. There must be a danger that the trespass avoids which is 'immediate and obvious' and the circumstances must be such that 'a reasonable person would conclude that there was no alternative to the act of trespass'[108].

The claimant lacks a right to immediate possession

4.99 The claimant's right must be to *immediate* possession. If a landowner has granted a lease to someone else which has not been brought to an end and trespassers enter the land, then it is only the subordinate leaseholder who has a right to immediate possession and not the initial landowner. Hence the landowner cannot bring a possession claim[109]. This situation can arise where a leaseholder has moved away or does not wish to be involved in proceedings, thereby thwarting the superior titleholder's possession claim.

Procedural failures

4.100 Significant procedural failings include a failure to name a defendant[110], failure to properly serve documents or a claim drafted too widely and relating to land not solely occupied by trespassers. If there are no other defences then relying on procedural grounds will typically only delay proceedings whilst the fault is rectified. Even then an adjournment is only likely where a party can demonstrate they would suffer prejudice should proceedings continue uninterrupted, for example where the procedural failing means the defendant has not been given sufficient opportunity to collate evidence to rebut an assertion made by the claimant. However, if procedural failings are sufficiently egregious, the court may require the landowner to restart proceedings from scratch as a debt of justice (*ex debito justitiae*)[111].

---

108 *Monsanto v Tilley* [2000] Env LR 313, CA, per Stuart-Smith LJ at para 33.
109 *Wirral Borough Council v Smith* (1982) 43 P & CR 312 or for an older case see *Doe d Wawn v Horn* (1838) 3 M & W 333.
110 This may include bringing a claim against 'persons unknown' when the names of some of those in occupation are known. However, the defendant will need to demonstrate prejudice to rely on this failing in any way.
111 See *Sun Street Property Ltd v Persons Unknown* [2011] EWHC 3432 (Ch), (2012), Times, 16 January.

Public law/Human Rights Act defences

4.101   Where possession is sought by a public body, such as a local authority, the decision to bring possession proceedings can be challenged either on traditional administrative law grounds or as a breach of the European Convention of Human Rights, actionable under s 6 of the Human Rights Act 1998.

4.102   A detailed description of public law defences is beyond the scope of this book. In general, a decision of a public body may be challenged on the following grounds:

- when the decision is so unreasonable that no reasonable decision-maker could have made it;

- when the decision-maker failed to consider relevant matters or took into account irrelevant matters;

- when the decision-maker made an error of law;

- when it has inflexibly adopted a blanket policy without regard to the specific facts of the case;

- when the decision-maker has failed to follow some published policy relating to the matter on which the defendant has relied[112].

4.103   The decision by a local authority to bring possession proceedings is in principle amenable to the challenges above. Such challenges may be used to defeat the possession claim and may be considered by the court dealing with that claim rather than issued as separate proceedings[113]. It is important to emphasise that public law challenges will examine the decision-making of the local authority and will rarely involve a detailed assessment of the factual basis on which the occupiers wish to remain in possession. Judicial review is a complex area and occupiers are advised to seek legal advice if they believe they have grounds for such a defence.

4.104   Another means to challenge the decisions of public bodies is to use the Human Rights Act 1998 (HRA 1998). Under s 6(1) of the HRA 1998, 'it is

---

112   On rare occasions it may be possible to rely on a statement by an official from the authority that those in occupation will be allowed to stay until a certain date. Much will depend on the status of the person making the promise and whether it was sufficiently clear and unequivocal. If a verbal offer is made then written confirmation should be sought. In any event those who witnessed the offer should make a contemporaneous note.

113   *Doherty v Birmingham City Council* [2008] UKHL 57, [2009] 1 AC 367 at paras 56, 123 and 157 and *Manchester City Council v Pinnock* [2010] UKSC 45, [2011] HLR 7 at para 81. Where a public law defence raised in county court proceedings shows some merit then this may introduce sufficient complexity to warrant a transfer of the case to the High Court.

unlawful for a public authority to act in a way which is incompatible with a Convention right'. A list of the relevant Convention rights can be found at Annex B. Under s 7(1) a person whose Convention rights have or will be breached may rely on those rights 'in any legal proceedings'. The impact of ss 6(1) and 7(1) on decisions to bring possession proceedings has a complex recent legal history. The Supreme Court decisions in *Manchester City Council v Pinnock*[114] and the subsequent case of *Hounslow London Borough Council v Powell*[115] have brought some clarification, although areas of uncertainty remain.

4.105 As Lord Neuberger MR stated in *Pinnock*, if domestic 'law is to be compatible with Article 8 [the right to a private and family life] ... the court must have the power to assess the proportionality of making the order, and, in making that assessment, to resolve any relevant dispute of fact'[116]. Similar arguments apply to defences based on Articles 10 and 11 (rights to freedom of expression and association[117]). Following another statement of Lord Neuberger in *Hall v Mayor of London*[118]:

'save possibly in very unusual and clear circumstances, Article 11, and Article 10, should be capable of being invoked to enable the merits of the particular case to be considered'[119].

4.106 Challenges based on human rights grounds in occupation cases will typically involve an assessment of the proportionality of the interference with the Article 10/11 rights of the demonstrators when balanced against the need to maintain order, the rights of others to use public spaces or the property rights of others (including the local authority itself)[120]. Whilst it is to be hoped that a

---

114 [2010] UKSC 45.
115 [2011] UKSC 8.
116 Para 49.
117 *Hall* was decided after argument had been heard in *Pinnock*, but before judgment was handed down. An example of a post-*Pinnock* case where Article 10/11 was given full ventilation in argument is *City of London v Samede* [2012] EWHC 34 (QB). For comments suggesting that the margin of appreciation given to state bodies in legislation that impinges on Article 10/11 is significantly less than in Article 8 possession cases, see *Tabernacle v Secretary of State for Defence* [2009] EWCA 23 at 50.
118 [2010] EWCA Civ 817.
119 Para 42. The permission decision of the Court of Appeal in the OccupyLSX case (*City of London Corporation v Samede* [2012] EWCA Civ 160) also confirms that Articles 10 and 11 are engaged in occupations.
120 It has been assumed that those in occupation are not seeking to rely on their right to private life under Article 8 on the basis that the occupation site is their 'home'. The applicability of Article 8 to cases where trespassers have been living on land for only a limited time but have no alternative 'home' is a complex question. The traveller cases of *Ward v Hillingdon London Borough Council* [2001] HRLR 40 and *Brighton and Hove City Council v Chrissy Alleyn* (unreported, 5 April 2011) support the view that Article 8 is engaged in eviction proceedings under its 'family life' aspects.

local authority will carry out such a balancing exercise before deciding to seek possession, the ultimate assessment of proportionality is for the court to make[121]. Therefore, considering human rights-based challenges will typically involve the court in examination of the facts of the case to a greater extent than traditional public law challenges. Where a human rights challenge has some merit it may be possible to seek a longer adjournment in order for a defendant to gather the relevant evidence needed to make out their case.

4.107 Even though the courts will be required to make an assessment of disputed facts in considering human rights defences, it is only those facts which are relevant to the possession claim which will be examined. The courts will be extremely unlikely to give more than a cursory examination of the substantive matter about which activists are demonstrating. Provided that the court is satisfied that the occupiers are genuinely exercising their Article 10/11 rights, by expressing sincerely held views about matters which are not obviously trivial, then it will not be necessary to deal with the content of the demonstration any further[122]. Whilst, this may frustrate those activists who wish to use the court process to highlight aspects of their cause, the rationale for the courts' approach is that freedom of speech should be afforded to all, irrespective of content and, in any event, the courts should not be the arbiters of what views are acceptable[123].

4.108 Given the potential advantage of delay to occupiers, a question arises as to not just when a defence based on Article 10/11 will ultimately succeed, but

---

121 See *Belfast City Council v Miss Behavin Ltd* [2007] UKHL 19, [2007] 1 WLR 1420 and *Hall v Mayor of London* [2010] EWCA Civ 817 (at 43).

122 In *City of London Corporation v Samede* [2012] EWCA Civ 160 the Court of Appeal highlighted the length of time devoted to occupiers explaining in court the causes for which they were demonstrating and stated that '[i]n strict principle, little if any court time need be taken up with such evidence'. The court suggested that judges should use case management powers to limit the amount of time such cases take, though a blanket ban excluding such evidence was not correct. For an earlier example of the general approach of the courts to attempts by activists to require the court to rule on the substantive matter prompting the demonstration see the judgment of Mummery LJ in *Monsanto plc v Tilly* [2000] Env LR 313, CA.

123 The European Court has indicated that some forms of protest deserve a particularly high degree of protection under Article 10. Where a protest engages with 'a debate on a matter of general concern and [constitute] political and militant expression … a high level of protection of the right to freedom of expression is required under Article 10' (*Lindon v France* (2008) 46 EHRR 35). There are nonetheless legal limits on freedom of speech, particularly where it incites violence. For an example of the general approach of the courts to attempts by activists to require the court to rule on the substantive matter prompting the demonstration see the judgment of Mummery LJ in *Monsanto v Tilly* [2000] Env LR 313, CA. In *City of London Corporation v Samede* [2012] EWCA Civ 160, the Court of Appeal confirmed that the 'general character' of the views expressed should be taken into account when assessing the proportionality of interference with Article 10 and 11 (at 41). However, this was not a factor which 'trumps all others' (at 41).

when the court should allow such proportionality arguments to even be made. In *Pinnock*, Lord Neuberger MR stated that the fact that the local authority is entitled to possession and will, in the absence of evidence to the contrary, be assumed to be acting within its duties was 'strong evidence' that making a possession order was proportionate. However, it was 'unsafe and unhelpful to invoke exceptionality as a guide' to when proportionality should be more carefully scrutinised by the courts[124]. Nonetheless, when a human rights point was raised:

> '[The] court should initially consider it summarily, and if, as will no doubt often be the case, the court is satisfied that, even if the facts relied on are made out, the point would not succeed, it should be dismissed. Only if the court is satisfied that it could affect the order that the court might make should the point be further entertained'.

4.109 In *Powell*, it was emphasised that 'the threshold for raising an arguable case on proportionality was a high one which would succeed only in a small proportion of cases'[125]. However, these comments arise in the case of possession proceedings against tenants whose Article 8 rights already provide some procedural protection[126]. In possession cases outside of the mainstream, the courts may be required to show more vigilance in assessing a local authority's claim to have acted proportionately.

4.110 The Human Rights Act 1998 does not extend the duty to act compatibly with the European Convention to private bodies. Therefore, where an occupation is on private land, it is not possible to argue that the *landowner's* failure to allow freedom of expression breaches Articles 10/11 and that this should defeat the possession order. However, the HRA 1998 does require the *court* to act compatibly with Article 10/11 and since a possession order is granted by the court, arguably the court must take Article 10/11 into account when making its decision. By parity of reasoning, the court is similarly required to consider the landowner's right to peaceful enjoyment of possessions under Article 1 of Protocol 1 to the Convention. The result of the argument is that the court must balance these competing rights in private possession claims.

---

124 See paras 51–53. Lord Neuberger's example of a case when the courts should be slow to assume that the authorities' assessment of proportionality was correct is illuminating in the present context. He cites an example where 'the property is the only occupied part of a site intended for immediate development for community housing', in such a case '[t]he authority could rely on that factor, but would have to plead it and adduce evidence to support it' (*Pinnock* at 53).

125 Para 35.

126 See *Powell* at 90 and 92.

4.111   This indirect applicability of the HRA 1998 in private possession claims was explicitly left open in *Pinnock*[127], although Lord Neuberger acknowledged there was some limited support for the argument above from European jurisprudence[128]. At the time of writing, there are no significant reported domestic cases post-*Pinnock* on the applicability of arguments based on Article 10/11 in private possession claims. The matter was raised in the High Court decision in *Sun Street Property Ltd v Persons Unknown*[129]. In considering an application to set aside a possession order, Roth J assumed, without deciding, that the court was required to consider Article 10 and 11 rights in any possession hearing[130]. However, he held that those in occupation had alternative means to effectively exercise their Article 10/11 rights and therefore the defence to the possession claim could not succeed[131].

4.112   The primary European case on the applicability of human rights arguments to occupations on private land is that of *Appleby v UK*[132]. This was a case brought by protesters who wished to leaflet and collect signatures for a petition in a private shopping mall but were prevented from doing so due to rules banning all political activities in the mall. The European Court of Human Rights held that there was no breach of Article 10/11 because there were alternative means by which the appellants could communicate their message. However, the European Court did leave open the possibility that 'where a bar on access to private property has the effect of preventing any effective exercise of freedom of expression or it can be said that the essence of the right has been destroyed'[133] the State might need to restrict private property rights in order to allow for freedom of expression[134].

4.113   The case law regarding Article 10/11 defences in private possession proceedings is in a state of development. However, what is clear is that in the domestic courts the threshold for raising an arguable human rights defence against a private landowner will be set significantly higher than for claims brought by public authorities. It is only in truly exceptional circumstances that

---

127   See para 50.
128   In *Pinnock*, Lord Neuberger MR referred to *Belchikova v Russia* (Application No 2408/06, 25 March 2010) where the European Court accepted that Article 8 applied to a private possession claim, although the case was ultimately ruled inadmissible on other grounds. That the point is still open was acknowledged by Arden LJ in *Murphy v Wyatt* [2011] EWCA Civ 408, [2011] HLR 29.
129   [2011] EWHC 3432 (Ch), (2012) Times, 16 January.
130   Para 28.
131   Para 32.
132   (2003) 37 EHRR 783.
133   *Appleby v UK* [2003] 37 EHRR 783 at para 50.
134   See also *Khurshid Mustafa and Tazibachi v Sweden* (Application No 23882/06, 16 December 2008); *Belchikova v Russia* (Application No 2408/06) and *Zehentner v Austria* (Application No 20082/02).

reliance on Article 10/11 rights will ever be sufficient to defer the right to possession of a private landowner for even a brief period.

Universities and the Human Rights Act 1998

The position of universities as public authorities under HRA 1998 is unclear[135]. The preferable view is that universities are **hybrid authorities** for the purposes of the HRA 1998, s 6(3): they exercise functions, some of which, but not all, are of a public nature. Private acts of such bodies lie outside the scope of the HRA 1998. The question then arises whether a decision by a university to seek possession of land on its own campus is an act which is public or private in nature? Arguably, since the admission of large numbers of students onto its campus for the purpose of education is a public function, decisions concerning the management of that space are not private in nature and must comply with the European Convention.

A further piece of legislation supporting the applicability of freedom of expression arguments in possession claims brought by universities is the Education (No 2) Act 1986, s 43, which provides for 'Freedom of speech in universities, polytechnics and colleges' as follows:

'(1) Every individual and body of persons concerned in the government of any establishment to which this section applies shall take such steps as are reasonably practicable to ensure that freedom of speech within the law is secured for members, students and employees of the establishment and for visiting speakers'.

Section 43 requires universities to develop codes of practice regarding meetings and other activities on campus. Clearly regard should be had to such guidance when defending a campus occupation.

Proportionality arguments in possession claims

4.114   Once it is established that human rights arguments apply in a given possession claim, the court will be required to examine the proportionality of making a possession order. The concept of proportionality and the basic scope

---

135   See *The Chancellor, Masters & Scholars of the University of Cambridge v HM Revenue and Customs* [2009] EWHC 434 (Ch), a charity tax case, for some discussion of the complexities involved. See Mead, *The New Law of Peaceful Protest* (2010), pp 48–49 for academic discussion.

of Articles 10 and 11 are discussed elsewhere in this book[136]. When applied to occupations, the court will be required to balance the occupiers' right to protest with the right of the landowner to peaceful enjoyment of his possessions, the rights of others to move freely, and the need to prevent public disorder. Much will depend on the facts of a particular case, in particular the level of disruption to others, the time for which the occupation has already been in place and the likely total duration. However, some guidance can be taken from the domestic and European case law. In addition to Strasbourg cases, guidance may also be taken from the Office for Democratic Institutions and Human Rights ('ODIHR') within the Organization for Security and Co-Operation in Europe ('OSCE')[137]. ODHIR has recently published *Guidelines on Freedom of Peaceful Assembly* which give guidance on the factors that should be considered by member states of the OSCE when managing assemblies[138].

Location

4.115   The importance of giving significant weight to the occupiers' chosen location was emphasised in *Hall*. However, the European Court held in *Rai, Allmond & 'Negotiate Now' v UK*[139] that the availability of other areas for demonstrating supported the proportionality of banning certain protests in a particular high-profile location (in that case it was Trafalgar Square).

4.116   The OSCE Guidelines on Freedom of Assembly are clear that priority should, where possible, be given to the occupiers' choice of location:

'In particular, the state should always seek to facilitate public assemblies at the organizers' preferred location, where this is a public place that is ordinarily accessible to the public ...'[140].

4.117   Moreover, the occupiers have a legitimate need for 'sight and sound' of their intended audience:

'Public assemblies are held to convey a message to a particular target person, group or organization. Therefore, as a general rule, assemblies should be facilitated within "sight and sound" of their target audience'[141].

---

136 See Key Concepts in Appendix E.
137 The United Kingdom has been a member of the OSCE and its predecessor institutions since the signing of the Helsinki Final Act in 1975.
138 *Guidelines on Freedom of Peaceful Assembly* (2nd edn, 2010) OSCE/ODIHR.
139 (1995) 19 EHRR CD93.
140 Explanatory Notes, para 19.
141 Guidelines, para 3.5.

Duration

4.118   Clearly the length of time that an occupation has already been in place will affect the court's assessment of how much of an opportunity those involved have already had to exercise Article 10/11 rights. However, if a protest has been in place for a long duration without significant disruption or other ill effects, and particularly if no previous attempts have been made to remove it, then this should count in favour of allowing it to continue[142].

4.119   Where a demonstration takes place on the road, the comment by Lord Clyde in *Director of Public Prosecutions v Jones*[143] is relevant: 'if the occupation becomes more than reasonably transitional in terms of either time or space, then it may come to exceed the right to use the highway [to protest]'[144]. However, he also noted that 'what is reasonable or usual may develop and change from one period of history to another'[145].

4.120   There have been relatively few ECHR cases regarding long-duration occupations. In the case of *Cisse v France*[146], the eviction of an occupation that had been present for two months at a church was held to be proportionate. However, it is significant that the case was held to engage Article 11(1) because this demonstrates that the European Court do not appear to impose a strict time limit on what may count as an 'assembly' for the purposes of Article 11.

Manner and form

4.121   It is not uncommon for those bringing proceedings against occupiers to target their objections solely to the camped nature of the protest, stating that they will permit other forms of protest to continue. Clearly, the possibility of other forms of protest will always weigh against allowing an occupation to continue. However, in *Tabernacle v Secretary of State for Defence*[147] it was held that in assessing proportionality the court must be alive to the possibility that the 'manner and form' may constitute the actual nature and quality of the protest; it may have acquired a symbolic force inseparable from the protesters' message.

---

142   See *Tablernacle v Secretary of State for Defence* [2009] EWCA Civ 23 at 41. The case concerned the Aldermaston Women's Peace Camp which had taken place one weekend a month for 23 years at the time of appeal. The camp is still running (as is the Aldermaston Atomic Weapons Establishment against which it was formed).
143   [1999] 2 AC 240.
144   Para 281.
145   Para 279.
146   Application No 51346/99.
147   [2009] EWCA Civ 23. The Court of Appeal confirmed this approach in the OccupyLSX case (*City of London Corporation v Samede* [2012] EWCA Civ 160).

4.122 The wider context of a protest may also impact on the alternative methods available to protesters to assemble and express their views. Thus, in the case defended by UCL students when occupying the Jeremy Bentham room and part of the Slade School of Arts in December 2010, the defendants raised fears and concerns about policing tactics used on recent marches, including the use of kettling and horse charges. The students argued, ultimately unsuccessfully, that the occupation was a necessary means by which to express their views as it was a safe space for protesters.

4.123 As with the choice of location, the OSCE Guidelines state that priority should, where possible, be given to the manner and form of the occupiers' choosing.

Obstruction

4.124 For occupations in public spaces, the extent of any disruption caused is the key factor in any proportionality assessment. The court may need to look at physical disruption, economic disruption, noise issues, health and safety concerns (especially fire and sanitation), difficulties in policing, planning control violations and any other factor that is raised in a given case. The statement of Laws LJ in *Tabernacle* is worth considering:

> 'Rights worth having are unruly things. Demonstrations and protests are liable to be a nuisance. They are liable to be inconvenient and tiresome, or at least perceived as such by others who are out of sympathy with them'[148].

4.125 The fact that members of the public do not ordinarily use a particular location is relevant[149]. Where an occupation occurs on a highway, those in occupation may rely on the public's right to make reasonable use of the highway provided that this use is not inconsistent with the primary right to pass and repass[150]. The size of the road and the relative size of the disruption are relevant[151]. In *Haw* a tent which covered 2ft of an 11ft wide pavement was held not to be an unreasonable use of the pavement.

4.126 ECHR cases clearly establish that a degree of disruption is inevitable in many protests and that this should be tolerated. *Surgey Kuznetsov v Russia*[152] concerned a picket for two hours a day over three days outside a courthouse where the organiser was prosecuted for an administrative offence. The

---

148 At para 43.
149 *Haw v Westminster Magistrates' Court* [2007] EWHC 2960 (Admin), [2008] QB 888.
150 *Director of Public Prosecutions v Jones* [1999] 2 AC 240.
151 *Director of Public Prosecutions v Jones* [1999] 2 AC 240 at 256.
152 Application No 10877/04.

European Court held that there was a violation of Article 11, it did emphasise the short duration of the protest, but made comments which echo those of LJ Laws in *Tabernacle*:

> 'as a general principle, the Court reiterates that any demonstration in a public place inevitably causes a certain level of disruption to ordinary life, including disruption of traffic, and that it is important for the public authorities to show a certain degree of tolerance towards peaceful gatherings'[153].

4.127 Slightly stronger sentiments are expressed by in the OSCE Guidelines[154]:

> 'Participants in public assemblies have as much a claim to use such sites for a reasonable period as anyone else. Indeed, public protest, and freedom of assembly in general, should be regarded as equally legitimate uses of public space as the more routine purposes for which public space is used'.

Evictions and other consequences of losing

4.128 If the defences do not succeed then the court will make a possession order. The order itself will be made on form N26.

4.129 The case of *McPhail v Persons Unknown*[155] has long been held to be authority for the proposition that when a landowner seeks a possession order against those who entered land as trespassers there is no power for the court to suspend or defer the order[156]. This might be inconsistent with the Supreme Court decisions in *Pinnock* and *Powell* which require the court to consider human rights defences in certain possession claims. The rule in *McPhail* may

---

153 Other cases where similar comments have been made include: *Balcik v Turkey* (Application No 25/02); *Oya Ataman v Turkey* (Application No 74552/01) and *Patyi v Hungary* (Application No 5529/05). For a less liberal approach, see *Çiloğlu v Turkey* (Application No 73333/01), where the court noted that a gathering in a public place, held regularly every Saturday morning for over three years, had become an almost permanent event which had the effect of disrupting traffic and clearly caused a breach of the peace. The actions of the police in preventing further protest had therefore been proportionate.

154 Para 20.

155 [1973] Ch 447, CA.

156 References in court forms to Suspended Possession Orders only apply to certain former tenants. Whilst *McPhail* applied to the High Court, the case of *Swordheath Properties Ltd v Floydd* [1978] 1 All ER 721 confirmed that the situation was the same in the county court. However, the parties may agree to defer the enforcement of the order by consent.

therefore be subject of future legal challenge[157]. However, in practice, when faced with the possibility of losing a possession order altogether, most landowners are likely to be prepared to make an undertaking to the court not to enforce a possession order for a given period. This option should clearly be borne in mind during negotiations.

4.130   The court may also award damages if the claimant has sought them[158]. These are assessed to meet the loss suffered by the landowner or any profit made by the trespasser. Unless there is evidence to the contrary, they will be assessed at standard market rent. There is no requirement for the landowner to show that he would have let out the property[159].

4.131   It is possible to appeal against the making of a possession order. If the order was made by a district judge in the county court, then the appeal is to a circuit judge in the county court. If the order was made by a circuit judge then the appeal lies to a High Court judge. Appeals from the High Court lie to the Court of Appeal. Permission to appeal is required from either the initial judge (and so should be sought at the end of the hearing) or from the court to which the appeal is made. An application to stay the possession order should be made alongside any permission application. Those wishing to appeal are advised to seek legal advice and should carefully consider the cost implications of appeals and the danger of setting an unhelpful precedent for future cases.

Warrant for possession

4.132   A possession order is not itself enough for a landowner to evict trespassers. Lawful eviction requires either a warrant of possession issued in the county court or a writ of possession issued in the High Court. The granting of a possession order gives the landowner three months to apply for a warrant or

---

157   In *Kay v Lambeth London Borough Council* [2006] UKHL 10, [2006] 2 AC 465 Lord Bingham stated that the rule in *McPhail* 'must be relaxed … in order to comply with Article 8' (at para 36). Lord Bingham was, however, in the minority on this point. *Boyland & Son Ltd v Rand* [2006] EWCA Civ 1860, [2007] HLR 24 was a direct challenge to the rule in *McPhail* that failed because of the decision of the majority in *Kay*. However, *Pinnock* overruled certain portions of *Kay* and Lord Neuberger stated that 'if domestic law justifies an outright order for possession, the effect of Article 8 may, albeit in exceptional circumstances, justify … granting an extended order for possession' (para 62). The limits of any relaxation of *McPhail* should be assessed by comparison with the decision in *Powell* that the six-week limit on postponement of possession orders relating to non-secure tenancies on grounds of 'exceptional hardship' was complaint with Article 8 (see Lord Hope at para 64). The arguments above all apply *mutatis mutandis* to Articles 10 and 11.

158   Damages cannot be sought where a claimant applies for an IPO.

159   *Swordheath Properties Ltd v Tabet* [1979] 1 WLR 285.

writ[160]. The warrant or writ can be executed anytime up to a year after it has been issued. Once a possession order has been made, obtaining a warrant or writ is a largely administrative process. It is usually quicker in the High Court than the county court, but where a possession order is issued in the county court, it is possible to apply to the High Court for enforcement and thereby obtain a writ. It is worth making enquiries with the Advisory Service for Squatters about the situation regarding timescales in the local area. In addition, a protest may be deemed a special case and can therefore be expedited in relation to other claims. It is possible to apply to have a warrant set aside, but it is necessary to either show some procedural error or a significant change of circumstances that provides a substantive defence to the possession proceedings.

4.133 The warrant of possession gives authority for bailiffs to come to the property to execute it. High Court Enforcement Officers (previously known as sheriffs) execute writs. Those in occupation should be issued with a notice of eviction (form N54). It may also be possible to phone the bailiffs' office at the court who will often be willing to provide an update in circumstances where they have further information[161].

4.134 When bailiffs execute a warrant they may use reasonable force to gain entry and to remove all those in occupation of the land. The bailiffs can evict anyone who is on the premises, whether or not:

- they were part of the original trespassers;
- they took part in the court proceedings; and
- they moved in after the possession order was made[162].

4.135 If the police attend an eviction they can arrest those who break the law, in particular, by resisting bailiffs[163]. The police can also make arrests for breach of the peace, including, in principle, arrests when such a breach is imminent but has not yet occurred[164]. The role of the police ought to be limited to these specific roles, but in practice the line between making arrests and assisting the bailiffs can be difficult to discern. The police may also assist in the eviction of trespassers (even outside possession proceedings) relying on the power of a landowner to use self-help to remove a trespasser supplemented with the power

---

160 See Rules of the Supreme Court r 113.7 regarding procedures in the High Court and the County Court Rules, r 24.6(2) for proceedings in the county court. The landowner may apply out of time if the possession order has not been used within three months, but he will need a reason for the delay.
161 The court bailiffs will rarely have any information until at least a week after the possession order is issued, but high profile cases may be expedited.
162 *R v Wandsworth County Court, ex p Wandsworth London Borough Council* [1975] 1 WLR 1314.
163 See 'Criminal Law' above.
164 See para **3.168** ff.

for him to call others to his assistance in this[165]. However, should the landowner not actually have a right to remove the trespassers, the police would be liable for claims relating to the use of unlawful force.

Going back

4.136   The warrant for possession is satisfied once the owners get possession[166]. They need not use bailiffs for this; the warrant is exhausted the moment the property has been returned to the landowner's possession. Once satisfied, the warrant cannot be re-used against different occupiers: the landowners must start proceedings again.

4.137   However, if after a warrant is satisfied, a property is re-occupied by people with a 'plain and sufficient nexus' to those subject to the original possession proceedings, then the owner can apply for **warrant of restitution** which effectively revives the original warrant for possession[167]. There is no need to give notice of this application. The only remedy if the warrant of restitution was issued in error would be to apply to have it set aside and it would be necessary to negotiate with the bailiffs to get time to do this.

4.138   Failure to comply with a court order, including a possession order, also constitutes contempt of court and may be punished with imprisonment. Technically, the contempt arises from the point at which the possession order comes into effect and is not predicated on the service of a warrant of possession. If the landowner seeks to bring contempt proceedings then the possession order should have a 'penal notice' stating the potential consequences of non-compliance attached to it when it is served[168]. Contempt of court is a serious matter, and a custodial sentence is possible[169]. However, contempt proceedings are a last resort and claimants should first attempt the execution of a warrant or writ[170].

---

165   See *Porter v Metropolitan Police Commissioner* (20 October 1999, unreported).
166   The same applies for writs of possession, for convenience, the phrase 'warrant' will be used to cover both orders.
167   *Wiltshire County Council v Frazer (No 2)* [1986] 1 WLR 109.
168   In *Bell v Tuohy* [2002] EWCA Civ 423, [2002] 1 WLR 2703 it was held that impeding a bailiff executing a possession warrant constituted contempt of court, and this should normally found a contempt application. However, in some cases it is permitted to rely on non-compliance with the possession order itself. Although an order which could be enforced by committal should be endorsed with a penal notice, it is within the discretion of the county court to commit a person to prison even though there is no notice; however, this power is to be used sparingly (*Jolly v Hull* [2000] 2 FLR 69).
169   Contempt of court may be punished in the Crown Court with up to two years' imprisonment.
170   See *Bell v Tuohy,* para 59.

INJUNCTIONS

4.139   Apart from possession proceedings, the other form of civil litigation that an occupation is likely to face is a claim for an injunction. An injunction is a court order requiring a person or group either to do something, stop doing something or refrain from doing something. For example an injunction might require those in an occupation to provide access to a certain building, or to remove all tents from a certain area or not to set up an occupation at all. 'Mandatory' orders—requiring people to do certain things—are rare and most injunctions are phrased in negative, prohibiting terms.

4.140   Breach of the terms of the injunction is contempt of court and can be punished with a fine or imprisonment. Some injunctions can have a power of arrest attached to them, which will be set out in the relevant legislation.

4.141   Injunctions are an equitable remedy and the court has a large degree of flexibility in what terms should be imposed. One important principle is that the requirements imposed should be the least restrictive required in the circumstances.

4.142   In occupation cases, as well as challenging the evidence put forward for the injunction, those defending occupiers will typically rely on Article 10 and 11 grounds as well. Many of the human rights points raised in opposing an injunction are similar to those in possession proceedings, but since an injunction is a more flexible remedy than outright possession the arguments may become more nuanced. For example, noise limits may be placed on an occupation, the removal of tents may be limited to those over a given size or an injunction may be used to turn a continuous occupation into one that only takes place over weekends or other times.

How do injunctions arise?

4.143   Any application for an injunction must have some underlying claim on which it is sought. In occupations, the underlying basis may be a claim for relief from trespass or public nuisance. There are also a variety of statutory bases for injunctions, such as to prevent harassment[171], to prevent an obstruction of the highway[172], to prevent a breach of planning control[173] or to prevent various forms of environmental damage.

---

171   Protection from Harassment Act 1997, s 3A.
172   Highways Act 1980, s 37.
173   Town and Country Planning Act 1990, s 187B.

4.144 Injunctions that are sought on the basis of a claim such as trespass may, in principle, be sought by anyone who is in a position to bring the claim or has 'standing'. Injunctions that are sought on a statutory basis may generally only by sought by the relevant government body, which in most cases is the local authority[174]. Injunctions may be brought against anyone who may be the subject of a claim, including 'persons unknown'[175]. Injunctions can be sought against named individuals in a representative capacity provided that all those represented share the same interest in the matter[176].

A *taxonomy of injunctions*

4.145 Injunctions can be granted after a civil wrong has been committed, in order to prevent its repetition, or beforehand, as a *quia timet* injunction, to prevent apprehended unlawful conduct. Injunctions can also be subdivided into those which are sought as the final remedy once a claim has been fully heard and those which are granted as an interim relief before the final claim is decided. Given the length of time which civil ligation may take, interim injunctions are more significant than might at first appear. In urgent or exceptional cases an interim injunction can be granted before a substantive claim has been issued[177].

4.146 The final division is between those interim injunctions that are sought 'on notice' and those that are 'without notice'. Giving 'notice' means informing the person who is to be subject to the injunction that an application has been made, thereby allowing them to take part in proceedings to resist the granting of the injunction.

When should notice be given?

4.147 The normal procedure is that an application notice must be served at least three days before the hearing for the interim injunction[178]. However, the court may consider that less time is required if the case is urgent[179]. An application may be made without notice only when there is exceptional urgency

---

174 Anti-harassment injunctions are an exception to this principle because they may be sought by anyone who is a victim of the harassment (see PFHA 1997, s 3A(2)).
175 See *Hampshire Waste Services Ltd v Intending Trespassers upon Chineham Incinerator Site* [2003] EWHC 1738 (Ch), [2004] Env LR 9 and *Secretary of State for the Environment, Food and Rural Affairs v Meier* [2009] UKSC 11, [2009] 1 WLR 2780.
176 See *Heathrow Airport v Garman* [2007] EWHC 1957 (QB) where representation orders were refused for groups that did not have identical interests and aims, but were upheld for some unincorporated associations.
177 CPR 25.2(1)(a).
178 CPR 23.4 and 23.7(1)(b).
179 CPR 23.7(4).

or where 'it appears to the court that there is good reason for not giving notice'[180]. However, those seeking an injunction may not deliberately delay an application in order to prevent giving notice since: '[e]very application must be made as soon as it becomes apparent that it is necessary or desirable to make it'[181].

4.148   Section 12 of the Human Rights Act 1998 also restricts the granting of 'without notice' injunctions which might affect freedom of expression. It requires that 'all practicable steps' should be taken to notify the defendant unless there are 'compelling reasons' why he should not be notified. Moreover, if the only reason preventing formal notice being given is urgency, the person seeking an application must give those affected by it informal notice by contacting them through whatever reasonable means are available[182]. Applications for interim injunctions may be dealt with by a telephone hearing where both sides communicate with the judge on a conference call, although this is rare[183]. It should be remembered that to grant an interim injunction without notice 'is to grant an exceptional remedy'[184].

4.149   When an interim injunction is applied for without notice the court may either grant the injunction, dismiss it or relist the application to be heard at a later date[185]. If the interim injunction is granted without notice, unless the court orders otherwise, it must be served on the defendant as soon as practicable[186]. It should contain a 'return date' on which the defendant can be present for a hearing[187], alternatively a defendant served with a without notice injunction may make an application to set it aside within seven days[188]. An application to set aside a without notice injunction should be made using form N244. It should state on the form that the application to set aside is made pursuant to CPR 23.10. Assuming that the application to set aside the injunction is resisted by the other side, a hearing will be held to determine the matter.

---

180 CPR 25.3.
181 CPR 23A PD 2.7.
182 CPR 23APD.4.2.
183 A telephone hearing may be used in cases of extreme urgency and when the hearing must be held out of normal court hours (CPR 25PD.4.2).
184 *Moat Housing Group-South Ltd v Harris* [2005] EWCA Civ 287, [2006] QB 606 (paras 63 and 71).
185 CPR 23.11.
186 CPR 25PD.5.1.
187 CPR 25PD.5.1(3).
188 CPR 23.10(2).

4.150 When an injunction is brought against named defendants, service of the injunction itself and of notice should take place in the normal manner[189]. When an injunction is brought against 'persons unknown', particularly when it relates to a specific area of land, the court may make an order for alternative service[190]. Typically, this will involve attaching copies of the relevant documents in clear plastic wallets to stakes on the ground surrounding the relevant land and/or posting documents through the letterbox.

When will the court grant an injunction?

4.151 When an injunction is granted as a final remedy, the claimant will already have succeeded in winning the underlying claim on which the injunction is sought. The court has power to grant an injunction when it is '*just and convenient to do so*'[191]. When a *quia timet* injunction is sought the general test is that there must be a real and imminent risk of substantial damage[192].

4.152 Where an injunction is sought as an interim remedy, the court must decide whether to grant an injunction before the final claim is heard. The general test for granting an interim injunction is that from the case of *American Cyanamid v Ethicon Ltd*[193]. The court must decide the following factors[194]:

(a) is there a serious issue to be tried? (ie the underlying claim must not be frivolous or vexatious);

(b) if an injunction **is not** granted, would damages be an adequate remedy for the claimant if he goes on to win the underlying claim? (ie if the claimant could be adequately compensated financially then this is a factor suggesting an interim injunction is not necessary; in demonstration cases the claimant may have concerns that they will not be able to recover damages from defendants);

(c) if an injunction **is** granted, would damages be an adequate compensation to the defendant should he defeat the underlying claim? (ie if the defendant could not be compensated financially if he ultimately defeats the claim then this is a factor suggesting that an injunction should not be granted; in many demonstration cases, damages will not be an adequate

---

189 See CPR 6.3 and CPR 6.20 for methods of service. This includes sending by first class post to a person's usual or last known address (CPR 6.9(2) and CPR 6.20(1)). Alternatively personal service, taking the documents to the person to be served, may be used (CPR 6.11 and CPR 6.22).
190 See CPR 6.15 and CPR 6.27.
191 Senior Courts Act 1981, s 37(1) and County Courts Act 1984, s 38.
192 *Fletcher v Bealey* [1884 F 983], (1885) LR 28 Ch D 688.
193 [1975] AC 396.
194 If an interim injunction is also a *quia timet* injunction then the requirement of a real and imminent risk of substantial damage must also be met.

remedy for the defendant. It is often a requirement that the claimant gives an undertaking to pay the defendant's costs if unsuccessful)[195];

(d)   where does the balance of convenience lie? (ie should the court allow matters to continue as they are until trial or should the court restrict the defendant's actions by making an injunction, where matters are finely balanced the court may consider the relative strength of each party's case in deciding this issue);

(e)   where all other factors are equal, the *status quo* should be preserved.

4.153   The test for an interim injunction is modified if granting the injunction will effectively dispose of the claim because by the time it comes to trial there will be nothing left to fight over: for example a demonstration may be planned for a certain date and if it does not take place then, the matter will be over. In circumstances like these, the court will consider the likelihood of the claimant succeeding at trial as a more significant factor in deciding whether to grant an injunction.

4.154   The test for an interim injunction will also be modified when fundamental rights of freedom of expression are at stake. Section 12 of the Human Rights Act 1998, which makes specific provision for freedom of expression cases, states that:

'12 Freedom of expression.

(1) This section applies if a court is considering whether to grant any relief which, if granted, might affect the exercise of the Convention right to freedom of expression.

…

(3) No such relief is to be granted so as to restrain publication before trial unless the court is satisfied that the applicant is likely to establish that publication should not be allowed.'

4.155   As Lord Nicholls said in *Cream Holdings Ltd v Banerjee*[196]:

'There can be no single, rigid standard governing all applications for interim restraint orders. Rather, on its proper construction the effect of section 12(3) is that the court is not to make an interim restraint order unless satisfied the applicant's prospects of success at the trial are

---

195   The person seeking the interim injunction must give an undertaking to compensate the defendant for any loss 'which the court considers the applicant should pay' CPR 25PD5.1(1)).
196   [2004] UKHL 44, [2005] 1 AC 253.

sufficiently favourable to justify such an order being made in the particular circumstances of the case. As to what degree of likelihood makes the prospects of success "sufficiently favourable", the general approach should be that courts will be exceedingly slow to make interim restraint orders where the applicant has not satisfied the court he will probably ("more likely than not") succeed at the trial. In general, that should be the threshold an applicant must cross before the court embarks on exercising its discretion, duly taking into account the relevant jurisprudence on article 10 and any countervailing Convention rights.'

This approach from *Cream Holdings* has been adopted in demonstration cases[197].

Grounds for injunctions

4.156   Injunctions may be sought on a large number of different grounds and it is only possible to cover those most commonly used in occupation cases here.

Prevention of crime

4.157   Local authorities can bring an injunction to restrain an action which would be a breach of criminal law[198]. However, this is a power to be used sparingly. A local authority also has the power to bring any proceedings where it considers it expedient 'for the promotion or protection of the interests of the inhabitants of their area'.

Trespass

4.158   In addition to a possession order, an injunction may be sought to prevent an actual or planned trespass[199]. Given the potential sanctions that come with it, a court should ordinarily only be prepared to make an injunction to prevent trespass where it would, in principle, be prepared to imprison those

---

197   *Christopher David Hall v Save Newchurch Guinea Pigs (Campaign) and sixteen others* [2005] EWHC 372 (QB) and *University of Oxford v Broughton* [2004] EWHC 2543 (QB).
198   Local Government Act 1972, s 222. *Stoke on Trent City Council v B&Q (Retail) Ltd* [1984] AC 754.
199   See *Secretary of State for the Environment, Food and Rural Affairs v Meier* [2009] UKSC 11, [2009] 1 WLR 2780.

concerned for breach[200]. However, there may be situations where, for personal factors relating to the defendants, imprisonment is unlikely and yet an injunction is justified due to its deterrent effect[201]. The test for a *quia timet* interim injunction to prevent trespass in a protest case is not settled. In *Heathrow Airport v Garman*[202] it was argued that an injunction should only be granted if it was necessary and proportionate to protect a legitimate aim and not simply on the balance of convenience. The court did not need to decide the matter because both tests were met.

Harassment

4.159   As Gross J stated in *EDO MBM Technology Ltd v Campaign to Smash EDO*: '[t]here is understandable concern that an Act passed to combat stalking should not be used to clamp down on rights of protest and expression'[203]. Notwithstanding these comments, the Protection from Harassment Act 1997 (PHA 1997) has regularly been used to obtain injunctions against demonstrators.

4.160   Section 1(1) of the PHA 1997 states that a person must not pursue a course of conduct which amounts to harassment of another and which he knows amounts to harassment of another. 'Harassment' includes causing a person alarm or distress, but is not further defined in the PHA 1997[204]. In relation to the same word in the Public Order Act 1986 it has been said that it does not require emotional disturbance and although the impact does not have to be grave, it should not be trivial[205].

4.161   Section 1(1A) of the PHA 1997[206] significantly widens this offence to include a course of conduct that involves harassment of two or more people and which the defendant knows involves harassment of those people. It also requires that the defendant intends by that action to persuade any person:

(a)   not to do something that he is entitled or required to do; or

(b)   to do something that he is not under any obligation to do.

---

200 See Lord Bingham's statement at para 32 in *South Bucks District Council v Porter* [2003] UKHL 26, [2003] 2 AC 558. Whilst *Porter* was a planning case, the principle was confirmed subject to a caveat regarding deterrence in *Meier* (see Lord Neuberger at 83).
201 *Meier* at 83.
202 [2007] EWHC 1957 (QB).
203 [2005] EWHC 837 (QB).
204 PHA 1997, s 7.
205 *Southard v Director of Public Prosecutions* [2006] EWHC 3449 (Admin), [2007] ACD 53.
206 Inserted by Serious Organised Crime and Police Act 2005.

4.162   Breach of s 1(1) or (1A) is a criminal offence. However, the Act also makes specific provision for injunctions to be granted to prevent an actual or apprehended breach of s 1(1) or (1A). Such injunctions may carry the power of arrest for breach of their terms. The terms of an injunction granted can be wide and include much conduct that it not unlawful in itself[207]. It is a defence to show that 'in the particular circumstances the pursuit of the course of conduct was reasonable'[208].

4.163   An injunction may be sought by any person who is the victim of the harassment or anyone who was intended to be persuaded through the harassment under s 1(1A). Whilst victims of harassment are limited to natural persons, corporate bodies may apply for injunctions as those sought to be persuaded under s 1(1A)(c)[209].

4.164   Since the effect of the injunctions granted under the Act is to create criminal liability for breach of the order[210], there is a strong argument that they should only be granted when the matters complained of are proved to the criminal standard. However, the authorities are in conflict on this point. Some adopt various civil standards for interim applications under the Act and the full criminal standard for final injunctions. Others distinguish between proving facts already existing and assessing the risk of future conduct[211].

Highway and planning

4.165   A local authority is entitled to seek an injunction under the Highways Act 1980 (HA 1980), s 130 to 'protect the rights of the public to the use and enjoyment of the highway' and to prevent an unreasonable obstruction of the highway[212].

4.166   Under the Town and Country Planning Act 1990 (TCPA 1990), s 187B(1), the local planning authority may apply for an injunction where it

---

207   *Christopher David Hall v Save Newchurch Guinea Pigs (Campaign) and sixteen others* [2005] EWHC 372 (QB).
208   PHA 1997, s 1(3)(c).
209   See *SmithKline Beecham plc v Avery* [2009] EWHC 1488 (QB), [2011] Bus LR D40.
210   See PHA 1997, ss 3(6) and 3A(3).
211   In *Jones v Hipgrave* [2004] EWHC 2901 (QB) the court adopted the civil standard for all civil proceedings under the Act including granting an injunction. In *EDO MBM Technology Ltd v Campaign to Smash EDO* [2005] EWHC 837 (QB) it was held that when assessing an apprehended future act it was not a matter of applying a particular standard, but that the court should 'proceed with caution'. In *Oxford University v Mr Robin Webb* [2006] EWHC 2490 (QB) the court adopted the standard of 'a high degree of confidence' for establishing the relevant facts at an interim stage. Finally, in *Heathrow Airport Ltd v Garman* [2007] EWHC 1957 (QB) the court adopted the criminal standard for an application for a final order under the Act.
212   HA 1980, s 137.

'considers it necessary or expedient for any actual or apprehended breach of planning control to be restrained'. The court may grant such an injunction if it thinks it 'appropriate for the purpose of restraining the breach'[213]. Factors the court will consider in a planning injunction include the degree and flagrancy of the breach, the urgency of the situation, health and safety considerations, previous planning decisions and whether conventional enforcement measures have been tried[214].

4.167   A material change of use of buildings or land constitutes 'development' for the purposes of the TCPA 1990. Planning permission is required for any development of land unless the use is lawful or immune from enforcement[215]. A change from highway, public space or open land to a camped occupation for more than 28 days would constitute a material change of use for planning purposes. However, uses that are ancillary to the existing primary use do not constitute a material change.

4.168   As an addition or alternative to an injunction, where a local planning authority apprehends there has been a breach of planning control, they may issue an enforcement notice[216]. The enforcement notice must state the matters which appear to breach planning control and specify the steps required to remedy the breach[217]. The enforcement notice must specify a date, not less than 28 days after it is served, when it will take effect[218]. Failure to comply with an enforcement notice after it has come into effect is a criminal offence punishable with a fine[219]. Unlike an injunction under s 187B, there is an automatic right to appeal against an enforcement notice which will stay the imposition of criminal sanctions until the appeal is determined[220]. However only a person having an interest in the land to which the enforcement relates or a 'relevant occupier' may appeal[221]. A 'relevant occupier' is a person who was in occupation with a

---

213   TCPA 1990, s 187B(2).
214   *South Buckinghamshire District Council v Porter (No 1)* [2003] UKHL 26, [2003] 2 AC 558.
215   TCPA 1990, ss 57 and 191. Building work or the change of use to a single dwelling house is immune after four years. All other development is immune after 10 years (TCPA 1990, s 171B). Some minor development, such as putting up gates or walls below certain heights, is automatically given planning permission as permitted development. Camping is generally permitted in planning terms for up to 28 days (Town and Country Planning (General Permitted Development) Order 1995, SI 1995/418).
216   TCPA 1990, s 172(1).
217   TCPA 1990, s 173.
218   TCPA 1990, s 172(3).
219   TCPA 1990, s 179. In the magistrates' courts the fine is up to £20,000; the fine is unlimited in the Crown Court.
220   TCPA 1990, s 175(4).
221   TCPA 1990, s 174(1).

licence when the enforcement notice was served and who continues in that position when the appeal is brought[222].

4.169 It is unusual for planning powers to be used against protesters, but it has occurred[223]. The range of factors that may be relied upon in deciding planning cases may allow planning authorities to obtain injunctions under planning control where other methods don't succeed.

ASBOs and ASBIs

4.170 An Anti-social Behaviour Order (ASBO) is a form of quasi-criminal court order that shares certain similarities with an injunction. The magistrates' court has power to grant an ASBO if it is satisfied that the person concerned has acted in an anti-social manner[224] and that such an order is necessary to protect relevant persons from future acts by him. Local authorities, county councils, the police and a range of other public bodies are able to apply for ASBOs[225]. Before granting an ASBO, the court must be satisfied to the criminal standard that anti-social behaviour has occurred, but the further test—whether the order is necessary—is a matter of judgment[226]. Like an anti-harassment injunction, the terms of an ASBO can be quite broad. Breach of an ASBO is a criminal offence and may be punished by up to five years' imprisonment[227]. It is a defence to show that the allegedly anti-social acts relied on were reasonable in the circumstances.

4.171 A Housing Action Trust, a local authority, a non-profit registered provider of social housing or a registered social landlord can apply under the Housing Act 1996, ss 153A–153E for an Anti-social Behaviour Injunction (ASBI). If the person against whom the injunction is sought is engaging, has engaged or threatens to engage in housing-related conduct capable of causing a nuisance or annoyance to:

(a) a person with a right to reside in or occupy housing accommodation owned or managed by one of the landlords above or other housing accommodation in the same neighbourhood; or

---

222 TCPA 1990, s 174(6). It is suggested that an occupier whose Article 10/11 rights were infringed by the planning authority through the issuing of an enforcement notice in situations where he was unable to appeal against the enforcement notice under s 174 would be able to challenge the decision to issue the notice by means of judicial review.
223 *City of London v Samede* [2012] EWHC 34 (QB).
224 An 'anti-social manner' means a manner that caused or was likely to cause harassment, alarm or distress to one or more persons not of the same household as him (CDA 1998, s 1).
225 See CDA 1998, s 1(1A). It is also possible for the relevant body to apply for an interim ASBO.
226 *R (on the application of McCann) v Crown Court at Manchester* [2002] UKHL 39.
227 CDA 1998, s 1(10).

(b)   a person engaged in lawful activity in, or in the neighbourhood of, such housing accommodation; or

(c)   a person employed in connection with the exercise of a relevant landlord's housing management functions;

then an ASBI can be sought to prohibit that person from engaging in specified housing-related anti-social conduct. In practice, the person against whom the injunction is sought is likely to be a tenant or a member of the tenant's household, but it could include occupiers on a social landlord's land. If the conduct consists of, or includes, the use or threatened use of violence and there is a significant risk of harm to one of the people mentioned above, then the court may prohibit the injuncted person from entering or being in a specified premises or area and/or may attach a power of arrest. An injunction may also be granted to prevent premises being used for unlawful purposes[228].

Other grounds

4.172   There are a range of other grounds under which an injunction may be obtained against an occupation, including as part of a claim in nuisance or under environmental protection legislation. Given the potentially severe sanctions for breach of an injunction, occupiers facing injunction proceedings should be advised to seek specialist legal advice wherever possible.

Conclusion

4.173   This chapter has given an overview of the law surrounding occupations. Given the increased ease of mass coordination through mobile phones and social networking tools, this is a developing area of protest and the law is changing in turn. However, both activists and the law build upon a rich tradition. It is hoped that the law adapts in order to sustain what has historically been an inspiring and effective form of protest.

---

228   HA 1996, s 153B.

Chapter 5

Holding the police to account

5.1   Police conduct at protests has come under increasing scrutiny in recent years. Controversial tactics such as kettling, the use of excessive and unnecessary force against demonstrators and the criminalisation of young people through the misapplication of police powers derived from anti-social behaviour legislation have all been the subject of complaints and claims against the police, in some cases even leading to criminal prosecutions.

5.2   The law surrounding these issues is complex and constantly developing, and it is a particularly specialist area. There are a vast number of tactical considerations that arise in the course of a complaint or civil action against the police, and this chapter cannot encompass all these matters. Protesters should be advised to seek specialist legal advice on such matters where possible. However, the ongoing cuts to the Legal Aid budget mean that public funding is increasingly difficult to obtain and formal legal advice may therefore not always be immediately available. In addition, whilst complaints and claims against the police are usually argued only after criminal cases have concluded, there are numerous evidential and strategic issues that protesters and practitioners should bear in mind from the very outset.

5.3   This chapter is therefore designed to give an insight into the potential proceedings that may arise out of poor policing at protests, including what actions can be taken following criminal investigations of, and prosecutions against, protesters. It covers the key touchstones of the complaint and litigation routes that may be available, with the aim of increasing the prospects of successfully holding the police to account for any wrongdoing later down the line, and to ensure vital opportunities and evidence are not inadvertently lost.

WHICH REMEDY?

5.4   The two main remedies a protester may wish to consider if they feel they have been mistreated by the police are a complaint against the police, or a claim for compensation. Another alternative in certain circumstances may be to bring judicial review proceedings, which are discussed at para **5.220**. In all cases, the standard of proof is a civil one. This means that the burden of proof is

213

upon the complainant or claimant to establish that their account should be preferred on the balance of probabilities, ie that it is more likely than not that the allegations they make are true. This should be distinguished from the criminal standard of proof, whereby the prosecution must prove the allegation(s) beyond reasonable doubt. Complaints and civil actions are distinct processes, although they are interrelated in that success or failure in one can influence the outcome of the other. The details of each remedy are discussed in more detail below.

5.5   The easiest way to identify whether either (or both) of these mechanisms will offer the right legal remedy, is to establish the primary aim of any action and develop a strategy on that basis. The need for a coherent approach to any form of legal action in this area cannot be over-emphasised. The two methods can also be pursued alongside each other, but there are advantages and disadvantages to each route that should be considered in advance.

Complaints overview

5.6   A complaint is made against individual officers and most frequently arises out of an alleged breach of the police's professional standards. These standards are known as the Standards of Professional Behaviour ('the Standards') and are set out in the Police (Conduct) Regulations 2008[1].

5.7   A complaint can, if successful, result in disciplinary action being taken against individual officers and, in a very rare number of cases, can lead to a criminal prosecution being brought against the subjects of a complaint. An apology can be offered in the course of the complaint procedure, but there is no power to award any financial compensation. A complaint may therefore be appropriate where concerns are raised about the individual actions of a particular officer, or group of officers, where it is felt that a mark should be made against their record. For example where, in the course of a demonstration, an officer acted in a heavy-handed or abusive manner, a protester may well decide that they wish to lodge a complaint against that particular officer so that his conduct does not go unnoticed.

5.8   Complaints may, however, be a less appropriate and effective course of action (or sole course of action) if the issue complained of is a broader institutional or force-wide concern. For example, where it is clear that individual officers are simply carrying out orders in the course of policing a march (perhaps by preventing protesters from taking a certain route or by systematically seeking to obtain protesters' details) a complaint against the individual officers is unlikely to meaningfully hold the police to account. In

---

1   Police (Conduct) Regulations 2008, SI 2008/2864, Schedule.

those circumstances, a complaint could still be made about the decision-making at a higher level or a civil action or judicial review should be considered to challenge the lawfulness of the police's actions.

5.9   The vast majority of complaints will be investigated by serving police officers at the Professional Standards Department ('PSD') of the relevant force. This is often met with disappointment by complainants, and concerns about the impartiality of the PSD are common. At the conclusion of the PSD investigation a report will be produced, setting out the complaints and the decisions reached. The quality and detail of these reports vary greatly from force to force and investigating officer to investigating officer. The report can only be as good as the investigation carried out, and it is worth noting that a report is often signed off by an officer of considerably more senior rank than the officer carrying out the actual investigatory work. These investigations can take a matter of weeks, or a number of months depending on the circumstances of the individual case.

5.10   If a protester is unhappy about the outcome of a complaint investigation by the PSD, an appeal can be lodged to the Independent Police Complaints Commission (IPCC). The IPCC was created following the introduction of the Police Reform Act 2002 and came into being on 1 April 2004. It replaced the Police Complaints Authority, which was created as part of the Police and Criminal Evidence Act 1984, and had been the subject of heavy criticism as a result of its limited powers and perceived lack of independence. However, the IPCC has itself not escaped criticism and a prominent network of lawyers acting for complainants cited a 'pattern of favouritism towards the police' when it resigned from the IPCC's advisory body in 2008[2]. The IPCC sought to refute this criticism, stating it would 'robustly defend' its independence and impartiality[3].

5.11   Whilst there are numerous tactical considerations that arise in the course of a complaint investigation, the process is designed to be navigated for non-lawyers. Protesters may therefore decide to pursue a complaint without formal legal representation. Certainly where there is no risk of a criminal prosecution against the protester, and where they do not intend to take any other legal action that may be prejudiced by decisions taken in the course of the complaint process, this is a viable option and the overview of the complaint process below will be of assistance in doing so. Similarly, where practitioners represent protesters in criminal matters, but do not have the expertise to pursue a civil action or judicial review, the information below should provide a synopsis of the various stages and evidential issues a complainant is likely to encounter.

---

2   www.guardian.co.uk/politics/2008/feb/25/police.law1.
3   www.guardian.co.uk/commentisfree/2008/feb/27/police.

Civil actions overview

5.12   Entirely distinct from the complaint process, protesters may wish to pursue a private law action against the police on the basis of a range of tortious or statutory causes of action. This is known as a 'civil action' or 'claim against the police', and is also referred to as 'litigation against the police'. It is a remedy that must be pursued through the county courts or in the High Court (and the higher civil courts on appeal). If successful, a claimant can be awarded damages, or compensation. The level of damages depends entirely on the circumstances of the case and is, to a large extent, at the discretion of the court. Civil actions are significantly more complex to pursue. Although the courts do not prevent individuals from bringing their cases without formal legal representation (protesters can act as 'litigants in person') there are so many technical hurdles and pitfalls that cases brought without specialist legal assistance are rarely successful, and often extremely stressful.

5.13   One of the most significant disadvantages of civil actions, unlike complaints, is that they can carry a significant cost risk. This is because it is a general rule of civil litigation that the losing party pays the winning party's costs. If a claimant therefore brings a claim against the police, and either loses at trial or chooses (or is forced) to discontinue the claim, the police may be entitled to enforce the costs of defending that claim against the claimant (although legally aided clients will usually be protected from such a risk, see para **5.21**). It is also worth noting that civil actions can take considerably longer than complaints to conclude, and it is not unusual for a case to last more than three years from start to finish.

5.14   However, there are significant advantages of bringing a civil claim over pursuing a complaint against the police. (Alternatively, pursuing the two remedies in conjunction is a common and often effective approach.) The first advantage is that, where cases go to trial, the final outcome is determined by an independent member of the judiciary or in certain cases a jury, either of which—unlike the police officers investigating complaints—have no formal professional ties to the police force that is the subject of the claim.

5.15   The second advantage is that, during the course of the case, assessments of legal issues are made by police lawyers, not police officers. Whilst these people are employed solely to protect the interests of the force being sued, they are one step removed from day-to-day policing activity and often will cast a fresh pair of eyes over a case which was dismissed during the complaints process, and realise there are legal weaknesses in the police's defence which require a change in their approach.

5.16   Third, civil actions are not brought against individual officers but against the Chief Constable of the relevant police force (or against the Commissioner of Police of the Metropolis, in the case of the Metropolitan

Police). He or she is vicariously liable (legally responsible) for the actions of individual officers in the force, providing these actions were carried out in the purported performance of their police functions. This is a particularly significant consideration where the police behaviour the subject of the complaint or claim is perceived as an institutional issue, as may be the case in large scale police actions in the course of protests where decisions are frequently taken at a senior policing level.

5.17   Further, civil actions, once issued at court, become public proceedings. This in itself can provide significant leverage against the police, who will often wish to avoid the adverse media attention. It also, of course, allows activists who wish to bring claims in part to highlight concerns about policing tactics during protests to raise the profile of any campaign around those concerns.

5.18   One final key advantage to consider is that civil actions are the main mechanism by which to obtain financial compensation (whilst damages can occasionally be awarded in judicial review proceedings this is unusual and not the primary purpose of such a challenge). Compensation or damages can be important in two contexts. First, compensation will of course financially benefit the claimant. Where the case includes a claim for a serious assault, the value may be quite substantial, and can greatly assist, especially where the claimant has not been able to work and has dependents. Compensation can also represent a recognition of a grievance suffered at the hands of the police, particularly where a complaint has been dismissed. In addition, however, civil actions, and the scope within them to secure financial compensation, allow for a greater range of funding mechanisms which are discussed in more detail below.

Judicial review overview

5.19   Finally, it is worth briefly mentioning judicial review proceedings, which are a public law remedy used to challenge decisions made by public bodies. These are discussed in more detail at para **5.220**, as they are often ancillary to or arising out of decisions made in the course of a civil action or complaint.

5.20   Judicial review may be a more appropriate means to challenge the police where the matter raises novel points of law or is of wider public importance. In certain circumstances, judicial review may be used to challenge higher-level decisions concerning either the policing of a particular demonstration or general policies adopted by the police.

Pros and cons of pursuing a police complaint over civil action

Pros:

- No risk of costs being awarded against protester
- Quicker
- Easier to navigate without a solicitor
- Can lead to disciplinary action of officers
- Can assist with obtaining Legal Aid
- Relatively simple appeal system to IPCC

Cons:

- Low success rate
- Usually police investigating police
- Protesters have to put their account on record at an early stage and usually without having had sight of independent evidence
- Delay of civil action
- No mechanism by which to afford financial compensation

FUNDING COMPLAINTS AND CIVIL ACTIONS AGAINST THE POLICE

Legal Aid

5.21   By far the most attractive method of funding a case against the police is by way of public funding (Legal Aid). Not only does it mean the complainant/claimant does not need to make any, or any significant, financial contribution, but it also offers protection for the claimant in the event a civil action is brought and is ultimately unsuccessful. This is because it is extremely unusual for a costs order to be enforced against a legally aided client.

5.22   The availability of Legal Aid is predominantly determined by the Access to Justice Act 1999 (AJA 1999), and the Funding Code. Legal Aid was, at the time of writing, administered by the Legal Services Commission (LSC) although a Bill had been tabled with proposals to abolish the LSC[4]. The LSC website contains detailed guidance on the Funding Code and Legal Aid in civil cases[5].

5.23   Legal Aid is available in principle for both complaints and civil actions against the police. Similarly, judicial review can be funded by way of Legal Aid. However, only law firms with a contract to carry out this specialist area of work will be able to offer assistance under the Legal Aid scheme. Most of the claimant-only firms rated in the independent guides to the legal profession (Legal 500 and Chambers & Partners) had Legal Aid contracts at the time of writing, although the constant threat of Legal Aid cuts means there is a great deal of uncertainty for the future.

5.24   There are two levels of Legal Aid which apply in broad terms to all the legal remedies a protester may want to pursue to hold police to account: Legal Help and a Certificate of Legal Aid. The former allows a legal practitioner to carry out some initial investigations in the case, but does cover any significant fees (like barrister's fees) or court costs (such as the issue fee). Legal Help therefore would cover the costs of running a complaint, and the initial steps required as part of a civil action. However, it is very unlikely to be sufficient to fund a civil action to conclusion, particularly because civil actions against the police rarely settle before proceedings are issued at court. Activists may also want to bear in mind that many law firms are reluctant to run a police complaint without the prospect of a civil action on the horizon, because in practice Legal Help rates are so low that firms sometimes make a loss on these cases. In practice, therefore, a firm is more likely to take on a case where there is a possibility of a civil action or judicial review somewhere along the line.

5.25   To qualify for Legal Help, the applicant must pass a means test, which assesses both the applicant's capital and income. At the time of writing, the capital limit for all cases against the police is £8,000; any applicant with savings or assets over this amount (including money in bonds or ISAs) will automatically be ineligible. Capital includes equity in a home over £100,000, and all equity in a home which is not the primary residence. The income test is more complicated, although those in receipt of 'passported' benefits (income support, income-based jobseeker's allowance, income-based employment support allowance and guarantee credit) automatically pass the means test. Further details can be found in Volume 2F of the Funding Code, and a helpful online eligibility calculator can be accessed on either the LSC or the Ministry of Justice websites.

---

4   See the Legal Aid, Sentencing and Punishment of Offenders Bill.
5   www.legalservices.gov.uk/civil/guidance/funding_code.asp.

5.26   As public funding cuts start to bite, Legal Aid is increasingly difficult to obtain and practitioners are reporting more and more knock backs from the LSC. To avoid any unnecessary delays or complications later in Legal Aid applications, full and detailed documentary evidence should be obtained to confirm all income and outgoings. This will include payslips, rental agreements and letters from the Department of Work and Pensions or Jobcentre to confirm receipt of benefits. Eligibility for assistance under the Legal Help scheme is assessed by the solicitors firm itself.

5.27   The next stage of Legal Aid requires a legal advisor to make a funding application to the LSC on behalf of the applicant. There are different types of funding certificates, including certificates for emergency funding, investigative help and full representation. The fine detail of this is outside the scope of this book. However, all applications for certificates contain a merits test, alongside the means test set out above. The merits assessment is effectively a cost-benefit test, whereby the LSC compares the costs of bringing the claim to the likely value of the claim, in the context of the prospects of success. To this end, a legal advisor will have to make an initial assessment of the merits of the case in accordance with five categories, listed A to E, which each have a correlating percentage setting out the merits (80% and above, 60–80% etc). Depending on the outcome of this assessment, a correlating 'cost-benefit' ratio is applied. For example, category B puts the chance of success of a case at 60–80%. To pass the merits test, a legal advisor will have to confirm that the likely damages to be awarded in the event of success will exceed the costs of bringing the claim by a ratio of 2:1. The greater the prospects of success, the lower the ratio required. In practice, claims with less than 50% prospect of success are unlikely to receive public funding, as are claims that are worth less than £5,000.

5.28   The types of claims that can be brought against police, what a protester must establish, and what compensation a successful claimant is likely to achieve, are touched upon in para **5.155**. It is worth noting at this stage, however, that claims for stand-alone breaches of human rights are traditionally low in value, and therefore a lot of protest cases may fall at this early hurdle. The value of a claim is likely to increase as a result of any serious and enduring injury, lengthy periods of detention, or intentional wrongdoing on the part of the police.

5.29   Nevertheless, many claims against the police arising in the context of protests will be important, not just to the individual involved, but the public as a whole. Fortunately, there are provisions in the Funding Code that recognise that cases against state agents such as the police do not solely benefit the individual claimant, and are often not pursued merely for financial benefit. The Funding Code therefore provides for representations to be made on the basis that the case is of 'overwhelming importance to the client' and of general public interest. Protesters should ensure such representations are made by legal advisors in detail and with supporting evidence where possible. In practice, those firms of solicitors that specialise in actions against the police will be fully apprised of the Funding Code provisions.

Conditional Fee Agreements: no win, no fee

5.30   An alternative means to fund a case is by way of a Conditional Fee Agreement (CFA). This is an arrangement whereby a solicitor (and sometimes a barrister) agrees to carry out work on a case without any fees being paid upfront on the basis that, if successful, the fees (and an uplift on those fees known as a 'success fee') can be recovered from the losing party, namely the police. Because payment of the legal costs is contingent on the case concluding in the claimant's favour, a CFA is unlikely to be available for high-risk or test cases. Free-standing complaints cannot be funded by CFA, although complaints made in conjunction with a civil action may be covered by the CFA.

5.31   However, CFAs are not without cost or risk to the individual. First, there are a number of costs or disbursements that will be incurred as part of a claim, such as court fees and counsel's fees (unless the barrister agrees to carry out work under a CFA as well). These can be quite significant and may have to be paid up front by the claimant, although different firms are prepared to agree different terms with their clients. Most significantly, a CFA, unlike Legal Aid, does not afford any protection against costs being enforced in the event the case is unsuccessful. This means that consideration should be given to an After the Event (ATE) insurance policy to protect against a costs order.

5.32   Solicitors are required to provide detailed advice and explanations of all the terms to any client before a CFA is signed, and protesters should ensure they are entirely comfortable with the terms before they sign them. In practice, a legal advisor will be carrying out an assessment of the merits and value of the claim in a very similar way as is described for Legal Aid applications above, and cases with less than 65% prospect of success will rarely be suitable for CFAs.

Private

5.33   Of course, claims against the police can be privately funded. The costs of this, however, are likely to be very significant and entirely prohibitive for most people. In addition, as with CFA's, there is no protection against costs in the event the case does not succeed, although ATE insurance can be taken out in privately funded cases. It is also worth noting that, in the event that the case is successful, all reasonable costs are recoverable from the defendant and a claimant should receive most of the funds paid out.

5.34   It is impossible to give any kind of accurate estimate as to the costs of a generic civil action. However, it would not be at all unusual for a claimant to be looking at a five figure sum for the costs of their preparing and presenting their own case, which will often be matched or exceeded by the costs of the defendant in the event the claimant loses.

Insurance

5.35   Protesters should check any insurance policies for legal expenses insurance. Some insurers will fund the cost of claims against the police, usually if there is a significant personal injury aspect to the claim (which may be the case if, for example, a protester was assaulted by police). Enquiries should be made directly of the insurer. Most legal advisors will do this on the claimant's behalf. Many insurers do not have the legal expertise to assess the costs and merits of a case against the police, simply because they are very unusual. Protesters should therefore ensure insurers have been provided ample time to consider the case, and this is best done by bringing the existence of any insurance policy to a legal advisor's attention as soon as possible.

Trade union

5.36   Trade union membership almost invariably includes cover for free legal assistance in the case of a personal injury claim. Some trade unions will fund claims against the police, but it depends on the individual circumstances of the case. It is certainly worth making enquiries of a local legal representative.

Group litigation

5.37   Where a claim arises in circumstances in which a large group of demonstrators are all affected by the actions of the police then it may be worth considering ways in which legal costs and risks can be shared across the group. This may be done either by applying for a formal Group Litigation Order[6] or under a more informal agreement with the legal representatives. Where the individual claims are not worth enough to qualify for Legal Aid (even when taking into account the exception for matters of 'overwhelming importance') then it may be possible to parcel up the claims in order to meet the threshold. Alternatively, it may be possible to fund a claim privately or via a CFA using this method. Specialist advice should be sought from a solicitor about the different options.

---

6   Group Litigation Orders are covered in the Civil Procedure Rules 1998, rr 19.10–19.15.

COMPLAINTS AGAINST THE POLICE

5.38   Any complaint against a police officer, including a complaint alleging criminal behaviour, must be pursued through the formal complaints procedure. This procedure, and the various practical requirements for complaint investigations, are found in the Police Reform Act 2002 (as amended) (PRA 2002), the Police (Conduct) Regulations 2008[7], the Police (Complaints and Misconduct) Regulations 2004[8] (as amended) and in detailed Home Office guidance.

5.39   In addition the IPCC has issued statutory guidance (the IPCC Guidance) pursuant to the PRA 2002, s 22 which collates a lot of the requirements in the Act and Regulations above. However, the IPCC Guidance is not binding, and on occasions police forces have taken quite contrary positions to those recommended by the IPCC. Some of the key provisions of all these documents have been set out below.

Who can complain about whom

5.40   A complaint can be made against any person serving with the police, such as police officers, police staff members or special constables[9]. Other than special constables, a complaint cannot be made against people volunteering for the police, nor can a complaint be made against employees of private companies who have been contracted by the police force to carry out police functions, known as 'designated staff'[10].

5.41   Designated staff are increasingly being used to privatise certain roles, often acting as custody assistants and escorting detained persons from the police station to court. Although the provisions detailed below do not apply to designated staff, individual companies may have their own complaint procedures. For ease of reference, this chapter uses the term 'officer' as a short-form for all police staff as, in the context of protests, police officers are the most likely subject of a complaint.

5.42   A complaint can be made by any member of the public who has either been the victim of the conduct complained of, has witnessed such conduct, or has been adversely affected by the conduct[11]. Therefore, a fellow protester can complain about the actions of one or more officers even if they themselves were not the victim of those actions, although without the evidence of the victim the

---

7   SI 2008/2864.
8   SI 2004/643.
9   IPCC Guidance, para 22.
10 IPCC Guidance, para 23.
11 PRA 2002, s 12(1).

likelihood of the complaint being upheld will be significantly reduced. If an individual does wish to complain in this context they should therefore identify other potential witnesses to bolster prospects of success.

5.43 A complainant can authorise a third party, such as a solicitor, to act on their behalf during the complaint process, providing the appropriate form of authority is used. Copies of all documentation sent and received as part of the complaint should be carefully retained, as they may become significant as part of any appeal, subsequent civil action or judicial review.

How to complain

5.44 Making a complaint is quite straightforward and can be done in various ways. A complaint can be made in person at the police station, over the telephone or in writing. It can also be lodged directly to the Professional Standards Department (PSD) of the relevant force, which is likely to result in the swiftest processing of the complaint. The details of each force's PSD can be found on the IPCC's website[12]. In addition, a complaint can be lodged online via the IPCC's website. For evidential reasons, it is advisable to lodge a complaint online or in writing. If a complaint is going to be lodged by post it is recommended this is done by recorded delivery. If it is lodged electronically via the IPCC's website a printout of the confirmation of receipt should be retained.

Subjects of complaint

5.45 A complaint must arise out of the conduct of a person serving with the police[13]. A complaint does not have to amount to misconduct nor does it have to allege a failure to meet the Standards of Professional Behaviour (the Standards)[14]. That said, where possible, complaints should be framed as a breach of the Standards to improve the prospects of the complaint being upheld.

5.46 The Standards can be found on the IPCC's website[15] and in Annex C of this book. The Standards include requirements that police officers:

- are honest, act with integrity and do not compromise or abuse their position;

- act with self-control and tolerance, treating members of the public and colleagues with respect and courtesy;

---

12 www.ipcc.gov.uk/en/Pages/professional_standards_contact_details.aspx.
13 IPCC Guidance, para 14.
14 As set out in the Police (Conduct) Regulations 2008, Schedule.
15 www.ipcc.gov.uk/en/Pages/standofprofbehaviour.aspx.

- act with fairness and impartiality. They do not discriminate unlawfully or unfairly;

- only use force to the extent that it is necessary, proportionate and reasonable in all the circumstances;

- treat information with respect and access or disclose it only in the proper course of police duties.

A complaint can list as many or few of the Standards of Professional Behaviour as is appropriate.

5.47   Once a complaint is made (providing it is made correctly and in a timely fashion) the relevant police force has a duty to either record it or provide the reasons why it has decided not to record the complaint. The circumstances in which the police do not have to record a complaint include if the complaint:

- is part of another complaint which they have already recorded;

- has been withdrawn by the person who made it;

- is about 'direction and control' matters (see para **5.49**)[16].

5.48   The IPCC expects a force to make a decision regarding whether or not to record the complaint within 10 working days[17] and inform the complainant of the same. If the force fails to do so a complainant may make an appeal to the IPCC[18].

5.49   In the context of protests, a common reason to refuse to record a complaint is that it pertains to direction and control matters. Paragraph 25 of the IPCC Guidance considers the term 'direction and control' to include the following strategic or operational management action:

- the drafting of local operational policing policies and the process leading to their approval;

- decisions about the configuration and organisation of policing resources, eg recruitment decisions, where officers or police staff should be located, how they should be managed or trained and what equipment should be procured for them;

- the level of general policing standards in the area, eg the fact that one basic command unit's (BCU) detection rate is lower than that of its neighbours or of the adjoining force.

---

16   PRA 2002, s 14(1).
17   IPCC Guidance, para 100.
18   IPCC Guidance, paras 133–136.

5.50   Paragraph 27 of the IPCC Guidance states that:

'Complaints about operational deployment and direction decisions and actions taken by police supervisors and managers should generally be treated as "direction and control" matters. However, the exemption should not be used where one or both of the following conditions apply:

- the complaint is that the decision or action does not itself comply with current force policy and practice or the law;

- the conduct of the police manager responsible for the deployment is so closely associated with the actions of others whose conduct is subject to complaint that the manner in which they were deployed or directed forms part of the complaint requiring resolution and cannot be separated or distinguished from it'.

5.51   The interpretation of 'direction and control' matters is highly relevant to complaints arising out of protests as it is frequently cited as the reason not to record a complaint in this context, for example complaints pertaining to the decision to impose a kettle. At the time of writing, the Administrative Court had rejected an application for judicial review by the Commissioner of Police of the Metropolis challenging the findings of the IPCC on appeal in a kettling case[19]. The IPCC upheld an appeal that the Metropolitan Police's PSD had wrongly determined that the complaint of a student detained (and seriously injured) in a kettle during the protests against the rise in tuition fees on 9 November 2010 was a 'direction and control' matter. As it stands therefore, it appears that both the IPCC and the courts are prepared to employ a fairly strict interpretation of those matters that fall within this category. In a subsequent complaint, also arising out of the student protests, where the PSD sought to avoid an investigation on the basis that the complaint pertained to 'direction and control' matters, the IPCC have recently decided to carry out an independent investigation. Decisions by police forces to not record a complaint on the basis that it amounts to a direction and control issue should therefore, where possible, be robustly challenged. The IPCC Guidance sets out that where there is any doubt about whether or not a complaint should be recorded, it should be treated as a complaint until it becomes clear on further investigation that it is not[20]. If a force ultimately decides that the complaint does not need to be recorded, the complainant should be given the opportunity to appeal the decision not to record the complaint to the IPCC.

---

19   Administrative Court reference CO/8725/2011.
20   SG 96.

Examples of issues which be complained about

- Excessive or unlawful use of force;

- Discriminatory/derogatory remarks or swearing/impoliteness;

- Detention in custody for excessive periods;

- Unlawful detention: eg no grounds for arrest or not informed of reason for arrest;

- Unlawful acts

What to include in a complaint

5.52   In general terms, the more information and detail that is included in a complaint, the more likely it is to succeed. Detailed accounts will improve the credibility of the complaint, and will make it easier for it to be investigated. Certainly, detailed descriptions of the officers involved (particularly where their names or badge numbers are not known) and their whereabouts and actions will at least enable the investigation to identify the subjects of the complaint, and whether there are any credible accounts to refute the complaint. Similarly, details as to the time and location of an incident will assist the investigation. This is particularly the case in the context of protests, where there will be a large number of officers and demonstrators in a small space. Protesters should therefore try to make detailed and contemporaneous notes of the events where possible.

5.53   However, it is worth noting that the account provided at this early stage will be made available throughout any subsequent civil action. This inevitably creates some tension because, no matter how honest and contemporaneous an account is, there will always be gaps and discrepancies in someone's recollection. This may not appear to be significant at the outset, but the police will have access to a much greater amount of evidence (from police officers, other witnesses, CCTV footage etc) than a complainant does at the time of making a statement and any discrepancy can be exploited and utilised as a basis to undermine a complainant's credibility. Similarly, if a protester provides an account during the course of a complaint, and subsequently provides a slightly different account as part of a civil action, that difference may well be amplified by the defendant police force in an effort to weaken the reliability of the evidence against them. The same of course applies to any discrepancy between accounts provided at the police station or during the course of a criminal trial, and subsequent accounts given as part of the complaint or civil action.

5.54   There is therefore no hard and fast rule as to how much detail a complainant should include in their statement. On the one hand, detail will enhance the credibility of an account and improve prospects of a complaint being upheld. On the other hand, a detailed yet inadvertently inaccurate account can damage prospects of success of both the complaint and any subsequent civil action. An experienced legal representative will be able to advise on a case-by-case basis. For protesters without legal representatives or practitioners who do not specialise in this area, it may be prudent to err on the side of caution and avoid including any detail of which the complainant is not absolutely certain.

5.55   In addition, the details of a complaint can be fleshed out by taking steps early on to obtain and preserve supporting evidence. It is worth ensuring that anybody who can provide an account that will assist the complaint does so, and that some key issues are covered, including:

- time, place and circumstances of the incident;

- sequence of events;

- when the witness became aware of the incident;

- descriptions of police officers involved, including badge numbers if available;

- actions of the complainant;

- what was said and done by all those involved.

5.56   If the complaint relates to an assault, the investigating officer allocated by the PSD will ask for medical evidence to be provided. There is no obligation to provide this as part of the complaint, but if it is available it is likely to enhance the prospects of the complaint being upheld. If the complainant can establish that they did in fact incur an injury at or around the time alleged, for example by providing a note from a GP or A&E records, then the complainant can at least establish that the injury exists, although the manner in which it was sustained and the lawfulness of any actions that caused it must of course still be proven. A failure to provide medical evidence can lead to the investigating officer drawing an inference that the injury cannot be evidenced, which may cause the complaint to fail. Medical evidence should, however, be scrutinised carefully for irrelevant or unhelpful information. Certainly there is usually no need to provide any comprehensive medical overview at the complaint stage.

5.57   As well as covering the substance of the complaint (as set out above for any witnesses to the incident) the complaint should include:

- those Standards of Professional Behaviour that have been breached and the factual background that has led to the allegation;

- the police force complained about;

- if made to the IPCC, consent to pass details of the complaint to the police force concerned for consideration.

The mode of investigation

5.58   Once a complaint has been recorded, a decision needs to be made as to who will investigate it. The nature and seriousness of the complaint are the primary factors a decision-maker will consider. In the vast majority of cases an officer in the relevant police force's Professional Standards Department will investigate the complaint. However, unless the nature of the complaint is particularly serious—for example where the conduct complained of has resulted in a serious injury—many forces will first ask whether the complainant is prepared to deal with the matter by way of local resolution.

5.59   Local resolution can only be pursued with the agreement of the person making the complaint. It usually involves a meeting with a senior police officer where the complainant has an opportunity to voice their grievances, which can result in the police apologising for the fact the complainant has found reason to complain. It does not usually involve an apology for the actions of the officer(s) the subject of the complaint, and cannot lead to disciplinary proceedings against an individual police officer or member or staff. Significantly, if at the end of the local resolution process the complainant is unsatisfied with the outcome, there is **no right to appeal** to the IPCC[21] about the outcome of the investigation, although a complainant can appeal the conduct of the local resolution process within 28 days of the date on which he or she thinks the police did not follow the agreed process[22]. It is therefore often not the most appropriate mode of investigation for the purposes of complaints arising in the context of protests.

5.60   The next level of investigation is local investigation, whereby the investigation is conducted by a police investigator who may be part of the PSD or may be attached to the local police division. This is by far the most common mode of investigation, and can be conducted with or without the complainant's consent. Because this is the most likely mode of investigation to arise out of complaints made in the context of protests, the local investigation process has been set out in detail below at para **5.69**.

5.61   If a complaint is more serious, it may be referred to the IPCC. The police must refer complaints to the IPCC where someone has died or been

---

21 IPCC Guidance, para 294.
22 Police (Complaints and Misconduct) Regulations 2004, SI 2004/643 (as amended), reg 9.

seriously injured[23] following direct of indirect contact with the police[24], or where the complaint includes the following allegations[25]:

- serious assault by a member of the police service;

- serious sexual assault by a member of the police service;

- serious corruption;

- any criminal offence or conduct aggravated by discriminatory behaviour.

5.62   The IPCC Guidance provides a non-exhaustive list of the types of injury which are likely to be considered a result of a serious assault[26]. These include:

- loss or breaking of a tooth or teeth;

- temporary loss of sensory functions (which may include loss of consciousness);

- extensive or multiple bruising;

- displaced broken nose;

- minor fractures;

- minor, but not merely superficial, cuts of a sort probably requiring medical attention (eg stitches);

- psychiatric injury that is more than fear, distress or panic (such injury will be proved by appropriate expert advice).

5.63   These injuries should be distinguished from those which are identified in the IPCC Guidance as not requiring a referral to the IPCC[27], such as grazes, scratches, abrasions, minor bruising, swellings, reddening of the skin, superficial cuts or a black eye. If any of the more serious injuries have been sustained, this fact should be clearly identified and evidence provided in support, for example in the form of photographs or medical notes.

5.64   The Guidance defines discriminatory behaviour as including discrimination based on[28]:

---

23   As defined in IPCC Guidance, para 216.
24   Police Reform Act 2002 (as amended), Sch 3, para 4(1)(a).
25   Police (Complaints and Misconduct) Regulations 2004, regs 2(2) and 5(1).
26   IPCC Guidance, para 206.
27   IPCC Guidance, para 208.
28   IPCC Guidance, para 213. See also Annex B of the IPCC Guidance.

- race;

- gender;

- religion;

- actual or perceived sexual orientation;

- physical or mental disability;

- age.

In addition, the Equality Act 2010 (para **5.210**) identifies further protected characteristics which, although not explicitly listed in the Guidance, are most likely to be included. The Equality Act 2010 prohibits discrimination based on marriage or civil partnership, gender reassignment and pregnancy or maternity.

5.65   If the complaint therefore entails an allegation falling within this category, it should be robustly stated from the outset that the expectation is that the matter will be referred to the IPCC for consideration. Complainants do occasionally encounter a reluctance on the part of the police to make a referral to the IPCC. It is worth reminding the police that the Guidance and Regulations quite clearly state that the matter **must** be referred to the IPCC where there is an **allegation** of the above nature; there is no requirement for the complainant to establish from the outset that such behaviour in fact occurred. The IPCC Guidance also requires the police to be mindful of any allegations that engage ECHR, Articles 2 and 3[29] (respectively the right to life, and the right to be free from torture, inhuman and degrading treatment or punishment).

5.66   If the matter is referred, the IPCC may decide to conduct a supervised, managed or independent investigation. Supervised and managed investigations seem to be increasingly unpopular with the IPCC and are unusual. An independent investigation is highly unlikely to occur except in the case of death or near death in custody, or in 'incidents that cause the greatest level of public concern'[30]. Further information about these modes of investigation can be found on the IPCC's website.

5.67   The IPCC may, and often does, instruct the police to investigate the complaint themselves even if a force has referred it to the IPCC. It may therefore seem fairly fruitless to force a referral to the IPCC in the first instance, and indeed a complainant may decide the delay this process will cause conflicts with their aims. In these circumstances it is nonetheless worth recording in writing the fact that submissions were made about the need for a referral to the IPCC as the failure to properly investigate a complaint may be reflected in aggravated damages sought as part of a civil action.

---

29 IPCC Guidance, para 221.
30 IPCC Guidance, para 240.

5.68   Continued refusal to refer the complaint to the IPCC for a decision on the mode of investigation may be challengeable by way of judicial review. Similarly, a decision by the IPCC to allow the police force to investigate the complaint themselves may be subject to judicial review, although the limited resources of the IPCC to carry out independent investigations suggests that only the most striking refusals to do so would be subject to a successful challenge. It is worth noting, however, that the IPCC has in the past been criticised for failing to promptly take over investigations—for example, when it did not formally remove the City of London Police from the investigation into the death of newspaper vendor Ian Tomlinson on 1 April 2009 during the G20 summit protests.

The local investigation process

5.69   If a decision is made, either by the PSD or the IPCC, that the complaint is suitable for local investigation, an investigating officer (IO) will be appointed to collate and consider all the evidence. On conclusion of this process, s/he will set out his or her findings in a final report.

5.70   In practice, however, the IO will rely on a complainant to suggest lines of enquiry, such as obtaining information from witnesses, especially where a complainant provides a statement naming friends or acquaintances as witnesses. In those circumstances a complainant (or his/her legal representative) may either seek to obtain statements from witnesses themselves or provide contact details for the IO to take a statement. Where a complainant is legally represented it is often beneficial for the representative to take the statements to ensure that any aspects which support the complainant's case are adequately covered.

5.71   Because there will be some inevitable delay between the date of the incident and the commencement of the investigation (see in particular para **5.97** where a complainant is also the subject of a criminal investigation), protesters should try to obtain and/or ensure the preservation of evidence that may otherwise be lost. Whilst it is ultimately the responsibility of the IO to secure evidence, this does not always occur in a timely fashion.

5.72   In the course of the investigation, and unless otherwise agreed, the IO should write to the complainant or their representative every 28 days to inform them of progress made[31]. They may also contact the complainant for further information. If a legal representative has been appointed any requests for further information should be made through the representative. Where a detailed witness statement has not been provided as part of the complaint, the

---

31   IPCC Guidance, para 399.

IO might ask to interview the complainant. The complainant can agree to this, or provide a written statement. However, it is worth noting that some IOs are keener to progress investigations expeditiously than others. If no statement or account is forthcoming, it is not unusual for IOs to conclude their investigation without sight of all the relevant evidence in support of the complaint, which would clearly prejudice the prospects of the complaint being upheld.

5.73   Depending on the nature and seriousness of a complaint, the IO may carry out full interviews with the officer(s) who are the subject of the complaint, or simply make telephone enquiries. An IO will usually not obtain the officers' accounts until he or she has collated a 'proportionate' amount of evidence from the complainant and other sources. What is proportionate will again depend on the nature and seriousness of the complaint and is to a large degree within the discretion of the IO (although decisions can on occasion be challenged by way of judicial review, see para **5.241**).

What information should be provided during and on conclusion of the investigation

5.74   On conclusion of the investigation, the IO will produce a written report setting out the findings, and whether the complaints have been upheld or not. A copy of this report should be made available to the complainant, should set out what evidence has been obtained in the course of an investigation, and explain how the findings in the report have been reached[32].

5.75   Key to the investigation will be the statements obtained from the victim and witnesses to the event. These are rarely automatically provided to a complainant at the time of the report, although copies can and usually should be requested immediately. There is, however, a direct conflict between the IPCC Guidance and the practice implemented by the overwhelming majority of forces on whether these statements should be provided to the complainant. The IPCC Guidance clearly advocates maximum transparency as part of the complaint process[33], stating that:

> 'The IPCC adopts a working policy that information should be made available unless there is a valid restriction or constraint on doing so, such as the real risk of harm that might result. It expects the police to employ the same principle when determining whether information should be disclosed'[34].

---

32 IPCC Guidance, para 534.
33 IPCC Guidance, para 255.
34 IPCC Guidance, para 257.

5.76 In practice, this means that the IPCC Guidance encourages that copies of statements or other underlying evidence should be provided if this can be done without incurring unreasonable expense[35] and providing the provision of such documents does not fall foul of the 'harm test'[36]. The harm test provides that disclosure shall not occur where:

'The appropriate authority considers that preventing disclosure to him is:

(a) necessary for the purpose of preventing the premature or inappropriate disclosure of information that is relevant to, or may be used in, any criminal proceedings;

(b) necessary in the interests of national security;

(c) necessary for the purpose of the prevention or detection of crime, or the apprehension or prosecution of offenders;

(d) necessary for the purpose of the prevention or detection of misconduct by other police officers or police staff members or their apprehension for such matters;

(e) justified on the grounds that providing the information would involve disproportionate effort in comparison to the seriousness of the allegations against the officer concerned;

(f) necessary and proportionate for the protection of the welfare and safety of any informant or witness; or

(g) otherwise in the public interest'[37].

5.77 These broad grounds afford the officer in charge of disclosure a large degree of discretion as to whether or not to provide a complainant with further information. However, the Statutory Guidance does set some robust limits to the harm test[38] and explicitly states that the concept of harm cannot be used to justify non-disclosure on the basis of:

'potential damage to a force's reputation or morale which might be caused by the disclosure or publication of information, such as the findings of an investigation, showing a criminal offence, misconduct or poor performance to have occurred ...'[39].

---

35 IPCC Guidance, para 535.
36 Set out in the Police (Conduct) Regulations 2008, reg 4 and applicable by virtue of the IPCC Guidance, paras C1 and C2.
37 Police (Conduct) Regulations 2008, reg 4.
38 IPCC Guidance, Annex C.
39 IPCC Guidance, Annex C4.

5.78   Similarly, the Guidance states that the risk of harm 'must be a real and significant one and not merely fanciful or theoretical'[40]. A non-exhaustive list of what may legitimately result in a conclusion that disclosure would infringe the harm test is set out in the Statutory Guidance at C9 and C10.

5.79   The non-disclosure of documents is a controversial and much disputed topic in a far broader legal context than just protest law. However, it is worth noting here that, whilst it is inherently difficult to challenge the non-disclosure of a document when the basis for it being withheld is not conveyed, legal challenges have been successful over time. Non-disclosure should therefore not be accepted at face value, and a rationale should be sought in the context of the Statutory Guidance, with consideration being given to a challenge by way of judicial review in the event that the answers obtained are unsatisfactory.

5.80   Similar principles apply to the provision of other evidence such as CCTV footage[41]. In addition, disclosure of CCTV footage may also be said to be subject to the provisions of the Data Protection Act if it shows other people who have not consented to its disclosure.

5.81   If a complaint is upheld, the police force may take disciplinary action against the officers who are the subject of the complaint. The type of action taken will depend on the seriousness of the complaint, and include (in order of severity):

- constructive words of advice;
- formal (written) warning;
- suspension;
- fines;
- reduction in rank;
- dismissal.

5.82   If the conduct complained of amounts to a criminal offence, the matter should also be referred to the Crown Prosecution Service so that consideration can be given to a criminal prosecution of the officers. In practice, criminal prosecutions of police officers are extremely rare.

Appealing the outcome of a local investigation

5.83   Complainants have a right of appeal to the IPCC following a local investigation. Unlike in the local resolution process, such an appeal can arise

---

40 IPCC Guidance, Annex C7.
41 IPCC Guidance, para 539.

out of a dissatisfaction with the outcome of the investigation and need not solely relate to procedural matters. An appeal can be made on the basis that the complainant:

(a)   has not been provided with adequate information about the findings of the investigation;

(b)   has not been provided with adequate information about any proposals of the appropriate authority to take, or not to take, action in consequence of the report;

(c)   disagrees with the findings of the investigation;

(d)   disagrees with any proposal of the appropriate authority to take, or not to take, action in respect of any of the matters dealt with in the report of the investigation[42];

(e)   disagrees with the decision not to refer the report to the CPS.

5.84   At the time of lodging the appeal the relevant heads should be listed, and where possible the rationale for the basis of the appeal. For example, if on the basis of the IO's report a protester disagrees with the findings of the investigation because inappropriate weight has been afforded to the account of the police, whilst the evidence of independent witnesses appears to have been too easily discarded, these facts should be set out as part of the appeal. There is no subsequent opportunity to appeal a decision by the IPCC (although their decision may be challenged by way of judicial review: see para **5.220**) so it is important to include all relevant heads of appeal and all factual and legal arguments at this stage.

5.85   It is essential to note that such an appeal must be received by the IPCC within 28 days of the date of the local investigation decision[43]. The period runs from the date the decision is sent, not the date the letter is received or considered[44]. Although the IPCC does have a discretion to allow appeals outside of this 28 day period[45], this discretion is rarely exercised, and only in special circumstances where it is just to do so. The IPCC will sometimes also accept further submissions after the 28 day deadline, provided the appeal is lodged in time and provided the further information is received before the IPCC has commenced its considerations. However there is no requirement to do so, and where at all possible all information should be provided from the outset.

5.86   Once the appeal is lodged, the IPCC will confirm receipt and allocate the appeal to a caseworker. The caseworker will not carry out a fresh

---

42   Police Reform Act 2002, Sch 3, para 25(2).
43   Police Reform Act 2002 (as amended), Sch 3, para 25.
44   Police (Complaints and Misconduct) Regulations 2004, reg 10.
45   Police (Complaints and Misconduct) Regulations 2004, reg 10(8).

investigation. They will not re-interview witnesses, or seek to obtain further evidence. Instead, they will consider the quality of the investigation already carried out by reviewing the evidence obtained and the decisions reached by the IO.

5.87 The IPCC can consider grounds of appeal not mentioned by the complainant, but does not have to do so. It is therefore important to include all relevant heads of appeal, even if they pertain to the same factual events or findings. For example, the investigation may result in a finding that no misconduct has occurred because the IO has determined, on the balance of probabilities, that an officer did not strike a protester with a baton in the course of a demonstration. In those circumstances an appeal could be lodged both on the basis that the complainant disagrees with the findings that there was no unlawful use of force, and further disagrees with the consequential failure to bring disciplinary proceedings.

5.88 The IPCC has regularly suffered extensive backlogs in dealing with appeals, so a complainant should be aware that it can take several months for the IPCC to reach an appeal decision. Once the IPCC has considered the case the appeal decision will be communicated in writing. If the appeal is upheld, the IPCC will give instructions to the chief police officer or police authority about what they should do about the complaint. The police must follow these instructions.

5.89   In deciding an appeal the IPCC may:

(a)   direct the appropriate authority to release information (subject to the harm test);

(b)   review the findings, without further investigation, which may result in the IPCC upholding the findings in whole or in part or substituting its own findings;

(c)   direct the appropriate authority to reinvestigate the complaint, subject to the nature of the original complaint, the evidence available and how the investigation has been handled;

(d)   recommend and, if this is resisted direct, the appropriate authority to take misconduct or disciplinary action;

(e)   recommend the appropriate authority take other action[46].

---

46 IPCC Guidance, para 521 and Police Reform Act 2002 (as amended), Sch 3, para 25(5), (6), (8) and (9).

5.90   In practice, the IPCC frequently directs the police to release further information and/or reinvestigate the complaint. The IPCC can give any directions it considers appropriate to ensure that the complainant is properly informed[47].

5.91   It is not unheard of that a complaint is returned to the relevant force to review its findings in the context of the IPCC's decision and that subsequently the police force maintains its original position, even in circumstances where the IPCC have upheld an appeal. The significance of this will depend on the basis of the appeal and the basis upon which the appeal was upheld. For example, if an appeal is upheld solely on the basis that inadequate information was given to the complainant, the police can remedy this by simply providing further information whilst ultimately maintaining that no misconduct occurred, and therefore still dismiss the complaint. If, however, the IPCC uphold an appeal because a force incorrectly applied the law, or because a certain finding of fact was untenable on the evidence available, a force should review the substantial basis for the complaint. If the force nonetheless refuses to uphold the complaint, a challenge by way of judicial review should be considered.

5.92   By way of example, a protester may make a complaint that excessive force was used in the course of dispersing a demonstration. The officer conducting the investigation may conclude that, on the evidence available to them, the protester was behaving unreasonably because he did not comply with a lawful request to leave the area, and that therefore the level of force used was necessary and proportionate. The IO may nonetheless fail to (adequately) summarise the evidence of the officers who are the subject of the complaint, and fail to provide an adequate description of the CCTV footage available. The protester could therefore lodge an appeal on the basis that s/he has not been given sufficient information about the reasons for the decision, that they disagree with the finding that the original request was lawful, and further or in the alternative that in any event they complied with the request. The IPCC caseworker will review the evidence, and may agree with the protester that the original request was unlawful (although note that this is the type of policing decision that may fall into the 'direction and control' category) and that further there is insufficient evidence to support the assertion that the protester did not comply with the request. The appeal would then be upheld and could be returned to the force, only for the force to provide further information without changing their original decision to dismiss the complaint.

5.93   In those circumstances a protester may wish to consider challenging the decision by way of judicial review, or alternatively may decide simply to proceed with a civil action for claims including assault and battery (see

---

47   Police Reform Act 2002 (as amended), Sch 3, para 25(6).

para **5.156**). What course of action should be pursued will depend to a great extent on what the protester's desired outcomes are, and whether a civil action is viable in the circumstances.

5.94   Where an appeal against a decision not to refer a report to the CPS for consideration of a criminal prosecution is upheld, the IPCC can direct the appropriate authority to refer the matter to the CPS[48].

5.95   If an appeal is not upheld, the IPCC must explain how and why it reached this decision. There is no further appeal route against the IPCC's decision as the IPCC is *functus officio*, which effectively means that it has no legal authority to review or reverse its own decisions once they have been formally communicated because its duties and functions have been completed. The only avenue open to a complainant in those circumstances is to challenge the decision by way of judicial review. It is important to note, however, that a challenge by way of judicial review can only be mounted against the decisions made by the IPCC, and cannot include grounds that should have been raised as part of the complaint or appeal but were not. For this reason, it is worth erring on the side of caution when drafting an appeal and including as many reasonable grounds as possible, to ensure all options are kept open for a challenge at a later stage.

When to complain

5.96   An important consideration in many protest-related complaints is when to complain. Whilst there is no official time limit on making a complaint, it is strongly recommended that any complaint is lodged within 12 months of the incident occurring. If more than 12 months have passed, and there is no good reason for the delay or injustice would be likely to be caused by it, then the police force concerned may not consider the complaint. In practice, many forces will automatically make an application for dispensation (see para **5.103**) where a complaint is made outside of the 12 month period.

5.97   In evidential terms, the sooner a complaint is lodged the better. However, there may be good reason to postpone making a complaint. A frequent consideration for both practitioners and protesters will be whether to lodge a complaint on arrival at the police station where the protester has been arrested following the incident which has given rise to the complaint. Whilst making the complaint on arrival at the police station may lend credibility to the allegation, it may also adversely affect the outcome of the criminal investigation. Although the lodging of a complaint plainly should not impact on the police's decision to pursue an investigation or prosecution, a protester may

---

48   Police Reform Act 2002 (as amended), Sch 3, para 25(9)(a).

wish to err on the side of caution and avoid the risk of aggravating the situation by making counter allegations to the police. In practice, lodging a complaint at the police station may also result in a lengthier period in the police station, even if only to deal with the practicalities of recording the complaint.

5.98 To illustrate these points with an example, suppose that a clash between police and protesters occurs on a demonstration, during which the complainant was struck with a baton. The complainant's account is that she was peacefully taking part in the demonstration when the clash erupted without warning. She was caught up in the upheaval and merely wished to leave the area. However, as the complainant attempted to do so, police officers were pushing and using batons on the protesters. The situation became increasingly heated, and in an attempt to protect herself from baton strikes, the complainant pushed a police officer. The complainant sustained serious bruising but she was arrested for assaulting an officer in the execution of his duty and taken to the police station, alongside a number of other protesters. At the police station, the protester wishes to lodge a complaint for assault. As part of that complaint she would argue that the officers were acting unlawfully and using excessive force, and that the protester merely acted in self-defence to an unlawful assault by the police. Whilst such a complaint may be entirely legitimately lodged at the police station, a complainant may nonetheless choose to await the outcome of the criminal investigation prior to lodging a complaint (providing the investigation concludes within 12 months of the incident) so as to ensure there is no additional motivation to bring charges against her.

5.99 It should be noted that there is no evidence beyond anecdotal accounts that the police have been moved by such improper motivations to bring charges, but it is clear that complainants often decide to minimise the risk of charges being brought. Particularly in examples such as the one above, a successful prosecution in which a criminal court makes findings against a protester on the basis that the police were acting lawfully and/or the protester did assault the officer(s) would make the prospects of a subsequent complaint being upheld almost nil. Whether or not the police (and the CPS) are actually influenced by a complaint having been lodged when making a charging decision does not take away from the fact that a successful prosecution is likely to protect individual officers from a complaint against them being upheld.

5.100 In practice, complainants are therefore often advised against lodging a complaint until the outcome of the criminal investigation is known. This does carry an additional complication in that a complainant may be criticised for failing to raise the conduct complained of at the earliest opportunity. It must be for the complainant to decide whether or not they would prefer to take the risk of potentially increasing the prospects of a prosecution being brought or the risk of the credibility of their account being diminished when the complaint is investigated. These competing factors must be weighed up on a case-by-case basis depending, amongst other factors, on the strength of the evidence against them in the criminal investigation, and on the available evidence in the complaint. In the event that a complainant decides to postpone lodging the complaint, they may wish to make a detailed, signed and dated complaint statement to their legal representative, setting out not only the basis of the complaint, but also the reasons for not raising it at the police station. As lodging a complaint at the police station may also extend the time spent in custody, this could be noted as a legitimate reason for the decision.

5.101   If criminal charges are brought against the protester, the police have a power to suspend the complaint investigation pending the outcome of the criminal proceedings where it would prejudice such proceedings[49]. This is known as holding the complaint *sub judice*. In practice, a complaint will always be suspended to allow criminal proceedings to take place. Providing the complaint is lodged within the 12 month period, this should not in theory affect the outcome of the complaint. In practice, however, the complainant can be disadvantaged, because the quality of evidence is likely to deteriorate with the passage of time. Whilst the police have a duty to ensure evidence is secured both before and while the investigation is suspended[50] it is nonetheless advisable that, where possible and without interfering with the criminal proceedings, the complainant should also take steps to secure and preserve evidence. Whilst a failure on the part of the police to preserve evidence can lead to an adverse inference being drawn against them (for example, that the evidence was intentionally destroyed or lost) an absence of evidence will rarely assist as much as positive evidence in support of an allegation.

5.102   The period of suspension of a complaint investigation should cease when the complainant/defendant is convicted or acquitted in the ongoing criminal proceedings. There will not normally be any prejudice caused by continuing the investigation before sentencing and therefore the complaint investigation should resume once a determination of guilt or innocence is made[51].

Dispensation and discontinuance

5.103   When a police force considers, before an investigation has started, that no further action should be taken in relation to a complaint it may make an application for dispensation to the IPCC, seeking permission not to investigate a complaint. This may arise where:

(a)   more than 12 months have elapsed between the incident, or the latest

---

49   Police (Complaints and Misconduct) Regulations 2004, reg 16.
50   IPCC Guidance, para 153.
51   IPCC Guidance, para 159.

incident, giving rise to the complaint and the making of the complaint and either that no good reason for the delay has been shown or that injustice would be likely to be caused by the delay;

(b) the matter is already the subject of a complaint;

(c) the complaint discloses neither the name and address of the complainant nor that of any other interested person and it is not reasonably practicable to ascertain such a name or address;

(d) the complaint is vexatious, oppressive or otherwise an abuse of the procedures for dealing with complaints;

(e) the complaint is repetitious; or

(f) it is not reasonably practicable to complete the investigation of the complaint or any other procedures under Schedule 3 to the PRA 2002[52].

5.104 The police must notify the complainant of such an application for dispensation[53] and a complainant may then wish to make representations to the IPCC that dispensation should not be granted. The IPCC expects the police to notify the complainant of the application for dispensation within five days of it being made to the IPCC[54].

5.105 Where a police force wishes to discontinue a complaint when the investigation has already commenced, it can apply to the IPCC for a discontinuance on the following grounds:

(a) the complainant refuses to cooperate to the extent that the Commission considers that it is not reasonably practicable to continue the investigation;

(b) the complainant has agreed the complaint may be subjected to local resolution;

(c) the Commission considers the complaint to be vexatious, oppressive or otherwise an abuse of the procedures for dealing with complaints or conduct matters;

(d) the complaint is repetitious, as defined in reg 3(3); or

(e) the complaint is one of which the Commission otherwise considers is such as to make it not reasonably practicable to proceed with the investigation[55].

---

52 Police (Complaints and Misconduct) Regulations 2004, reg 3(2).
53 Police Reform Act 2002 (as amended), Sch 3, para 7(2) and Police (Complaints and Misconduct) Regulations 2004, reg 3(2).
54 IPCC Guidance, para 382.
55 Police (Complaints and Misconduct) Regulations 2004, reg 7.

5.106 When applying for a discontinuance, the appropriate authority must send a copy of the application form to the complainant on the same day that it is sent to the IPCC[56].

CIVIL ACTIONS AGAINST THE POLICE

Introduction

5.107 Civil actions against the police, also known as claims or litigation against the police, are legal proceedings brought through the civil court system. Their primary function is to obtain compensation, also referred to as damages, but there are a number of other advantages to bringing a civil action that may make this a particularly attractive option to activists seeking to hold the police to account (as set out at paras **5.14–5.18**).

5.108 Civil actions come in many different shapes and sizes, known as causes of action. These are the heads of claim under which damages are sought, and each cause of action has a distinct legal test that needs to be met if the claim is to succeed. Some causes of action are set out in statute (such as the law surrounding discrimination) but many are based on definitions developed over the years through case law, known as common law torts.

5.109 Civil actions are entirely discrete from the complaint process discussed above, although the timing and outcome of a civil action will usually be affected if a complaint has been lodged. For example, a successful complaint is likely to increase the prospects of success of a civil action, and is therefore also likely to improve the chances of the police settling a civil case before trial.

5.110 However, not every set of circumstances giving rise to a complaint will also give rise to a civil action, and there are many more practical hurdles and tactical considerations in litigation than in the complaint process. Whereas the complaint process is designed to enable complainants to navigate the system without formal legal representation, litigation is far more complex and risky. It is predominantly the domain of lawyers, and even the most robust litigants in person often feel isolated and intimidated by the process. Certainly the police will always have formal legal representation when action is taken against them, either in the form of in-house lawyers, or increasingly by way of external law firms. Furthermore, this area of law is constantly developing, with new cases coming out very frequently which impact not only on the substantive elements of the case, but also on the procedural requirements. A failure to keep abreast of the law can therefore be fatal to a case.

---

56 Police (Complaints and Misconduct) Regulations 2004, reg 7(5).

5.111   For all these reasons, protesters who are contemplating a civil action are strongly recommended to seek formal legal representation as soon as possible. Most reputable firms are listed in the independent guides, which rank law firms on the basis of feedback from clients and other professionals, including *Chambers & Partners* and the *Legal 500*[57].

5.112   However, there are real limitations on the availability of lawyers in this area. Not only is the demand greater than the supply, but further Legal Aid will usually only be available for cases of a relatively high value, and only to those with very limited financial means[58]. Where Legal Aid is not available, activists will have to consider other funding options. A Conditional Fee Agreement (CFA) may be a viable alternative[59], also known as a 'no win, no fee' agreement. But the nature of CFAs is such that they are unattractive to firms where the prospects of success are limited or unclear, which will often be the case in protest cases as they normally engage novel and developing areas of law. Pursuing civil actions on a privately paid basis is prohibitively costly, and will only be viable for a handful of people. Similarly, funding a case by way of insurance is relatively uncommon, particularly in protest cases where the causes of action and factual circumstances are often alien to insurance companies. Unfortunately, this means that there is a huge gap between those who are able to secure legal assistance and those who require it and access to justice through civil actions may be limited.

5.113   A basic understanding of the most relevant aspects of this area of law may therefore be of great assistance to activists. Whilst the complexity of police actions means that this chapter can only ever provide a basic overview of some of its most common features, it should assist protesters in maximising the prospects of success by taking early steps to preserve evidence, and further should enable them to better convey the key facets of their case to potential legal advisors.

5.114   This section therefore has a number of aims. First, it provides an overview of the procedures and time-frames involved in suing the police for damages, which will assist in deciding whether the process is one on which protesters wish to embark. Second, it will enable protesters and their (criminal) legal advisors to better frame any enquiry they wish to put to a specialist firm. Third, the practicalities of a protester's route through the various aspects of the legal system means that evidential and procedural steps may need to be taken before any criminal case is concluded and therefore, in practice, before they instruct a specialist police actions solicitor.

---

57   Search in the civil liberties and human rights and/or police law sections.
58   For more information on the tests for Legal Aid see para **5.21**.
59   See para **5.30**.

5.115   More than anything, the purpose of this section is therefore to provide some basic guidance to ensure protesters and practitioners are aware of what the various prerequisites and hallmarks of a successful civil action are, so that opportunities are not missed.

5.116   Finally, this section is intended to provide an accessible, albeit potted, overview of the law in order to equip protesters with the tools required to ensure the police are held to account.

Practicalities

5.117   One of the greatest obstacles in bringing claims against the police is funding. As set out above, almost all methods of funding an action of this nature will require a combination of 'reasonable prospects of success' and seeking to recover damages, although the latter can be overcome where the case engages significant public interest and/or human rights issues. However, there are some other significant practical considerations that any protesters should be aware of from the outset.

Time limits and limitation

5.118   One of the first considerations in any civil action is the deadline by which proceedings must be brought. These deadlines are known as limitation periods and are set out in statute and interpreted in case law. For tortious claims (such as assault, false imprisonment and malicious prosecution) the general provisions in the Limitation Act 1980 apply. For statutory claims, such as claims under the Human Rights Act 1998 (HRA 1998) or Equality Act 2010 (EA 2010), the statutes themselves contain provisions for the limitation period[60]. Many of the heads of claim have different limitation periods, by which time proceedings must be commenced at court. It is essential that a claim is issued within the limitation period. A failure to issue a claim within the limitation period is likely to result in a claim being time-barred and a claimant being prevented from pursuing a claim. Although the court has a discretion to allow claims out of time in certain circumstances[61], applications of this nature are frequently denied and claims should therefore be issued within time if at all possible.

5.119   The relevant limitation periods are listed under each head of claim below. They run from the date that the cause of action arises. In many cases this will be the date of the actual incident—for example the date a protester was

---

60   See for example HRA 1998, s 7(5) and EA 2010, s 118.
61   Limitation Act 1980, s 33; HRA 1998, s 7(5)(b) and EA 2010, s 118(1)(b) and the procedural requirements thereunder.

assaulted or arrested—although in other cases limitation may run from the 'date of knowledge', for example in a claim for negligence.

5.120   It should be noted that some limitation periods are extremely tight, and are likely to expire before the conclusion of a criminal case or complaint investigation. The shortest limitation period of six months less one day applies to all types of discrimination claims, except those brought under Article 14 of the European Convention on Human Rights (ECHR) actionable by virtue of the HRA 1998, in which case the limitation period is one year less one day.

5.121   There are two notable exceptions to the limitation rule. The first is that where the claimant is a minor (under 18 years old) any limitation period determined by the Limitation Act 1980 will not start running until they have reached 18. This exception does not apply to claims brought under the HRA 1998[62] and (although the law had yet to be tested on the issue at the time of writing) is also unlikely to apply to other causes of action which have specific time limits contained in the statute itself, such as the EA 2010. To err on the side of caution, specialist advice should be sought well in advance of any expiration of the limitation period.

5.122   The second exception applies where 'any fact relevant to the plaintiff's right of action has been deliberately concealed from him by the defendant'[63] or where there has been a 'deliberate commission of a breach of duty in circumstances in which it is unlikely to be discovered for some time amounts to deliberate concealment of the facts involved in that breach of duty'[64].

5.123   In practice, bringing a claim outside of the limitation period allows a defendant to raise a limitation defence. A court could therefore accept the claim in the first instance and the defendant would have to seek to have the claim struck out on the basis that it was brought out of time. Defendants are, however, almost invariably alive to the issue and it is only in most unusual circumstances that such a defence will not be raised. This also means that the court will often only consider the issue of limitation, and whether the claim should be allowed out of time, some way down the litigation route by which time a lot of time, energy and money may have been invested by the claimant.

Preparatory work and securing evidence

5.124   Even before proceedings are commenced a considerable amount of preparatory work needs to be undertaken. This may include identifying the correct defendant and causes of action and securing funding. Whilst emergency

---

62   *M (a minor by his litigation friend LT) v Ministry of Justice* [2009] EWCA Civ 419.
63   Limitation Act 1980, s 32(1)(b).
64   Limitation Act 1980, s 32(2).

procedures for obtaining Legal Aid are available, a claimant is likely to encounter greater difficulties in securing legal representation if the limitation period is fast approaching. Prompt enquiries should therefore be made of a specialist practitioner if a protester is considering bringing a civil action.

5.125 Even where limitation is not due to expire in the immediate future, urgent steps may be required to secure evidence. In general terms, the quality and availability of evidence is likely to deteriorate rapidly. Both claimants' and witnesses' recollection of events will fade with the passage of time. Detailed statements should therefore be taken as soon as possible.

5.126 Evidence such as CCTV footage can be crucial to the success of a case, and depending on the location and provenance of the footage, it can be lost in a matter of days or weeks. Similarly, documentary evidence is likely to be lost over time. Different types of documents in the possession of the police must be retained for different periods, so to ensure crucial documentary evidence is not lost, its disclosure should be sought or its preservation should be requested at the earliest opportunity.

5.127 CCTV footage belonging to the local council (such as CCTV footage of a public place) can be requested under the Data Protection Act 1998, as can documentary evidence held by the police and third parties. In the case of the police, a Subject Access Request can be made, which usually incurs a fee of £10.00. The type of documents that should be requested will depend on the case, but may include:

(a)   custody records;

(b)   property records;

(c)   search records;

(d)   CCTV footage of the custody suite;

(e)   notebooks of officers involved in the incident;

(f)   written and/or tape recorded records of interview;

(g)   photographs;

(h)   Police National Computer (PNC) records, which will contain, *inter alia*, details of previous arrests, cautions, charges and convictions;

(i)   records of any 999 calls;

(j)   Computer Aided Dispatch (CAD) records, which may record information passed between police controllers and officers;

(k)   in the case of the Metropolitan Police, Crime Report Information System (CRIS) records, which will include a record of the steps taken by the police in the course of the investigation including, for example, dates on which decisions to charge were taken (or similar records in the case of other forces).

A catch-all provision should be made in any Subject Access Request for all other documents in the police's possession created as a result of the incident, or even all other documents in the police's possession pertaining to the claimant.

5.128   There will be a section on the custody record which summarises the relevant findings following any examination by the Forensic Medical Examiner (or FME) at the police station, but in addition the FME may have made separate notes of the consultation which are medical in confidence. Like all medical records, claimants are entitled to copies of records made by a doctor at the police station or FME. These can be obtained directly from the doctor, whose details should be provided by the police.

5.129   Certain documents may not necessarily be disclosable during the early stages of a case, but their preservation should nonetheless be sought. This should be done in writing to the police station where the claimant was detained, or where the police officers involved are based. To ensure receipt, and proof of receipt, such requests should be made in writing and sent by fax or recorded delivery where possible. A copy of the letter can be sent to the police force's solicitors to ensure they are aware of the fact the preservation of documents has been sought. Although documents may still go missing, this correspondence may be helpful in due course, for example when, in the later stages of litigation, the claimant is asking a court to draw an inference that documents were intentionally destroyed.

5.130   If a protester has also been prosecuted, documentation should also be sought from the courts. Magistrates' courts do not tape-record trials, but court clerks will often keep their notes and magistrates and judges will often place notes recording the reasons for their verdict on the file. These can be very helpful if the court made comments in the course of a criminal case criticising the officers' behaviour, eg in concluding the officers were not acting in the execution of their duty or questioning the credibility of their evidence. Whilst these comments will not be binding in a civil action, they do provide an indication as to how a court is likely to view the police's evidence. In addition, courts keep formal records of the outcome of a case, and a print out of the same can usually be obtained. Copies of all documents should also be requested from any legal representative involved in the criminal matter, including any solicitor or police station representative who attended the police station, barristers representing the claimant in criminal hearings, and of course criminal solicitors.

The Civil Procedure Rules and Pre-Action Protocols

5.131 Even before a claim is issued, a claimant is required to carry out certain steps under the Civil Procedure Rules 1998 (CPR 1998)[65]. Claimants should note that failure to comply with the CPR 1998 may result in a claim failing altogether. Whilst the detail of the rules is outside of the scope of this book, it is worth considering some of the key provisions in the CPR to get a general flavour of their importance and purpose.

5.132 The overriding objective of the CPR 1998 is to deal with cases justly, and is set out at para 1.1:

'(1) These Rules are a new procedural code with the overriding objective of enabling the court to deal with cases justly.

(2) Dealing with a case justly includes, so far as is practicable:

(a)   ensuring that the parties are on an equal footing;

(b)   saving expense;

(c)   dealing with the case in ways which are proportionate:

    (i)   to the amount of money involved;

    (ii)   to the importance of the case;

    (iii)   to the complexity of the issues; and

    (iv)   to the financial position of each party;

(d)   ensuring that it is dealt with expeditiously and fairly; and

(e)   allotting to it an appropriate share of the court's resources, while taking into account the need to allot resources to other cases'.

5.133 This important provision may be invoked to both hinder and assist activists. For example, in the course of possession proceedings, those seeking possession of land will attempt to rely on the provisions regarding saving expense and ensuring that cases are dealt with expeditiously to achieve the swift return of their land. Protesters acting as litigants in person could in turn request modification of the court procedure to assist them, for example under provisions seeking to ensure that the parties are on equal footing.

5.134 The CPR 1998 also seek to limit the unnecessary use of court resources. One of the practical implications of this is that parties are expected to

---

65   www.justice.gov.uk/guidance/courts-and-tribunals/courts/procedure-rules/civil/.

try to resolve disputes without recourse to the court where possible. To this end, many types of cases have a specific 'pre-action protocol' (PAP) which prescribes specific steps the parties should take before engaging the court, including the better and earlier exchange of information 'to put the parties in a position where they may be able to settle cases fairly and early without litigation'[66].

5.135   Whilst there is no specific PAP for cases against the police, many police forces propose the use of the PAP for personal injury claims[67], especially where the claim involves an element of personal injury. However, this PAP is not necessarily the most advantageous for claimants and it should not necessarily be accepted as applicable on face value. Specialist police action solicitors and the Metropolitan Police have, for some years, been in discussions over developing a specific agreed PAP, but no agreement has been reached.

5.136   Nevertheless, in general terms, the court will expect a claimant to afford the defendant time to consider the allegations being made, and to ascertain whether the matter can be resolved without recourse to the courts. The most common and practicable way to do this is to send the defendant a letter of claim as soon as it is possible to detail the claim in a realistic manner.

Letters of claim

5.137   Letters of claim are very important documents, and can significantly impact upon the prospects of a case. They are often the first formal expression of the claimant's case, detailing the allegations and the legal basis for the claim. It is essential that a letter of claim correctly reflects the facts of the case, as any subsequent variation of the claimant's account in later documents may be relied upon by the defendant to undermine the claimant's credibility.

5.138   The PAP for personal injury cases sets out what information a letter of claim should contain. Only some of this will be relevant to police actions. Certainly, a letter of claim should include a summary of facts. It should also set out any loss, damage or injury suffered and detail the law upon which the claimant will seek to rely. A claimant can also request the disclosure of documents as part of the response to the letter of claim, and it is therefore an important opportunity to obtain further information that may greatly assist the claim. To ensure this opportunity is fully exploited, the letter of claim should contain a list of specific documents to be disclosed.

---

66   PI PAP 1.2.
67   www.justice.gov.uk/guidance/courts-and-tribunals/courts/procedure-rules/civil/contents/
    protocols/prot_pic.htm.

5.139 Once a letter of claim has been provided, the defendant is expected to provide a letter of response, setting out whether the claim is accepted or denied, and the basis upon which this position is taken as well as providing any disclosure (reasonably) requested. The time period for a response depends on the circumstances of a case, but will usually be somewhere between one and three months.

5.140 The amount of information the defendant provides in practice varies from police force to police force, although reasonable requests for relevant documents that require only proportionate searches should be disclosed. Of course, what is reasonable, relevant and proportionate will differ from case to case. However, where disclosure is very unforthcoming, the CPR 1998 do allow a party to apply to the court (even before issuing proceedings) to seek disclosure[68]. Such an application can also be made, in certain circumstances, against a third party[69]. A failure to comply with the CPR, or an abuse of the procedures by, for example, making inappropriate or premature applications, can result in cost sanctions.

5.141 It should be noted that whilst compliance with the CPR 1998 is exceptionally important, it cannot be relied upon to defend an application to have a claim dismissed because it was issued outside of the limitation period. If the limitation period is due to expire in the immediate future, proceedings should be issued and the period between issue and service should be utilised to comply with the PAP or a stay in proceedings should be sought.

5.142 A stay in proceedings will temporarily pause the case and suspend the timetable with which a case would otherwise need to comply. The court has a wide range of 'case management' powers under CPR 1998, r 3, and can grant a stay following an application by consent between the parties, or, if one of the parties refuses to agree to a stay, without such consent. In practice, where defendants are approached in a timely fashion and with a reasonable explanation, most police forces will consider agreeing a stay to allow the exchange of information. In recent months, however, defendants seem increasingly reluctant to agree to a stay and approaches on this issue should be made well in advance of the expiration of any deadline.

Issuing proceedings and next steps

5.143 Proceedings are commenced by issuing a claim form (form N1) at court[70]. The claim form must contain various pieces of information, including the name and address of the claimant and the defendant. The defendant in any

---

68 CPR 31.16.
69 CPR 31.17.
70 CPR 7.

civil action is the Chief Constable of the relevant police force, or in the case of the Metropolitan Police, the Commissioner of Police of the Metropolis. Civil actions against the police are not issued against named individual police officers. The claim form must also provide a basic summary of the claim, including the heads of claim where possible. In most circumstances, issuing a claim incurs a fee (which depends on the court in which the claim is being issued and the anticipated value of the claim). Claimants in receipt of certain benefits or on low income may be able to obtain a fee exemption using form EX160.

5.144 Once a claim has been issued, a timetable is set in motion which must be adhered to. This timetable is again detailed in the CPR. Any claim form must be served on the defendant within four months of the date of issue. There are specific rules regarding how the claim form, and any other formal documents (also known as pleadings), must be served[71]. Failure to serve a claim form will make a claim extinct and it will be as if the claim was never issued in the first place, although the court, in certain circumstances, can extend time for service of the claim form[72].

5.145 Once the claim form is served, a further document known as the particulars of claim must be served upon the defendant within 14 days of service of the claim form, or within four months of the date of issue, whichever occurs first[73]. The particulars of claim may be served alongside the claim form at any point within the four month period, and in fact can be provided to the court at the time of issue. In certain circumstances, the court can approve a different timetable for service of the particulars of claim.

Particulars of claim

5.146 The particulars of claim must include various pieces of information, and be presented in a particular format. For example, it must contain a concise statement of the facts on which the claimant relies[74] and be verified by a statement of truth[75]. Certain documents upon which a claimant wishes to rely must be provided at the same time as the particulars of claim, for example medical evidence and proof of any loss of earnings claim.

---

71 CPR 7.5.
72 CPR 7.6.
73 CPR 7.4.
74 CPR Pt 16, in particular CPR 16.4.
75 Part 22.

Defence

5.147   The CPR 1998 then place various obligations on the defendant who must, if he proposes to defend the claim, serve a defence within 14 days of service of the particulars of claim and supporting evidence[76], unless an acknowledgement of service is provided within 14 days[77], in which case the defence is due within 28 days of service of the particulars of claim. The defendant may make a formal request for further information, seeking information or clarification which is 'reasonably necessary and proportionate to enable the first party to prepare his own case or to understand the case he has to meet'.

Case management

5.148   Thereafter both parties file a document known as an allocation questionnaire (sent by the court) within the timeline provided for by the court. This document details various issues to assist the court with managing the case, such as the estimated duration of the trial, the number and type of witnesses (witnesses of fact, expert witnesses etc) and the costs incurred to date[78]. Often both parties will then attempt to agree a timetable for the case to progress, known as directions. These will provide for the full exchange of information, including disclosure[79], further expert evidence and witness statements, and a timeframe for the actual trial. If a timetable cannot be agreed between the parties, the court can hold a hearing (increasingly done by telephone) known as a case management conference (CMC) to determine what directions should be made. Upon serving the allocation questionnaire, the claimant may also serve a reply to the defence under CPR 1998, r 15.8.

5.149   There are a great number of other requirements with which the parties must comply, and the above summary merely provides a cursory overview of some of the key provisions.

Other pre-trial considerations

5.150   In practice, many actions against the police settle before going to trial, usually as a result of an offer of compensation by the defendant in return for which the claimant agrees to permanently discontinue the case. Settlement has advantages and disadvantages for the claimant, which are likely to be more pronounced in protest cases. The main advantages of settling a case for the

---

76   CPR 15.4.
77   CPR 10.1.
78   CPR 26.
79   In accordance with CPR 31.6.

claimant are that it provides a swifter resolution of the matter, and certainty as to the outcome. One of the main disadvantages is that a negotiated settlement often does not entail an admission of liability or even an apology. Depending on the terms of the settlement, it may also prevent the claimant from publicising the outcome of the case.

5.151   In protest cases, where the financial value of the claim is unlikely to be very substantial and compensation is not usually the primary motivation for bringing the case, settlement may therefore seem an unattractive prospect. However, as set out above, the CPR 1998 encourages early settlement without the need to seek recourse to the courts. The CPR contains various provisions which firmly push parties in that proposed direction. For example, either party can make a settlement offer in the format provided for under r 36 of the CPR 1998, commonly known as a 'Part 36 offer'. In summary, r 36 puts in place severe cost implications where parties refuse to accept an offer which, at trial, transpires to have been reasonable. This means that Part 36 offers must be taken very seriously. For legally aided clients, there is an added responsibility to justify ongoing funding by ensuring that litigation is conducted reasonably. In practice, an appropriate financial offer will often have to be accepted, or Legal Aid will be withdrawn.

5.152   It is therefore essential to consider from the outset what the aims of litigation are and whether they can realistically be achieved. Whilst financial value is not the sole factor that a court or the LSC will consider, it is certainly a very significant one. Another important factor in protest cases will often be the infringements of fundamental rights, but this does not mean that all protest-related cases where a breach of human rights is alleged will avoid the general restrictions of the CPR and public funding requirements.

5.153   There are mechanisms by which non-financial aims can be achieved in the course of settlement, and these should be given consideration early on. There are no hard and fast rules as to what can and cannot form part of the terms of settlement. Whilst admissions of liability are rare in actions against the police in all but the strongest cases, apologies are more often forthcoming. The distinction between the two need not always be as great as first appears, and sometimes a form of wording can be agreed which achieves the desired aim, particularly where the terms of settlement do not contain a confidentiality clause preventing the outcome from being publicised.

5.154   In cases of individual wrongdoing, such as officers displaying discriminatory behaviour which was not, or not adequately, addressed in the course of a complaint, an impact statement can be drawn up on behalf of the claimant, and its consideration by the officers and possibly their supervisors can form part of a negotiated settlement.

Heads of claim

5.155   As with the complaint system, it is for the claimant to make out the relevant legal and evidential requirements in a claim against the police, because the burden is on the claimant to prove, on the balance of probabilities, that their allegations are substantiated. There are a large number of potential causes of action available to protesters, depending on the circumstances of the case. Some of the most common causes of action arising out of protests, and the limitations that apply to them, have been set out in brief terms below.

Assault and battery

5.156   These are technically two separate causes of action, but in practice they are almost always pleaded simultaneously and are sometimes, erroneously, treated as almost interchangeable. Battery is the intentional or reckless application of force resulting in physical touching. The claimant does not need to suffer injury as a result of the force for it to amount to a battery (although whether or not an injury resulted, and the degree of such injury, will impact on the value of the claim and therefore also the availability of public funding).

5.157   In the context of protests, the following could all amount to a battery if the application of force was unjustified:

- pushing/touching by police in the course of the imposition of a kettle or police line;

- any touching as a result of unlawful searches carried out;

- handcuffing in the course of an arrest;

- taking of DNA/fingerprints at the police station.

5.158   Clearly, more extreme applications of force may also amount to a battery, such as:

- shield or baton strikes;

- CS gas or pepper spray;

- force used in the application of police dogs;

- horse charges.

5.159   Assault, in contrast to battery, does not even require any physical contact. The claimant need only establish that the defendant committed an act which caused the claimant to reasonably apprehend that the defendant intended to immediately commit a battery.

5.160   An assault may arise in the context of demonstrations and marches where protesters reasonably believe they will be subjected to immediate force, for example as a result of horse charges, or where lines of riot police rush at protesters. Taken together then, assault and battery can be defined as the infliction, or reasonable apprehension of the immediate infliction, of unlawful hostile force[80].

5.161   However not all use of force by police will amount to an assault or battery, as the police have wide powers to use force in the course of searching, arresting, and detaining people. The use of force becomes unlawful in broadly two circumstances:

(a)   where it was unlawful to apply any force at all because the police were not acting within their powers; or

(b)   notwithstanding that it was lawful to apply force, the extent of that force was unreasonable.

5.162   Whether or not the police were acting within their powers will depend on whether the relevant power was properly exercised. The power to arrest and the power to stop and search are discussed respectively at paras **1.74** and **1.161**. For example, where a search is conducted on a protester under the auspices of the Criminal Justice and Public Order Act 1994, s 60[81], but no valid authorisation for such a search is in place, the search will be unlawful and all force used as a result will amount to a battery. Similarly, if a protester is stopped for a search under PACE 1984, s 1, but the officer has no reasonable grounds to suspect that s/he was in possession of a stolen or prohibited article, such a search would be unlawful. Note that, in the case of a stop and search, a failure to comply with PACE Code A will not necessarily make a search unlawful[82].

5.163   As set out at para **1.168**, an arrest will only be lawful if:

(i)   an officer has reasonable grounds to suspect the person being arrested has, or is about to, commit an offence[83], and

(ii)   the person being arrested is informed of the fact they are under arrest, provided it is reasonably practicable to do so[84]; and

(iii)   an officer has reasonable grounds for believing that it is necessary to arrest the person in question for a reason listed in PACE 1984, s 24(5) (see paras **1.174** and **1.175**).

---

80 See for example *Collins v Wilcock* [1984] 1 WLR 1172 and *Wilson v Pringle* [1987] QB 237.
81 See para **1.106**.
82 PACE 1984, s 67(10).
83 PACE 1984, s 24.
84 PACE 1984, s 28.

If these conditions are made out, the police are entitled to use reasonable force to execute the arrest[85]. However, if any of these conditions is not made out, the police will not be lawfully exercising their powers. Any physical contact made as part of, or after, the arrest will therefore amount to a battery. For example, where a police officer arrests a protester on suspicion that they have caused criminal damage in the course of a demonstration, but lacks sufficient evidence to reasonably support such a suspicion, the arrest may be unlawful.

5.164   If an officer uses force, even minimal force, without the intention of arresting an individual, but solely for the purpose of detaining them for further conversation and to complete enquiries, the officer is acting unlawfully. In *Ludlow v Burgess*[86], the court stated that:

'Here is a detention of a man against his will without arrest. On any view that is unlawful and a serious interference with a citizen's liberty and in those circumstances it cannot be an act performed in the execution of a police officer's duty ...'

5.165   Further, in *Wood v Director of Public Prosecutions*[87] Latham LJ stated at para 7 that:

'Where a police officer restrains a person, but does not at that time intend or purport to arrest him, then he is committing an assault, even if an arrest would have been justified'.

5.166   In addition to the various powers set out in Chapter 1, which carry a power to use reasonable force in the execution of each particular duty, the police (like all members of the public) also have a have a power to use such force as is reasonable in the circumstances to prevent crime[88]. This is most frequently relied upon when police officers claim to be acting in self-defence. This could be relevant where, for example, the police were in attendance at a demonstration but not actively policing, ie not attempting to impose a kettle or arrest or search someone, and claimed to have used force in response to being attacked by a protester.

5.167   The second manner in which the use of force by police officers can amount to a battery is where an officer is lawfully applying force in the execution of their duty, but the degree of force used is excessive. What amounts to an excessive amount of force will depend greatly on the circumstances. For example, where a protester is arrested for obstructing a highway and is doing so

---

85   PACE 1984, s 117.
86   (1982) 75 CAR 227.
87   [2008] EWHC 1056 (Admin).
88   Criminal Law Act 1967, s 3.

entirely peacefully without any threat of violence but equally is not responding to requests to move, an officer would be entitled to use reasonable force to arrest that person and take them to a police station to be processed. Such force may entail lifting the protester up to remove them from the road. However, the officer would not be justified in applying baton or shield strikes or kicks. Similarly, if the protester (having been moved out of the road) subsequently fully cooperates and complies with requests to get into a police van, the application of handcuffs could amount to an excessive use of force.

5.168   Much more ambiguous, however, are arrests in the course of rapidly escalating events, which will often be the case where large-scale protests are taking place. In those circumstances, the application of handcuffs is less likely to be considered excessive. Similarly, if a protester has for example linked their arms through a railing and is refusing to cooperate with requests to desist from doing so, the police may be entitled to apply considerable force to ensure the protester releases his grip.

5.169   In principle, officers are trained to use the minimum amount of force necessary, and then to employ increasing levels of force on an escalating scale if their initial efforts are fruitless. Officers are, however, often afforded a degree of discretion by the courts, and they do not have to religiously follow each step in the scale.

5.170   A claim for assault and battery needs to be issued within three years of the date of the incident.

False imprisonment

5.171   *Halsbury's Laws of England* states that 'To compel a person to remain in a given place is an imprisonment'. There are two elements to the tort of false imprisonment. First, the claimant must establish on the balance of probabilities, the fact that he or she was detained. The burden then shifts to the defendant to establish that there was lawful authority to justify the detention[89].

5.172   The police have a power to detain individuals if they are lawfully exercising their powers of arrest, or for the purposes of a stop and search, as well as a power to detain at the police station following arrest. If the power is not lawfully exercised then all or part of the period for which someone is detained could amount to false imprisonment (alongside any force being used amounting to a battery).

---

89 See for example *Lumba v Secretary of State for the Home Department* [2011] UKSC 12, para 65 and *Clerk & Lindsell on Torts* (20th edn).

5.173 For example, if no reasonable grounds existed to suspect a protester of committing an offence, the arrest and entire subsequent detention may become unlawful because the arrest did not comply with the requirements set out in PACE 1984, s 24[90]. If, conversely, an arrest is established to be unlawful because a police officer failed to inform a protester of the reasons for their arrest as soon as it became reasonably practicable to do so (contrary to PACE 1984, s 28) the arrest will be unlawful up to the point the provisions under PACE 1984, s 28 are complied with, which will usually be at the point the protester is booked into police custody and the custody sergeant informs them of the basis for their arrest and detention.

5.174 The powers of police to detain protesters in a 'kettle' (alongside bystanders who are inadvertently caught up in the containment) are discussed above in detail at para **1.131** ff.

5.175 A claim for false imprisonment may also arise where a protester's detention is initially lawful, but where they are subsequently detained for longer than necessary, or for longer than is authorised in PACE 1984[91]. Whether a detention is for an unreasonably long period will depend on the individual circumstances, and the reasons upon which the police have formed the view that an arrest was necessary (as required by PACE 1984, s 24(5)). The most common justification (under PACE 1984, s 24(5)(e)) is 'to allow the prompt and effective investigation of the offence or of the conduct of the person in question'. This reason is often cited where, for example, an individual is detained for the purposes of being interviewed, or where a search of their house is being carried out. If the detention continues after those investigatory steps have been completed, it may amount to a false imprisonment. The reasons for an arrest should be noted on the front page of the custody record.

5.176 In recent years, claims for false imprisonment have also been brought (some successfully) by way of a challenge to the necessity of an arrest as required by PACE 1984, s 24(5) arguing that the detention amounted to false imprisonment from the outset because the arrest was not necessary for the purpose noted. Such a challenge may arise, for example, where a protester is arrested for the purpose of conducting an interview, but the protester made it clear that they were willing to attend the police station and be interviewed voluntarily. This alone may not make the arrest unlawful, but claims can be considered in these circumstances.

---

90 See para **1.168**.
91 See para **1.201**.

5.177   A claim for false imprisonment must be issued within six years of the date of the incident, or three years of the date of the incident if it contains a claim for personal injury (for example, a psychiatric injury as a result of the detention).

Malicious prosecution

5.178   The tort of malicious prosecution should be considered by protesters who have been subject to a criminal prosecution and where the criminal case has ultimately been terminated in their favour. A case will be considered to have terminated in someone's favour if the prosecution is discontinued by the CPS before or during the criminal trial, if the case is dismissed by the court (for example after half-time submissions) or if the protester is ultimately acquitted or succeeds in quashing the conviction on appeal. It may also apply where a protester has accepted a bindover[92] providing the bindover was agreed by the defence in advance of the trial and the prosecution subsequently offered no evidence[93]. A claim for malicious prosecution can sometimes be brought where the claimant has pleaded guilty to some (usually lesser) offences, and is acquitted of others.

5.179   However, a claim for malicious prosecution cannot be brought in all cases which have concluded in the protester's favour, and in fact is only likely to succeed in a very small number of circumstances. This is because a claimant must establish not only that a prosecution was instigated and concluded in their favour, but that the police lacked 'reasonable and probable cause' in bringing the prosecution, and that they acted maliciously.

5.180   In *Hicks v Faulkner*[94] Judge Hawkins interpreted the requirement of 'reasonable and probable cause' to mean:

> '[An] honest belief in the guilt of the accused based upon a full conviction, founded on reasonable grounds, of the existence of a state of circumstances which, assuming them to be true, would reasonably lead any ordinary prudent and cautious man, placed in the position of the accuser, to the conclusion that the person charged was probably guilty of the crime imputed'.

5.181   To establish a lack of reasonable and probable cause a claimant would have to establish either that the prosecutor did not believe in the guilt of the claimant, or that 'a person of ordinary prudence and caution would not

---

92   See para **3.183**.

93   *Hourihane v Metropolitan Police Commissioner* (1994) Times, 27 December, CA.

94   (1878) 8 QBD, para 167, as cited by the European Court of Human Rights in *Osman v United Kingdom* (2000) 29 EHRR 245.

conclude in the light of the facts honestly believed at the time that the claimant was probably guilty of the relevant offence'.

5.182   In addition to establishing a lack of reasonable and probable cause, a claimant must prove that the police acted maliciously in that their motive was one which was other than that of simply instituting a prosecution for the purpose of bringing a person to justice[95]. However, a lack of honest belief cannot be inferred simply from a malicious motive in bringing the prosecution[96].

5.183   Both these elements of the tort are therefore clearly difficult to establish, and careful consideration should be given to the realistic prospects of success before a claim is instigated. In particular, claimants often feel understandably aggrieved when they are acquitted and a judge makes comments about the limited evidence to support the allegation, or the credibility of the officers' account. Whilst these factors may indicate a more sinister underlying motive, a prosecution brought for a proper cause but on limited evidence will not amount to a malicious prosecution (although in rare circumstances it could amount to negligence). Protesters should also bear in mind the different burdens and standards of proof in criminal and civil proceedings: a claimant may not be able to establish on the balance of probabilities that the police acted without reasonable and probable cause, and with malice, simply because the prosecution were not able to establish beyond reasonable doubt that the person prosecuted committed an offence.

5.184   However, claims for malicious prosecution can attract substantial damages and play an important role in holding the police to account. They should certainly be considered in circumstances where a claimant believes the officers fabricated evidence in support of a prosecution, for example a charge of assaulting or obstructing a police officer, to cover up their own wrongdoings.

5.185   It should also be noted that a claim for malicious prosecution is not actionable per se, which means that a claim can only be brought if the claimant can establish damage has resulted from the prosecution. The type of damage for which a claim can be brought is limited to damage to property, reputation, freedom or person. This will include financial losses (for example loss of earnings) or psychiatric injury caused by the prosecution. Damage to reputation will not arise out of all prosecutions, and will often depend on the type and circumstances of the charge. For example, charges brought for offences that allege dishonesty are more likely to be considered by the court to be capable of causing damage to reputation. In relation to loss of liberty, it will be sufficient if

---

95   *Stevens v Midland Counties Railway Co* (1854) 10 Ex, para 352.
96   *Glinski v McIver* [1962] AC 726.

a claimant can establish that they were prosecuted for an offence punishable by loss of liberty. The claimant does not necessarily need to establish an actual loss of liberty[97].

5.186 A claim for malicious prosecution must be issued within six years of the date of the criminal proceedings concluding in the claimant's favour, or three years in the event of the claim including a personal injury element.

Claims under the HRA 1998

5.187 The Human Rights Act 1998 (HRA 1998) brought into legal effect the fundamental rights and freedoms contained in the European Convention on Human Rights (ECHR). As a consequence, it is unlawful for a public authority to act in a way which is incompatible with a Convention right[98]. Police forces, and the officers employed by them, will amount to public authorities for the purpose of the HRA 1998, as indeed will courts who are under a duty, wherever possible, to interpret English law in a manner that is compatible with the ECHR. If a public authority acts in a way that is incompatible with the ECHR a person may bring proceedings against the authority if he can establish that he is a victim of that unlawful act[99]. A person may also rely on a Convention right in any other legal proceedings[100], such as when defending a criminal prosecution[101] or bringing a claim for judicial review[102]. The courts have a discretion to award damages in a civil action for breaches of Convention rights if they are necessary to afford just satisfaction, but in practice these damages are often relatively low, and sometimes add only nominal value to a tortious claim arising out of the same facts.

5.188 In some cases, bringing a claim under the HRA 1998 in addition to a tortious claim will therefore serve little purpose, and may simply cause procedural difficulties because of the short limitation period. This may be the case with Article 5, which significantly overlaps with the law on false imprisonment. However, sometimes reliance on the HRA 1998 is invaluable, especially where the Convention right covers or includes a factual scenario not previously tested or considered in common law. In addition, only those cases that have pleaded breaches of Convention rights in the domestic courts can be brought before the European Court[103].

---

97 *Whiffen v Bailey & Romford Urban District Council* [1915] 1 KB 600, CA.
98 HRA 1998, s 6(1).
99 Section 7(1).
100 Ibid.
101 See para **3.121**.
102 See para **5.220**.
103 Applications to the European Court are well beyond the scope of this book. However, it is worth noting that only a fraction of domestic cases are afforded permission to bring a

5.189   The rights and freedoms in the ECHR can be categorised into absolute rights, which can never be limited, and qualified rights which can be balanced and limited in order to ensure other people's rights and freedoms are not infringed. Most of the relevant rights and freedoms to protest law are qualified. This means that a public authority is entitled to limit them in certain circumstances.

5.190   *Article 5: the right to liberty and security of person.* Article 5 enshrines the right to liberty and is an absolute right, but one which contains a finite list of exceptions. Article 5(1) sets out:

> 'Everyone has the right to liberty and security of person. No one shall be deprived of his liberty save in the following cases and in accordance with a procedure prescribed by law:

> (a)   the lawful detention of a person after conviction by a competent court;

> (b)   the lawful arrest or detention of a person for non-compliance with the lawful order of a court or in order to secure the fulfilment of any obligation prescribed by law;

> (c)   the lawful arrest or detention of a person effected for the purpose of bringing him before the competent legal authority on reasonable suspicion of having committed an offence or when it is reasonably considered necessary to prevent his committing an offence or fleeing after having done so;

> (d)   the detention of a minor by lawful order for the purpose of educational supervision or his lawful detention for the purpose of bringing him before the competent legal authority;

> (e)   the lawful detention of persons for the prevention of the spreading of infectious diseases, of persons of unsound mind, alcoholics or drug addicts or vagrants;

> (f)   the lawful arrest or detention of a person to prevent his effecting an unauthorised entry into the country or of a person against whom action is being taken with a view to deportation or extradition'.

5.191   In civil actions, the remit of Article 5 overlaps significantly (and sometimes entirely) with the law on false imprisonment. Sometimes it will add little or nothing to a claim for false imprisonment and is not even pleaded,

---

challenge before the European Court, and one crucial precondition of those cases is that all domestic remedies have been exhausted prior to making the application.

particularly where limitation has passed. However, some cases have explicitly underlined the importance of Article 5 in the context of considering the lawfulness of an arrest. So, for example, in *Al-Fayed v Metropolitan Police Commissioner* the judge emphasised that:

> '... it seems to me that it is necessary to bear in mind that the right to liberty under Article 5 was engaged and that any decision to arrest had to take into account the importance of this right ...'[104].

5.192   However, he went on to say that:

> '... It has to be remembered that the protection provided by Article 5 is against arbitrary arrest. The European Court of Human Rights in *Fox, Campbell and Hartley* held that the protection required by the article was met by the requirement that there must be "reasonable grounds" for the arrest. I do not therefore consider that Article 5 required the court to evaluate the exercise of discretion in any different way from the exercise of any other executive discretion, although it must do so ... in the light of the important right to liberty which was at stake'.

5.193   These comments exemplify the slightly ambiguous use of Convention rights in civil actions. Clearly, in *Al-Fayed* the judge saw fit to mention Article 5, and appeared to place some considerable importance on its applicability in the context of a challenge to the legality of an arrest. Nevertheless, the judgment stops short of suggesting Article 5 afforded the claimant any additional protection above and beyond those contained in the common law.

5.194   Article 5 also contains some procedural safeguards, such as the right to be informed promptly of arrest[105] and the right to be brought promptly before a court[106] which, in broad terms, also mirror the procedural domestic requirements. Article 5 has, however, been an important provision in the context of protest law, and in particular in relation to the police's use of kettling.

5.195   *Article 8: Right to respect for private and family life.* Article 8 of the ECHR states:

> '1 Everyone has the right to respect for his private and family life, his home and his correspondence.

---

104   [2004] EWCA Civ 1579, para 43.
105   Article 5(2).
106   Article 5(3).

2 There shall be no interference by a public authority with the exercise of this right except such as is in accordance with the law and is necessary in a democratic society in the interests of national security, public safety or the economic well-being of the country, for the prevention of disorder or crime, for the protection of health or morals, or for the protection of the rights and freedoms of others'.

5.196   Article 8(2) makes it clear that this is a qualified right, which can be restricted in a broad range of circumstances. Article 8 can be a very useful provision in the context of protest law, and has (amongst many other things) been used to challenge the application of stop and search laws[107]. Activists may also, for example, seek to rely on Article 8 to challenge the retention of films, photographs and data on the Police National Computer.

5.197   *Article 10: Freedom of expression.* Article 10 sets out that:

'1 Everyone has the right to freedom of expression. This right shall include freedom to hold opinions and to receive and impart information and ideas without interference by public authority and regardless of frontiers. This article shall not prevent States from requiring the licensing of broadcasting, television or cinema enterprises.

2 The exercise of these freedoms, since it carries with it duties and responsibilities, may be subject to such formalities, conditions, restrictions or penalties as are prescribed by law and are necessary in a democratic society, in the interests of national security, territorial integrity or public safety, for the prevention of disorder or crime, for the protection of health or morals, for the protection of the reputation or rights of others, for preventing the disclosure of information received in confidence, or for maintaining the authority and impartiality of the judiciary'.

5.198   Like Article 8, Article 10 is a qualified right by virtue of Article 10(2). The relevance of Article 10 in the context of protest law is immediately obvious, and it has been pleaded extensively by activists seeking to express their political views[108] and in the course of the 'McLibel' case[109], albeit with varying degrees of success.

5.199   Article 10 has also successfully been utilised (alongside Article 11) in the context of defensive action on behalf of political activists. In *Vogt v*

---

107   See for example Case 4158/05 *Gillan and Quinton v United Kingdom* [2010] ECHR 28.
108   See for example *Appleby v United Kingdom* (2003) 37 EHRR 783.
109   *Steel and Morris v United Kingdom* (2005) 41 EHRR 22.

Germany[110] the European Court held that Articles 10 and 11 the ECHR were violated when Ms Vogt was dismissed from her post as a result of her membership of the German Communist Party.

5.200 The European Court has indicated that some forms of protest deserve a particularly high degree of protection under Article 10. Where a protest engages with 'a debate on a matter of general concern and [constitutes] political and militant expression … a high level of protection of the right to freedom of expression is required under Article 10'[111].

5.201 *Article 11: the freedom of assembly and association.* Article 11 sets out that:

'1 Everyone has the right to freedom of peaceful assembly and to freedom of association with others, including the right to form and to join trade unions for the protection of his interests.

2 No restrictions shall be placed on the exercise of these rights other than such as are prescribed by law and are necessary in a democratic society in the interests of national security or public safety, for the prevention of disorder or crime, for the protection of health or morals or for the protection of the rights and freedoms of others. This article shall not prevent the imposition of lawful restrictions on the exercise of these rights by members of the armed forces, of the police or of the administration of the State'.

5.202 Again, like Articles 8 and 10, Article 11 is a qualified right by virtue of Article 11(2). It has been extensively and successfully applied in the context of demonstrations. It applies to a range of protests, including marches, sit-ins and meetings. Before Article 11 there was no explicit common law right to protest, although there was no common law prohibition on protest either. In *Bączkowski v Poland*[112] the European Court held that the banning of an LGBT pride parade in Warsaw was in violation of Article 11 of the European Convention on Human Rights, holding that:

'This obligation is of particular importance for persons holding unpopular views or belonging to minorities, because they are more vulnerable to victimisation'[113].

---

110 (1996) 21 EHRR 205.
111 *Lindon v France* (2008) 46 EHRR 35.
112 Application No 1543/06 (2009) 48 EHRR 19.
113 *Bączkowski v Poland* (Application No 1543/06) (2009) 48 EHRR 19, para 64.

5.203   The right also covers the freedom to form and join trade unions and other associations and has been successfully invoked to protect strike action. In *Demir and Baykara v Turkey*[114] the European Court affirmed the fundamental right of workers to engage in collective bargaining and take collective action.

5.204   Articles 5, 8, 10 and 11 were pleaded in many of the recent domestic protest cases, such as *R (on the application of Hannah McClure and Joshua Moos) v Commissioner of Police of the Metropolis*[115] and *Castle v Commissioner of Police of the Metropolis*[116], both discussed in more detail at para **1.152** ff.

5.205   *Article 14: Prohibition on discrimination.* Article 14 contains a prohibition on discrimination in respect of rights under the Convention. Whilst Article 14 specifically prohibits discrimination based on 'sex, race, colour, language, religion, political or other opinion, national or social origin, association with a national minority, property, birth or other status'. 'Other status' leaves the door open for the court to rule that discrimination has occurred on the basis of other characteristics, as it has in the past with, for example, sexual orientation.

5.206   Article 14 is however a 'parasitic' right, and cannot be relied upon in isolation. It affords for the enjoyment of other rights free from the constraints of discrimination and an applicant must therefore prove discrimination in the enjoyment of a specific right that is guaranteed elsewhere in the Convention.

5.207   Some of the cases referred to above pleaded Article 14 in conjunction with other articles, for example *Bączkowski v Poland*[117], in which the applicant argued not only an infringement of his rights under Article 11, but persuaded the court that a breach of Article 14 had occurred, because other marches on the same day had not been subject to the same conditions as the gay rights march and were allowed to take place.

5.208   By virtue of the HRA 1998, s 7 all proceedings under the HRA 1998 must be brought within the period of one year beginning with the date on which the act complained of took place. The same section does afford the courts a discretion to extend that time limit to a period it 'considers equitable having regard to all the circumstances'.

---

114   [2008] ECHR 1345.
115   [2012] EWCA Civ 12.
116   [2011] EWHC 2317 (Admin).
117   Application No 1543/06 (2009) 48 EHRR 19.

Other claims: discrimination, breaches of the Data Protection Act, harassment

5.209   There are many more potential causes of action than those listed in this book that protesters may wish to consider when bringing a claim against the police. They are simply too numerous to cover in their entirety, and certainly to cover in any detail. However, some additional heads of claim are very briefly summarised below, simply to reflect the scope for potential legal action.

5.210   *Discrimination.* In addition to the provisions under the ECHR, Article 14 (which can only be relied upon in the context of the enjoyment of another Convention right) domestic law does afford for protection from discrimination. Until recently, there were a number of separate laws prohibiting discrimination on the basis of *inter alia* race[118], gender[119] and disability[120]. However, much of the anti-discrimination law has now been consolidated in the Equality Act 2010, most of which came into force on 1 October 2010. It sets out various protected characteristics[121] and lists the types of conduct that is prohibited in relation to those characteristics[122]. The protected characteristics include religion or belief, which explicitly includes a reference to a lack of belief[123], but notably make no reference to political views or opinions.

5.211   The Equality Act 2010 makes provisions for the complainant to send the potential defendant a questionnaire to seek further information, which can be useful not only to obtain an insight into the defendant's position, but also because a failure to answer a question can lead to the court drawing an inference against the defendant.

5.212   Claims for discrimination under the Equality Act 2010 must be brought within six months of the date of the act to which the claim relates, or such other period as the court thinks just and equitable[124]. The questionnaire should also be submitted before the expiration of the six months time limit.

5.213   *Data Protection Act 1998.* The Data Protection Act 1998 (DPA 1998) developed a set of 'data protection principles'[125] governing the handling of personal data and 'sensitive personal data'[126]. Sensitive personal data includes

---

118   Race Relations Act 1976 as amended by the Race Relations (Amendment) Act 2000.
119   Sex Discrimination Act 1975.
120   Disability Discrimination Act 1995.
121   Equality Act 2010, Ch 1.
122   Equality Act 2010, Ch 2.
123   Equality Act 2010, s 10(2).
124   Equality Act 2010, s 118.
125   DPA 1998, Sch 1.
126   As defined by the DPA 1998, s 2.

information about an individual's political opinions[127]. The principles include a requirement for information to be accurate and kept up to date[128] and for information to be obtained and processed only for one or more specified and lawful purposes, and for it not to be further processed in any manner incompatible with that purpose or those purposes[129].

5.214   An individual may be able to recover compensation if a data controller breaches certain requirements set out in the Act. Compensation will usually only be awarded if the individual has suffered damage as a result of the breach. A person can, however, also claim for distress if the data was collected for a 'special purpose'[130] or if the victim of the breach has suffered both damage and distress[131].

5.215   Activists may wish to consider the provisions of the DPA 1998 if they are concerned that the police are passing information about their political activities to third parties, or are otherwise using the information in a manner other than that envisaged by the Act. Similarly, if the police fail to ensure that records kept are accurate (for example where they have wrongly recorded an arrest resulting in a conviction rather than no charge) the DPA 1998 can be used to rectify the matter, and in certain circumstances obtain compensation.

5.216   In addition, the DPA 1998 entitles individuals to:

- obtain copies of information held against them;

- be told whether any personal data is being processed;

- be given a description of the personal data, the reasons it is being processed, and whether it will be given to any other organisations or people;

- be given a copy of the information comprising the data; and

- be given details of the source of the data (where this is available)[132].

The right is triggered by making a written request and paying a fee.

5.217   *Harassment.* Under the Protection from Harassment Act 1997 an individual may be able to bring a claim against the police where officers' actions have caused alarm or distress to a person. The Act imposes both criminal and civil liability for harassment. Whilst a claim for harassment may

---

127   DPA 1998, s 2(b).
128   DPA 1998, Sch 1, para 4.
129   DPA 1998, Sch 1, para 2.
130   As defined in the DPA 1998, s 3.
131   DPA 1998, s 13.
132   DPA 1998, s 7.

appear to be a viable alternative where the police's conduct falls short of one of heads of claim set out above, these cases often fail. This is because the Act provides for various defences on which the police will often seek to rely, including where they can show that the course of conduct

'(a)   ... was pursued for the purpose of preventing or detecting crime,

(b)   ... was pursued under any enactment or rule of law or to comply with any condition or requirement imposed by any person under any enactment, or

(c)   ... that in the particular circumstances the pursuit of the course of conduct was reasonable'[133].

5.218   In particular, the first and last of these defences afford the police a considerable amount of leeway in their actions. However, activists may wish to consider a claim for harassment if, for example, police are repeatedly attending their home or stopping and searching them without any apparent lawful basis.

Costs

5.219   As set out above, a major consideration for activists contemplating any civil action must be the potential cost implications. The importance of this consideration cannot be over-emphasised, as legal costs in these cases mount incredibly swiftly and can become very significant indeed. Courts can, and very frequently do, order costs to be paid by the losing party, and where an activist brings a civil action or judicial review claim without the protection of Legal Aid or After the Event insurance, they can face cost orders of tens of thousands of pounds. Specific legal advice should therefore always be sought before bringing proceedings.

JUDICIAL REVIEW PROCEEDINGS

5.220   Judicial review is a means by which to challenge the lawfulness of the exercise of power by public bodies through the courts. Applications for judicial review are heard by the Administrative Court section of the High Court. The relevance of judicial review in the context of criminal proceedings is discussed at para **2.120**. This section considers judicial review in further detail in the context of police accountability. However, as with civil actions, public law challenges by way of judicial review are complex legal proceedings, and

---

133   PHA 1997, s 1(3).

activists should seek tailored advice from specialist solicitors at the earliest opportunity.

Judicial review claims can only be brought where it is alleged that the public authority being challenged has made an error, or errors, of law. The issue is always confined to legal argument and it is very rare indeed for the court to hear evidence or decide contested issues of fact. In practice, the account of the facts as put forward by the public authority will most often have to be accepted and the argument will centre on whether the public authority's actions, given those facts, amounted to an error of law.

Preliminary considerations

5.221 Before even commencing judicial review proceedings, the person bringing the claim (known as a claimant, as with civil actions) should carefully consider whether judicial review is the most appropriate mechanism by which to challenge a decision.

Public bodies

5.222 Judicial review proceedings can only be brought against public bodies, which can include private companies carrying out public functions. Decisions made by the police, CPS and IPCC will certainly fall within the definition.

Standing or sufficient interest

5.223 Judicial review proceedings can only be brought by a claimant who has sufficient interest in bringing a claim[134]. This is unlikely to cause a protester any difficulty where the decision directly impacts on a determination in the context of their criminal matter or police complaint. However, for activists who wish to utilise judicial review to challenge the lawfulness of public bodies in a broader sense this can pose problems. Fortunately, the courts have taken a fairly lenient view of the issue.

5.224 In *R v Secretary of State for Foreign Affairs, ex p The World Development Movement*[135] the World Development Movement (WDM) was held to be entitled to challenge the decision of Britain's Foreign Secretary to spend over £2 million on a development project to build a hydroelectric dam in Malaysia. It was decided in that case that the WDM were best placed to mount

---

134 Senior Courts Act 1981, s 31(3).
135 [1995] 1 WLR 386, [1995] 1 All ER 611.

the challenge. The case also cited another judgment[136] which raised concerns about the implications of preventing pressure groups from bringing judicial review proceedings, stating that 'a grave lacuna in our system of public law' could arise:

> 'if a pressure group, like the federation, or even a public spirited taxpayer, were prevented … from bringing the matter to the attention of the court to vindicate the rule of law and get the unlawful conduct stopped'.

5.225 Where the application includes a challenge on the basis of Convention rights the claimant will also have to establish that s/he is a victim for the purpose of the HRA 1998[137].

Alternative remedies

5.226 Judicial review will, however, rarely be the most appropriate course of action where there are alternative remedies available, such as where a statutory right of appeal exists. For example, in theory a challenge could be brought against the Professional Standards Department of a police force following an unlawful decision made by the PSD in the context of a complaint investigation. However, in those circumstances the complainant has an obvious appeal route to the IPCC and therefore a judicial review is unlikely to be the most appropriate route by which to challenge the decision.

5.227 In addition, protesters will often be presented with a factual background that incorporates both public law elements (best challenged by judicial review) and private law elements (best challenged by way of a civil action). Careful consideration should be given as to which remedy is most appropriate, and which will offer the best prospects of success in the circumstances. In some cases, the best course of action will be to mount a civil action and a public law challenge in tandem.

Funding

5.228 In principle, Legal Aid is available for judicial review challenges, subject to the same means and merits tests set out at para **5.21**. Because the primary aim of a judicial review is not to obtain financial compensation, the cost/benefit test does not apply in the same strict financial terms. A claimant will still have to show that the decision which is the subject of the proposed challenge is sufficiently significant (either to them, or the wider public) to merit

---

136 *R v Inland Revenue Commissioners, ex p National Federation of Self Employed and Small Businesses Ltd* [1982] AC 617.
137 HRA 1998, s 7.

public funding. Trivial, technical challenges are unlikely to attract Legal Aid. However, costs mount up very quickly in judicial review proceedings, and Legal Aid is therefore reluctantly granted. To maximise prospects of obtaining Legal Aid, all efforts made to exhaust alternative remedies should be emphasised in the funding application.

5.229   Neither a Conditional Fee Agreement (CFA) nor funding by way of insurance is likely to be available in judicial review proceedings. Therefore the only option in the absence of Legal Aid will be to fund the matter privately (either as an individual or as a group), but with punitively high costs of bringing the claim, and the substantial risk of becoming liable for the defendant's costs in the event the case is lost, this is rarely a viable alternative.

5.230   If the claim relates to an issue of significant wider public interest (and in practice is therefore likely to attract publicity), it is sometimes possible to find lawyers who will act *pro bono* (for free) to cover the costs of the claimant. That only leaves the risk of having to pay defendant's costs in the event of a loss. In extreme circumstances, the court may be willing to grant a Protective Costs Order (PCO) to an individual or group bringing the action. A PCO is an order made by the court at the outset of proceedings which provides that the party applying for the order shall, regardless of the outcome of the proceedings, either not be liable at all for the other party's costs or be liable only for a fixed proportion thereof[138]. In practice, the courts are much more likely to limit the costs than remove cost liability altogether. The court will take into consideration various factors when assessing an application for a PCO, including whether the challenge raises issues of general public importance, whether the public interest requires that those issues should be resolved and whether the applicant has a private interest in the outcome of the case. It will also consider the financial resources of both parties, and whether proceedings would be discontinued but for the PCO.

Time limits

5.231   The time limit for submitting an application for judicial review is very strict, and shorter than any of the other civil limitation periods discussed in this book. An application for judicial review must be brought promptly, and in any event within three months from the date of the decision challenged[139]. A claim for judicial review can be refused if there is undue delay, even if it is brought within three months. An ignorance of the time limits will not prevent the claim from failing if it is brought out of time.

---

138   See *R v Lord Chancellor, ex p Child Poverty Action Group* [1999] 1 WLR 347.
139   Senior Courts Act 1981, s 31(6) and CPR 54.5.

Civil Procedure Rules 1998

5.232   Judicial review proceedings have their own distinct set of rules in the CPR at CPR 54, as well as a separate Pre-Action Protocol. The rules set out time limits for serving and responding to the claim. In addition, r 54.4 sets out that, even prior to any substantive hearing, the court must grant permission to allow a claim to progress. Many claims are refused permission at this stage. There are provisions that allow for the renewal of the permission application, but many claims are nevertheless refused permission. As with civil actions, a failure to comply with some of the provisions in CPR 54 can lead to the claim failing in its entirety.

Political considerations

5.233   A final issue to consider when contemplating judicial review proceedings is the broader ramifications of an action. Judicial review can be a very important tool for activists seeking to challenge the abuse of power by the police. It can deliver favourable judgments that impact upon policing tactics on a national scale, and has the ability to cause tangible improvements to people's lives. However, an unfavourable judgment can have very real and negative implications on protesters' rights. Whilst this can apply equally in civil actions commenced in the High Court, such cases are rare in the context of protest law and the issue is therefore much more likely to arise in a public law context.

FAQ: Civil action or judicial review?

Advantages of a civil action:

- Lengthier time limit by which to lodge proceedings

- No permission required from the court

- Commonplace use of oral and written evidence

Advantages of judicial review:

- Quality of decision-making in Administrative Court is often superior

- Proceedings likely to conclude more swiftly

- Low value of a claim less likely to affect Legal Aid

- Non-pecuniary nature of remedies means less likely to enable defendant to force settlement by 'paying off' the claimant

---

- Cases are reported and can significantly influence policing tactics
- Can generate wider publicity

Legal grounds for challenge

5.234 Lord Diplock in *CCSU v Minister for the Civil Service*[140] categorised three grounds for judicial review:

(a)   illegality;

(b)   irrationality;

(c)   procedural impropriety.

5.235 Whilst these grounds have been expanded in subsequent years, and in particular following the advent of the HRA 1998, they remain the predominant bases for challenges by way of judicial review. The first two grounds are most relevant in the context of protest law, and are discussed briefly below.

Illegality

5.236 Challenges on the basis of illegality are broadly brought where a public body exceeds or abuses its powers. This may occur where the police:

- act without legal authority[141];
- use their powers for an improper or unauthorised purpose[142];
- make a decision based on an error in law[143] or which is incompatible with the ECHR[144].

Irrationality

5.237 Challenges brought on the basis of irrationality relate to the quality of the decision-making itself, rather than (as with a challenge brought on the basis of illegality) the limits placed on the decision-maker's powers. A claimant must reach a very high threshold to successfully challenge a decision on the grounds that it was irrational.

---

140 [1985] AC 374.
141 *Attorney General v Fulham Corpn* [1921] 1 Ch 440.
142 *Congreve v Home Office* [1976] QB 629.
143 *Anisminic Ltd v Foreign Compensation Commission* [1969] 2 AC 147.
144 Contrary to the HRA 1998, s 6(1).

5.238   'Irrationality' was defined in the case of *Associated Provincial Picture House Ltd v Wednesbury Corpn*[145] in which Lord Greene MR stated that in very limited circumstances, the court would be entitled to interfere and review the quality of the decision making even where a public body had not acted unlawfully. This would apply where a public body had 'come to a conclusion so unreasonable that no reasonable authority could have come to it'.

5.239   This has subsequently become known as '*Wednesbury* unreasonableness'. That the test is a high one, and the court will only interfere in exceptional circumstances, was emphasised by Lord Diplock in *CCSU v Minister for the Civil Service*[146], referring to an irrational decision as one:

> 'which is so outrageous in its defiance of logic or of accepted moral standards that no sensible person who had applied his mind to the question to be decided could have arrived at it'.

5.240   The court therefore does not review the decision on the basis of what a reasonable public body would do in the circumstances, but only on the basis of what no reasonable public body could do. There is authority to suggest that this very high threshold may be more easily achieved where Convention rights are engaged[147].

Types of decision that may be challengeable by way of judicial review

5.241   The types of decisions that therefore may be challengeable by way of judicial review in the context of protests and complaints/civil actions against the police include:

(a)   a decision by the LSC to refuse Legal Aid;

(b)   a decision by the PSD to refuse to refer a complaint to the IPCC;

(c)   a decision by the IPCC that a complaint can be appropriately investigated by the PSD;

(d)   a decision to refuse to obtain or accept further evidence in the course of a complaint investigation;

(e)   a decision to refuse to provide disclosure, either by the PSD or the IPCC, in the course of or at the conclusion of a complaint investigation;

(f)   a decision by the IPCC to refuse to allow an out of time complaint;

---

145   [1948] 1 KB 223.
146   Ibid.
147   See for example *R v Ministry of Defence, ex p Smith* [1996] 1 All ER 257.

(g)   a decision by the IPCC not to uphold an appeal;

(h)   a decision by the police force/PSD not to amend the findings of an investigation following a successful appeal to the IPCC.

Remedies/relief sought

5.242   If a challenge for judicial review is successful, the Administrative Court may make various orders, which can compel a public body to review the decision the subject of the challenge, quash or nullify the decision the subject of the challenge, or prohibit a public body from taking specific action.

5.243   The court can also make a declaration, a form of judgment which clarifies the respective rights and obligations of the parties. Although a declaration does not order the parties to carry out or refrain from any action in particular, it can be a useful tool, for example when the aim of the challenge is to influence police force's actions in the future. A declaration that a particular decision was unlawful could also resolve the legal position in any ancillary civil action. The court also has the power to award financial compensation in limited circumstances, including where the claimant has successfully established a breach of Convention rights.

5.244   These remedies are at the discretion of the court, which means that, even if it finds for the claimant, it is not obliged to award any of the remedies.

Costs

5.245   The court can, and usually will, determine the issue of costs at the conclusion of a case. The normal position applies whereby the losing party is likely to be ordered to pay the winning party's costs. As with civil actions, such an order cannot be enforced against a legally aided client without the permission of the court.

Annex A

Flowcharts

A.1   Pre-trial procedure for summary only offence **or** either way offences which stay in the magistrates's court.

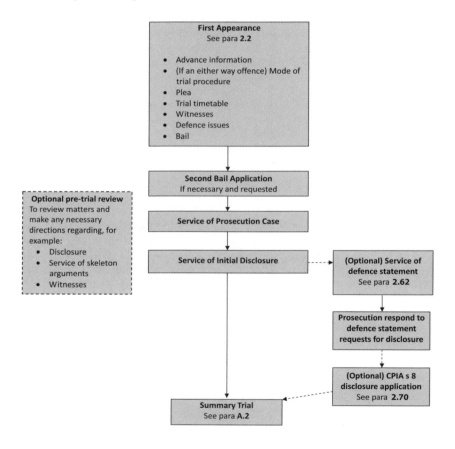

A.2   Stages in a summary trial.

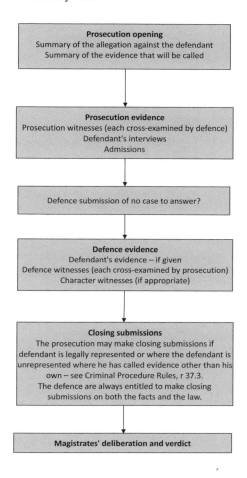

A.3   Appeal routes for summary only offence **or** either way offences which stay in the magistrates' court.

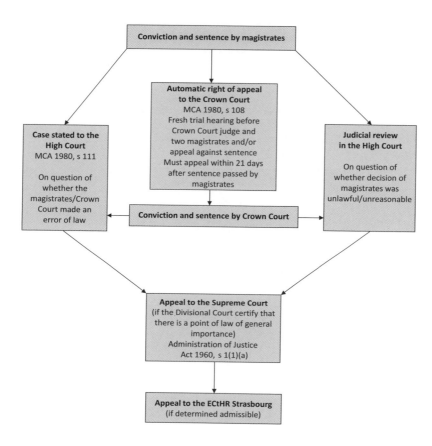

Extracts from relevant legislation

Human Rights Act 1998

1998 c 42

Introduction

B.1

1 The Convention Rights

(1)   In this Act 'the Convention rights' means the rights and fundamental freedoms set out in—

(a)   Articles 2 to 12 and 14 of the Convention,

(b)   Articles 1 to 3 of the First Protocol, and

(c)   [Article 1 of the Thirteenth Protocol],

as read with Articles 16 to 18 of the Convention.

(2)   Those Articles are to have effect for the purposes of this Act subject to any designated derogation or reservation (as to which see sections 14 and 15).

(3)   The Articles are set out in Schedule 1.

(4)   The [Secretary of State] may by order make such amendments to this Act as he considers appropriate to reflect the effect, in relation to the United Kingdom, of a protocol.

(5)   In subsection (4) 'protocol' means a protocol to the Convention—

(a)   which the United Kingdom has ratified; or

(b)   which the United Kingdom has signed with a view to ratification.

(6)   No amendment may be made by an order under subsection (4) so as to come into force before the protocol concerned is in force in relation to the United Kingdom.

Amendment
  Sub-s (1): in para (c) words 'Article 1 of the Thirteenth Protocol' in square brackets substituted by SI 2004/1574, art 2(1) (date in force: 22 June 2004: see SI 2004/1574, art 1).

Sub-s (4): words 'Secretary of State' in square brackets substituted by SI 2003/1887, art 9, Sch 2, para 10(1) (date in force: 19 August 2003: see SI 2003/1887, art 1(2)).

B.2

2 Interpretation of Convention rights

(1) A court or tribunal determining a question which has arisen in connection with a Convention right must take into account any—

(a) judgment, decision, declaration or advisory opinion of the European Court of Human Rights,

(b) opinion of the Commission given in a report adopted under Article 31 of the Convention,

(c) decision of the Commission in connection with Article 26 or 27(2) of the Convention, or

(d) decision of the Committee of Ministers taken under Article 46 of the Convention,

whenever made or given, so far as, in the opinion of the court or tribunal, it is relevant to the proceedings in which that question has arisen.

(2) Evidence of any judgment, decision, declaration or opinion of which account may have to be taken under this section is to be given in proceedings before any court or tribunal in such manner as may be provided by rules.

(3) In this section 'rules' means rules of court or, in the case of proceedings before a tribunal, rules made for the purposes of this section—

(a) by ... [the Lord Chancellor or] the Secretary of State, in relation to any proceedings outside Scotland;

(b) by the Secretary of State, in relation to proceedings in Scotland; or

(c) by a Northern Ireland department, in relation to proceedings before a tribunal in Northern Ireland—

(i) which deals with transferred matters; and

(ii) for which no rules made under paragraph (a) are in force.

Amendment
Sub-s (3): in para (a) words omitted repealed by SI 2003/1887, art 9, Sch 2, para 10(2) (date in force: 19 August 2003: see SI 2003/1887, art 1(2)); in para (a) words 'the Lord Chancellor or' in square brackets inserted by SI 2005/3429, art 8, Schedule, para 3 (date in force: 12 January 2006: see SI 2005/3429, art 1(2)).

Legislation

B.3

3 Interpretation of legislation

(1)   So far as it is possible to do so, primary legislation and subordinate legislation must be read and given effect in a way which is compatible with the Convention rights.

(2)   This section—

   (a)   applies to primary legislation and subordinate legislation whenever enacted;

   (b)   does not affect the validity, continuing operation or enforcement of any incompatible primary legislation; and

   (c)   does not affect the validity, continuing operation or enforcement of any incompatible subordinate legislation if (disregarding any possibility of revocation) primary legislation prevents removal of the incompatibility.

B.4

4 Declaration of incompatibility

(1)   Subsection (2) applies in any proceedings in which a court determines whether a provision of primary legislation is compatible with a Convention right.

(2)   If the court is satisfied that the provision is incompatible with a Convention right, it may make a declaration of that incompatibility.

(3)   Subsection (4) applies in any proceedings in which a court determines whether a provision of subordinate legislation, made in the exercise of a power conferred by primary legislation, is compatible with a Convention right.

(4)   If the court is satisfied—

   (a)   that the provision is incompatible with a Convention right, and

   (b)   that (disregarding any possibility of revocation) the primary legislation concerned prevents removal of the incompatibility,

it may make a declaration of that incompatibility.

(5)   In this section 'court' means—

   [(a)   the Supreme Court;]

   (b)   the Judicial Committee of the Privy Council;

   (c)   the [Court Martial Appeal Court];

    (d)   in Scotland, the High Court of Justiciary sitting otherwise than as a trial court or the Court of Session;

    (e)   in England and Wales or Northern Ireland, the High Court or the Court of Appeal;

    [(f)   the Court of Protection, in any matter being dealt with by the President of the Family Division, the Vice-Chancellor or a puisne judge of the High Court].

(6)   A declaration under this section ('a declaration of incompatibility')—

    (a)   does not affect the validity, continuing operation or enforcement of the provision in respect of which it is given; and

    (b)   is not binding on the parties to the proceedings in which it is made.

Amendment
Sub-s (5): para (a) substituted by the Constitutional Reform Act 2005, s 40(4), Sch 9, Pt 1, para 66(1), (2) (date in force: 1 October 2009: see SI 2009/1604, art 2(d)); in para (c) words 'Court Martial Appeal Court' in in square brackets substituted by the Armed Forces Act 2006, s 378(1), Sch 16, para 156 (date in force (for certain purposes): 28 March 2009: see SI 2009/812, art 3(a), (b), (for remaining purposes): 31 October 2009: see SI 2009/1167, art 4); para (f) inserted by the Mental Capacity Act 2005, s 67(1), Sch 6, para 43 (date in force: 1 October 2007: see SI 2007/1897, art 2(1)(d)).

B.5

5   Right of Crown to intervene

(1)   Where a court is considering whether to make a declaration of incompatibility, the Crown is entitled to notice in accordance with rules of court.

(2)   In any case to which subsection (1) applies—

    (a)   a Minister of the Crown (or a person nominated by him),

    (b)   a member of the Scottish Executive,

    (c)   a Northern Ireland Minister,

    (d)   a Northern Ireland department,

is entitled, on giving notice in accordance with rules of court, to be joined as a party to the proceedings.

(3)   Notice under subsection (2) may be given at any time during the proceedings.

(4)   A person who has been made a party to criminal proceedings (other than in Scotland) as the result of a notice under subsection (2) may, with leave, appeal to the [Supreme Court] against any declaration of incompatibility made in the proceedings.

(5)   In subsection (4)—

'criminal proceedings' includes all proceedings before the *Courts-Martial Appeal Court* [Court Martial Appeal Court]; and

'leave' means leave granted by the court making the declaration of incompatibility or by the [Supreme Court].

Amendment

Sub-s (4): words 'Supreme Court' in square brackets substituted by the Constitutional Reform Act 2005, s 40(4), Sch 9, Pt 1, para 66(1), (3).

Sub-s (5): in definition 'criminal proceedings' words 'Courts-Martial Appeal Court' in italics repealed and subsequent words in square brackets substituted by the Armed Forces Act 2006, s 378(1), Sch 16, para 157 (date in force (for certain purposes): 28 March 2009: see SI 2009/812, art 3(a), (b), (for remaining purposes): to be appointed: see the Armed Forces Act 2006, s 383(2)); in definition 'leave' words 'Supreme Court' in square brackets substituted by the Constitutional Reform Act 2005, s 40(4), Sch 9, Pt 1, para 66(1), (3) (date in force: 1 October 2009: see SI 2009/1604, art 2(d)).

Public authorities

B.6

6   Acts of public authorities

(1)   It is unlawful for a public authority to act in a way which is incompatible with a Convention right.

(2)   Subsection (1) does not apply to an act if—

(a)   as the result of one or more provisions of primary legislation, the authority could not have acted differently; or

(b)   in the case of one or more provisions of, or made under, primary legislation which cannot be read or given effect in a way which is compatible with the Convention rights, the authority was acting so as to give effect to or enforce those provisions.

(3)   In this section 'public authority' includes—

(a)   a court or tribunal, and

(b)   any person certain of whose functions are functions of a public nature,

but does not include either House of Parliament or a person exercising functions in connection with proceedings in Parliament.

(4)   …

(5)   In relation to a particular act, a person is not a public authority by virtue only of subsection (3)(b) if the nature of the act is private.

(6)   'An act' includes a failure to act but does not include a failure to—

(a)   introduce in, or lay before, Parliament a proposal for legislation; or

(b)   make any primary legislation or remedial order.

Amendment
    Sub-s (4): repealed by the Constitutional Reform Act 2005, ss 40(4), 146, Sch 9, Pt 1, para 66(1), (4), Sch 18, Pt 5 (date in force: 1 October 2009: see SI 2009/1604, art 2(d)).

B.7

7 Proceedings

(1)   A person who claims that a public authority has acted (or proposes to act) in a way which is made unlawful by section 6(1) may—

(a)   bring proceedings against the authority under this Act in the appropriate court or tribunal, or

(b)   rely on the Convention right or rights concerned in any legal proceedings,

but only if he is (or would be) a victim of the unlawful act.

(2)   In subsection (1)(a) 'appropriate court or tribunal' means such court or tribunal as may be determined in accordance with rules; and proceedings against an authority include a counterclaim or similar proceeding.

(3)   If the proceedings are brought on an application for judicial review, the applicant is to be taken to have a sufficient interest in relation to the unlawful act only if he is, or would be, a victim of that act.

(4)   If the proceedings are made by way of a petition for judicial review in Scotland, the applicant shall be taken to have title and interest to sue in relation to the unlawful act only if he is, or would be, a victim of that act.

(5)   Proceedings under subsection (1)(a) must be brought before the end of—

(a)   the period of one year beginning with the date on which the act complained of took place; or

(b)   such longer period as the court or tribunal considers equitable having regard to all the circumstances,

but that is subject to any rule imposing a stricter time limit in relation to the procedure in question.

(6)   In subsection (1)(b) 'legal proceedings' includes—

(a)   proceedings brought by or at the instigation of a public authority; and

(b)   an appeal against the decision of a court or tribunal.

(7)   For the purposes of this section, a person is a victim of an unlawful act only if he would be a victim for the purposes of Article 34 of the Convention if proceedings were brought in the European Court of Human Rights in respect of that act.

(8)   Nothing in this Act creates a criminal offence.

(9)   In this section 'rules' means—

   (a)   in relation to proceedings before a court or tribunal outside Scotland, rules made by ... [the Lord Chancellor or] the Secretary of State for the purposes of this section or rules of court,

   (b)   in relation to proceedings before a court or tribunal in Scotland, rules made by the Secretary of State for those purposes,

   (c)   in relation to proceedings before a tribunal in Northern Ireland—

      (i)   which deals with transferred matters; and

      (ii)   for which no rules made under paragraph (a) are in force,

      rules made by a Northern Ireland department for those purposes,

and includes provision made by order under section 1 of the Courts and Legal Services Act 1990.

(10)   In making rules, regard must be had to section 9.

(11)   The Minister who has power to make rules in relation to a particular tribunal may, to the extent he considers it necessary to ensure that the tribunal can provide an appropriate remedy in relation to an act (or proposed act) of a public authority which is (or would be) unlawful as a result of section 6(1), by order add to—

   (a)   the relief or remedies which the tribunal may grant; or

   (b)   the grounds on which it may grant any of them.

(12)   An order made under subsection (11) may contain such incidental, supplemental, consequential or transitional provision as the Minister making it considers appropriate.

(13)   'The Minister' includes the Northern Ireland department concerned.

Amendment
   Sub-s (9): in para (a) words omitted repealed by SI 2003/1887, art 9, Sch 2, para 10(2) (date in force: 19 August 2003: see SI 2003/1887, art 1(2)).
   Sub-s (9): in para (a) words 'the Lord Chancellor or' in square brackets inserted by SI 2005/3429, art 8, Schedule, para 3 (date in force: 12 January 2006: see SI 2005/3429, art 1(2)).

B.8

8   Judicial remedies

(1)   In relation to any act (or proposed act) of a public authority which the court finds is (or would be) unlawful, it may grant such relief or remedy, or make such order, within its powers as it considers just and appropriate.

(2)   But damages may be awarded only by a court which has power to award damages, or to order the payment of compensation, in civil proceedings.

(3)   No award of damages is to be made unless, taking account of all the circumstances of the case, including—

   (a)   any other relief or remedy granted, or order made, in relation to the act in question (by that or any other court), and

   (b)   the consequences of any decision (of that or any other court) in respect of that act,

the court is satisfied that the award is necessary to afford just satisfaction to the person in whose favour it is made.

(4)   In determining—

   (a)   whether to award damages, or

   (b)   the amount of an award,

the court must take into account the principles applied by the European Court of Human Rights in relation to the award of compensation under Article 41 of the Convention.

(5)   A public authority against which damages are awarded is to be treated—

   (a)   in Scotland, for the purposes of section 3 of the Law Reform (Miscellaneous Provisions) (Scotland) Act 1940 as if the award were made in an action of damages in which the authority has been found liable in respect of loss or damage to the person to whom the award is made;

   (b)   for the purposes of the Civil Liability (Contribution) Act 1978 as liable in respect of damage suffered by the person to whom the award is made.

(6)   In this section—

   'court' includes a tribunal;

   'damages' means damages for an unlawful act of a public authority; and

   'unlawful' means unlawful under section 6(1).

B.9

9   Judicial acts

(1)   Proceedings under section 7(1)(a) in respect of a judicial act may be brought only—

   (a)   by exercising a right of appeal;

   (b)   on an application (in Scotland a petition) for judicial review; or

(c)   in such other forum as may be prescribed by rules.

(2)   That does not affect any rule of law which prevents a court from being the subject of judicial review.

(3)   In proceedings under this Act in respect of a judicial act done in good faith, damages may not be awarded otherwise than to compensate a person to the extent required by Article 5(5) of the Convention.

(4)   An award of damages permitted by subsection (3) is to be made against the Crown; but no award may be made unless the appropriate person, if not a party to the proceedings, is joined.

(5)   In this section—

> 'appropriate person' means the Minister responsible for the court concerned, or a person or government department nominated by him;

> 'court' includes a tribunal;

> 'judge' includes a member of a tribunal, a justice of the peace [(or, in Northern Ireland, a lay magistrate)] and a clerk or other officer entitled to exercise the jurisdiction of a court;

> 'judicial act' means a judicial act of a court and includes an act done on the instructions, or on behalf, of a judge; and

> 'rules' has the same meaning as in section 7(9).

Amendment
Sub-s (5): in definition 'judge' words '(or, in Northern Ireland, a lay magistrate)' in square brackets inserted by the Justice (Northern Ireland) Act 2002, s 10(6), Sch 4, para 39 (date in force: 1 April 2005: see the Justice (Northern Ireland) Act 2002 (Commencement No 8) Order 2005, SR 2005/109, art 2, Schedule).

Remedial action

B.10

10   Power to take remedial action

(1)   This section applies if—

(a)   a provision of legislation has been declared under section 4 to be incompatible with a Convention right and, if an appeal lies—

    (i)   all persons who may appeal have stated in writing that they do not intend to do so;

    (ii)   the time for bringing an appeal has expired and no appeal has been brought within that time; or

(iii)   an appeal brought within that time has been determined or abandoned; or

(b)   it appears to a Minister of the Crown or Her Majesty in Council that, having regard to a finding of the European Court of Human Rights made after the coming into force of this section in proceedings against the United Kingdom, a provision of legislation is incompatible with an obligation of the United Kingdom arising from the Convention.

(2)   If a Minister of the Crown considers that there are compelling reasons for proceeding under this section, he may by order make such amendments to the legislation as he considers necessary to remove the incompatibility.

(3)   If, in the case of subordinate legislation, a Minister of the Crown considers—

(a)   that it is necessary to amend the primary legislation under which the subordinate legislation in question was made, in order to enable the incompatibility to be removed, and

(b)   that there are compelling reasons for proceeding under this section,

he may by order make such amendments to the primary legislation as he considers necessary.

(4)   This section also applies where the provision in question is in subordinate legislation and has been quashed, or declared invalid, by reason of incompatibility with a Convention right and the Minister proposes to proceed under paragraph 2(b) of Schedule 2.

(5)   If the legislation is an Order in Council, the power conferred by subsection (2) or (3) is exercisable by Her Majesty in Council.

(6)   In this section 'legislation' does not include a Measure of the Church Assembly or of the General Synod of the Church of England.

(7)   Schedule 2 makes further provision about remedial orders.

European Convention on Human Rights and Fundamental Freedoms

B.11

Article 5

1   Everyone has the right to liberty and security of person. No one shall be deprived of his liberty save in the following cases and in accordance with a procedure prescribed by law:

(a)   the lawful detention of a person after conviction by a competent court;

(b)   the lawful arrest or detention of a person for non-compliance with the lawful order of a court or in order to secure the fulfilment of any obligation prescribed by law;

(c)   the lawful arrest or detention of a person effected for the purpose of bringing him before the competent legal authority of reasonable suspicion of having committed and offence or when it is reasonably considered necessary to prevent his committing an offence or fleeing after having done so;

(d)   the detention of a minor by lawful order for the purpose of educational supervision or his lawful detention for the purpose of bringing him before the competent legal authority;

(e)   the lawful detention of persons for the prevention of the spreading of infectious diseases, of persons of unsound mind, alcoholics or drug addicts, or vagrants;

(f)   the lawful arrest or detention of a person to prevent his effecting an unauthorized entry into the country or of a person against whom action is being taken with a view to deportation or extradition.

2   Everyone who is arrested shall be informed promptly, in a language which he understands, of the reasons for his arrest and the charge against him.

3   Everyone arrested or detained in accordance with the provisions of paragraph 1(c) of this article shall be brought promptly before a judge or other officer authorized by law to exercise judicial power and shall be entitled to trial within a reasonable time or to release pending trial. Release may be conditioned by guarantees to appear for trial.

4   Everyone who is deprived of his liberty by arrest or detention shall be entitled to take proceedings by which the lawfulness of his detention shall be decided speedily by a court and his release ordered if the detention is not lawful.

5   Everyone who has been the victim of arrest or detention in contravention of the provisions of this article shall have an enforceable right to compensation.

B.12

Article 6

1   In the determination of his civil rights and obligations or of any criminal charge against him, everyone is entitled to a fair and public hearing within a reasonable time by an independent and impartial tribunal established by law. Judgement shall be pronounced publicly by the press and public may be excluded from all or part of the trial in the interest of morals, public order or national security in a democratic society, where the interests of juveniles or the

protection of the private life of the parties so require, or the extent strictly necessary in the opinion of the court in special circumstances where publicity would prejudice the interests of justice.

2   Everyone charged with a criminal offence shall be presumed innocent until proved guilty according to law.

3   Everyone charged with a criminal offence has the following minimum rights:

   (a)   to be informed promptly, in a language which he understands and in detail, of the nature and cause of the accusation against him;

   (b)   to have adequate time and the facilities for the preparation of his defence;

   (c)   to defend himself in person or through legal assistance of his own choosing or, if he has not sufficient means to pay for legal assistance, to be given it free when the interests of justice so require;

   (d)   to examine or have examined witnesses against him and to obtain the attendance and examination of witnesses on his behalf under the same conditions as witnesses against him;

   (e)   to have the free assistance of an interpreter if he cannot understand or speak the language used in court.

B.13

Article 7

1   No one shall be held guilty of any criminal offence on account of any act or omission which did not constitute a criminal offence under national or international law at the time when it was committed. Nor shall a heavier penalty be imposed than the one that was applicable at the time the criminal offence was committed.

2   This article shall not prejudice the trial and punishment of any person for any act or omission which, at the time when it was committed, was criminal according the general principles of law recognized by civilized nations.

B.14

Article 8

1   Everyone has the right to respect for his private and family life, his home and his correspondence.

2   There shall be no interference by a public authority with the exercise of this right except such as is in accordance with the law and is necessary in a democratic society in the interests of national security, public safety or the

economic well-being of the country, for the prevention of disorder or crime, for the protection of health or morals, or for the protection of the rights and freedoms of others.

B.15

Article 9

1 Everyone has the right to freedom of thought, conscience and religion; this right includes freedom to change his religion or belief, and freedom, either alone or in community with others and in public or private, to manifest his religion or belief, in worship, teaching, practice and observance.

2 Freedom to manifest one's religion or beliefs shall be subject only to such limitations as are prescribed by law and are necessary in a democratic society in the interests of public safety, for the protection of public order, health or morals, or the protection of the rights and freedoms of others.

B.16

Article 10

1 Everyone has the right to freedom of expression. This right shall include freedom to hold opinions and to receive and impart information an ideas without interference by public authority and regardless of frontiers. This article shall not prevent States from requiring the licensing of broadcasting, television or cinema enterprises.

2 The exercise of these freedoms, since it carries with it duties and responsibilities, may be subject to such formalities, conditions, restrictions or penalties as are prescribed by law and are necessary in a democratic society, in the interests of national security, territorial integrity or public safety, for the prevention of disorder or crime, for the protection of health or morals, for the protection of the reputation or the rights of others, for preventing the disclosure of information received in confidence, or for maintaining the authority and impartiality of the judiciary.

B.17

Article 11

1 Everyone has the right to freedom of peaceful assembly and to freedom of association with others, including the right to form and to join trade unions for the protection of his interests.

2 No restrictions shall be placed on the exercise of these rights other than such as are prescribed by law and are necessary in a democratic society in the interests of national security or public safety, for the prevention of disorder or crime, for the protection of health or morals or for the protection of the rights

and freedoms of others. This article shall not prevent the imposition of lawful restrictions on the exercise of these rights by members of the armed forces, of the police or of the administration of the State.

B.18

Protocol   1 Enforcement of certain Rights and Freedoms not included in Section I of the Convention

The Governments signatory hereto, being Members of the Council of Europe,

Being resolved to take steps to ensure the collective enforcement of certain rights and freedoms other than those already included in Section I of the Convention for the Protection of Human Rights and Fundamental Freedoms signed at Rome on 4th November, 1950 (hereinafter referred to as 'the Convention'),

Have agreed as follows:

B.19

Article 1

Every natural or legal person is entitled to the peaceful enjoyment of his possessions. No one shall be deprived of his possessions except in the public interest and subject to the conditions provided for by law and by the general principles of international law.

The preceding provisions shall not, however, in any way impair the right of a State to enforce such laws as it deems necessary to control the use of property in accordance with the general interest or to secure the payment of taxes or other contributions or penalties.

Public Order Act 1986

1986 c 64

Part I
New Offences

B.20

1   Riot

(1)   Where 12 or more persons who are present together use or threaten unlawful violence for a common purpose and the conduct of them (taken together) is such as would cause a person of reasonable firmness present at the

scene to fear for his personal safety, each of the persons using unlawful violence for the common purpose is guilty of riot.

(2)　It is immaterial whether or not the 12 or more use or threaten unlawful violence simultaneously.

(3)　The common purpose may be inferred from conduct.

(4)　No person of reasonable firmness need actually be, or be likely to be, present at the scene.

(5)　Riot may be committed in private as well as in public places.

(6)　A person guilty of riot is liable on conviction on indictment to imprisonment for a term not exceeding ten years or a fine or both.

B.20A

2　Violent disorder

(1)　Where 3 or more persons who are present together use or threaten unlawful violence and the conduct of them (taken together) is such as would cause a person of reasonable firmness present at the scene to fear for personal safety, each of the persons using or threatening unlawful violence is guilty of violent disorder.

(2)　It is immaterial whether or not the 3 or more use or threaten unlawful violence simultaneously.

(3)　No person of reasonable firmness need actually be, or be likely to be, present at the scene.

(4)　Violent disorder may be committed in private as well as in public places.

(5)　A person guilty of violent disorder is liable on conviction on indictment to imprisonment for a term not exceeding 5 years or a fine or both, or on summary conviction to imprisonment for a term not exceeding 6 months or a fine not exceeding the statutory maximum or both.

B.21

3　Affray

(1)　A person is guilty of affray if he uses or threatens unlawful violence towards another and his conduct is such as would cause a person of reasonable firmness present at the scene to fear for his personal safety.

(2)　Where 2 or more persons use or threaten the unlawful violence, it is the conduct of them taken together that must be considered for the purposes of subsection (1).

(3)　For the purposes of this section a threat cannot be made by the use of words alone.

(4)   No person of reasonable firmness need actually be, or be likely to be, present at the scene.

(5)   Affray may be committed in private as well as in public places.

(6)   ...

(7)   A person guilty of affray is liable on conviction on indictment to imprisonment for a term not exceeding 3 years or a fine or both, or on summary conviction to imprisonment for a term not exceeding 6 months or a fine not exceeding the statutory maximum or both.

Amendment
> Sub-s (6): repealed by the Serious Organised Crime and Police Act 2005, ss 111, 174(2), Sch 7, Pt 1, para 26(1), (2), Sch 17, Pt 2 (date in force: 1 January 2006: see SI 2005/3495, art 2(1)(m), (t), (u)(xxvi)).

B.22

4   Fear or provocation of violence

(1)   A person is guilty of an offence if he—

(a)   uses towards another person threatening, abusive or insulting words or behaviour, or

(b)   distributes or displays to another person any writing, sign or other visible representation which is threatening, abusive or insulting,

with intent to cause that person to believe that immediate unlawful violence will be used against him or another by any person, or to provoke the immediate use of unlawful violence by that person or another, or whereby that person is likely to believe that such violence will be used or it is likely that such violence will be provoked.

(2)   An offence under this section may be committed in a public or a private place, except that no offence is committed where the words or behaviour are used, or the writing, sign or other visible representation is distributed or displayed, by a person inside a dwelling and the other person is also inside that or another dwelling.

(3)   ...

(4)   A person guilty of an offence under this section is liable on summary conviction to imprisonment for a term not exceeding 6 months or a fine not exceeding level 5 on the standard scale or both.

Amendment
> Sub-s (3): repealed by the Serious Organised Crime and Police Act 2005, ss 111, 174(2), Sch 7, Pt 1, para 26(1), (3), Sch 17, Pt 2 (date in force: 1 January 2006: see SI 2005/3495, art 2(1)(m), (t), (u)(xxvi)).

B.23

[4A   Intentional harassment, alarm or distress]

[(1)   A person is guilty of an offence if, with intent to cause a person harassment, alarm or distress, he—

(a)   uses threatening, abusive or insulting words or behaviour, or disorderly behaviour, or

(b)   displays any writing, sign or other visible representation which is threatening, abusive or insulting,

thereby causing that or another person harassment, alarm or distress.

(2)   An offence under this section may be committed in a public or a private place, except that no offence is committed where the words or behaviour are used, or the writing, sign or other visible representation is displayed, by a person inside a dwelling and the person who is harassed, alarmed or distressed is also inside that or another dwelling.

(3)   It is a defence for the accused to prove—

(a)   that he was inside a dwelling and had no reason to believe that the words or behaviour used, or the writing, sign or other visible representation displayed, would be heard or seen by a person outside that or any other dwelling, or

(b)   that his conduct was reasonable.

(4)   …

(5)   A person guilty of an offence under this section is liable on summary conviction to imprisonment for a term not exceeding 6 months or a fine not exceeding level 5 on the standard scale or both.]

Amendment
  Inserted by the Criminal Justice and Public Order Act 1994, s 154.
    Sub-s (4): repealed by the Serious Organised Crime and Police Act 2005, ss 111, 174(2), Sch 7, Pt 1, para 26(1), (4), Sch 17, Pt 2 (date in force: 1 January 2006: see SI 2005/3495, art 2(1)(m), (t), (u)(xxvi)).

B.24

5   Harassment, alarm or distress

(1)   A person is guilty of an offence if he—

(a)   uses threatening, abusive or insulting words or behaviour, or disorderly behaviour, or

(b)   displays any writing, sign or other visible representation which is threatening, abusive or insulting, within the hearing or sight of a person likely to be caused harassment, alarm or distress thereby.

(2)   An offence under this section may be committed in a public or a private place, except that no offence is committed where the words or behaviour are used, or the writing, sign or other visible representation is displayed, by a person inside a dwelling and the other person is also inside that or another dwelling.

(3)   It is a defence for the accused to prove—

   (a)   that he had no reason to believe that there was any person within hearing or sight who was likely to be caused harassment, alarm or distress, or

   (b)   that he was inside a dwelling and had no reason to believe that the words or behaviour used, or the writing, sign or other visible representation displayed, would be heard or seen by a person outside that or any other dwelling, or

   (c)   that his conduct was reasonable.

(4)   ...

(5)   ...

(6)   A person guilty of an offence under this section is liable on summary conviction to a fine not exceeding level 3 on the standard scale.

Amendment
   Sub-ss (4), (5): repealed by the Serious Organised Crime and Police Act 2005, ss 111, 174(2), Sch 7, Pt 1, para 26(1), (5), Sch 17, Pt 2 (date in force: 1 January 2006: see SI 2005/3495, art 2(1)(m), (t), (u)(xxvi)).

B.25

6   Mental element: miscellaneous

(1)   A person is guilty of riot only if he intends to use violence or is aware that his conduct may be violent.

(2)   A person is guilty of violent disorder or affray only if he intends to use or threaten violence or is aware that his conduct may be violent or threaten violence.

(3)   A person is guilty of an offence under section 4 only if he intends his words or behaviour, or the writing, sign or other visible representation, to be threatening, abusive or insulting, or is aware that it may be threatening, abusive or insulting.

(4)   A person is guilty of an offence under section 5 only if he intends his words or behaviour, or the writing, sign or other visible representation, to be

threatening, abusive or insulting, or is aware that it may be threatening, abusive or insulting or (as the case may be) he intends his behaviour to be or is aware that it may be disorderly.

(5)   For the purposes of this section a person whose awareness is impaired by intoxication shall be taken to be aware of that of which he would be aware if not intoxicated, unless he shows either that his intoxication was not self-induced or that it was caused solely by the taking or administration of a substance in the course of medical treatment.

(6)   In subsection (5) 'intoxication' means any intoxication, whether caused by drink, drugs or other means, or by a combination of means.

(7)   Subsections (1) and (2) do not affect the determination for the purposes of riot or violent disorder of the number of persons who use or threaten violence.

B.26

7   Procedure: miscellaneous

(1)   No prosecution for an offence of riot or incitement to riot may be instituted except by or with the consent of the Director of Public Prosecutions.

(2)   For the purposes of the rules against charging more than one offence in the same count or information, each of sections 1 to 5 creates one offence.

(3)   If on the trial on indictment of a person charged with violent disorder or affray the jury find him not guilty of the offence charged, they may (without prejudice to section 6(3) of the Criminal Law Act 1967) find him guilty of an offence under section 4.

(4)   The Crown Court has the same powers and duties in relation to a person who is by virtue of subsection (3) convicted before it of an offence under section 4 as a magistrates' court would have on convicting him of the offence.

B.27

8   Interpretation

(1)   In this Part—

'dwelling' means any structure or part of a structure occupied as a person's home or as other living accommodation (whether the occupation is separate or shared with others) but does not include any part not so occupied, and for his purpose 'structure' includes a tent, caravan, vehicle, vessel or other temporary or movable structure;

'violence' means any violent conduct, so that—

(a)   except in the context of affray, it includes violent conduct towards property as well as violent conduct towards persons, and

(b)   it is not restricted to conduct causing or intended to cause injury or damage but includes any other violent conduct (for example, throwing at or towards a person a missile of a kind capable of causing injury which does not hit or falls short).

B.28

10   Construction of other instruments

(1)   In the Riot (Damages) Act 1886 ... (compensation for riot damage) 'riotous' and 'riotously' shall be construed in accordance with section 1 above.

(2)   In Schedule 1 to the Marine Insurance Act 1906 (form and rules for the construction of certain insurance policies) 'rioters' in rule 8 and 'riot' in rule 10 shall, in the application of the rules to any policy taking effect on or after the coming into force of this section, be construed in accordance with section 1 above unless a different intention appears.

(3)   'Riot' and cognate expressions in any enactment in force before the coming into force of this section (other than the enactments mentioned in subsections (1) and (2) above) shall be construed in accordance with section 1 above if they would have been construed in accordance with the common law offence of riot apart from this Part.

(4)   Subject to subsections (1) to (3) above and unless a different intention appears, nothing in this Part affects the meaning of 'riot' or any cognate expression in any enactment in force, or other instrument taking effect, before the coming into force of this section.

Amendment
Sub-s (1): words omitted repealed by the Merchant Shipping Act 1995, s 314(1), Sch 12.

Part II
Processions and Assemblies

B.29

11   Advance notice of public processions

(1)   Written notice shall be given in accordance with this section of any proposal to hold a public procession intended—

(a)   to demonstrate support for or opposition to the views or actions of any person or body of persons,

(b)   to publicise a cause or campaign, or

(c)   to mark or commemorate an event,

unless it is not reasonably practicable to give any advance notice of the procession.

(2)   Subsection (1) does not apply where the procession is one commonly or customarily held in the police area (or areas) in which it is proposed to be held or is a funeral procession organised by a funeral director acting in the normal course of his business.

(3)   The notice must specify the date when it is intended to hold the procession, the time when it is intended to start it, its proposed route, and the name and address of the person (or of one of the persons) proposing to organise it.

(4)   Notice must be delivered to a police station—

   (a)   in the police area in which it is proposed the procession will start, or

   (b)   where it is proposed the procession will start in Scotland and cross into England, in the first police area in England on the proposed route.

(5)   If delivered not less than 6 clear days before the date when the procession is intended to be held, the notice may be delivered by post by the recorded delivery service; but section 7 of the Interpretation Act 1978 (under which a document sent by post is deemed to have been served when posted and to have been delivered in the ordinary course of post) does not apply.

(6)   If not delivered in accordance with subsection (5), the notice must be delivered by hand not less than 6 clear days before the date when the procession is intended to be held or, if that is not reasonably practicable, as soon as delivery is reasonably practicable.

(7)   Where a public procession is held, each of the persons organising it is guilty of an offence if—

   (a)   the requirements of this section as to notice have not been satisfied, or

   (b)   the date when it is held, the time when it starts, or its route, differs from the date, time or route specified in the notice.

(8)   It is a defence for the accused to prove that he did not know of, and neither suspected nor had reason to suspect, the failure to satisfy the requirements or (as the case may be) the difference of date, time or route.

(9)   To the extent that an alleged offence turns on a difference of date, time or route, it is a defence for the accused to prove that the difference arose from circumstances beyond his control or from something done with the agreement of a police officer or by his direction.

(10)   A person guilty of an offence under subsection (7) is liable on summary conviction to a fine not exceeding level 3 on the standard scale.

B.30

12   Imposing conditions on public processions

(1)   If the senior police officer, having regard to the time or place at which and the circumstances in which any public procession is being held or is intended to be held and to its route or proposed route, reasonably believes that—

    (a)   it may result in serious public disorder, serious damage to property or serious disruption to the life of the community, or

    (b)   the purpose of the persons organising it is the intimidation of others with a view to compelling them not to do an act they have a right to do, or to do an act they have a right not to do,

he may give directions imposing on the persons organising or taking part in the procession such conditions as appear to him necessary to prevent such disorder, damage, disruption or intimidation, including conditions as to the route of the procession or prohibiting it from entering any public place specified in the directions.

(2)   In subsection (1) 'the senior police officer' means—

    (a)   in relation to a procession being held, or to a procession intended to be held in a case where persons are assembling with a view to taking part in it, the most senior in rank of the police officers present at the scene, and

    (b)   in relation to a procession intended to be held in a case where paragraph (a) does not apply, the chief officer of police.

(3)   A direction given by a chief officer of police by virtue of subsection (2)(b) shall be given in writing.

(4)   A person who organises a public procession and knowingly fails to comply with a condition imposed under this section is guilty of an offence, but it is a defence for him to prove that the failure arose from circumstances beyond his control.

(5)   A person who takes part in a public procession and knowingly fails to comply with a condition imposed under this section is guilty of an offence, but it is a defence for him to prove that the failure arose from circumstances beyond his control.

(6)   A person who incites another to commit an offence under subsection (5) is guilty of an offence.

(7)   ...

(8)   A person guilty of an offence under subsection (4) is liable on summary conviction to imprisonment for a term not exceeding 3 months or a fine not exceeding level 4 on the standard scale or both.

(9)   A person guilty of an offence under subsection (5) is liable on summary conviction to a fine not exceeding level 3 on the standard scale.

(10)   A person guilty of an offence under subsection (6) is liable on summary conviction to imprisonment for a term not exceeding 3 months or a fine not exceeding level 4 on the standard scale or both, *notwithstanding section 45(3) of the Magistrates' Courts Act 1980 (inciter liable to same penalty as incited)*.

(11)   In Scotland this section applies only in relation to a procession being held, and to a procession intended to be held in a case where persons are assembling with a view to taking part in it.

Amendment

Sub-s (7): repealed by the Serious Organised Crime and Police Act 2005, ss 111, 174(2), Sch 7, Pt 1, para 26(1), (6), Sch 17, Pt 2 (date in force: 1 January 2006: see SI 2005/3495, art 2(1)(m), (t), (u)(xxvi)).

Sub-s (10): words from 'notwithstanding section 45(3)' to the end repealed, in relation to England and Wales, by the Serious Crime Act 2007, ss 63(2), 92, Sch 6, Pt 2, paras 58(1), (2), (3)(a), Sch 14 (date in force: 1 October 2008: see SI 2008/2504, art 2(a), (i)(v)).

B.31

13   Prohibiting public processions

(1)   If at any time the chief officer of police reasonably believes that, because of particular circumstances existing in any district or part of a district, the powers under section 12 will not be sufficient to prevent the holding of public processions in that district or part from resulting in serious public disorder, he shall apply to the council of the district for an order prohibiting for such period not exceeding 3 months as may be specified in the application the holding of all public processions (or of any class of public procession so specified) in the district or part concerned.

(2)   On receiving such an application, a council may with the consent of the Secretary of State make an order either in the terms of the application or with such modifications as may be approved by the Secretary of State.

(3)   Subsection (1) does not apply in the City of London or the metropolitan police district.

(4)   If at any time the Commissioner of Police for the City of London or the Commissioner of Police of the Metropolis reasonably believes that, because of particular circumstances existing in his police area or part of it, the powers under section 12 will not be sufficient to prevent the holding of public processions in that area or part from resulting in serious public disorder, he may with the consent of the Secretary of State make an order prohibiting for such period not exceeding 3 months as may be specified in the order the holding of all public processions (or of any class of public procession so specified) in the area or part concerned.

(5)   An order made under this section may be revoked or varied by a subsequent order made in the same way, that is, in accordance with subsections (1) and (2) or subsection (4), as the case may be.

(6)   Any order under this section shall, if not made in writing, be recorded in writing as soon as practicable after being made.

(7)   A person who organises a public procession the holding of which he knows is prohibited by virtue of an order under this section is guilty of an offence.

(8)   A person who takes part in a public procession the holding of which he knows is prohibited by virtue of an order under this section is guilty of an offence.

(9)   A person who incites another to commit an offence under subsection (8) is guilty of an offence.

(10)   ...

(11)   A person guilty of an offence under subsection (7) is liable on summary conviction to imprisonment for a term not exceeding 3 months or a fine not exceeding level 4 on the standard scale or both.

(12)   A person guilty of an offence under subsection (8) is liable on summary conviction to a fine not exceeding level 3 on the standard scale.

(13)   A person guilty of an offence under subsection (9) is liable on summary conviction to imprisonment for a term not exceeding 3 months or a fine not exceeding level 4 on the standard scale or both, ...

Amendment

Sub-s (10): repealed by the Serious Organised Crime and Police Act 2005, ss 111, 174(2), Sch 7, Pt 1, para 26(1), (7), Sch 17, Pt 2 (date in force: 1 January 2006: see SI 2005/3495, art 2(1)(m), (t), (u)(xxvi)).

Sub-s (13): words omitted repealed by the Serious Crime Act 2007, ss 63(2), 92, Sch 6, Pt 2, paras 58(1), (2), (3)(b), Sch 14 (date in force: 1 October 2008: see SI 2008/2504, art 2(a), (i)(v)).

B.32

14   Imposing conditions on public assemblies

(1)   If the senior police officer, having regard to the time or place at which and the circumstances in which any public assembly is being held or is intended to be held, reasonably believes that—

   (a)   it may result in serious public disorder, serious damage to property or serious disruption to the life of the community, or

   (b)   the purpose of the persons organising it is the intimidation of others with a view to compelling them not to do an act they have a right to do, or to do an act they have a right not to do, he may give directions imposing on the persons organising or taking part in the assembly such conditions as to the place at which the assembly may be (or continue to be) held, its maximum duration, or the maximum number of persons who may constitute it, as appear to him necessary to prevent such disorder, damage, disruption or intimidation.

(2)   In subsection (1) 'the senior police officer' means—

    (a)   in relation to an assembly being held, the most senior in rank of the police officers present at the scene, and

    (b)   in relation to an assembly intended to be held, the chief officer of police.

(3)   A direction given by a chief officer of police by virtue of subsection (2)(b) shall be given in writing.

(4)   A person who organises a public assembly and knowingly fails to comply with a condition imposed under this section is guilty of an offence, but it is a defence for him to prove that the failure arose from circumstances beyond his control.

(5)   A person who takes part in a public assembly and knowingly fails to comply with a condition imposed under this section is guilty of an offence, but it is a defence for him to prove that the failure arose from circumstances beyond his control.

(6)   A person who incites another to commit an offence under subsection (5) is guilty of an offence.

(7)   ...

(8)   A person guilty of an offence under subsection (4) is liable on summary conviction to imprisonment for a term not exceeding 3 months or a fine not exceeding level 4 on the standard scale or both.

(9)   A person guilty of an offence under subsection (5) is liable on summary conviction to a fine not exceeding level 3 on the standard scale.

(10)   A person guilty of an offence under subsection (6) is liable on summary conviction to imprisonment for a term not exceeding 3 months or a fine not exceeding level 4 on the standard scale or both, *notwithstanding section 45(3) of the Magistrates' Courts Act 1980.*

Amendment

    Sub-s (7): repealed by the Serious Organised Crime and Police Act 2005, ss 111, 174(2), Sch 7, Pt 1, para 26(1), (8), Sch 17, Pt 2 (date in force: 1 January 2006: see SI 2005/3495, art 2(1)(m), (t), (u)(xxvi)).

    Sub-s (10): words 'notwithstanding section 45(3) of the Magistrates' Courts Act 1980' in italics repealed, in relation to England and Wales, by the Serious Crime Act 2007, ss 63(2), 92, Sch 6, Pt 2, para 58(1), (2), (3)(c), Sch 14 (date in force: 1 October 2008: see SI 2008/2504, art 2(a), (i)(v)).

B.33

[14A   Prohibiting trespassory assemblies]

[(1)   If at any time the chief officer of police reasonably believes that an assembly is intended to be held in any district at a place on land to which the public has no right of access or only a limited right of access and that the assembly—

(a)   is likely to be held without the permission of the occupier of the land or to conduct itself in such a way as to exceed the limits of any permission of his or the limits of the public's right of access, and

(b)   may result—

(i)   in serious disruption to the life of the community, or

(ii)   where the land, or a building or monument on it, is of histori-cal, architectural, archaeological or scientific importance, in significant damage to the land, building or monument,

he may apply to the council of the district for an order prohibiting for a specified period the holding of all trespassory assemblies in the district or a part of it, as specified.

(2)   On receiving such an application, a council may—

(a)   in England and Wales, with the consent of the Secretary of State make an order either in the terms of the application or with such modifications as may be approved by the Secretary of State; or

(b)   in Scotland, make an order in the terms of the application.

(3)   Subsection (1) does not apply in the City of London or the metropolitan police district.

(4)   If at any time the Commissioner of Police for the City of London or the Commissioner of Police of the Metropolis reasonably believes that an assembly is intended to be held at a place on land to which the public has no right of access or only a limited right of access in his police area and that the assembly—

(a)   is likely to be held without the permission of the occupier of the land or to conduct itself in such a way as to exceed the limits of any permission of his or the limits of the public's right of access, and

(b)   may result—

(i)   in serious disruption to the life of the community, or

(ii)   where the land, or a building or monument on it, is of histori-cal, architectural, archaeological or scientific importance, in significant damage to the land, building or monument, he may with the consent of the Secretary of State make an order prohibiting for a specified period the holding of all trespassory assemblies in the area or a part of it, as specified.

(5)   An order prohibiting the holding of trespassory assemblies operates to prohibit any assembly which—

>   (a)   is held on land to which the public has no right of access or only a limited right of access, and

>   (b)   takes place in the prohibited circumstances, that is to say, without the permission of the occupier of the land or so as to exceed the limits of any permission of his or the limits of the public's right of access.

(6)   No order under this section shall prohibit the holding of assemblies for a period exceeding 4 days or in an area exceeding an area represented by a circle with a radius of 5 miles from a specified centre.

(7)   An order made under this section may be revoked or varied by a subsequent order made in the same way, that is, in accordance with subsection (1) and (2) or subsection (4), as the case may be.

(8)   Any order under this section shall, if not made in writing, be recorded in writing as soon as practicable after being made.

(9)   In this section and sections 14B and 14C—

>   'assembly' means an assembly of 20 or more persons;

>   'land' means land in the open air;

>   'limited', in relation to a right of access by the public to land, means that their use of it is restricted to use for a particular purpose (as in the case of a highway or road) or is subject to other restrictions;

>   'occupier' means—

>   >   (a)   in England and Wales, the person entitled to possession of the land by virtue of an estate or interest held by him; or

>   >   (b)   in Scotland, the person lawfully entitled to natural possession of the land,

>   and in subsections (1) and (4) includes the person reasonably believed by the authority applying for or making the order to be the occupier;

>   'public' includes a section of the public; and

>   'specified' means specified in an order under this section.

[(9A)   In relation to Scotland, the references in this section to the public's rights (or limited right) of access do not include any right which the public or any member of the public may have by way of access rights within the meaning of the Land Reform (Scotland) Act 2003 (asp 2).]

(10)   In relation to Scotland, the references in subsection (1) above to a district and to the council of the district shall be construed—

(a)   as respects applications before 1st April 1996, as references to the area of a regional or islands authority and to the authority in question; and

(b)   as respects applications on and after that date, as references to a local government area and to the council for that area.

(11)   In relation to Wales, the references in subsection (1) above to a district and to the council of the district shall be construed, as respects applications on and after 1st April 1996, as references to a county or county borough and to the council for that county or county borough.]

Amendment
    Inserted by the Criminal Justice and Public Order Act 1994, s 70.
      Sub-s (9A): inserted by the Land Reform (Scotland) Act 2003, s 99, Sch 2, para 9 (date in force: 9 February 2005: see SSI 2005/17, art 2(b)).

B.34

[14B   Offences in connection with trespassory assemblies and arrest therefor]

[(1)   A person who organises an assembly the holding of which he knows is prohibited by an order under section 14A is guilty of an offence.

(2)   A person who takes part in an assembly which he knows is prohibited by an order under section 14A is guilty of an offence.

(3)   In England and Wales, a person who incites another to commit an offence under subsection (2) is guilty of an offence.

(4)   ...

(5)   A person guilty of an offence under subsection (1) is liable on summary conviction to imprisonment for a term not exceeding 3 months or a fine not exceeding level 4 on the standard scale or both.

(6)   A person guilty of an offence under subsection (2) is liable on summary conviction to a fine not exceeding level 3 on the standard scale.

(7)   A person guilty of an offence under subsection (3) is liable on summary conviction to imprisonment for a term not exceeding 3 months or a fine not exceeding level 4 on the standard scale or both, *notwithstanding section 45(3) of the Magistrates' Courts Act 1980.*

(8) Subsection (3) above is without prejudice to the application of any principle of Scots Law as respects art and part guilt to such incitement as is mentioned in that subsection.]

Amendment

> Inserted by the Criminal Justice and Public Order Act 1994, s 70.
>
> Sub-s (4): repealed by the Serious Organised Crime and Police Act 2005, ss 111, 174(2), Sch 7, Pt 1, para 26(1), (9), Sch 17, Pt 2 (date in force: 1 January 2006: see SI 2005/3495, art 2(1)(m), (t), (u)(xxvi)).
>
> Sub-s (7): words 'notwithstanding section 45(3) of the Magistrates' Courts Act 1980' in italics repealed, in relation to England and Wales, by the Serious Crime Act 2007, ss 63(2), 92, Sch 6, Pt 2, paras 58(1), (2), (3)(d), Sch 14 (date in force: 1 October 2008: see SI 2008/2504, art 2(a), (i)(v)).

B.35

[14C   Stopping persons from proceeding to trespassory assemblies]

[(1)   If a constable in uniform reasonably believes from proceedings that a person is on his way to an assembly within the area to which an order under section 14A applies which the constable reasonably believes is likely to be an assembly which is prohibited by that order, he may, subject to subsection (2) below—

(a)   stop that person, and

(b)   direct him not to proceed in the direction of the assembly.

(2)   The power conferred by subsection (1) may only be exercised within the area to which the order applies.

(3)   A person who fails to comply with a direction under subsection (1) which he knows has been given to him is guilty of an offence.

(4)   ...

(5)   A person guilty of an offence under subsection (3) is liable on summary conviction to a fine not exceeding level 3 on the standard scale.]

Amendment

> Inserted by the Criminal Justice and Public Order Act 1994, s 71.
>
> Sub-s (4): repealed by the Serious Organised Crime and Police Act 2005, ss 111, 174(2), Sch 7, Pt 1, para 26(1), (10), Sch 17, Pt 2 (date in force: 1 January 2006: see SI 2005/3495, art 2(1)(m), (t), (u)(xxvi)).

B.36

15   Delegation

(1)   The chief officer of police may delegate, to such extent and subject to such conditions as he may specify, any of his functions under sections 12 to [14A] to [an] assistant chief constable; and references in those sections to the person delegating shall be construed accordingly.

(2)   Subsection (1) shall have effect in the City of London and the metropolitan police district as if '[an] assistant chief constable' read 'an assistant commissioner of police'.

Amendment
>   Sub-s (1): number in square brackets substituted by the Criminal Justice and Public Order Act 1994, s 168(2), Sch 10, para 60; word in square brackets substituted by the Police and Magistrates' Courts Act 1994, s 44, Sch 5, Part II, para 37.
>   Sub-s (2): word in square brackets substituted by the Police and Magistrates' Courts Act 1994, s 44, Sch 5, Part II, para 37.

B.37

16   Interpretation

In this Part—

>   'the City of London' means the City as defined for the purposes of the Acts relating to the City of London police;

>   'the metropolitan police district' means that district as defined in section 76 of the London Government Act 1963;

>   'public assembly' means an assembly of *20* [2] or more persons in a public place which is wholly or partly open to the air;

>   'public place' means—

>   (a)   any highway, or in Scotland any road within the meaning of the Roads (Scotland) Act 1984, and

>   (b)   any place to which at the material time the public or any section of the public has access, on payment or otherwise, as of right or by virtue of express or implied permission;

>   'public procession' means a procession in a public place.

Amendment
>   In definition 'public assembly' reference to '20' in italics repealed and subsequent reference in square brackets substituted, in relation to England and Wales, by the Anti-social Behaviour Act 2003, s 57 (date in force: 20 January 2004: see SI 2003/3300, art 2(e)(i)).

Police Reform and Social Responsibility Act 2011

2011 c 13

Part 3
Parliament Square Garden and Surrounding Area

Repeal of SOCPA 2005 provisions

B.38

141 Demonstrations in vicinity of Parliament: repeal of SOCPA 2005 provisions

(1) Sections 132 to 138 of the Serious Organised Crime and Police Act 2005 (which regulate demonstrations and use of loudspeakers in the vicinity of Parliament) are repealed.

(2) The public assemblies in relation to which section 14 of the Public Order Act 1986 applies, as a consequence of the repeal of section 132(6) of the Serious Organised Crime and Police Act 2005, include public assemblies which started, or were being organised, before this section comes into force.

Controls on activities in Parliament Square Garden and adjoining pavements

B.39

142 Controlled area of Parliament Square

(1) For the purposes of this Part, the 'controlled area of Parliament Square' means the area of land that is comprised in—

(a) the central garden of Parliament Square, and

(b) the footways that immediately adjoin the central garden of Parliament Square.

(2) In subsection (1)—

'the central garden of Parliament Square' means the site in Parliament Square on which the Minister of Works was authorised by the Parliament Square (Improvements) Act 1949 to lay out the garden referred to in that Act as 'the new central garden';

'footway' has the same meaning as in the Highways Act 1980 (see section 329(1) of that Act).

B.40

143   Prohibited activities in controlled area of Parliament Square

(1)   A constable or authorised officer who has reasonable grounds for believing that a person is doing, or is about to do, a prohibited activity may direct the person—

    (a)   to cease doing that activity, or

    (b)   (as the case may be) not to start doing that activity.

(2)   For the purposes of this Part, a 'prohibited activity' is any of the following—

    (a)   operating any amplified noise equipment in the controlled area of Parliament Square;

    (b)   erecting or keeping erected in the controlled area of Parliament Square—

        (i)   any tent, or

        (ii)   any other structure that is designed, or adapted, (solely or mainly) for the purpose of facilitating sleeping or staying in a place for any period;

    (c)   using any tent or other such structure in the controlled area of Parliament Square for the purpose of sleeping or staying in that area;

    (d)   placing or keeping in place in the controlled area of Parliament Square any sleeping equipment with a view to its use (whether or not by the person placing it or keeping it in place) for the purpose of sleeping overnight in that area;

    (e)   using any sleeping equipment in the controlled area of Parliament Square for the purpose of sleeping overnight in that area.

(3)   But an activity is not to be treated as a 'prohibited activity' within subsection (2) if it is done—

    (a)   for police, fire and rescue authority or ambulance purposes,

    (b)   by or on behalf of a relevant authority, or

    (c)   by a person so far as authorised under section 147 to do it (authorisation for operation of amplified noise equipment).

(4)   In subsection (2)(a) 'amplified noise equipment' means any device that is designed or adapted for amplifying sound, including (but not limited to)—

    (a)   loudspeakers, and

    (b)   loudhailers.

(5)   In subsection (3)(b) 'relevant authority' means any of the following—

(a)   a Minister of the Crown or a government department,

(b)   the Greater London Authority, or

(c)   Westminster City Council.

(6)   It is immaterial for the purposes of a prohibited activity—

(a)   in the case of an activity within subsection (2)(b) or (c) of keeping a tent or similar structure erected or using a tent or similar structure, whether the tent or structure was first erected before or after the coming into force of this section;

(b)   in the case of an activity within subsection (2)(d) or (e) of keeping in place any sleeping equipment or using any such equipment, whether the sleeping equipment was first placed before or after the coming into force of this section.

(7)   In this section 'sleeping equipment' means any sleeping bag, mattress or other similar item designed, or adapted, (solely or mainly) for the purpose of facilitating sleeping in a place.

(8)   A person who fails without reasonable excuse to comply with a direction under subsection (1) commits an offence and is liable on summary conviction to a fine not exceeding level 5 on the standard scale.

B.41

144   Directions under section 143: further provision

(1)   A direction requiring a person to cease doing a prohibited activity may include a direction that the person does not start doing that activity again after having ceased it.

(2)   A direction requiring a person not to start doing a prohibited activity continues in force until—

(a)   the end of such period beginning with the day on which the direction is given as may be specified by the constable or authorised officer giving the direction, or

(b)   if no such period is specified, the end of the period of 90 days beginning with the day on which the direction is given.

(3)   A period specified under subsection (2)(a) may not be longer than 90 days.

(4)   A direction may be given to a person to cease operating, or not to start operating, any amplified noise equipment only if it appears to the constable or authorised officer giving the direction that the following condition is met.

(5)   The condition is that the person is operating, or is about to operate, the equipment in such a manner as to produce sound that other persons in or in the

vicinity of the controlled area of Parliament Square can hear or are likely to be able to hear.

(6)   A direction—

(a)   may be given orally,

(b)   may be given to any person individually or to two or more persons together, and

(c)   may be withdrawn or varied by the person who gave it.

(7)   In this section—

'amplified noise equipment' has the meaning given by section 143(4);

'direction' means a direction given under section 143(1).

B.42

145   Power to seize property

(1)   A constable or authorised officer may seize and retain a prohibited item that is on any land in the controlled area of Parliament Square if it appears to that constable or officer that the item is being, or has been, used in connection with the commission of an offence under section 143.

(2)   A constable may seize and retain a prohibited item that is on any land outside of the controlled area of Parliament Square if it appears to the constable that the item has been used in connection with the commission of an offence under section 143.

(3)   A 'prohibited item' is any item of a kind mentioned in section 143(2).

(4)   A constable may use reasonable force, if necessary, in exercising a power of seizure under this section.

(5)   An item seized under this section must be returned to the person from whom it was seized—

(a)   no later than the end of the period of 28 days beginning with the day on which the item was seized, or

(b)   if proceedings are commenced against the person for an offence under section 143 before the return of the item under paragraph (a), at the conclusion of those proceedings.

(6)   If it is not possible to return an item under subsection (5) because the name or address of the person from whom it was seized is not known—

(a)   the item may be returned to any other person appearing to have rights in the property who has come forward to claim it, or

(b)   if there is no such person, the item may be disposed of or destroyed at any time after the end of the period of 90 days beginning with the day on which the item was seized.

(7)   Subsections (5)(b) and (6) do not apply if a court makes an order under section 146(1)(a) for the forfeiture of the item.

(8)   The references in subsections (1) and (2) to an item that is 'on' any land include references to an item that is in the possession of a person who is on any such land.

B.43

146   Power of court on conviction

(1)   The court may do either or both of the following on the conviction of a person ('P') of an offence under section 143—

    (a)   make an order providing for the forfeiture of any item of a kind mentioned in subsection (2) of that section that was used in the commission of the offence;

    (b)   make such other order as the court considers appropriate for the purpose of preventing P from engaging in any prohibited activity in the controlled area of Parliament Square.

(2)   An order under subsection (1)(b) may (in particular) require P not to enter the controlled area of Parliament Square for such period as may be specified in the order.

(3)   Power of the court to make an order under this section is in addition to the court's power to impose a fine under section 143(8).

B.44

147   Authorisation for operation of amplified noise equipment

(1)   The responsible authority for any land in the controlled area of Parliament Square may authorise a person in accordance with this section to operate on that land any amplified noise equipment (as defined by section 143(4)).

(2)   An application for authorisation must be made to the responsible authority by or on behalf of the person (or persons) seeking the authorisation.

(3)   The responsible authority may—

    (a)   determine the form in which, and the manner in which, an application is to be made;

    (b)   specify the information to be supplied in connection with an application;

    (c)   require a fee to be paid for determining an application.

(4)   If an application is duly made to a responsible authority, the authority must—

    (a)   determine the application, and

    (b)   give notice in writing to the applicant of the authority's decision within the period of 21 days beginning with the day on which the authority receives the application.

(5)   The notice must specify—

    (a)   the person (or persons) authorised (whether by name or description),

    (b)   the kind of amplified noise equipment to which the authorisation applies,

    (c)   the period to which the authorisation applies, and

    (d)   any conditions to which the authorisation is subject.

(6)   The responsible authority may at any time—

    (a)   withdraw an authorisation given to a person under this section, or

    (b)   vary any condition to which an authorisation is subject.

(7)   Variation under subsection (6)(b) includes—

    (a)   imposing a new condition,

    (b)   removing an existing condition, or

    (c)   altering any period to which a condition applies.

(8)   The exercise of a power under subsection (6) to withdraw an authorisation or to vary a condition is effected by the responsible authority giving notice in writing to the applicant.

B.45

148   Meaning of 'authorised officer' and 'responsible authority'

(1)   This section applies for the purposes of this Part.

(2)   'Authorised officer', in relation to any land in the controlled area of Parliament Square, means—

    (a)   an employee of the responsible authority for that land who is authorised in writing by the authority for the purposes of this Part, and

    (b)   any other person who, under arrangements made with the responsible authority (whether by that or any other person), is so authorised for the purposes of this Part.

(3) 'Responsible authority', in relation to any land in the controlled area of Parliament Square, means—

    (a)   the Greater London Authority, for any land comprised in the central garden of Parliament Square (as defined by section 142(2)), and

    (b)   Westminster City Council, for any other land.

B.46

149 Effect of Part on byelaws

(1)   In section 385 of the Greater London Authority Act 1999 (byelaws), after subsection (6) insert—

'(6A)   Byelaws under this section may not be made as respects Parliament Square Garden for the purpose of prohibiting a particular activity so far as that activity is a prohibited activity for the purposes of Part 3 of the Police Reform and Social Responsibility Act 2011 (see section 143(2) of that Act).'.

(2)   Any byelaw made under section 385 of the Greater London Authority Act 1999 before the date on which section 143 above comes into force ceases to have effect on that date so far as the byelaw makes provision prohibiting, as respects the controlled area of Parliament Square, a particular activity that is a prohibited activity for the purposes of this Part.

(3)   Nothing in this Part restricts the making of any byelaw under section 235(1) of the Local Government Act 1972 (power of councils to make byelaws) for the purpose of prohibiting, as respects the controlled area of Parliament Square, a particular activity except so far as the activity is a prohibited activity for the purposes of this Part.

Police and Criminal Evidence Act 1984

1984 c 60

Part I
Powers to Stop and Search

B.47

1 Power of constable to stop and search persons, vehicles etc

(1)   A constable may exercise any power conferred by this section—

    (a)   in any place to which at the time when he proposes to exercise the power the public or any section of the public has access, on payment or otherwise, as of right or by virtue of express or implied permission; or

(b)   in any other place to which people have ready access at the time when he proposes to exercise the power but which is not a dwelling.

(2)   Subject to subsection (3) to (5) below, a constable—

(a)   may search—

(i)   any person or vehicle;

(ii)   anything which is in or on a vehicle,

for stolen or prohibited articles[, any article to which subsection (8A) below applies or any firework to which subsection (8B) below applies]; and

(b)   may detain a person or vehicle for the purpose of such a search.

(3)   This section does not give a constable power to search a person or vehicle or anything in or on a vehicle unless he has reasonable grounds for suspecting that he will find stolen or prohibited articles[, any article to which subsection (8A) below applies or any firework to which subsection (8B) below applies].

(4)   If a person is in a garden or yard occupied with and used for the purposes of a dwelling or on other land so occupied and used, a constable may not search him in the exercise of the power conferred by this section unless the constable has reasonable grounds for believing—

(a)   that he does not reside in the dwelling; and

(b)   that he is not in the place in question with the express or implied permission of a person who resides in the dwelling.

(5)   If a vehicle is in a garden or yard occupied with and used for the purposes of a dwelling or on other land so occupied and used, a constable may not search the vehicle or anything in or on it in the exercise of the power conferred by this section unless he has reasonable grounds for believing—

(a)   that the person in charge of the vehicle does not reside in the dwelling; and

(b)   that the vehicle is not in the place in question with the express or implied permission of a person who resides in the dwelling.

(6)   If in the course of such a search a constable discovers an article which he has reasonable grounds for suspecting to be a stolen or prohibited article[, an article to which subsection (8A) below applies or a firework to which subsection (8B) below applies], he may seize it.

(7)   An article is prohibited for the purposes of this Part of this Act if it is—

(a)   an offensive weapon; or

(b)   an article—

   (i)   made or adapted for use in the course of or in connection with an offence to which this sub-paragraph applies; or

   (ii)   intended by the person having it with him for such use by him or by some other person.

(8)   The offences to which subsection (7)(b)(i) above applies are—

   (a)   burglary;

   (b)   theft;

   (c)   offences under section 12 of the Theft Act 1968 (taking motor vehicle or other conveyance without authority); …

   [(d)   fraud (contrary to section 1 of the Fraud Act 2006)][; and

   (e)   offences under section 1 of the Criminal Damage Act 1971 (destroying or damaging property)].

[(8A)   This subsection applies to any article in relation to which a person has committed, or is committing or is going to commit an offence under section 139 of the Criminal Justice Act 1988.]

[(8B)   This subsection applies to any firework which a person possesses in contravention of a prohibition imposed by fireworks regulations.

(8C)   In this section—

   (a)   'firework' shall be construed in accordance with the definition of 'fireworks' in section 1(1) of the Fireworks Act 2003; and

   (b)   'fireworks regulations' has the same meaning as in that Act.]

(9)   In this Part of this Act 'offensive weapon' means any article—

   (a)   made or adapted for use for causing injury to persons; or

   (b)   intended by the person having it with him for such use by him or by some other person.

Amendment

Sub-s (2): in para (a) words from ', any article to' to '(8B) below applies' in square brackets (originally inserted by the Criminal Justice Act 1988, s 140(1)) substituted by the Serious Organised Crime and Police Act 2005, s 115(1), (2) (date in force: 1 July 2005: see SI 2005/1521, art 3(1)(f)).

Sub-s (3): words from ', any article to' to '(8B) below applies' in square brackets (originally enacted by the Criminal Justice Act 1988, s 140(1)) substituted by the Serious Organised Crime and Police Act 2005, s 115(1), (3) (date in force: 1 July 2005: see SI 2005/1521, art 3(1)(f)).

Sub-s (6): words ', an article to' to '(8A) below applies' in square brackets (originally inserted by the Criminal Justice Act 1988, s 140(1)) substituted by the Serious Organised Crime and Police Act 2005, s 115(1), (4) (date in force: 1 July 2005: see SI 2005/1521, art 3(1)(f)).

Sub-s (8): in para (c) word omitted repealed by the Criminal Justice Act 2003, s 332, Sch 37, Pt 1 (date in force: 20 January 2004: see SI 2004/81, art 2(1), (2)(g)(i));: para (d) substituted by the Fraud Act 2006, s 14(1), Sch 1, para 21 (date in force: 15 January 2007: see SI 2006/3200, art 2); para (e) and word '; and' immediately preceding it inserted by the Criminal Justice Act 2003, s 1(2) (date in force: 20 January 2004: see SI 2004/81, art 2(1), (2)(a)).

Sub-s (8A): inserted by the Criminal Justice Act 1988, s 140(1).

Sub-ss (8B), (8C): inserted by the Serious Organised Crime and Police Act 2005, s 115(1), (5) (date in force: 1 July 2005: see SI 2005/1521, art 3(1)(f)).

B.48

2   Provisions relating to search under section 1 and other powers

(1)   A constable who detains a person or vehicle in the exercise—

    (a)   of the power conferred by section 1 above; or

    (b)   of any other power—

        (i)   to search a person without first arresting him; or

        (ii)   to search a vehicle without making an arrest,

need not conduct a search if it appears to him subsequently—

    (i)   that no search is required; or

    (ii)   that a search is impracticable.

(2)   If a constable contemplates a search, other than a search of an unattended vehicle, in the exercise—

    (a)   of the power conferred by section 1 above; or

    (b)   of any other power, except the power conferred by section 6 below and the power conferred by section 27(2) of the Aviation Security Act 1982—

        (i)   to search a person without first arresting him; or

        (ii)   to search a vehicle without making an arrest,

it shall be his duty, subject to subsection (4) below, to take reasonable steps before he commences the search to bring to the attention of the appropriate person—

    (i)   if the constable is not in uniform, documentary evidence that he is a constable; and

    (ii)   whether he is in uniform or not, the matters specified in subsection (3) below;

and the constable shall not commence the search until he has performed that duty.

(3)   The matters referred to in subsection (2)(ii) above are—

(a)   the constable's name and the name of the police station to which he is attached;

(b)   the object of the proposed search;

(c)   the constable's grounds for proposing to make it; and

(d)   the effect of section 3(7) or (8) below, as may be appropriate.

(4)   A constable need not bring the effect of section 3(7) or (8) below to the attention of the appropriate person if it appears to the constable that it will not be practicable to make the record in section 3(1) below.

(5)   In this section 'the appropriate person' means—

(a)   if the constable proposes to search a person, that person; and

(b)   if he proposes to search a vehicle, or anything in or on a vehicle, the person in charge of the vehicle.

(6)   On completing a search of an unattended vehicle or anything in or on such a vehicle in the exercise of any such power as is mentioned in subsection (2) above a constable shall leave a notice—

(a)   stating that he has searched it;

(b)   giving the name of the police station to which he is attached;

(c)   stating that an application for compensation for any damage caused by the search may be made to that police station; and

(d)   stating the effect of section 3(8) below.

(7)   The constable shall leave the notice inside the vehicle unless it is not reasonably practicable to do so without damaging the vehicle.

(8)   The time for which a person or vehicle may be detained for the purposes of such a search is such time as is reasonably required to permit a search to be carried out either at the place where the person or vehicle was first detained or nearby.

(9)   Neither the power conferred by section 1 above nor any other power to detain and search a person without first arresting him or to detain and search a vehicle without making an arrest is to be construed—

(a)   as authorising a constable to require a person to remove any of his clothing in public other than an outer coat, jacket or gloves; or

(b)   as authorising a constable not in uniform to stop a vehicle.

(10)   This section and section 1 above apply to vessels, aircraft and hovercraft as they apply to vehicles.

B.49

3   Duty to make records concerning searches

(1)   Where a constable has carried out a search in the exercise of any such power as is mentioned in section 2(1) above, other than a search—

   (a)   under section 6 below; or

   (b)   under section 27(2) of the Aviation Security Act 1982,

[a record of the search shall be made] in writing unless it is not practicable to do so.

[(2)   If a record of a search is required to be made by subsection (1) above—

   (a)   in a case where the search results in a person being arrested and taken to a police station, the constable shall secure that the record is made as part of the person's custody record;

   (b)   in any other case, the constable shall make the record on the spot, or, if that is not practicable, as soon as practicable after the completion of the search.]

(3)   ...

(4)   ...

(5)   ...

(6)   The record of a search of a person or a vehicle—

   (a)   shall state—

      (i)   the object of the search;

      (ii)   the grounds for making it;

      (iii) the date and time when it was made;

      (iv)   the place where it was made;

      [(v) except in the case of a search of an unattended vehicle, the ethnic origins of the person searched or the person in charge of the vehicle searched (as the case may be); and]

   (b)   shall identify the constable [who carried out the search].

[(6A)   The requirement in subsection (6)(a)(v) above for a record to state a person's ethnic origins is a requirement to state—

   (a)   the ethnic origins of the person as described by the person, and

   (b)   if different, the ethnic origins of the person as perceived by the constable.]

(7)   [If a record of a search of a person has been made under this section,] the person who was searched shall be entitled to a copy of the record if he asks for one before the end of the period specified in subsection (9) below.

(8)   If—

(a)   the owner of a vehicle which has been searched or the person who was in charge of the vehicle at the time when it was searched asks for a copy of the record of the search before the end of the period specified in subsection (9) below; and

[(b)   a record of the search of the vehicle has been made under this section,]

the person who made the request shall be entitled to a copy.

(9)   The period mentioned in subsections (7) and (8) above is the period of [3 months] beginning with the date on which the search was made.

(10)   The requirements imposed by this section with regard to records of searches of vehicles shall apply also to records of searches of vessels, aircraft and hovercraft.

Amendment

Sub-s (1): words 'a record of the search shall be made' in square brackets substituted by the Crime and Security Act 2010, s 1(1), (2) (date in force: 7 March 2011: see SI 2011/414, art 2(a)).

Sub-s (2): substituted by the Crime and Security Act 2010, s 1(1), (3) (date in force: 7 March 2011: see SI 2011/414, art 2(a)).

Sub-ss (3)–(5): repealed by the Crime and Security Act 2010, s 1(1), (4) (date in force: 7 March 2011: see SI 2011/414, art 2(a)).

Sub-s (6): para (a)(v) substituted, for para (a)(v), (vi) as originally enacted, by the Crime and Security Act 2010, s 1(1), (5)(a) (date in force: 7 March 2011: see SI 2011/414, art 2(a)); in para (b) words 'who carried out the search' in square brackets substituted by the Crime and Security Act 2010, s 1(1), (5)(b) (date in force: 7 March 2011: see SI 2011/414, art 2(a)).

Sub-s (6A): inserted by the Crime and Security Act 2010, s 1(1), (6) (date in force: 7 March 2011: see SI 2011/414, art 2(a)).

Sub-s (7): words from 'If a record' to 'under this section,' in square brackets substituted by the Crime and Security Act 2010, s 1(1), (7) (date in force: 7 March 2011: see SI 2011/414, art 2(a)).

Sub-s (8): para (b) substituted by the Crime and Security Act 2010, s 1(1), (8) (date in force: 7 March 2011: see SI 2011/414, art 2(a)).

Sub-s (9): words '3 months' in square brackets substituted by the Crime and Security Act 2010, s 1(1), (9) (date in force: 7 March 2011: see SI 2011/414, art 2(a)).

Part II
Powers of Entry, Search and Seizure

Search warrants

B.50

8   Power of justice of the peace to authorise entry and search of premises

(1)   If on an application made by a constable a justice of the peace is satisfied that there are reasonable grounds for believing—

(a)   that [an indictable offence] has been committed; and

(b)   that there is material on premises [mentioned in subsection (1A) below] which is likely to be of substantial value (whether by itself or together with other material) to the investigation of the offence; and

(c)   that the material is likely to be relevant evidence; and

(d)   that it does not consist of or include items subject to legal privilege, excluded material or special procedure material; and

(e)   that any of the conditions specified in subsection (3) below applies [in relation to each set of premises specified in the application],

he may issue a warrant authorising a constable to enter and search the premises.

[(1A)   The premises referred to in subsection (1)(b) above are—

(a)   one or more sets of premises specified in the application (in which case the application is for a 'specific premises warrant'); or

(b)   any premises occupied or controlled by a person specified in the application, including such sets of premises as are so specified (in which case the application is for an 'all premises warrant').

(1B)   If the application is for an all premises warrant, the justice of the peace must also be satisfied—

(a)   that because of the particulars of the offence referred to in paragraph (a) of subsection (1) above, there are reasonable grounds for believing that it is necessary to search premises occupied or controlled by the person in question which are not specified in the application in order to find the material referred to in paragraph (b) of that subsection; and

(b)   that it is not reasonably practicable to specify in the application all the premises which he occupies or controls and which might need to be searched.]

[(1C) The warrant may authorise entry to and search of premises on more than one occasion if, on the application, the justice of the peace is satisfied that it is necessary to authorise multiple entries in order to achieve the purpose for which he issues the warrant.

(1D) If it authorises multiple entries, the number of entries authorised may be unlimited, or limited to a maximum.]

(2) A constable may seize and retain anything for which a search has been authorised under subsection (1) above.

(3) The conditions mentioned in subsection (1)(e) above are—

(a) that it is not practicable to communicate with any person entitled to grant entry to the premises;

(b) that it is practicable to communicate with a person entitled to grant entry to the premises but it is not practicable to communicate with any person entitled to grant access to the evidence;

(c) that entry to the premises will not be granted unless a warrant is produced;

(d) that the purpose of a search may be frustrated or seriously prejudiced unless a constable arriving at the premises can secure immediate entry to them.

(4) In this Act 'relevant evidence', in relation to an offence, means anything that would be admissible in evidence at a trial for the offence.

(5) The power to issue a warrant conferred by this section is in addition to any such power otherwise conferred.

[(6) This section applies in relation to a relevant offence (as defined in section 28D(4) of the Immigration Act 1971) as it applies in relation to [an indictable offence]].

[(7) Section 4 of the Summary Jurisdiction (Process) Act 1881 (execution of process of English courts in Scotland) shall apply to a warrant issued on the application of an officer of Revenue and Customs under this section by virtue of section 114 below.]

Amendment

Sub-s (1): in para (a) words 'an indictable offence' in square brackets substituted by the Serious Organised Crime and Police Act 2005, s 111, Sch 7, Pt 3, para 43(1), (3) (date in force: 1 January 2006: see SI 2005/3495, art 2(1)(m)); in para (b) words 'mentioned in subsection (1A) below' in square brackets substituted by the Serious Organised Crime and Police Act 2005, s 113(1), (2), (3)(a) (date in force: 1 January 2006: see SI 2005/3495, art 2(1)(n)); in para (e) words 'in relation to each set of premises specified in the application' in square brackets inserted by the Serious Organised Crime and Police Act 2005, s 113(1), (2), (3)(b) (date in force: 1 January 2006: see SI 2005/3495, art 2(1)(n)).

Sub-ss (1A), (1B): inserted by the Serious Organised Crime and Police Act 2005, s 113(1), (2), (4) (date in force: 1 January 2006: see SI 2005/3495, art 2(1)(n)).

Sub-ss (1C), (1D): inserted by the Serious Organised Crime and Police Act 2005, s 114(1), (2) (date in force: 1 January 2006: see SI 2005/3495, art 2(1)(n)).

Sub-s (6): inserted by the Immigration and Asylum Act 1999, s 169(1), Sch 14, para 80(1), (2) (date in force: 14 February 2000: see SI 2000/168, art 2, Schedule); words 'an indictable offence' in square brackets substituted by the Serious Organised Crime and Police Act 2005, s 111, Sch 7, Pt 3, para 43(1), (3) (date in force: 1 January 2006: see SI 2005/3495, art 2(1)(m)).

Sub-s (7): inserted by the Finance Act 2007, s 86 (date in force: this amendment came into force on 19 July 2007 (date of Royal Assent of the Finance Act 2007) in the absence of any specific commencement provision).

B.51

9   Special provisions as to access

(1)   A constable may obtain access to excluded material or special procedure material for the purposes of a criminal investigation by making an application under Schedule 1 below and in accordance with that Schedule.

(2)   Any Act (including a local Act) passed before this Act under which a search of premises for the purposes of a criminal investigation could be authorised by the issue of a warrant to a constable shall cease to have effect so far as it relates to the authorisation of searches—

(a)   for items subject to legal privilege; or

(b)   for excluded material; or

(c)   for special procedure material consisting of documents or records other than documents.

[(2A)   Section 4 of the Summary Jurisdiction (Process) Act 1881 (c 24) (which includes provision for the execution of process of English courts in Scotland) and section 29 of the Petty Sessions (Ireland) Act 1851 (c 93) (which makes equivalent provision for execution in Northern Ireland) shall each apply to any process issued by a circuit judge under Schedule 1 to this Act as it applies to process issued by a magistrates' court under the Magistrates' Courts Act 1980 (c 43).]

Amendment
Sub-s (2A): inserted by the Criminal Justice and Police Act 2001, s 86(1) (date in force: 1 August 2001: see SI 2001/2223, art 3(e)).

B.52

10   Meaning of 'items subject to legal privilege'

(1)   Subject to subsection (2) below, in this Act 'items subject to legal privilege' means—

(a)   communications between a professional legal adviser and his client or any person representing his client made in connection with the giving of legal advice to the client;

(b) communications between a professional legal adviser and his client or any person representing his client or between such an adviser or his client or any such representative and any other person made in connection with or in contemplation of legal proceedings and for the purposes of such proceedings; and

(c) items enclosed with or referred to in such communications and made—

(i) in connection with the giving of legal advice; or

(ii) in connection with or in contemplation of legal proceedings and for the purposes of such proceedings,

when they are in the possession of a person who is entitled to possession of them.

(2) Items held with the intention of furthering a criminal purpose are not items subject to legal privilege.

B.53

11 Meaning of 'excluded material'

(1) Subject to the following provisions of this section, in this Act 'excluded material' means—

(a) personal records which a person has acquired or created in the course of any trade, business, profession or other occupation or for the purposes of any paid or unpaid office and which he holds in confidence;

(b) human tissue or tissue fluid which has been taken for the purposes of diagnosis or medical treatment and which a person holds in confidence;

(c) journalistic material which a person holds in confidence and which consists—

(i) of documents; or

(ii) of records other than documents.

(2) A person holds material other than journalistic material in confidence for the purposes of this section if he holds it subject—

(a) to an express or implied undertaking to hold it in confidence; or

(b) to a restriction on disclosure or an obligation of secrecy contained in any enactment, including an enactment contained in an Act passed after this Act.

(3)   A person holds journalistic material in confidence for the purposes of this section if—

    (a)   he holds it subject to such an undertaking, restriction or obligation; and

    (b)   it has been continuously held (by one or more persons) subject to such an undertaking, restriction or obligation since it was first acquired or created for the purposes of journalism.

B.54

12   Meaning of 'personal records'

In this Part of this Act 'personal records' means documentary and other records concerning an individual (whether living or dead) who can be identified from them and relating—

    (a)   to his physical or mental health;

    (b)   to spiritual counselling or assistance given or to be given to him; or

    (c)   to counselling or assistance given or to be given to him, for the purposes of his personal welfare, by any voluntary organisation or by any individual who—

        (i)   by reason of his office or occupation has responsibilities for his personal welfare; or

        (ii)   by reason of an order of a court has responsibilities for his supervision.

B.55

13   Meaning of 'journalistic material'

(1)   Subject to subsection (2) below, in this Act 'journalistic material' means material acquired or created for the purposes of journalism.

(2)   Material is only journalistic material for the purposes of this Act if it is in the possession of a person who acquired or created it for the purposes of journalism.

(3)   A person who receives material from someone who intends that the recipient shall use it for the purposes of journalism is to be taken to have acquired it for those purposes.

B.56

14   Meaning of 'special procedure material'

(1)   In this Act 'special procedure material' means—

(a)   material to which subsection (2) below applies; and

(b)   journalistic material, other than excluded material.

(2)   Subject to the following provisions of this section, this subsection applies to material, other than items subject to legal privilege and excluded material, in the possession of a person who—

(a)   acquired or created it in the course of any trade, business, profession or other occupation or for the purpose of any paid or unpaid office; and

(b)   holds it subject—

(i)   to an express or implied undertaking to hold it in confidence; or

(ii)   to a restriction or obligation such as is mentioned in section 11(2)(b) above.

(3)   Where material is acquired—

(a)   by an employee from his employer and in the course of his employment; or

(b)   by a company from an associated company,

it is only special procedure material if it was special procedure material immediately before the acquisition.

(4)   Where material is created by an employee in the course of his employment, it is only special procedure material if it would have been special procedure material had his employer created it.

(5)   Where material is created by a company on behalf of an associated company, it is only special procedure material if it would have been special procedure material had the associated company created it.

(6)   A company is to be treated as another's associated company for the purposes of this section if it would be so treated under [section 449 of the Corporation Tax Act 2010].

Amendment
Sub-s (6): words 'section 449 of the Corporation Tax Act 2010' in square brackets substituted by the Corporation Tax Act 2010, s 1177, Sch 1, Pt 2, para 193; for transitional provisions and savings see s 1180(1), Sch 2, Pts 1, 2 thereto (date in force: this amendment has effect for corporation tax purposes for accounting periods ending on or after 1 April 2010: see the Corporation Tax Act 2010, s 1184(1)(a); this amendment has effect for income tax and capital gains tax purposes for the tax year 2010–11 and subsequent tax years: see the Corporation Tax Act 2010, s 1184(1)(b)).

B.57

15   Search warrants—safeguards

(1)   This section and section 16 below have effect in relation to the issue to constables under any enactment, including an enactment contained in an Act passed after this Act, of warrants to enter and search premises; and an entry on or search of premises under a warrant is unlawful unless it complies with this section and section 16 below.

(2)   Where a constable applies for any such warrant, it shall be his duty—

    (a)   to state—

        (i)   the ground on which he makes the application; ...

        (ii)   the enactment under which the warrant would be issued; [and]

      [(iii)   if the application is for a warrant authorising entry and search on more than one occasion, the ground on which he applies for such a warrant, and whether he seeks a warrant authorising an unlimited number of entries, or (if not) the maximum number of entries desired;]

    [(b)   to specify the matters set out in subsection (2A) below; and]

    (c)   to identify, so far as is practicable, the articles or persons to be sought.

[(2A)   The matters which must be specified pursuant to subsection (2)(b) above are—

    [(a)   if the application relates to one or more sets of premises specified in the application, each set of premises which it is desired to enter and search;]

    (b)   [if the application relates to any premises occupied or controlled by a person specified in the application—]

        (i)   as many sets of premises which it is desired to enter and search as it is reasonably practicable to specify;

        (ii)   the person who is in occupation or control of those premises and any others which it is desired to enter and search;

      (iii)   why it is necessary to search more premises than those specified under sub-paragraph (i); and

      (iv)   why it is not reasonably practicable to specify all the premises which it is desired to enter and search.]

(3)   An application for such a warrant shall be made ex parte and supported by an information in writing.

(4) The constable shall answer on oath any question that the justice of the peace or judge hearing the application asks him.

(5) A warrant shall authorise an entry on one occasion only [unless it specifies that it authorises multiple entries].

[(5A) If it specifies that it authorises multiple entries, it must also specify whether the number of entries authorised is unlimited, or limited to a specified maximum.]

(6) A warrant—

    (a) shall specify—

        (i) the name of the person who applies for it;

        (ii) the date on which it is issued;

        (iii) the enactment under which it is issued; and

        [(iv) each set of premises to be searched, or (in the case of an all premises warrant) the person who is in occupation or control of premises to be searched, together with any premises under his occupation or control which can be specified and which are to be searched; and]

    (b) shall identify, so far as is practicable, the articles or persons to be sought.

[(7) Two copies shall be made of a [warrant] (see section 8(1A)(a) above) which specifies only one set of premises and does not authorise multiple entries; and as many copies as are reasonably required may be made of any other kind of warrant.]

(8) The copies shall be clearly certified as copies.

Amendment

    Sub-s (2): in para (a)(i) word omitted repealed by the Serious Organised Crime and Police Act 2005, ss 114(1), (3), (4)(a), 174(2), Sch 17, Pt 2 (date in force: 1 January 2006: see SI 2005/3495, art 2(1)(n), (t), (u)(xxiv)); in para (a)(ii) word 'and' in square brackets inserted by the Serious Organised Crime and Police Act 2005, s 114(1), (3), (4)(b) (date in force: 1 January 2006: see SI 2005/3495, art 2(1)(n)); para (a)(iii) inserted by the Serious Organised Crime and Police Act 2005, s 114(1), (3), (4)(c) (date in force: 1 January 2006: see SI 2005/3495, art 2(1)(n)); para (b) substituted by the Serious Organised Crime and Police Act 2005, s 113(1), (5), (6) (date in force: 1 January 2006: see SI 2005/3495, art 2(1)(n)).

    Sub-s (2A): inserted by the Serious Organised Crime and Police Act 2005, s 113(1), (5), (7) (date in force: 1 January 2006: see SI 2005/3495, art 2(1)(n)); para (a) substituted by SI 2005/3496, art 7(1), (2)(a) (date in force: 1 January 2006: see SI 2005/3496, art 1(1)); in para (b) words from 'if the application' to 'in the application—' in square brackets substituted by SI 2005/3496, art 7(1), (2)(b) (date in force: 1 January 2006: see SI 2005/3496, art 1(1)).

    Sub-s (5): words 'unless it specifies that it authorises multiple entries' in square brackets inserted by the Serious Organised Crime and Police Act 2005, s 114(1), (3), (5) (date in force: 1 January 2006: see SI 2005/3495, art 2(1)(n)).

    Sub-s (5A): inserted by the Serious Organised Crime and Police Act 2005, s 114(1), (3), (6) (date in force: 1 January 2006: see SI 2005/3495, art 2(1)(n)).

Sub-s (6): para (a)(iv) substituted by the Serious Organised Crime and Police Act 2005, s 113(1), (5), (8) (date in force: 1 January 2006: see SI 2005/3495, art 2(1)(n)).

Sub-s (7): substituted by the Serious Organised Crime and Police Act 2005, s 114(1), (3), (7) (date in force: 1 January 2006: see SI 2005/3495, art 2(1)(n)); word 'warrant' in square brackets substituted by SI 2005/3496, art 7(1), (3) (date in force: 1 January 2006: see SI 2005/3496, art 1(1)).

B.58

16   Execution of warrants

(1)   A warrant to enter and search premises may be executed by any constable.

(2)   Such a warrant may authorise persons to accompany any constable who is executing it.

[(2A)   A person so authorised has the same powers as the constable whom he accompanies in respect of—

    (a)   the execution of the warrant, and

    (b)   the seizure of anything to which the warrant relates.

(2B)   But he may exercise those powers only in the company, and under the supervision, of a constable.]

(3)   Entry and search under a warrant must be within [three months] from the date of its issue.

[(3A)   If the warrant is an all premises warrant, no premises which are not specified in it may be entered or searched unless a police officer of at least the rank of inspector has in writing authorised them to be entered.]

[(3B)   No premises may be entered or searched for the second or any subsequent time under a warrant which authorises multiple entries unless a police officer of at least the rank of inspector has in writing authorised that entry to those premises.]

(4)   Entry and search under a warrant must be at a reasonable hour unless it appears to the constable executing it that the purpose of a search may be frustrated on an entry at a reasonable hour.

(5)   Where the occupier of premises which are to be entered and searched is present at the time when a constable seeks to execute a warrant to enter and search them, the constable—

    (a)   shall identify himself to the occupier and, if not in uniform, shall produce to him documentary evidence that he is a constable;

    (b)   shall produce the warrant to him; and

    (c)   shall supply him with a copy of it.

(6)   Where—

(a)   the occupier of such premises is not present at the time when a constable seeks to execute such a warrant; but

(b)   some other person who appears to the constable to be in charge of the premises is present,

subsection (5) above shall have effect as if any reference to the occupier were a reference to that other person.

(7)   If there is no person present who appears to the constable to be in charge of the premises, he shall leave a copy of the warrant in a prominent place on the premises.

(8)   A search under a warrant may only be a search to the extent required for the purpose for which the warrant was issued.

(9)   A constable executing a warrant shall make an endorsement on it stating—

(a)   whether the articles or persons sought were found; and

(b)   whether any articles were seized, other than articles which were sought [and,

unless the warrant is a … warrant specifying one set of premises only, he shall do so separately in respect of each set of premises entered and searched, which he shall in each case state in the endorsement].

[(10)   A warrant shall be returned to the appropriate person mentioned in subsection (10A) below—

(a)   when it has been executed; or

(b)   in the case of a specific premises warrant which has not been executed, or an all premises warrant, or any warrant authorising multiple entries, upon the expiry of the period of three months referred to in subsection (3) above or sooner.

(10A)   The appropriate person is—

(a)   if the warrant was issued by a justice of the peace, the designated officer for the local justice area in which the justice was acting when he issued the warrant;

(b)   if it was issued by a judge, the appropriate officer of the court from which he issued it.]

(11)   A warrant which is returned under subsection (10) above shall be retained for 12 months from its return—

(a)   by the [designated officer for the local justice area], if it was returned under paragraph (i) of that subsection; and

(b)   by the appropriate officer, if it was returned under paragraph (ii).

(12)   If during the period for which a warrant is to be retained the occupier of [premises] to which it relates asks to inspect it, he shall be allowed to do so.

Amendment

Sub-ss (2A), (2B): inserted by the Criminal Justice Act 2003, s 2 (date in force: 20 January 2004: see SI 2004/81, art 2(1), (2)(a)).

Sub-s (3): words 'three months' in square brackets substituted by the Serious Organised Crime and Police Act 2005, s 114(1), (8)(a) (date in force: 1 January 2006: see SI 2005/3495, art 2(1)(n)).

Sub-s (3A): inserted by the Serious Organised Crime and Police Act 2005, s 113(1), (9)(a) (date in force: 1 January 2006: see SI 2005/3495, art 2(1)(n)).

Sub-s (3B): inserted by the Serious Organised Crime and Police Act 2005, s 114(1), (8)(b) (date in force: 1 January 2006: see SI 2005/3495, art 2(1)(n)).

Sub-s (9): words from 'and, unless the warrant' to 'in the endorsement' in square brackets inserted by the Serious Organised Crime and Police Act 2005, s 113(1), (9)(b) (date in force: 1 January 2006: see SI 2005/3495, art 2(1)(n)); words omitted repealed by SI 2005/3496, art 8 (date in force: 1 January 2006: see SI 2005/3496, art 1(1)).

Sub-ss (10), (10A): substituted, for sub-s (10) as originally enacted, by the Serious Organised Crime and Police Act 2005, s 114(1), (8)(c) (date in force: 1 January 2006: see SI 2005/3495, art 2(1)(n)).

Sub-s (11): in para (a) words 'designated officer for the local justice area' in square brackets substituted by the Courts Act 2003, s 109(1), Sch 8, para 281(1), (3) (date in force: 1 April 2005: see SI 2005/910, art 3(y); for transitional provisions see SI 2005/911, arts 2–5).

Sub-s (12): word 'premises' in square brackets substituted by the Serious Organised Crime and Police Act 2005, s 113(1), (9)(c) (date in force: 1 January 2006: see SI 2005/3495, art 2(1)(n)).

Entry and search without search warrant

B.59

17   Entry for purpose of arrest etc

(1)   Subject to the following provisions of this section, and without prejudice to any other enactment, a constable may enter and search any premises for the purpose—

    (a)   of executing—

        (i)   a warrant of arrest issued in connection with or arising out of criminal proceedings; or

        (ii)   a warrant of commitment issued under section 76 of the Magistrates' Courts Act 1980;

    (b)   of arresting a person for an [indictable] offence;

    (c)   of arresting a person for an offence under—

        (i)   section 1 (prohibition of uniforms in connection with political objects) ... of the Public Order Act 1936;

        (ii)   any enactment contained in sections 6 to 8 or 10 of the

Criminal Law Act 1977 (offences relating to entering and remaining on property);

[(iii) section 4 of the Public Order Act 1986 (fear or provocation of violence);]

[(iiia) section 4 (driving etc when under influence of drink or drugs) or 163 (failure to stop when required to do so by constable in uniform) of the Road Traffic Act 1988;

(iiib) section 27 of the Transport and Works Act 1992 (which relates to offences involving drink or drugs);]

[(iv) section 76 of the Criminal Justice and Public Order Act 1994 (failure to comply with interim possession order);]

[(v) any of sections 4, 5, 6(1) and (2), 7 and 8(1) and (2) of the Animal Welfare Act 2006 (offences relating to the prevention of harm to animals);]

[(ca) of arresting, in pursuance of section 32(1A) of the Children and Young Persons Act 1969, any child or young person who has been remanded or committed to local authority accommodation under section 23(1) of that Act;

[(caa) of arresting a person for an offence to which section 61 of the Animal Health Act 1981 applies;]

(cb) of recapturing any person who is, or is deemed for any purpose to be, unlawfully at large while liable to be detained—

    (i)   in a prison, remand centre, young offender institution or secure training centre, or

    (ii) in pursuance of [section 92 of the Powers of Criminal Courts (Sentencing) Act 2000] (dealing with children and young persons guilty of grave crimes), in any other place;]

(d) of recapturing [any person whatever] who is unlawfully at large and whom he is pursuing; or

(e) of saving life or limb or preventing serious damage to property.

(2) Except for the purpose specified in paragraph (e) of subsection (1) above, the powers of entry and search conferred by this section—

(a) are only exercisable if the constable has reasonable grounds for believing that the person whom he is seeking is on the premises; and

(b) are limited, in relation to premises consisting of two or more separate dwellings, to powers to enter and search—

    (i)   any parts of the premises which the occupiers of any dwelling comprised in the premises use in common with the occupiers of any other such dwelling; and

(ii)   any such dwelling in which the constable has reasonable grounds for believing that the person whom he is seeking may be.

(3)   The powers of entry and search conferred by this section are only exercisable for the purposes specified in subsection (1)(c)(ii) [or (iv)] above by a constable in uniform.

(4)   The power of search conferred by this section is only a power to search to the extent that is reasonably required for the purpose for which the power of entry is exercised.

(5)   Subject to subsection (6) below, all the rules of common law under which a constable has power to enter premises without a warrant are hereby abolished.

(6)   Nothing in subsection (5) above affects any power of entry to deal with or prevent a breach of the peace.

Amendment

Sub-s (1): in para (b) word 'indictable' in square brackets substituted by the Serious Organised Crime and Police Act 2005, s 111, Sch 7, Pt 3, para 43(1), (4) (date in force: 1 January 2006: see SI 2005/3495, art 2(1)(m)); in para (c)(i) words omitted repealed by the Public Order Act 1986, s 40(3), Sch 3; para (c)(iii) inserted by the Public Order Act 1986, s 40(2), Sch 2, para 7; para (c)(iiia), (iiib) substituted, for para (c)(iiia) (as inserted by the Police Reform Act 2002, s 49(2)), by the Serious Organised Crime and Police Act 2005, s 111, Sch 7, Pt 4, para 58(a) (date in force: 1 January 2006: see SI 2005/3495, art 2(1)(m)); para (c)(iv) inserted by the Criminal Justice and Public Order Act 1994, s 168(2), Sch 10, para 53(a); para (c)(v) inserted by the Animal Welfare Act 2006, s 24 (date in force (in relation to Wales): 27 March 2007: see SI 2007/1030, art 2(1)(e); (in relation to England): 6 April 2007: see SI 2007/499, art 2(2)(g)); paras (ca), (cb) inserted by the Prisoners (Return to Custody) Act 1995, s 2(1); para (caa) inserted by the Serious Organised Crime and Police Act 2005, s 111, Sch 7, Pt 4, para 58(b) (date in force: 1 January 2006: see SI 2005/3495, art 2(1)(m)); in para (cb)(ii) words 'section 92 of the Powers of Criminal Courts (Sentencing) Act 2000' in square brackets substituted by the Powers of Criminal Courts (Sentencing) Act 2000, s 165(1), Sch 9, para 95 (date in force: 25 August 2000: see the Powers of Criminal Courts (Sentencing) Act 2000, s 168(1)); in para (d) words 'any person whatever' in square brackets substituted by the Prisoners (Return to Custody) Act 1995, s 2(1).

Sub-s (3): words in square brackets inserted by the Criminal Justice and Public Order Act 1994, s 168(2), Sch 10, para 53(b).

B.60

18   Entry and search after arrest

(1)   Subject to the following provisions of this section, a constable may enter and search any premises occupied or controlled by a person who is under arrest for an [indictable] offence, if he has reasonable grounds for suspecting that there is on the premises evidence, other than items subject to legal privilege, that relates—

(a)   to that offence; or

(b)   to some other [indictable] offence which is connected with or similar to that offence.

(2)   A constable may seize and retain anything for which he may search under subsection (1) above.

(3)   The power to search conferred by subsection (1) above is only a power to search to the extent that is reasonably required for the purpose of discovering such evidence.

(4)   Subject to subsection (5) below, the powers conferred by this section may not be exercised unless an officer of the rank of inspector or above has authorised them in writing.

[(5)   A constable may conduct a search under subsection (1)—

(a)   before the person is taken to a police station or released on bail under section 30A, and

(b)   without obtaining an authorisation under subsection (4),

if the condition in subsection (5A) is satisfied.

(5A)   The condition is that the presence of the person at a place (other than a police station) is necessary for the effective investigation of the offence.]

(6)   If a constable conducts a search by virtue of subsection (5) above, he shall inform an officer of the rank of inspector or above that he has made the search as soon as practicable after he has made it.

(7)   An officer who—

(a)   authorises a search; or

(b)   is informed of a search under subsection (6) above, shall make a record in writing—

(i)   of the grounds for the search; and

(ii)   of the nature of the evidence that was sought.

(8)   If the person who was in occupation or control of the premises at the time of the search is in police detention at the time the record is to be made, the officer shall make the record as part of his custody record.

Amendment
Sub-s (1): word 'indictable' in square brackets in both places it occurs substituted by the Serious Organised Crime and Police Act 2005, s 111, Sch 7, Pt 3, para 43(1), (5). (date in force: 1 January 2006: see SI 2005/3495, art 2(1)(m)).
Sub-ss (5), (5A): substituted, for sub-s (5) as originally enacted, by the Criminal Justice Act 2003, s 12, Sch 1, paras 1, 2 (date in force: 20 January 2004: see SI 2004/81, art 2(1), (2)(a)).

Annex B *Extracts from relevant legislation*

Seizure etc

B.61

19 General power of seizure etc

(1) The powers conferred by subsections (2), (3) and (4) below are exercisable by a constable who is lawfully on any premises.

(2) The constable may seize anything which is on the premises if he has reasonable grounds for believing—

(a) that it has been obtained in consequence of the commission of an offence; and

(b) that it is necessary to seize it in order to prevent it being concealed, lost, damaged, altered or destroyed.

(3) The constable may seize anything which is on the premises if he has reasonable grounds for believing—

(a) that it is evidence in relation to an offence which he is investigating or any other offence; and

(b) that it is necessary to seize it in order to prevent the evidence being concealed, lost, altered or destroyed.

(4) The constable may require any information which is [stored in any electronic form] and is accessible from the premises to be produced in a form in which it can be taken away and in which it is visible and legible [or from which it can readily be produced in a visible and legible form] if he has reasonable grounds for believing—

(a) that—

(i) it is evidence in relation to an offence which he is investigating or any other offence; or

(ii) it has been obtained in consequence of the commission of an offence; and

(b) that it is necessary to do so in order to prevent it being concealed, lost, tampered with or destroyed.

(5) The powers conferred by this section are in addition to any power otherwise conferred.

(6) No power of seizure conferred on a constable under any enactment (including an enactment contained in an Act passed after this Act) is to be taken to authorise the seizure of an item which the constable exercising the power has reasonable grounds for believing to be subject to legal privilege.

Amendment
Sub-s (4): words 'stored in any electronic form' in square brackets substituted by the Criminal
Justice and Police Act 2001, s 70, Sch 2, Pt 2, para 13(1)(a), (2)(a) (date in force: 1 April
2003: see SI 2003/708, art 2(c), (k)); words from 'or from which' to 'and legible form' in
square brackets inserted by the Criminal Justice and Police Act 2001, s 70, Sch 2, Pt 2,
para 13(1)(b), (2)(a) (date in force: 1 April 2003: see SI 2003/708, art 2(c), (k)).

B.62

20   Extension of powers of seizure to computerised information

(1)   Every power of seizure which is conferred by an enactment to which this
section applies on a constable who has entered premises in the exercise of a
power conferred by an enactment shall be construed as including a power to
require any information [stored in any electronic form] and accessible from the
premises to be produced in a form in which it can be taken away and in which it
is visible and legible [or from which it can readily be produced in a visible and
legible form].

(2)   This section applies—

    (a)   to any enactment contained in an Act passed before this Act;

    (b)   to sections 8 and 18 above;

    (c)   to paragraph 13 of Schedule 1 to this Act; and

    (d)   to any enactment contained in an Act passed after this Act.

Amendment
Sub-s (1): words 'stored in any electronic form' in square brackets substituted by the Criminal
Justice and Police Act 2001, s 70, Sch 2, Pt 2, para 13(1)(a), (2)(a) (date in force: 1 April
2003: see SI 2003/708, art 2(c), (k)); words from 'or from which' to 'and legible form' in
square brackets inserted by the Criminal Justice and Police Act 2001, s 70, Sch 2, Pt 2,
para 13(1)(b), (2)(a) (date in force: 1 April 2003: see SI 2003/708, art 2(c), (k)).

B.63

21   Access and copying

(1)   A constable who seizes anything in the exercise of a power conferred by
any enactment, including an enactment contained in an Act passed after this
Act, shall, if so requested by a person showing himself—

    (a)   to be the occupier of premises on which it was seized; or

    (b)   to have had custody or control of it immediately before the seizure,

provide that person with a record of what he seized.

(2)   The officer shall provide the record within a reasonable time from the
making of the request for it,

(3)   Subject to subsection (8) below, if a request for permission to be granted access to anything which—

(a)   has been seized by a constable; and

(b)   is retained by the police for the purpose of investigating an offence,

is made to the officer in charge of the investigation by a person who had custody or control of the thing immediately before it was so seized or by someone acting on behalf of such a person, the officer shall allow the person who made the request access to it under the supervision of a constable.

(4)   Subject to subsection (8) below, if a request for a photograph or copy of any such thing is made to the officer in charge of the investigation by a person who had custody or control of the thing immediately before it was so seized, or by someone acting on behalf of such a person, the officer shall—

(a)   allow the person who made the request access to it under the supervision of a constable for the purpose of photographing or copying it; or

(b)   photograph or copy it, or cause it to be photographed or copied.

(5)   A constable may also photograph or copy, or have photographed or copied, anything which he has power to seize, without a request being made under subsection (4) above.

(6)   Where anything is photographed or copied under subsection (4)(*b*) above, the photograph or copy shall be supplied to the person who made the request.

(7)   The photograph or copy shall be so supplied within a reasonable time from the making of the request.

(8)   There is no duty under this section to grant access to, or to supply a photograph or copy of, anything if the officer in charge of the investigation for the purposes of which it was seized has reasonable grounds for believing that to do so would prejudice—

(a)   that investigation;

(b)   the investigating of an offence other than the offence for the purposes of investigating which the thing was seized; or

(c)   any criminal proceedings which may be brought as a result of—

(i)   the investigation of which he is in charge; or

(ii)   any such investigation as is mentioned in paragraph (*b*) above.

[(9)   The references to a constable in subsections (1), (2), (3)(a) and (5) include a person authorised under section 16(2) to accompany a constable executing a warrant.]

Amendment
Sub-s (9): inserted by the Criminal Justice Act 2003, s 12, Sch 1, paras 1, 3 (date in force: 20 January 2004: see SI 2004/81, art 2(1), (2)(a)).

B.64

22 Retention

(1) Subject to subsection (4) below, anything which has been seized by a constable or taken away by a constable following a requirement made by virtue of section 19 or 20 above may be retained so long as is necessary in all the circumstances.

(2) Without prejudice to the generality of subsection (1) above—

(a) anything seized for the purposes of a criminal investigation may be retained, except as provided by subsection (4) below,—

(i) for use as evidence at a trial for an offence; or

(ii) for forensic examination or for investigation in connection with an offence; and

(b) anything may be retained in order to establish its lawful owner, where there are reasonable grounds for believing that it has been obtained in consequence of the commission of an offence.

(3) Nothing seized on the ground that it may be used—

(a) to cause physical injury to any person;

(b) to damage property;

(c) to interfere with evidence; or

(d) to assist in escape from police detention or lawful custody,

may be retained when the person from whom it was seized is no longer in police detention or the custody of a court or is in the custody of a court but has been released on bail.

(4) Nothing may be retained for either of the purposes mentioned in subsection (2)(*a*) above if a photograph or copy would be sufficient for that purpose.

(5) Nothing in this section affects any power of a court to make an order under section 1 of the Police (Property) Act 1897.

[(6) This section also applies to anything retained by the police under section 28H(5) of the Immigration Act 1971.]

[(7) The reference in subsection (1) to anything seized by a constable includes anything seized by a person authorised under section 16(2) to accompany a constable executing a warrant.]

Amendment
Sub-s (6): inserted by the Immigration and Asylum Act 1999, s 169(1), Sch 14, para 80(1), (3) (date in force: 14 February 2000: see SI 2000/168, art 2, Schedule).
Sub-s (7): inserted by the Criminal Justice Act 2003, s 12, Sch 1, paras 1, 4 (date in force: 20 January 2004: see SI 2004/81, art 2(1), (2)(a)).

Supplementary

B.65

23 Meaning of 'premises' etc

In this Act—

'premises' includes any place and, in particular, includes—

    (a)   any vehicle, vessel, aircraft or hovercraft;

    (b)   any offshore installation;

    [(ba) any renewable energy installation;]

    (c)   any tent or movable structure; ...

'offshore installation' has the meaning given to it by section 1 of the Mineral Workings (Offshore Installations) Act 1971;

['renewable energy installation' has the same meaning as in Chapter 2 of Part 2 of the Energy Act 2004].

Amendment
In definition 'premises' para (ba) substituted, for word 'and' at end of para (b) as originally enacted, by the Energy Act 2004, s 103(2)(a) (date in force: 5 October 2004: see SI 2004/2575, art 2(1), Sch 1); in definition 'premises' in para (c) word omitted repealed by the Energy Act 2004, s 197(9), Sch 23, Pt 1 (date in force: 5 October 2004: see SI 2004/2575, art 2(1), Sch 1, Table); definition 'renewable energy installation' inserted by the Energy Act 2004, s 103(2)(b) (date in force: 5 October 2004: see SI 2004/2575, art 2(1), Sch 1).

Part III
Arrest

B.66

[24 Arrest without warrant: constables]

[(1)   A constable may arrest without a warrant—

    (a)   anyone who is about to commit an offence;

    (b)   anyone who is in the act of committing an offence;

    (c)   anyone whom he has reasonable grounds for suspecting to be about to commit an offence;

(d)   anyone whom he has reasonable grounds for suspecting to be committing an offence.

(2)   If a constable has reasonable grounds for suspecting that an offence has been committed, he may arrest without a warrant anyone whom he has reasonable grounds to suspect of being guilty of it.

(3)   If an offence has been committed, a constable may arrest without a warrant—

(a)   anyone who is guilty of the offence;

(b)   anyone whom he has reasonable grounds for suspecting to be guilty of it.

(4)   But the power of summary arrest conferred by subsection (1), (2) or (3) is exercisable only if the constable has reasonable grounds for believing that for any of the reasons mentioned in subsection (5) it is necessary to arrest the person in question.

(5)   The reasons are—

(a)   to enable the name of the person in question to be ascertained (in the case where the constable does not know, and cannot readily ascertain, the person's name, or has reasonable grounds for doubting whether a name given by the person as his name is his real name);

(b)   correspondingly as regards the person's address;

(c)   to prevent the person in question—

(i)   causing physical injury to himself or any other person;

(ii)   suffering physical injury;

(iii)   causing loss of or damage to property;

(iv)   committing an offence against public decency (subject to subsection (6)); or

(v)   causing an unlawful obstruction of the highway;

(d)   to protect a child or other vulnerable person from the person in question;

(e)   to allow the prompt and effective investigation of the offence or of the conduct of the person in question;

(f)   to prevent any prosecution for the offence from being hindered by the disappearance of the person in question.

(6)   Subsection (5)(c)(iv) applies only where members of the public going about their normal business cannot reasonably be expected to avoid the person in question.]

Annex B *Extracts from relevant legislation*

Amendment

Substituted, together with s 24A, for this section as originally enacted, by the Serious Organised Crime and Police Act 2005, s 110(1); for effect see s 110(4) thereof (date in force: 1 January 2006: see SI 2005/3495, art 2(1)(m)).

B.67

[24A   Arrest without warrant: other persons]

[(1)   A person other than a constable may arrest without a warrant—

  (a)   anyone who is in the act of committing an indictable offence;

  (b)   anyone whom he has reasonable grounds for suspecting to be committing an indictable offence.

(2)   Where an indictable offence has been committed, a person other than a constable may arrest without a warrant—

  (a)   anyone who is guilty of the offence;

  (b)   anyone whom he has reasonable grounds for suspecting to be guilty of it.

(3)   But the power of summary arrest conferred by subsection (1) or (2) is exercisable only if—

  (a)   the person making the arrest has reasonable grounds for believing that for any of the reasons mentioned in subsection (4) it is necessary to arrest the person in question; and

  (b)   it appears to the person making the arrest that it is not reasonably practicable for a constable to make it instead.

(4)   The reasons are to prevent the person in question—

  (a)   causing physical injury to himself or any other person;

  (b)   suffering physical injury;

  (c)   causing loss of or damage to property; or

  (d)   making off before a constable can assume responsibility for him.

[(5)   This section does not apply in relation to an offence under Part 3 or 3A of the Public Order Act 1986.]]

Amendment

Substituted, together with s 24, for s 24 as originally enacted, by the Serious Organised Crime and Police Act 2005, s 110(1); for effect see s 110(4) thereof (date in force: 1 January 2006: see SI 2005/3495, art 2(1)(m)).

Sub-s (5): inserted by the Racial and Religious Hatred Act 2006, s 2 (date in force: 1 October 2007: see SI 2007/2490, art 2(1)).

B.68

28 Information to be given on arrest

(1)   Subject to subsection (5) below, where a person is arrested, otherwise than by being informed that he is under arrest, the arrest is not lawful unless the person arrested is informed that he is under arrest as soon as is practicable after his arrest.

(2)   Where a person is arrested by a constable, subsection (1) above applies regardless of whether the fact of the arrest is obvious.

(3)   Subject to subsection (5) below, no arrest is lawful unless the person arrested is informed of the ground for the arrest at the time of, or as soon as is practicable after, the arrest.

(4)   Where a person is arrested by a constable, subsection (3) above applies regardless of whether the ground for the arrest is obvious.

(5)   Nothing in this section is to be taken to require a person to be informed—

(a)   that he is under arrest; or

(b)   of the ground for the arrest,

if it was not reasonably practicable for him to be so informed by reason of his having escaped from arrest before the information could be given.

B.69

29 Voluntary attendance at police station etc

Where for the purpose of assisting with an investigation a person attends voluntarily at a police station or at any other place where a constable is present or accompanies a constable to a police station or any such other place without having been arrested—

(a)   he shall be entitled to leave at will unless he is placed under arrest;

(b)   he shall be informed at once that he is under arrest if a decision is taken by a constable to prevent him from leaving at will.

B.70

30 Arrest elsewhere than at police station

[(1)   Subsection (1A) applies where a person is, at any place other than a police station—

(a)   arrested by a constable for an offence, or

(b)   taken into custody by a constable after being arrested for an offence by a person other than a constable.

(1A)   The person must be taken by a constable to a police station as soon as practicable after the arrest.

(1B)   Subsection (1A) has effect subject to section 30A (release on bail) and subsection (7) (release without bail).]

(2)   Subject to subsections (3) and (5) below, the police station to which an arrested person is taken under [subsection (1A)] above shall be a designated police station.

(3)   A constable to whom this subsection applies may take an arrested person to any police station unless it appears to the constable that it may be necessary to keep the arrested person in police detention for more than six hours.

(4)   Subsection (3) above applies—

> (a)   to a constable who is working in a locality covered by a police station which is not a designated police station; and

> (b)   to a constable belonging to a body of constables maintained by an authority other than a police authority.

(5)   Any constable may take an arrested person to any police station if—

> (a)   either of the following conditions is satisfied—

>> (i)   the constable has arrested him without the assistance of any other constable and no other constable is available to assist him;

>> (ii)   the constable has taken him into custody from a person other than a constable without the assistance of any other constable and no other constable is available to assist him; and

> (b)   it appears to the constable that he will be unable to take the arrested person to a designated police station without the arrested person injuring himself, the constable or some other person.

(6)   If the first police station to which an arrested person is taken after his arrest is not a designated police station, he shall be taken to a designated police station not more than six hours after his arrival at the first police station unless he is released previously.

[(7)   A person arrested by a constable at any place other than a police station must be released without bail if the condition in subsection (7A) is satisfied.

(7A)   The condition is that, at any time before the person arrested reaches a police station, a constable is satisfied that there are no grounds for keeping him under arrest or releasing him on bail under section 30A.]

(8)   A constable who releases a person under subsection (7) above shall record the fact that he has done so.

(9)   The constable shall make the record as soon as is practicable after the release.

[(10)   Nothing in subsection (1A) or in section 30A prevents a constable delaying taking a person to a police station or releasing him on bail if the condition in subsection (10A) is satisfied.

(10A)   The condition is that the presence of the person at a place (other than a police station) is necessary in order to carry out such investigations as it is reasonable to carry out immediately.

(11)   Where there is any such delay the reasons for the delay must be recorded when the person first arrives at the police station or (as the case may be) is released on bail.]

(12)   Nothing in [subsection (1A) or section 30A] above shall be taken to affect—

(a)   paragraphs 16(3) or 18(1) of Schedule 2 to the Immigration Act 1971;

(b)   section 34(1) of the Criminal Justice Act 1972; or

[(c)   any provision of the Terrorism Act 2000.]

(13)   Nothing in subsection (10) above shall be taken to affect paragraph 18(3) of Schedule 2 to the Immigration Act 1971.

Amendment

Sub-ss (1), (1A), (1B): substituted, for sub-s (1) as originally enacted, by the Criminal Justice Act 2003, s 4(1), (2) (date in force: 20 January 2004: see SI 2004/81, art 2(1), (2)(a)).

Sub-s (2): words 'subsection (1A)' in square brackets substituted by the Criminal Justice Act 2003, s 4(1), (3) (date in force: 20 January 2004: see SI 2004/81, art 2(1), (2)(a)).

Sub-ss (7), (7A): substituted, for sub-s (7) as originally enacted, by the Criminal Justice Act 2003, s 4(1), (4) (date in force: 20 January 2004: see SI 2004/81, art 2(1), (2)(a)).

Sub-ss (10), (10A), (11): substituted, for sub-ss (10), (11) as originally enacted, by the Criminal Justice Act 2003, s 4(1), (5) (date in force: 20 January 2004: see SI 2004/81, art 2(1), (2)(a)).

Sub-s (12): words 'subsection (1A) or section 30A' in square brackets substituted by the Criminal Justice Act 2003, s 4(1), (6) (date in force: 20 January 2004: see SI 2004/81, art 2(1), (2)(a)); para (c) substituted by the Terrorism Act 2000, s 125(1), Sch 15, para 5(1), (2) (date in force: 19 February 2001 (except in relation to a person detained prior to that date): see the Terrorism Act 2000, s 129(1)(b) and SI 2001/421, art 2).

B.71

[30A   Bail elsewhere than at police station]

[(1)   A constable may release on bail a person who is arrested or taken into custody in the circumstances mentioned in section 30(1).

(2)   A person may be released on bail under subsection (1) at any time before he arrives at a police station.

(3) A person released on bail under subsection (1) must be required to attend a police station.

[(3A) Where a constable releases a person on bail under subsection (1)—

(a) no recognizance for the person's surrender to custody shall be taken from the person,

(b) no security for the person's surrender to custody shall be taken from the person or from anyone else on the person's behalf,

(c) the person shall not be required to provide a surety or sureties for his surrender to custody, and

(d) no requirement to reside in a bail hostel may be imposed as a condition of bail.

(3B) Subject to subsection (3A), where a constable releases a person on bail under subsection (1) the constable may impose, as conditions of the bail, such requirements as appear to the constable to be necessary—

(a) to secure that the person surrenders to custody,

(b) to secure that the person does not commit an offence while on bail,

(c) to secure that the person does not interfere with witnesses or otherwise obstruct the course of justice, whether in relation to himself or any other person, or

(d) for the person's own protection or, if the person is under the age of 17, for the person's own welfare or in the person's own interests.

(4) Where a person is released on bail under subsection (1), a requirement may be imposed on the person as a condition of bail only under the preceding provisions of this section.]

(5) The police station which the person is required to attend may be any police station.]

Amendment
Inserted by the Criminal Justice Act 2003, s 4(1), (7) (date in force: 20 January 2004: see SI 2004/81, art 2(1), (2)(a)).
Sub-ss (3A), (3B), (4): substituted, for sub-s (4) as originally enacted, by the Police and Justice Act 2006, s 10, Sch 6, Pt 1, para 1, Pt 2, para 2 (date in force: 1 April 2007: see SI 2007/709, art 3(i)).

B.72

[30B Bail under section 30A: notices]

[(1) Where a constable grants bail to a person under section 30A, he must give that person a notice in writing before he is released.

(2) The notice must state—

(a)   the offence for which he was arrested, and

(b)   the ground on which he was arrested.

(3)   The notice must inform him that he is required to attend a police station.

(4)   It may also specify the police station which he is required to attend and the time when he is required to attend.

[(4A)   If the person is granted bail subject to conditions under section 30A(3B), the notice also—

(a)   must specify the requirements imposed by those conditions,

(b)   must explain the opportunities under sections 30CA(1) and 30CB(1) for variation of those conditions, and

(c)   if it does not specify the police station at which the person is required to attend, must specify a police station at which the person may make a request under section 30CA(1)(b).]

(5)   If the notice does not include the information mentioned in subsection (4), the person must subsequently be given a further notice in writing which contains that information.

(6)   The person may be required to attend a different police station from that specified in the notice under subsection (1) or (5) or to attend at a different time.

(7)   He must be given notice in writing of any such change as is mentioned in subsection (6) but more than one such notice may be given to him.]

Amendment
Inserted by the Criminal Justice Act 2003, s 4(1), (7) (date in force: 20 January 2004: see SI 2004/81, art 2(1), (2)(a)).
Sub-s (4A): inserted by the Police and Justice Act 2006, s 10, Sch 6, Pt 1, para 1, Pt 2, para 3 (date in force: 1 April 2007: see SI 2007/709, art 3(i)).

B.73

[30C   Bail under section 30A: supplemental]

[(1)   A person who has been required to attend a police station is not required to do so if he is given notice in writing that his attendance is no longer required.

(2)   If a person is required to attend a police station which is not a designated police station he must be—

(a)   released, or

(b)   taken to a designated police station,

not more than six hours after his arrival.

(3)   Nothing in the Bail Act 1976 applies in relation to bail under section 30A.

(4)   Nothing in section 30A or 30B or in this section prevents the re-arrest without a warrant of a person released on bail under section 30A if new evidence justifying a further arrest has come to light since his release.]

Amendment
Inserted by the Criminal Justice Act 2003, s 4(1), (7) (date in force: 20 January 2004: see SI 2004/81, art 2(1), (2)(a)).

B.74

[30CA   Bail under section 30A: variation of conditions by police]

[(1)   Where a person released on bail under section 30A(1) is on bail subject to conditions—

   (a)   a relevant officer at the police station at which the person is required to attend, or

   (b)   where no notice under section 30B specifying that police station has been given to the person, a relevant officer at the police station specified under section 30B(4A)(c),

may, at the request of the person but subject to subsection (2), vary the conditions.

(2)   On any subsequent request made in respect of the same grant of bail, subsection (1) confers power to vary the conditions of the bail only if the request is based on information that, in the case of the previous request or each previous request, was not available to the relevant officer considering that previous request when he was considering it.

(3)   Where conditions of bail granted to a person under section 30A(1) are varied under subsection (1)—

   (a)   paragraphs (a) to (d) of section 30A(3A) apply,

   (b)   requirements imposed by the conditions as so varied must be requirements that appear to the relevant officer varying the conditions to be necessary for any of the purposes mentioned in paragraphs (a) to (d) of section 30A(3B), and

   (c)   the relevant officer who varies the conditions must give the person notice in writing of the variation.

(4)   Power under subsection (1) to vary conditions is, subject to subsection (3)(a) and (b), power—

   (a)   to vary or rescind any of the conditions, and

   (b)   to impose further conditions.

(5)   In this section 'relevant officer', in relation to a designated police station, means a custody officer but, in relation to any other police station—

(a) means a constable ... who is not involved in the investigation of the offence for which the person making the request under subsection (1) was under arrest when granted bail under section 30A(1), if such a constable ... is readily available, and

(b) if no such constable ... is readily available—

    (i) means a constable other than the one who granted bail to the person, if such a constable is readily available, and

    (ii) if no such constable is readily available, means the constable who granted bail.]

Amendment
Inserted by the Police and Justice Act 2006, s 10, Sch 6, Pt 1, para 1, Pt 2, para 4 (date in force: 1 April 2007: see SI 2007/709, art 3(i)).
Sub-s (5): in para (a) words omitted repealed by the Policing and Crime Act 2009, s 112(1), (2), Sch 7, Pt 13, para 123(1), (2)(a)(i), Sch 8, Pt 13 (date in force: 12 January 2010: see the Policing and Crime Act 2009, s 116(6)(a)); in paras (a), (b) words omitted repealed by the Policing and Crime Act 2009, s 112(1), (2), Sch 7, Pt 13, para 123(1), (2)(a)(ii), (b), Sch 8, Pt 13 (date in force: 12 January 2010: see the Policing and Crime Act 2009, s 116(6)(a)).

B.75

[30CB   Bail under section 30A: variation of conditions by court]

[(1)   Where a person released on bail under section 30A(1) is on bail subject to conditions, a magistrates' court may, on an application by or on behalf of the person, vary the conditions if—

(a) the conditions have been varied under section 30CA(1) since being imposed under section 30A(3B),

(b) a request for variation under section 30CA(1) of the conditions has been made and refused, or

(c) a request for variation under section 30CA(1) of the conditions has been made and the period of 48 hours beginning with the day when the request was made has expired without the request having been withdrawn or the conditions having been varied in response to the request.

(2)   In proceedings on an application for a variation under subsection (1), a ground may not be relied upon unless—

(a) in a case falling within subsection (1)(a), the ground was relied upon in the request in response to which the conditions were varied under section 30CA(1), or

(b) in a case falling within paragraph (b) or (c) of subsection (1), the ground was relied upon in the request mentioned in that paragraph, but this does not prevent the court, when deciding the application, from considering different grounds arising out of a change in circumstances that has occurred since the making of the application.

(3)   Where conditions of bail granted to a person under section 30A(1) are varied under subsection (1)—

 (a)   paragraphs (a) to (d) of section 30A(3A) apply,

 (b)   requirements imposed by the conditions as so varied must be requirements that appear to the court varying the conditions to be necessary for any of the purposes mentioned in paragraphs (a) to (d) of section 30A(3B), and

 (c)   that bail shall not lapse but shall continue subject to the conditions as so varied.

(4)   Power under subsection (1) to vary conditions is, subject to subsection (3)(a) and (b), power—

 (a)   to vary or rescind any of the conditions, and

 (b)   to impose further conditions.]

Amendment
 Inserted by the Police and Justice Act 2006, s 10, Sch 6, Pt 1, para 1, Pt 2, para 4 (date in force: 1 April 2007: see SI 2007/709, art 3(i)).

B.76

[30D   Failure to answer to bail under section 30A]

[(1)   A constable may arrest without a warrant a person who—

 (a)   has been released on bail under section 30A subject to a requirement to attend a specified police station, but

 (b)   fails to attend the police station at the specified time.

(2)   A person arrested under subsection (1) must be taken to a police station (which may be the specified police station or any other police station) as soon as practicable after the arrest.

[(2A)   A person who has been released on bail under section 30A may be arrested without a warrant by a constable if the constable has reasonable grounds for suspecting that the person has broken any of the conditions of bail.

(2B)   A person arrested under subsection (2A) must be taken to a police station (which may be the specified police station mentioned in subsection (1) or any other police station) as soon as practicable after the arrest.]

(3)   In subsection (1), 'specified' means specified in a notice under subsection (1) or (5) of section 30B or, if notice of change has been given under subsection (7) of that section, in that notice.

(4)   For the purposes of—

(a)   section 30 (subject to the [obligations in subsections (2) and (2B)]), and

(b)   section 31,

an arrest under this section is to be treated as an arrest for an offence.]

Amendment

Inserted by the Criminal Justice Act 2003, s 4(1), (7) (date in force: 20 January 2004: see SI 2004/81, art 2(1), (2)(a)).

Sub-ss (2A), (2B): inserted by the Police and Justice Act 2006, s 10, Sch 6, Pt 1, para 1, Pt 2, para 5(1), (2) (date in force: 1 April 2007: see SI 2007/709, art 3(i)).

Sub-s (4): in para (a) words 'obligations in subsections (2) and (2B)' in square brackets substituted by the Police and Justice Act 2006, s 10, Sch 6, Pt 1, para 1, Pt 2, para 5(1), (3) (date in force: 1 April 2007: see SI 2007/709, art 3(i)).

B.77

31   Arrest for further offence

Where—

(a)   a person—

(i)   has been arrested for an offence; and

(ii)   is at a police station in consequence of that arrest; and

(b)   it appears to a constable that, if he were released from that arrest, he would be liable to arrest for some other offence,

he shall be arrested for that other offence.

B.78

32   Search upon arrest

(1)   A constable may search an arrested person, in any case where the person to be searched has been arrested at a place other than a police station, if the constable has reasonable grounds for believing that the arrested person may present a danger to himself or others.

(2)   Subject to subsections (3) to (5) below, a constable shall also have power in any such case—

(a)   to search the arrested person for anything—

(i)   which he might use to assist him to escape from lawful custody; or

(ii)   which might be evidence relating to an offence; and

[(b)   if the offence for which he has been arrested is an indictable offence, to enter and search any premises in which he was when arrested or immediately before he was arrested for evidence relating to the offence].

(3)   The power to search conferred by subsection (2) above is only a power to search to the extent that is reasonably required for the purpose of discovering any such thing or any such evidence.

(4)   The powers conferred by this section to search a person are not to be construed as authorising a constable to require a person to remove any of his clothing in public other than an outer coat, jacket or gloves [but they do authorise a search of a person's mouth].

(5)   A constable may not search a person in the exercise of the power conferred by subsection (2)(a) above unless he has reasonable grounds for believing that the person to be searched may have concealed on him anything for which a search is permitted under that paragraph.

(6)   A constable may not search premises in the exercise of the power conferred by subsection (2)(b) above unless he has reasonable grounds for believing that there is evidence for which a search is permitted under that paragraph on the premises.

(7)   In so far as the power of search conferred by subsection (2)(b) above relates to premises consisting of two or more separate dwellings, it is limited to a power to search—

  (a)   any dwelling in which the arrest took place or in which the person arrested was immediately before his arrest; and

  (b)   any parts of the premises which the occupier of any such dwelling uses in common with the occupiers of any other dwellings comprised in the premises.

(8)   A constable searching a person in the exercise of the power conferred by subsection (1) above may seize and retain anything he finds, if he has reasonable grounds for believing that the person searched might use it to cause physical injury to himself or to any other person.

(9)   A constable searching a person in the exercise of the power conferred by subsection (2)(a) above may seize and retain anything he finds, other than an item subject to legal privilege, if he has reasonable grounds for believing—

  (a)   that he might use it to assist him to escape from lawful custody; or

  (b)   that it is evidence of an offence or has been obtained in consequence of the commission of an offence.

(10)   Nothing in this section shall be taken to affect the power conferred by [section 43 of the Terrorism Act 2000].

Amendment

Sub-s (2): para (b) substituted by the Serious Organised Crime and Police Act 2005, s 111, Sch 7, Pt 3, para 43(1), (6) (date in force: 1 January 2006: see SI 2005/3495, art 2(1)(m)).

Sub-s (4): words 'but they do authorise a search of a person's mouth' in square brackets inserted by the Criminal Justice and Public Order Act 1994, s 59(2).

Sub-s (10): words 'section 43 of the Terrorism Act 2000' in square brackets substituted by the Terrorism Act 2000, s 125(1), Sch 15, para 5(1), (3) (date in force: 19 February 2001 (except in relation to a person detained prior to that date): see the Terrorism Act 2000, s 129(1)(b) and SI 2001/421, art 2).

Part IV
Detention

Detention—conditions and duration

B.79

34   Limitations on police detention

(1)   A person arrested for an offence shall not be kept in police detention except in accordance with the provisions of this Part of this Act.

(2)   Subject to subsection (3) below, if at any time a custody officer—

  (a)   becomes aware, in relation to any person in police detention, that the grounds for the detention of that person have ceased to apply; and

  (b)   is not aware of any other grounds on which the continued detention of that person could be justified under the provisions of this Part of this Act,

it shall be the duty of the custody officer, subject to subsection (4) below, to order his immediate release from custody.

(3)   No person in police detention shall be released except on the authority of a custody officer at the police station where his detention was authorised or, if it was authorised at more than one station, a custody officer at the station where it was last authorised.

(4)   A person who appears to the custody officer to have been unlawfully at large when he was arrested is not to be released under subsection (2) above.

(5)   A person whose release is ordered under subsection (2) above shall be released without bail unless it appears to the custody officer—

  (a)   that there is need for further investigation of any matter in connection with which he was detained at any time during the period of his detention; or

  [(b)   that, in respect of any such matter, proceedings may be taken against him or he may be reprimanded or warned under section 65 of the Crime and Disorder Act 1998,] and, if it so appears, he shall be released on bail.

(6)   For the purposes of this Part of this Act a person arrested under [section 6D of the Road Traffic Act 1988] [or section 30(2) of the Transport and Works Act 1992 (c 42)] is arrested for an offence.

[(7)   For the purposes of this Part a person who—

(a)   attends a police station to answer to bail granted under section 30A,

(b)   returns to a police station to answer to bail granted under this Part, or

(c)   is arrested under section 30D or 46A,

is to be treated as arrested for an offence and that offence is the offence in connection with which he was granted bail.]

[But this subsection is subject to section 47(6) (which provides for the calculation of certain periods, where a person has been granted bail under this Part, by reference to time when the person is in police detention only).]

[(8)   Subsection (7) does not apply in relation to a person who is granted bail subject to the duty mentioned in section 47(3)(b) and who either—

(a)   attends a police station to answer to such bail, or

(b)   is arrested under section 46A for failing to do so,

(provision as to the treatment of such persons for the purposes of this Part being made by section 46ZA).]

Amendment
   Sub-s (5): para (b) substituted by the Criminal Justice and Court Services Act 2000, s 56(2) (date in force: 1 February 2001: see SI 2000/3302, art 3(a)).
   Sub-s (6): words 'section 6D of the Road Traffic Act 1988' in square brackets substituted by the Railways and Transport Safety Act 2003, s 107, Sch 7, para 12 (date in force: 30 March 2004: see SI 2004/827, art 3(bb), (ii)); words 'or section 30(2) of the Transport and Works Act 1992 (c 42)' in square brackets inserted by the Police Reform Act 2002, s 53(1) (date in force: 1 April 2003: see SI 2003/808, art 2(d)).
   Sub-s (7): inserted by the Criminal Justice and Public Order Act 1994, s 29(3); substituted by the Criminal Justice Act 2003, s 12, Sch 1, paras 1, 5 (date in force: 20 January 2004: see SI 2004/81, art 2(1), (2)(a)); words from 'But this subsection' to 'police detention only).' in square brackets inserted by the Police (Detention and Bail) Act 2011, s 1(2) (date in force: 1 January 1986: see the Police (Detention and Bail) Act 2011, s 1(3)).
   Sub-s (8): inserted by the Police and Justice Act 2006, s 46(1), (2) (date in force (in relation to the local justice area of Lambeth and Southwark): 1 April 2007: see SI 2007/709, art 3(n); (in relation to certain local justice areas): 14 November 2008: see SI 2008/2785, art 2; (in relation to certain local justice areas): 3 October 2011: see SI 2011/2144, art 2(1)(b), (2); (for remaining purposes): to be appointed: see the Police and Justice Act 2006, s 53(1)(a)).

B.80

35   Designated police stations

(1)   The chief officer of police for each police area shall designate the police stations in his area which, subject to [sections 30(3) and (5), 30A(5) and

356

30D(2)], are to be the stations in that area to be used for the purpose of detaining arrested persons.

(2)   A chief officer's duty under subsection (1) above is to designate police stations appearing to him to provide enough accommodation for that purpose.

[(2A)   The Chief Constable of the British Transport Police Force may designate police stations which (in addition to those designated under subsection (1) above) may be used for the purpose of detaining arrested persons.]

(3)   Without prejudice to section 12 of the Interpretation Act 1978 (continuity of duties) a chief officer—

    (a)   may designate a station which was not previously designated; and

    (b)   may direct that a designation of a station previously made shall cease to operate.

(4)   In this Act 'designated police station' means a police station designated under this section.

Amendment
> Sub-s (1): words 'section 30(3) and (5), 30A(5) and 30D(2)' in square brackets substituted by the Criminal Justice Act 2003, s 12, Sch 1, paras 1, 6 (date in force: 20 January 2004: see SI 2004/81, art 2(1), (2)(a)).
>
> Sub-s (2A): inserted by the Anti-terrorism, Crime and Security Act 2001, s 101, Sch 7, paras 11, 12 (date in force: 14 December 2001: see the Anti-terrorism, Crime and Security Act 2001, s 127(2)(f)).

B.81

36   Custody officers at police stations

(1)   One or more custody officers shall be appointed for each designated police station.

(2)   A custody officer for [a police station designated under section 35(1) above] shall be appointed—

    (a)   by the chief officer of police for the area in which the designated police station is situated; or

    (b)   by such other police officer as the chief officer of police for that area may direct.

[(2A)   A custody officer for a police station designated under section 35(2A) above shall be appointed—

    (a)   by the Chief Constable of the British Transport Police Force; or

    (b)   by such other member of that Force as that Chief Constable may direct.]

[(3) No officer may be appointed a custody officer unless the officer is of at least the rank of sergeant.]

(4) An officer of any rank may perform the functions of a custody officer at a designated police station if a custody officer is not readily available to perform them.

(5) Subject to the following provisions of this section and to section 39(2) below, none of the functions of a custody officer in relation to a person shall be performed by [an officer] who at the time when the function falls to be performed is involved in the investigation of an offence for which that person is in police detention at that time.

(6) Nothing in subsection (5) above is to be taken to prevent a custody officer—

    (a) performing any function assigned to custody officers—

        (i) by this Act; or

        (ii) by a code of practice issued under this Act;

    (b) carrying out the duty imposed on custody officers by section 39 below;

    (c) doing anything in connection with the identification of a suspect; or

    (d) doing anything under [sections 7 and 8 of the Road Traffic Act 1988].

(7) Where an arrested person is taken to a police station which is not a designated police station, the functions in relation to him which at a designated police station would be the functions of a custody officer shall be performed—

    (a) by an officer who is not involved in the investigation of an offence for which he is in police detention, if [such an officer] is readily available; and

    (b) if no such officer is readily available, by the officer who took him to the station or any other officer.

[(7A) Subject to subsection (7B), subsection (7) applies where a person attends a police station which is not a designated station to answer to bail granted under section 30A as it applies where a person is taken to such a station.

(7B) Where subsection (7) applies because of subsection (7A), the reference in subsection (7)(b) to the officer who took him to the station is to be read as a reference to the officer who granted him bail.]

(8) References to a custody officer in [section 34 above or in] the following provisions of this Act include references to [an officer] other than a custody officer who is performing the functions of a custody officer by virtue of subsection (4) or (7) above.

(9)   Where by virtue of subsection (7) above an officer of a force maintained by a police authority who took an arrested person to a police station is to perform the functions of a custody officer in relation to him, the officer shall inform an officer who—

(a)   is attached to a designated police station; and

(b)   is of at least the rank of inspector,

that he is to do so.

(10)   The duty imposed by subsection (9) above shall be performed as soon as it is practicable to perform it.

[(11)   …]

Amendment

Sub-s (2): words 'a police station designated under section 35(1) above' in square brackets substituted by the Anti-terrorism, Crime and Security Act 2001, s 101, Sch 7, paras 11, 13(1), (2) (date in force: 14 December 2001: see the Anti-terrorism, Crime and Security Act 2001, s 127(2)(f)).

Sub-s (2A): inserted by the Anti-terrorism, Crime and Security Act 2001, s 101, Sch 7, paras 11, 13(1), (3) (date in force: 14 December 2001: see the Anti-terrorism, Crime and Security Act 2001, s 127(2)(f)).

Sub-s (3): substituted by the Policing and Crime Act 2009, s 112(1), Sch 7, Pt 13, paras 123(1), (3)(a) (date in force: 12 January 2010: see the Policing and Crime Act 2009, s 116(6)(a)).

Sub-s (5): words 'an officer' in square brackets substituted by the Policing and Crime Act 2009, s 112(1), Sch 7, Pt 13, paras 123(1), (3)(b) (date in force: 12 January 2010: see the Policing and Crime Act 2009, s 116(6)(a)).

Sub-s (6): words in square brackets in para (d) substituted by the Road Traffic (Consequential Provisions) Act 1988, s 4, Sch 3, para 27.

Sub-s (7): in para (a) words omitted repealed by the Policing and Crime Act 2009, s 112, Sch 7, Pt 13, paras 123(1), (3)(c)(i), Sch 8, pt 13 (date in force: 12 January 2010: see the Policing and Crime Act 2009, s 116(6)(a)); in para (a) words 'such an officer' in square brackets substituted by the Policing and Crime Act 2009, s 112(1), Sch 7, Pt 13, paras 123(1), (3)(c)(i) (date in force: 12 January 2010: see the Policing and Crime Act 2009, s 116(6)(a)).

Sub-ss (7A), (7B): inserted by the Criminal Justice Act 2003, s 12, Sch 1, paras 1, 7 (date in force: 20 January 2004: see SI 2004/81, art 2(1), (2)(a)).

Sub-s (8): words 'section 34 above or in' in square brackets inserted by the Serious Organised Crime and Police Act 2005, s 121(1), (5)(a) (date in force: 7 March 2011: see SI 2011/410, art 2(f)); words 'an officer' in square brackets substituted by the Policing and Crime Act 2009, s 112(1), Sch 7, Pt 13, paras 123(1), (3)(d) (date in force: 12 January 2010: see the Policing and Crime Act 2009, s 116(6)(a)).

Sub-s (11): inserted by the Serious Organised Crime and Police Act 2005, s 121(1), (6) (date in force: to be appointed); repealed by the Policing and Crime Act 2009, s 112(1), (2), Sch 7, Pt 13, paras 123(1), (3)(e), Sch 8, Pt 13 (date in force: 12 January 2010: see the Policing and Crime Act 2009, s 116(6)(a)).

B.82

37   Duties of custody officer before charge

(1)   Where—

(a)   a person is arrested for an offence—

   (i)   without a warrant; or

   (ii)   under a warrant not endorsed for bail, ...

(b)   ...

the custody officer at each police station where he is detained after his arrest shall determine whether he has before him sufficient evidence to charge that person with the offence for which he was arrested and may detain him at the police station for such period as is necessary to enable him to do so.

(2)   If the custody officer determines that he does not have such evidence before him, the person arrested shall be released either on bail or without bail, unless the custody officer has reasonable grounds for believing that his detention without being charged is necessary to secure or preserve evidence relating to an offence for which he is under arrest or to obtain such evidence by questioning him.

(3)   If the custody officer has reasonable grounds for so believing, he may authorise the person arrested to be kept in police detention.

(4)   Where a custody officer authorises a person who has not been charged to be kept in police detention, he shall, as soon as is practicable, make a written record of the grounds for the detention.

(5)   Subject to subsection (6) below, the written record shall be made in the presence of the person arrested who shall at that time be informed by the custody officer of the grounds for his detention.

(6)   Subsection (5) above shall not apply where the person arrested is, at the time when the written record is made—

   (a)   incapable of understanding what is said to him;

   (b)   violent or likely to become violent; or

   (c)   in urgent need of medical attention.

(7)   Subject to section 41(7) below, if the custody officer determines that he has before him sufficient evidence to charge the person arrested with the offence for which he was arrested, the person arrested—

   [(a)   [shall be—

      (i)   released without charge and on bail, or

      (ii)   kept in police detention,

      for the purpose] of enabling the Director of Public Prosecutions to make a decision under section 37B below,

   (b)   shall be released without charge and on bail but not for that purpose,

360

(c)   shall be released without charge and without bail, or

(d)   shall be charged].

[(7A)   The decision as to how a person is to be dealt with under subsection (7) above shall be that of the custody officer.

(7B)   Where a person is [dealt with under subsection (7)(a)] above, it shall be the duty of the custody officer to inform him that he is being released[, or (as the case may be) detained,] to enable the Director of Public Prosecutions to make a decision under section 37B below.]

(8)   Where—

(a)   a person is released under subsection (7)(b) [or (c)] above; and

(b)   at the time of his release a decision whether he should be prosecuted for the offence for which he was arrested has not been taken,

it shall be the duty of the custody officer so to inform him.

[(8A)   Subsection (8B) applies if the offence for which the person is arrested is one in relation to which a sample could be taken under section 63B below and the custody officer—

(a)   is required in pursuance of subsection (2) above to release the person arrested and decides to release him on bail, or

(b)   decides in pursuance of subsection (7)(a) or (b) above to release the person without charge and on bail.

(8B)   The detention of the person may be continued to enable a sample to be taken under section 63B, but this subsection does not permit a person to be detained for a period of more than 24 hours after the relevant time.]

(9)   If the person arrested is not in a fit state to be dealt with under subsection (7) above, he may be kept in police detention until he is.

(10)   The duty imposed on the custody officer under subsection (1) above shall be carried out by him as soon as practicable after the person arrested arrives at the police station or, in the case of a person arrested at the police station, as soon as practicable after the arrest.

(11)–(14)   …

(15)   In this Part of this Act—

'arrested juvenile' means a person arrested with or without a warrant who appears to be under the age of 17 …;

'endorsed for bail' means endorsed with a direction for bail in accordance with section 117(2) of the Magistrates' Courts Act 1980.

Amendment
Sub-s (1): words omitted repealed by the Criminal Justice and Public Order Act 1994, ss 29(4)(a), 168(3), Sch 11.

Sub-s (7): paras (a)–(d) substituted, for paras (a), (b) as originally enacted, by the Criminal Justice Act 2003, s 28, Sch 2, paras 1, 2(1), (2) (date in force: 29 January 2004: see SI 2004/81, art 4(1), (2)(c)); in para (a) words from 'shall be—' to 'for the purpose' in square brackets substituted by the Police and Justice Act 2006, s 11 (date in force: 15 January 2007: see SI 2006/3364, art 2(c)).

Sub-ss (7A), (7B): inserted by the Criminal Justice Act 2003, s 28, Sch 2, paras 1, 2(1), (3) (date in force: 29 January 2004: see SI 2004/81, art 4(1), (2)(c)).

Sub-s (7B): words 'dealt with under subsection (7)(a)' in square brackets substituted by the Police and Justice Act 2006, s 52, Sch 14, para 9(a) (date in force: 15 January 2007: see SI 2006/3364, art 2(j), (k) (as amended by SI 2007/29, art 2)); words ', or (as the case may be) detained,' in square brackets inserted by the Police and Justice Act 2006, s 52, Sch 14, para 9(b) (date in force: 15 January 2007: see SI 2006/3364, art 2(j), (k) (as amended by SI 2007/29, art 2)).

Sub-s (8): in para (a) words 'or (c)' in square brackets inserted by the Criminal Justice Act 2003, s 28, Sch 2, paras 1, 2(1), (4) (date in force: 29 January 2004: see SI 2004/81, art 4(1), (2)(c)).

Sub-ss (8A), (8B): inserted by the Drugs Act 2005, s 23(1), Sch 1, paras 1, 2 (date in force: 1 December 2005: see SI 2005/3053, art 2(1)(f)).

Sub-ss (11)–(14): repealed by the Criminal Justice Act 1991, ss 72, 101(2), Sch 13.

Sub-s (15): words omitted repealed by the Children Act 1989, s 108(7), Sch 15.

B.83

[37A   Guidance]

[(1)   The Director of Public Prosecutions may issue guidance—

(a)   for the purpose of enabling custody officers to decide how persons should be dealt with under section 37(7) above or 37C(2) [or 37CA(2)] below, and

(b)   as to the information to be sent to the Director of Public Prosecutions under section 37B(1) below.

(2)   The Director of Public Prosecutions may from time to time revise guidance issued under this section.

(3)   Custody officers are to have regard to guidance under this section in deciding how persons should be dealt with under section 37(7) above or 37C(2) [or 37CA(2)] below.

(4)   A report under section 9 of the Prosecution of Offences Act 1985 (report by DPP to Attorney General) must set out the provisions of any guidance issued, and any revisions to guidance made, in the year to which the report relates.

(5)   The Director of Public Prosecutions must publish in such manner as he thinks fit—

(a)   any guidance issued under this section, and

(b)   any revisions made to such guidance.

(6)   Guidance under this section may make different provision for different cases, circumstances or areas.]

Amendment
Inserted by the Criminal Justice Act 2003, s 28, Sch 2, paras 1, 3 (date in force: 29 January 2004: see SI 2004/81, art 4(1), (2)(c)).

Sub-s (1): in para (a) words 'or 37CA(2)' in square brackets inserted by the Police and Justice Act 2006, s 10, Sch 6, Pt 1, para 1, Pt 3, para 8(2) (date in force: 1 April 2007: see SI 2007/709, art 3(i)).

Sub-s (3): words 'or 37CA(2)' in square brackets inserted by the Police and Justice Act 2006, s 10, Sch 6, Pt 1, para 1, Pt 3, para 8(2) (date in force: 1 April 2007: see SI 2007/709, art 3(i)).

B.84

[37B   Consultation with the Director of Public Prosecutions]

[(1)   Where a person is [dealt with under section 37(7)(a)] above, an officer involved in the investigation of the offence shall, as soon as is practicable, send to the Director of Public Prosecutions such information as may be specified in guidance under section 37A above.

(2)   The Director of Public Prosecutions shall decide whether there is sufficient evidence to charge the person with an offence.

(3)   If he decides that there is sufficient evidence to charge the person with an offence, he shall decide—

(a)   whether or not the person should be charged and, if so, the offence with which he should be charged, and

(b)   whether or not the person should be given a caution and, if so, the offence in respect of which he should be given a caution.

(4)   The Director of Public Prosecutions [shall give notice] of his decision to an officer involved in the investigation of the offence.

[(4A)   Notice under subsection (4) above shall be in writing, but in the case of a person kept in police detention under section 37(7)(a) above it may be given orally in the first instance and confirmed in writing subsequently.]

(5)   If his decision is—

(a)   that there is not sufficient evidence to charge the person with an offence, or

(b)   that there is sufficient evidence to charge the person with an offence but that the person should not be charged with an offence or given a caution in respect of an offence,

a custody officer shall give the person notice in writing that he is not to be prosecuted.

(6)   If the decision of the Director of Public Prosecutions is that the person should be charged with an offence, or given a caution in respect of an offence, the person shall be charged or cautioned accordingly.

(7)   But if his decision is that the person should be given a caution in respect of the offence and it proves not to be possible to give the person such a caution, he shall instead be charged with the offence.

(8)   For the purposes of this section, a person is to be charged with an offence either—

[(a)   when he is in police detention at a police station (whether because he has returned to answer bail, because he is detained under section 37(7)(a) above or for some other reason), or]

(b)   in accordance with section 29 of the Criminal Justice Act 2003.

(9)   In this section 'caution' includes—

(a)   a conditional caution within the meaning of Part 3 of the Criminal Justice Act 2003,

[(aa) a youth conditional caution within the meaning of Chapter 1 of Part 4 of the Crime and Disorder Act 1998] and

(b)   a warning or reprimand under section 65 *of the Crime and Disorder Act 1998* [of that Act].]

Amendment

Inserted by the Criminal Justice Act 2003, s 28, Sch 2, paras 1, 3 (date in force (for the purposes of sub-ss (1)–(7), (9)(b)): 29 January 2004: see SI 2004/81, art 4(1), (2)(c); (for the purposes of sub-s (9)(a)): 3 July 2004: see SI 2004/1629, art 2(1), (2)(c); (for remaining purposes): 1 October 2007: see SI 2007/2874, art 2(1), (2)(a), (3)).

Sub-s (1): words 'dealt with under section 37(7)(a)' in square brackets substituted by the Police and Justice Act 2006, s 52, Sch 14, para 10(1), (2) (date in force: 15 January 2007: see SI 2006/3364, art 2(j), (k) (as amended by SI 2007/29, art 2)).

Sub-s (4): words 'shall give notice' in square brackets substituted by the Police and Justice Act 2006, s 52, Sch 14, para 10(1), (3) (date in force: 15 January 2007: see SI 2006/3364, art 2(j), (k) (as amended by SI 2007/29, art 2)).

Sub-s (4A): inserted by the Police and Justice Act 2006, s 52, Sch 14, para 10(1), (4) (date in force: 15 January 2007: see SI 2006/3364, art 2(j), (k) (as amended by SI 2007/29, art 2)).

Sub-s (8): para (a) substituted by the Police and Justice Act 2006, s 52, Sch 14, para 10(1), (5) (date in force: 15 January 2007: see SI 2006/3364, art 2(j), (k) (as amended by SI 2007/29, art 2)).

Sub-s (9): para (aa) inserted by the Criminal Justice and Immigration Act 2008, s 148, Sch 26, Pt 2, para 20(1)(a) (date in force (for certain purposes): 16 November 2009: see SI 2009/2780, art 2(1)(b), (d), (2); (for remaining purposes): to be appointed: see the Criminal Justice and Immigration Act 2008, s 153(7)).

Sub-s (9): in para (b) words 'of the Crime and Disorder Act 1998' in italics repealed and subsequent words in square brackets substituted by the Criminal Justice and Immigration Act 2008, s 148, Sch 26, Pt 2, para 20(1)(b) (date in force (for certain purposes): 16 November 2009: see SI 2009/2780, art 2(1)(b), (d), (2); (for remaining purposes): to be appointed: see the Criminal Justice and Immigration Act 2008, s 153(7)).

B.85

[37C   Breach of bail following release under section 37(7)(a)]

[(1)   This section applies where—

(a)   a person released on bail under section 37(7)(a) above or subsection (2)(b) below is arrested under section 46A below in respect of that bail, and

(b)   at the time of his detention following that arrest at the police station mentioned in section 46A(2) below, notice under section 37B(4) above has not been given.

(2)   The person arrested—

(a)   shall be charged, or

(b)   shall be released without charge, either on bail or without bail.

(3)   The decision as to how a person is to be dealt with under subsection (2) above shall be that of a custody officer.

(4)   A person released on bail under subsection (2)(b) above shall be released on bail subject to the same conditions (if any) which applied immediately before his arrest.]

Amendment
Inserted by the Criminal Justice Act 2003, s 28, Sch 2, paras 1, 3 (date in force: 29 January 2004: see SI 2004/81, art 4(1), (2)(c)).

B.86

[37CA   Breach of bail following release under section 37(7)(b)]

[(1)   This section applies where a person released on bail under section 37(7)(b) above or subsection (2)(b) below—

(a)   is arrested under section 46A below in respect of that bail, and

(b)   is being detained following that arrest at the police station mentioned in section 46A(2) below.

(2)   The person arrested—

(a)   shall be charged, or

(b)   shall be released without charge, either on bail or without bail.

(3)   The decision as to how a person is to be dealt with under subsection (2) above shall be that of a custody officer.

(4)   A person released on bail under subsection (2)(b) above shall be released on bail subject to the same conditions (if any) which applied immediately before his arrest.]

Amendment
Inserted by the Police and Justice Act 2006, s 10, Sch 6, Pt 1, para 1, Pt 3, para 8(1) (date in force: 1 April 2007: see SI 2007/709, art 3(i)).

B.87

[37D   Release [on bail under section 37]: further provision]

[(1)   Where a person is released on bail under section [37, 37C(2)(b) or 37CA(2)(b)] above, a custody officer may subsequently appoint a different time, or an additional time, at which the person is to attend at the police station to answer bail.

(2)   The custody officer shall give the person notice in writing of the exercise of the power under subsection (1).

(3)   The exercise of the power under subsection (1) shall not affect the conditions (if any) to which bail is subject.

(4)   Where a person released on bail under section 37(7)(a) or 37C(2)(b) above returns to a police station to answer bail or is otherwise in police detention at a police station, he may be kept in police detention to enable him to be dealt with in accordance with section 37B or 37C above or to enable the power under subsection (1) above to be exercised.

[(4A)   Where a person released on bail under section 37(7)(b) or 37CA(2)(b) above returns to a police station to answer bail or is otherwise in police detention at a police station, he may be kept in police detention to enable him to be dealt with in accordance with section 37CA above or to enable the power under subsection (1) above to be exercised.

(5)   If the person mentioned in subsection (4) or (4A) above is not in a fit state to enable him to be dealt with as mentioned in that subsection or to enable the power under subsection (1) above to be exercised, he may be kept in police detention until he is.]

(6)   Where a person is kept in police detention by virtue of subsection (4)[, (4A)] or (5) above, section 37(1) to (3) and (7) above (and section 40(8) below so far as it relates to section 37(1) to (3)) shall not apply to the offence in connection with which he was released on bail under section [37(7), 37C(2)(b) or 37CA(2)(b)] above.]

Amendment

Inserted by the Criminal Justice Act 2003, s 28, Sch 2, paras 1, 3 (date in force: 29 January 2004: see SI 2004/81, art 4(1), (2)(c)).

Section heading: words 'on bail under section 37' in square brackets substituted by the Police and Justice Act 2006, s 10, Sch 6, Pt 1, para 1, Pt 3, para 9(2) (date in force: 1 April 2007: see SI 2007/709, art 3(i)).

Sub-s (1): words '37, 37C(2)(b) or 37CA(2)(b)' in square brackets substituted by the Police and Justice Act 2006, s 10, Sch 6, Pt 1, para 1, Pt 3, para 9(1) (date in force: 1 April 2007: see SI 2007/709, art 3(i)).

Sub-ss (4A), (5): substituted, for sub-s (5), by the Police and Justice Act 2006, s 10, Sch 6, Pt 1, para 1, Pt 3, para 10(1), (2) (date in force: 1 April 2007: see SI 2007/709, art 3(i)).

Sub-s (6): reference to ', (4A)' in square brackets inserted by the Police and Justice Act 2006, s 10, Sch 6, Pt 1, para 1, Pt 3, para 10(1), (3)(a) (date in force: 1 April 2007: see SI 2007/709, art 3(i)); words '37(7), 37C(2)(b) or 37CA(2)(b)' in square brackets substituted by the Police and Justice Act 2006, s 10, Sch 6, Pt 1, para 1, Pt 3, para 10(1), (3)(b) (date in force: 1 April 2007: see SI 2007/709, art 3(i)).

B.88

38 Duties of custody officer after charge

(1) Where a person arrested for an offence otherwise than under a warrant endorsed for bail is charged with an offence, the custody officer shall[, subject to section 25 of the Criminal Justice and Public Order Act 1994,] order his release from police detention, either on bail or without bail, unless—

    (a)   if the person arrested is not an arrested juvenile—

        (i)   his name or address cannot be ascertained or the custody officer has reasonable grounds for doubting whether a name or address furnished by him as his name or address is his real name or address;

    [(ii)   the custody officer has reasonable grounds for believing that the person arrested will fail to appear in court to answer to bail;

      (iii)   in the case of a person arrested for an imprisonable offence, the custody officer has reasonable grounds for believing that the detention of the person arrested is necessary to prevent him from committing an offence;

    [(iiia) in a case where a sample may be taken from the person under section 63B below, the custody officer has reasonable grounds for believing that the detention of the person is necessary to enable the sample to be taken from him;]

      (iv)   in the case of a person arrested for an offence which is not an imprisonable offence, the custody officer has reasonable grounds for believing that the detention of the person arrested is necessary to prevent him from causing physical injury to any other person or from causing loss of or damage to property;

      (v)   the custody officer has reasonable grounds for believing that the detention of the person arrested is necessary to prevent him from interfering with the administration of justice or with the investigation of offences or of a particular offence; or

      (vi)   the custody officer has reasonable grounds for believing that the detention of the person arrested is necessary for his own protection;]

    (b)   if he is an arrested juvenile—

        (i)   any of the requirements of paragraph (a) above is satisfied [(but, in the case of paragraph (a)(iiia) above, only if the arrested juvenile has attained the minimum age)]; or

(ii)   the custody officer has reasonable grounds for believing that he ought to be detained in his own interests;

[(c)   the offence with which the person is charged is murder].

(2)   If the release of a person arrested is not required by subsection (1) above, the custody officer may authorise him to be kept in police detention [but may not authorise a person to be kept in police detention by virtue of subsection (1)(a)(iiia) after the end of the period of six hours beginning when he was charged with the offence].

[(2A)   The custody officer, in taking the decisions required by subsection (1)(a) and (b) above (except (a)(i) and (vi) and (b)(ii)), shall have regard to the same considerations as those which a court is required to have regard to in taking the corresponding decisions under paragraph [2(1)] of Part I of Schedule 1 to the Bail Act 1976 [(disregarding paragraph 2(2) of that Part)].]

(3)   Where a custody officer authorises a person who has been charged to be kept in police detention, he shall, as soon as practicable, make a written record of the grounds for the detention.

(4)   Subject to subsection (5) below, the written record shall be made in the presence of the person charged who shall at that time be informed by the custody officer of the grounds for his detention.

(5)   Subsection (4) above shall not apply where the person charged is, at the time when the written record is made—

(a)   incapable of understanding what is said to him;

(b)   violent or likely to become violent; or

(c)   in urgent need of medical attention.

[[(6)   Where a custody officer authorises an arrested juvenile to be kept in police detention under subsection (1) above, the custody officer shall, unless he certifies—

(a)   that, by reason of such circumstances as are specified in the certificate, it is impracticable for him to do so; or

(b)   in the case of an arrested juvenile who has attained the [age of 12 years], that no secure accommodation is available and that keeping him in other local authority accommodation would not be adequate to protect the public from serious harm from him,

secure that the arrested juvenile is moved to local authority accommodation.

(6A)   In this section—

'local authority accommodation' means accommodation provided by or on behalf of a local authority (within the meaning of the Children Act 1989);

['minimum age' means the age specified in [section 63B(3)(b) below]];

'secure accommodation' means accommodation provided for the purpose of restricting liberty;

['sexual offence' means an offence specified in Part 2 of Schedule 15 to the Criminal Justice Act 2003;

'violent offence' means murder or an offence specified in Part 1 of that Schedule;]

and any reference, in relation to an arrested juvenile charged with a violent or sexual offence, to protecting the public from serious harm from him shall be construed as a reference to protecting members of the public from death or serious personal injury, whether physical or psychological, occasioned by further such offences committed by him.]

(6B)   Where an arrested juvenile is moved to local authority accommodation under subsection (6) above, it shall be lawful for any person acting on behalf of the authority to detain him.]

(7)   A certificate made under subsection (6) above in respect of an arrested juvenile shall be produced to the court before which he is first brought thereafter.

[(7A)   In this section 'imprisonable offence' has the same meaning as in Schedule 1 to the Bail Act 1976.]

(8)   In this Part of this Act 'local authority' has the same meaning as in the [Children Act 1989].

Amendment

Sub-s (1): words ', subject to section 25 of the Criminal Justice and Public Order Act 1994,' in square brackets inserted by the Criminal Justice and Public Order Act 1994, s 168(2), Sch 10, para 54; para (a)(ii), (iii), (iv)–(vi) substituted, for para (a)(ii), (iii) as originally enacted, by the Criminal Justice and Public Order Act 1994, s 28(2); para (a)(iiia) (inserted by the Criminal Justice and Court Services Act 2000, s 57(1), (3)(a)) substituted by the Drugs Act 2005, s 23(1), Sch 1, paras 1, 3(a) (date in force: 1 December 2005: see SI 2005/3053, art 2(1)(f)); in para (b)(i) words from '(but, in the case' to 'the minimum age)' in square brackets inserted by the Criminal Justice Act 2003, s 5(1), (2)(a)(ii) (date in force (in so far as relating to Cleveland, Greater Manchester, Humberside, Merseyside, metropolitan police district, Nottinghamshire and West Yorkshire police areas): 1 August 2004: see SI 2004/1867, art 2; (for remaining purposes): 1 December 2005: see SI 2005/3055, art 2); para (c) inserted by the Coroners and Justice Act 2009, s 177(1), Sch 21, Pt 7, para 77 (date in force: 1 February 2010: see SI 2010/145, art 2(2), Schedule, paras 18(a), 25(b)).

Sub-s (2): words from 'but may not authorise' to 'charged with the offence' in square brackets inserted by the Criminal Justice and Court Services Act 2000, s 57(1), (3)(b) (date in force (in relation to Nottinghamshire, Staffordshire and Metropolitan police districts): 2 July 2001: see SI 2001/2232, art 2(f); (in relation to Bedfordshire, Devon and Cornwall, Lancashire, Merseyside, South Yorkshire, and North Wales police districts): 20 May 2002: see SI 2002/1149, art 2; (in relation to Avon and Somerset, Greater Manchester, Thames Valley and West Yorkshire police districts): 2 September 2002: see SI 2002/1862, art 2; (in relation to Cleveland and Humber police districts): 1 April 2003: see SI 2003/709, art 2; (in relation to Cambridgeshire, Leicestershire, Northumbria and West Midlands police districts): 1 April

2004: see SI 2004/780, art 2; (in relation to Gwent, Northamptonshire and South Wales police districts): 1 April 2005: see SI 2005/596, art 2; (for remaining purposes): 1 December 2005: see SI 2005/3054, art 2.

Sub-ss (2A), (7A): inserted by the Criminal Justice and Public Order Act 1994, s 28(3), (4).

Sub-s (2A): reference to '2(1)' in square brackets substituted by the Criminal Justice Act 2003, s 331, Sch 36, Pt 1, para 5(a) (date in force: 5 April 2004: see SI 2004/829, art 2(1), (2)(k)); words '(disregarding paragraph 2(2) of that Part)' in square brackets inserted by the Criminal Justice Act 2003, s 331, Sch 36, Pt 1, para 5(b) (date in force: 5 April 2004: see SI 2004/829, art 2(1), (2)(k)).

Sub-s (6): substituted, together with sub-s (6A), for existing sub-ss (6), (6A), by the Criminal Justice Act 1991, s 59; words in square brackets substituted by the Criminal Justice and Public Order Act 1994, s 24.

Sub-s (6A): inserted by the Children Act 1989, s 108(5), Sch 13, para 53(2); substituted, together with sub-s (6), for existing sub-ss (6), (6A), by the Criminal Justice Act 1991, s 59; definition 'minimum age' inserted by the Criminal Justice Act 2003, s 5(1), (2)(b) (date in force (in so far as relating to Cleveland, Greater Manchester, Humberside, Merseyside, metropolitan police district, Nottinghamshire and West Yorkshire police areas): 1 August 2004: see SI 2004/1867, art 2; (for remaining purposes): 1 December 2005: see SI 2005/3055, art 2); in definition 'minimum wage' words 'section 63B(3)(b) below' in square brackets substituted by the Drugs Act 2005, s 23(1), Sch 1, paras 1, 3(b) (date in force: 1 December 2005: see SI 2005/3053, art 2(1)(f)); definitions 'sexual offence' and 'violent offence' substituted by the Criminal Justice Act 2003, s 304, Sch 32, Pt 1, para 44 (date in force: 4 April 2005: see SI 2005/950, art 2(1), Sch 1, para 42(20)).

Sub-s (6B): inserted by the Children Act 1989, s 108(5), Sch 13, para 53(2).

Sub-s (8): words in square brackets substituted by the Children Act 1989, s 108(5), Sch 13, para 53(3).

B.89

39   Responsibilities in relation to persons detained

(1)   Subject to subsections (2) and (4) below, it shall be the duty of the custody officer at a police station to ensure—

    (a)   that all persons in police detention at that station are treated in accordance with this Act and any code of practice issued under it and relating to the treatment of persons in police detention; and

    (b)   that all matters relating to such persons which are required by this Act or by such codes of practice to be recorded are recorded in the custody records relating to such persons.

(2)   If the custody officer, in accordance with any code of practice issued under this Act, transfers or permits the transfer of a person in police detention—

    (a)   to the custody of a police officer investigating an offence for which that person is in police detention; or

    (b)   to the custody of an officer who has charge of that person outside the police station,

the custody officer shall cease in relation to that person to be subject to the duty imposed on him by subsection (1)(a) above; and it shall be the duty of the officer to whom the transfer is made to ensure that he is treated in accordance with the provisions of this Act and of any such codes of practice as are mentioned in subsection (1) above.

(3)   If the person detained is subsequently returned to the custody of the custody officer, it shall be the duty of the officer investigating the offence to report to the custody officer as to the manner in which this section and the codes of practice have been complied with while that person was in his custody.

(4)   If an arrested juvenile is [moved to local authority accommodation] under section 38(6) above, the custody officer shall cease in relation to that person to be subject to the duty imposed on him by subsection (1) above.

(5)   …

(6)   Where—

  (a)   an officer of higher rank than the custody officer […] gives directions relating to a person in police detention; and

  (b)   the directions are at variance—

    (i)   with any decision made or action taken by the custody officer in the performance of a duty imposed on him under this Part of this Act; or

    (ii)   with any decision or action which would but for the directions have been made or taken by him in the performance of such a duty,

the custody officer shall refer the matter at once to an officer of the rank of superintendent or above who is responsible for the police station for which the custody officer is acting as custody officer.

[(7)   …]

Amendment

  Sub-s (4): words in square brackets substituted by the Children Act 1989, s 108(5), Sch 13, para 54.

  Sub-s (5): repealed by the Children Act 1989, s 108(7), Sch 15.

  Sub-s (6): in para (a) words in square brackets inserted by the Serious Organised Crime and Police Act 2005, s 121(7)(a) (date in force: to be appointed) and repealed by the Policing and Crime Act 2009, s 112, Sch 7, Pt 13, para 123(1), (4)(a), Sch 8, Pt 13 (date in force: 12 January 2010: see the Policing and Crime Act 2009, s 116(6)(a)).

  Sub-s (7): inserted by the Serious Organised Crime and Police Act 2005, s 121(7)(b) (not in force) and repealed by the Policing and Crime Act 2009, s 112(1), (2), Sch 7, Pt 13, paras 123(1), (4)(b), Sch 8, Pt 13 (date in force: 12 January 2010: see the Policing and Crime Act 2009, s 116(6)(a)).

B.90

40   Review of police detention

(1)   Reviews of the detention of each person in police detention in connection with the investigation of an offence shall be carried out periodically in accordance with the following provisions of this section—

    (a)   in the case of a person who has been arrested and charged, by the custody officer; and

    (b)   in the case of a person who has been arrested but not charged, by an officer of at least the rank of inspector who has not been directly involved in the investigation.

(2)   The officer to whom it falls to carry out a review is referred to in this section as a 'review officer'.

(3)   Subject to subsection (4) below—

    (a)   the first review shall be not later than six hours after the detention was first authorised;

    (b)   the second review shall be not later than nine hours after the first;

    (c)   subsequent reviews shall be at intervals of not more than nine hours.

(4)   A review may be postponed—

    (a)   if, having regard to all the circumstances prevailing at the latest time for it specified in subsection (3) above, it is not practicable to carry out the review at that time;

    (b)   without prejudice to the generality of paragraph (a) above—

        (i)   if at that time the person in detention is being questioned by a police officer and the review officer is satisfied that an interruption of the questioning for the purpose of carrying out the review would prejudice the investigation in connection with which he is being questioned; or

        (ii)   if at that time no review officer is readily available.

(5)   If a review is postponed under subsection (4) above it shall be carried out as soon as practicable after the latest time specified for it in subsection (3) above.

(6)   If a review is carried out after postponement under subsection (4) above, the fact that it was so carried out shall not affect any requirement of this section as to the time at which any subsequent review is to be carried out.

(7)   The review officer shall record the reasons for any postponement of a review in the custody record.

(8)   Subject to subsection (9) below, where the person whose detention is under review has not been charged before the time of the review, section 37(1) to (6) above shall have effect in relation to him, but with [the modifications specified in subsection (8A).]

[(8A)   The modifications are—

(a)   the substitution of references to the person whose detention is under review for references to the person arrested;

(b)   the substitution of references to the review officer for references to the custody officer; and

(c)   in subsection (6), the insertion of the following paragraph after paragraph (a)—

'(aa) asleep;'.]

(9)   Where a person has been kept in police detention by virtue of section 37(9) [or 37D(5)] above, section 37(1) to (6) shall not have effect in relation to him but it shall be the duty of the review officer to determine whether he is yet in a fit state.

(10)   Where the person whose detention is under review has been charged before the time of the review, section 38(1) to [(6B)] above shall have effect in relation to him, with [the modifications specified in subsection (10A)].

[(10A)   The modifications are—

(a)   the substitution of a reference to the person whose detention is under review for any reference to the person arrested or to the person charged; and

(b)   in subsection (5), the insertion of the following paragraph after paragraph (a)—

'(aa) asleep;'.]

(11)   Where—

(a)   an officer of higher rank than the review officer gives directions relating to a person in police detention; and

(b)   the directions are at variance—

(i)   with any decision made or action taken by the review officer in the performance of a duty imposed on him under this Part of this Act; or

(ii)   with any decision or action which would but for the directions have been made or taken by him in the performance of such a duty,

373

the review officer shall refer the matter at once to an officer of the rank of superintendent or above who is responsible for the police station for which the review officer is acting as review officer in connection with the detention.

(12)   Before determining whether to authorise a person's continued detention the review officer shall give—

(a)   that person (unless he is asleep); or

(b)   any solicitor representing him who is available at the time of the review,

an opportunity to make representations to him about the detention.

(13)   Subject to subsection (14) below, the person whose detention is under review or his solicitor may make representations under subsection (12) above either orally or in writing.

(14)   The review officer may refuse to hear oral representations from the person whose detention is under review if he considers that he is unfit to make such representations by reason of his condition or behaviour.

Amendment

Sub-s (8): words 'the modifications specified in subsection (8A)' in square brackets substituted by the Police Reform Act 2002, s 52(1) (date in force: 1 April 2003: see SI 2003/808, art 2(d)).

Sub-s (8A): inserted by the Police Reform Act 2002, s 52(2) (date in force: 1 April 2003: see SI 2003/808, art 2(d)).

Sub-s (9): words 'or 37D(5)' in square brackets inserted by the Criminal Justice Act 2003, s 28, Sch 2, paras 1, 4 (date in force: 29 January 2004: see SI 2004/81, art 4(1), (2)(c)).

Sub-s (10): reference to '(6B)' in square brackets substituted by the Police Reform Act 2002, s 52(3)(a) (date in force: 1 April 2003: see SI 2003/808, art 2(d)); words 'the modifications specified in subsection (10A)' in square brackets substituted by the Police Reform Act 2002, s 52(3)(a) (date in force: 1 April 2003: see SI 2003/808, art 2(d)).

Sub-s (10A): inserted by the Police Reform Act 2002, s 52(4) (date in force: 1 April 2003: see SI 2003/808, art 2(d)).

B.91

[40A   Use of telephone for review under s 40]

[[(1)   A review under section 40(1)(b) may be carried out by means of a discussion, conducted by telephone, with one or more persons at the police station where the arrested person is held.

(2)   But subsection (1) does not apply if—

(a)   the review is of a kind authorised by regulations under section 45A to be carried out using video-conferencing facilities; and

(b)   it is reasonably practicable to carry it out in accordance with those regulations.]

(3)   Where any review is carried out under this section by an officer who is not present at the station where the arrested person is held—

(a)   any obligation of that officer to make a record in connection with the carrying out of the review shall have effect as an obligation to cause another officer to make the record;

(b)   any requirement for the record to be made in the presence of the arrested person shall apply to the making of that record by that other officer; and

(c)   the requirements under section 40(12) and (13) above for—

   (i)   the arrested person, or

   (ii)   a solicitor representing him,

to be given any opportunity to make representations (whether in writing or orally) to that officer shall have effect as a requirement for that person, or such a solicitor, to be given an opportunity to make representations in a manner authorised by subsection (4) below.

(4)   Representations are made in a manner authorised by this subsection—

(a)   in a case where facilities exist for the immediate transmission of written representations to the officer carrying out the review, if they are made either—

   (i)   orally by telephone to that officer; or

   (ii)   in writing to that officer by means of those facilities;

   and

(b)   in any other case, if they are made orally by telephone to that officer.

(5)   In this section 'video-conferencing facilities' has the same meaning as in section 45A below.]

Amendment

Inserted by the Criminal Justice and Police Act 2001, s 73(1), (2) (date in force: 1 April 2003: see SI 2003/708, art 2(d)).

Sub-ss (1), (2): substituted by the Criminal Justice Act 2003, s 6 (date in force: 20 January 2004: see SI 2004/81, art 2(1), (2)(a)).

B.92

41   Limits on period of detention without charge

(1)   Subject to the following provisions of this section and to sections 42 and 43 below, a person shall not be kept in police detention for more than 24 hours without being charged.

(2)   The time from which the period of detention of a person is to be calculated (in this Act referred to as 'the relevant time')—

(a)   in the case of a person to whom this paragraph applies, shall be—

(i)   the time at which that person arrives at the relevant police station; or

(ii)   the time 24 hours after the time of that person's arrest,

whichever is the earlier;

(b)   in the case of a person arrested outside England and Wales, shall be—

(i)   the time at which that person arrives at the first police station to which he is taken in the police area in England or Wales in which the offence for which he was arrested is being investigated; or

(ii)   the time 24 hours after the time of that person's entry into England and Wales,

whichever is the earlier;

(c)   in the case of a person who—

(i)   attends voluntarily at a police station; or

(ii)   accompanies a constable to a police station without having been arrested,

and is arrested at the police station, the time of his arrest;

[(ca)   in the case of a person who attends a police station to answer to bail granted under section 30A, the time when he arrives at the police station;]

(d)   in any other case, except where subsection (5) below applies, shall be the time at which the person arrested arrives at the first police station to which he is taken after his arrest.

(3)   Subsection (2)(a) above applies to a person if—

(a)   his arrest is sought in one police area in England and Wales;

(b)   he is arrested in another police area; and

(c)   he is not questioned in the area in which he is arrested in order to obtain evidence in relation to an offence for which he is arrested;

and in sub-paragraph (i) of that paragraph 'the relevant police station' means the first police station to which he is taken in the police area in which his arrest was sought.

(4)   Subsection (2) above shall have effect in relation to a person arrested under section 31 above as if every reference in it to his arrest or his being arrested were a reference to his arrest or his being arrested for the offence for which he was originally arrested.

(5)   If—

   (a)   a person is in police detention in a police area in England and Wales ('the first area'); and

   (b)   his arrest for an offence is sought in some other police area in England and Wales ('the second area'); and

   (c)   he is taken to the second area for the purposes of investigating that offence, without being questioned in the first area in order to obtain evidence in relation to it,

the relevant time shall be—

   (i)   the time 24 hours after he leaves the place where he is detained in the first area; or

   (ii)   the time at which he arrives at the first police station to which he is taken in the second area,

whichever is the earlier.

(6)   When a person who is in police detention is removed to hospital because he is in need of medical treatment, any time during which he is being questioned in hospital or on the way there or back by a police officer for the purpose of obtaining evidence relating to an offence shall be included in any period which falls to be calculated for the purposes of this Part of this Act, but any other time while he is in hospital or on his way there or back shall not be so included.

(7)   Subject to subsection (8) below, a person who at the expiry of 24 hours after the relevant time is in police detention and has not been charged shall be released at that time either on bail or without bail.

(8)   Subsection (7) above does not apply to a person whose detention for more than 24 hours after the relevant time has been authorised or is otherwise permitted in accordance with section 42 or 43 below.

(9)   A person released under subsection (7) above shall not be re-arrested without a warrant for the offence for which he was previously arrested unless new evidence justifying a further arrest has come to light since his release[; but this subsection does not prevent an arrest under section 46A below].

Amendment
   Sub-s (2): para (ca) inserted by the Criminal Justice Act 2003, s 12, Sch 1, paras 1, 8 (date in force: 20 January 2004: see SI 2004/81, art 2(1), (2)(a)).
   Sub-s (9): words in square brackets inserted by the Criminal Justice and Public Order Act 1994, s 29(4)(b).

B.93

42   Authorisation of continued detention

(1)   Where a police officer of the rank of superintendent or above who is responsible for the police station at which a person is detained has reasonable grounds for believing that—

(a)   the detention of that person without charge is necessary to secure or preserve evidence relating to an offence for which he is under arrest or to obtain such evidence by questioning him;

[(b)   an offence for which he is under arrest is an [indictable] offence; and]

(c)   the investigation is being conducted diligently and expeditiously,

he may authorise the keeping of that person in police detention for a period expiring at or before 36 hours after the relevant time.

(2)   Where an officer such as is mentioned in subsection (1) above has authorised the keeping of a person in police detention for a period expiring less than 36 hours after the relevant time, such an officer may authorise the keeping of that person in police detention for a further period expiring not more than 36 hours after that time if the conditions specified in subsection (1) above are still satisfied when he gives the authorisation.

(3)   If it is proposed to transfer a person in police detention to another police area, the officer determining whether or not to authorise keeping him in detention under subsection (1) above shall have regard to the distance and the time the journey would take.

(4)   No authorisation under subsection (1) above shall be given in respect of any person—

(a)   more than 24 hours after the relevant time; or

(b)   before the second review of his detention under section 40 above has been carried out.

(5)   Where an officer authorises the keeping of a person in police detention under subsection (1) above, it shall be his duty—

(a)   to inform that person of the grounds for his continued detention; and

(b)   to record the grounds in that person's custody record.

(6)   Before determining whether to authorise the keeping of a person in detention under subsection (1) or (2) above, an officer shall give—

(a)   that person; or

(b)   any solicitor representing him who is available at the time when it falls to the officer to determine whether to give the authorisation, an opportunity to make representations to him about the detention.

(7)   Subject to subsection (8) below, the person in detention or his solicitor may make representations under subsection (6) above either orally or in writing.

(8)   The officer to whom it falls to determine whether to give the authorisation may refuse to hear oral representations from the person in detention if he considers that he is unfit to make such representations by reason of his condition or behaviour.

(9)   Where—

> (a)   an officer authorises the keeping of a person in detention under subsection (1) above; and
>
> (b)   at the time of the authorisation he has not yet exercised a right conferred on him by section 56 or 58 below,

the officer—

> (i)   shall inform him of that right;
>
> (ii)   shall decide whether he should be permitted to exercise it;
>
> (iii)   shall record the decision in his custody record; and
>
> (iv)   if the decision is to refuse to permit the exercise of the right, shall also record the grounds for the decision in that record.

(10)   Where an officer has authorised the keeping of a person who has not been charged in detention under subsection (1) or (2) above, he shall be released from detention, either on bail or without bail, not later than 36 hours after the relevant time, unless—

> (a)   he has been charged with an offence; or
>
> (b)   his continued detention is authorised or otherwise permitted in accordance with section 43 below.

(11)   A person released under subsection (10) above shall not be re-arrested without a warrant for the offence for which he was previously arrested unless new evidence justifying a further arrest has come to light since his release[; but this subsection does not prevent an arrest under section 46A below].

Amendment
> Sub-s (1): para (b) substituted by the Criminal Justice Act 2003, s 7 (date in force: 20 January 2004: see SI 2004/81, art 2(1), (2)(a)); in para (b) word 'indictable' in square brackets substituted by the Serious Organised Crime and Police Act 2005, s 111, Sch 7, Pt 3, para 43(1), (7) (date in force: 1 January 2006: see SI 2005/3495, art 2(1)(m)).
> Sub-s (11): words in square brackets inserted by the Criminal Justice and Public Order Act 1994, s 29(4)(b).

43 Warrants of further detention

(1)   Where, on an application on oath made by a constable and supported by an information, a magistrates' court is satisfied that there are reasonable grounds for believing that the further detention of the person to whom the application relates is justified, it may issue a warrant of further detention authorising the keeping of that person in police detention.

(2)   A court may not hear an application for a warrant of further detention unless the person to whom the application relates—

    (a)   has been furnished with a copy of the information; and

    (b)   has been brought before the court for the hearing.

(3)   The person to whom the application relates shall be entitled to be legally represented at the hearing and, if he is not so represented but wishes to be so represented—

    (a)   the court shall adjourn the hearing to enable him to obtain representation; and

    (b)   he may be kept in police detention during the adjournment.

(4)   A person's further detention is only justified for the purposes of this section or section 44 below if—

    (a)   his detention without charge is necessary to secure or preserve evidence relating to an offence for which he is under arrest or to obtain such evidence by questioning him;

    (b)   an offence for which he is under arrest is [an indictable offence]; and

    (c)   the investigation is being conducted diligently and expeditiously.

(5)   Subject to subsection (7) below, an application for a warrant of further detention may be made—

    (a)   at any time before the expiry of 36 hours after the relevant time; or

    (b)   in a case where—

        (i)   it is not practicable for the magistrates' court to which the application will be made to sit at the expiry of 36 hours after the relevant time; but

        (ii)   the court will sit during the 6 hours following the end of that period,

    at any time before the expiry of the said 6 hours.

(6)   In a case to which subsection (5)(b) above applies—

(a)   the person to whom the application relates may be kept in police detention until the application is heard; and

(b)   the custody officer shall make a note in that person's custody record—

    (i)   of the fact that he was kept in police detention for more than 36 hours after the relevant time; and

    (ii)   of the reason why he was so kept.

(7)   If—

(a)   an application for a warrant of further detention is made after the expiry of 36 hours after the relevant time; and

(b)   it appears to the magistrates' court that it would have been reasonable for the police to make it before the expiry of that period,

the court shall dismiss the application.

(8)   Where on an application such as is mentioned in subsection (1) above a magistrates' court is not satisfied that there are reasonable grounds for believing that the further detention of the person to whom the application relates is justified, it shall be its duty—

(a)   to refuse the application; or

(b)   to adjourn the hearing of it until a time not later than 36 hours after the relevant time.

(9)   The person to whom the application relates may be kept in police detention during the adjournment.

(10)   A warrant of further detention shall—

(a)   state the time at which it is issued;

(b)   authorise the keeping in police detention of the person to whom it relates for the period stated in it.

(11)   Subject to subsection (12) below, the period stated in a warrant of further detention shall be such period as the magistrates' court thinks fit, having regard to the evidence before it.

(12)   The period shall not be longer than 36 hours.

(13)   If it is proposed to transfer a person in police detention to a police area other than that in which he is detained when the application for a warrant of further detention is made, the court hearing the application shall have regard to the distance and the time the journey would take.

(14)   Any information submitted in support of an application under this section shall state—

(a)   the nature of the offence for which the person to whom the application relates has been arrested;

(b)   the general nature of the evidence on which that person was arrested;

(c)   what inquiries relating to the offence have been made by the police and what further inquiries are proposed by them;

(d)   the reasons for believing the continued detention of that person to be necessary for the purposes of such further inquiries.

(15)   Where an application under this section is refused, the person to whom the application relates shall forthwith be charged or, subject to subsection (16) below, released, either on bail or without bail.

(16)   A person need not be released under subsection (15) above—

(a)   before the expiry of 24 hours after the relevant time; or

(b)   before the expiry of any longer period for which his continued detention is or has been authorised under section 42 above.

(17)   Where an application under this section is refused, no further application shall be made under this section in respect of the person to whom the refusal relates, unless supported by evidence which has come to light since the refusal.

(18)   Where a warrant of further detention is issued, the person to whom it relates shall be released from police detention, either on bail or without bail, upon or before the expiry of the warrant unless he is charged.

(19)   A person released under subsection (18) above shall not be re-arrested without a warrant for the offence for which he was previously arrested unless new evidence justifying a further arrest has come to light since his release[; but this subsection does not prevent an arrest under section 46A below.]

Amendment
Sub-s (4): in para (b) words 'an indictable offence' in square brackets substituted by the Serious Organised Crime and Police Act 2005, s 111, Sch 7, Pt 3, para 43(1), (8) (date in force: 1 January 2006: see SI 2005/3495, art 2(1)(m)).
Sub-s (19): words from '; but this subsection' to 'section 46A below.' in square brackets inserted by the Criminal Justice and Public Order Act 1994, s 29(4)(b).

B.95

44   Extension of warrants of further detention

(1)   On an application on oath made by a constable and supported by an information a magistrates' court may extend a warrant of further detention issued under section 43 above if it is satisfied that there are reasonable grounds for believing that the further detention of the person to whom the application relates is justified.

(2)   Subject to subsection (3) below, the period for which a warrant of further detention may be extended shall be such period as the court thinks fit, having regard to the evidence before it.

(3)   The period shall not—

(a)   be longer than 36 hours; or

(b)   end later than 96 hours after the relevant time.

(4)   Where a warrant of further detention has been extended under subsection (1) above, or further extended under this subsection, for a period ending before 96 hours after the relevant time, on an application such as is mentioned in that subsection a magistrates' court may further extend the warrant if it is satisfied as there mentioned; and subsections (2) and (3) above apply to such further extensions as they apply to extensions under subsection (1) above.

(5)   A warrant of further detention shall, if extended or further extended under this section, be endorsed with a note of the period of the extension.

(6)   Subsections (2), (3), and (14) of section 43 above shall apply to an application made under this section as they apply to an application made under that section.

(7)   Where an application under this section is refused, the person to whom the application relates shall forthwith be charged or, subject to subsection (8) below, released, either on bail or without bail.

(8)   A person need not be released under subsection (7) above before the expiry of any period for which a warrant of further detention issued in relation to him has been extended or further extended on an earlier application made under this section.

B.96

45   Detention before charge—supplementary

(1)   In sections 43 and 44 of this Act 'magistrates' court' means a court consisting of two or more justices of the peace sitting otherwise than in open court.

(2)   Any reference in this Part of this Act to a period of time or a time of day is to be treated as approximate only.

B.97

[45A   Use of video-conferencing facilities for decisions about detention]

[(1)   Subject to the following provisions of this section, the Secretary of State may by regulations provide that, in the case of an arrested person who is held in a police station, some or all of the functions mentioned in subsection (2) may be performed (notwithstanding anything in the preceding provisions of this Part) by an officer who—

(a)   is not present in that police station; but

(b)   has access to the use of video-conferencing facilities that enable him to communicate with persons in that station.

(2)   Those functions are—

(a)   the functions in relation to an arrested person taken to[, or answering to bail at,] a police station that is not a designated police station which, in the case of an arrested person taken to a station that is a designated police station, are functions of a custody officer under section 37, 38 or 40 above; and

(b)   the function of carrying out a review under section 40(1)(b) above (review, by an officer of at least the rank of inspector, of the detention of person arrested but not charged).

(3)   Regulations under this section shall specify the use to be made in the performance of the functions mentioned in subsection (2) above of the facilities mentioned in subsection (1) above.

(4)   Regulations under this section shall not authorise the performance of any of the functions mentioned in subsection (2)(a) above by such an officer as is mentioned in subsection (1) above unless he is a custody officer for a designated police station.

(5)   Where any functions mentioned in subsection (2) above are performed in a manner authorised by regulations under this section—

(a)   any obligation of the officer performing those functions to make a record in connection with the performance of those functions shall have effect as an obligation to cause another officer to make the record; and

(b)   any requirement for the record to be made in the presence of the arrested person shall apply to the making of that record by that other officer.

(6)   Where the functions mentioned in subsection (2)(b) are performed in a manner authorised by regulations under this section, the requirements under section 40(12) and (13) above for—

(a)   the arrested person, or

(b)   a solicitor representing him,

to be given any opportunity to make representations (whether in writing or orally) to the person performing those functions shall have effect as a requirement for that person, or such a solicitor, to be given an opportunity to make representations in a manner authorised by subsection (7) below.

(7)   Representations are made in a manner authorised by this subsection—

    (a)   in a case where facilities exist for the immediate transmission of written representations to the officer performing the functions, if they are made either—

        (i)   orally to that officer by means of the video-conferencing facilities used by him for performing those functions; or

        (ii)   in writing to that officer by means of the facilities available for the immediate transmission of the representations;

      and

    (b)   in any other case if they are made orally to that officer by means of the video-conferencing facilities used by him for performing the functions.

(8)   Regulations under this section may make different provision for different cases and may be made so as to have effect in relation only to the police stations specified or described in the regulations.

(9)   Regulations under this section shall be made by statutory instrument and shall be subject to annulment in pursuance of a resolution of either House of Parliament.

(10)   Any reference in this section to video-conferencing facilities, in relation to any functions, is a reference to any facilities (whether a live television link or other facilities) by means of which the functions may be performed with the officer performing them, the person in relation to whom they are performed and any legal representative of that person all able to both see and to hear each other.]

Amendment
> Inserted by the Criminal Justice and Police Act 2001, s 73(1), (3) (date in force: 1 April 2003: see SI 2003/708, art 2(d)).
>
>   Sub-s (2): in para (a) words ', or answering to bail at,' in square brackets inserted by the Criminal Justice Act 2003, s 12, Sch 1, paras 1, 9 (date in force: 20 January 2004: see SI 2004/81, art 2(1), (2)(a)).

Detention—miscellaneous

B.98

46   Detention after charge

(1)   Where a person—

    (a)   is charged with an offence; and

(b)   after being charged—

    (i)   is kept in police detention; or

    (ii)   is detained by a local authority in pursuance of arrangements made under section 38(6) above,

he shall be brought before a magistrates' court in accordance with the provisions of this section.

(2)   If he is to be brought before a magistrates' court [in the local justice] area in which the police station at which he was charged is situated, he shall be brought before such a court as soon as is practicable and in any event not later than the first sitting after he is charged with the offence.

(3)   If no magistrates' court [in that area] is due to sit either on the day on which he is charged or on the next day, the custody officer for the police station at which he was charged shall inform the [designated officer] for the area that there is a person in the area to whom subsection (2) above applies.

(4)   If the person charged is to be brought before a magistrates' court [in a local justice] area other than that in which the police station at which he was charged is situated, he shall be removed to that area as soon as is practicable and brought before such a court as soon as is practicable after his arrival in the area and in any event not later than the first sitting of a magistrates' court [in that area] after his arrival in the area.

(5)   If no magistrates' court [in that area] is due to sit either on the day on which he arrives in the area or on the next day—

(a)   he shall be taken to a police station in the area; and

(b)   the custody officer at that station shall inform the [designated officer] for the area that there is a person in the area to whom subsection (4) applies.

(6)   Subject to subsection (8) below, where [the designated officer for a local justice] area has been informed—

(a)   under subsection (3) above that there is a person in the area to whom subsection (2) above applies; or

(b)   under subsection (5) above that there is a person in the area to whom subsection (4) above applies,

[the designated officer] shall arrange for a magistrates' court to sit not later than the day next following the relevant day.

(7)   In this section ' the relevant day'—

(a)   in relation to a person who is to be brought before a magistrates' court [in the local justice] area in which the police station at which he was charged is situated, means the day on which he was charged; and

(b)   in relation to a person who is to be brought before a magistrates' court [in any other local justice] area, means the day on which he arrives in the area.

(8)   Where the day next following the relevant day is Christmas Day, Good Friday or a Sunday, the duty of the [designated officer] under subsection (6) above is a duty to arrange for a magistrates' court to sit not later than the first day after the relevant day which is not one of those days.

(9)   Nothing in this section requires a person who is in hospital to be brought before a court if he is not well enough.

Amendment

Sub-s (2): words 'in the local justice' in square brackets substituted by the Courts Act 2003, s 109(1), Sch 8, para 282(1), (2) (date in force: 1 April 2005: see SI 2005/910, art 3(y)).

Sub-s (3): words 'in that area' in square brackets substituted by the Courts Act 2003, s 109(1), Sch 8, para 282(1), (3)(a) (date in force: 1 April 2005: see SI 2005/910, art 3(y)); words 'designated officer' in square brackets substituted by the Courts Act 2003, s 109(1), Sch 8, para 282(1), (3)(b) (date in force: 1 April 2005: see SI 2005/910, art 3(y)).

Sub-s (4): words 'in a local justice' in square brackets substituted by the Courts Act 2003, s 109(1), Sch 8, para 282(1), (4)(a) (date in force: 1 April 2005: see SI 2005/910, art 3(y)); words 'in that area' in square brackets substituted by the Courts Act 2003, s 109(1), Sch 8, para 282(1), (4)(b) (date in force: 1 April 2005: see SI 2005/910, art 3(y)).

Sub-s (5): words 'in that area' in square brackets substituted by the Courts Act 2003, s 109(1), Sch 8, para 282(1), (5)(a) (date in force: 1 April 2005: see SI 2005/910, art 3(y)); in para (b) words 'designated officer' in square brackets substituted by the Courts Act 2003, s 109(1), Sch 8, para 282(1), (5)(b) (date in force: 1 April 2005: see SI 2005/910, art 3(y)).

Sub-s (6): words 'the designated officer for a local justice' in square brackets substituted by the Courts Act 2003, s 109(1), Sch 8, para 282(1), (6)(a) (date in force: 1 April 2005: see SI 2005/910, art 3(y)); words 'the designated officer' in square brackets substituted by the Courts Act 2003, s 109(1), Sch 8, para 282(1), (6)(b) (date in force: 1 April 2005: see SI 2005/910, art 3(y)).

Sub-s (7): in para (a) words 'in the local justice' in square brackets substituted by the Courts Act 2003, s 109(1), Sch 8, para 282(1), (7)(a) (date in force: 1 April 2005: see SI 2005/910, art 3(y)); in para (b) words 'for any other local justice' in square brackets substituted by the Courts Act 2003, s 109(1), Sch 8, para 282(1), (7)(b) (date in force: 1 April 2005: see SI 2005/910, art 3(y)).

Sub-s (8): words 'designated officer' in square brackets substituted by the Courts Act 2003, s 109(1), Sch 8, para 282(1), (8) (date in force: 1 April 2005: see SI 2005/910, art 3(y)).

B.99

[46ZA   Persons granted live link bail]

[(1)   This section applies in relation to bail granted under this Part subject to the duty mentioned in section 47(3)(b) ('live link bail').

(2)   An accused person who attends a police station to answer to live link bail is not to be treated as in police detention for the purposes of this Act.

(3)   Subsection (2) does not apply in relation to an accused person if—

(*a*)   *at any time before the beginning of proceedings in relation to a live link direction under section 57C of the Crime and Disorder Act 1998 in relation to him, he informs a constable that he does not intend to give his consent to the direction;*

(b)   *at any such time,* [at any time before the beginning of proceedings in relation to a live link direction under section 57C of the Crime and Disorder Act 1998 in relation to the accused person,] a constable informs him that a live link will not be available for his use for the purposes of that section;

(c)   *proceedings in relation to a live link direction under that section have begun but he does not give his consent to the direction;* or

(d)   the court determines for *any other reason* [any reason] not to give such a direction.

(4)   If *any of paragraphs (a) to (d) of subsection (3) apply* [paragraph (b) or (d) of subsection (3) applies] in relation to a person, he is to be treated for the purposes of this Part—

(a)   as if he had been arrested for and charged with the offence in connection with which he was granted bail, and

(b)   as if he had been so charged at the time when that paragraph first applied in relation to him.

(5)   An accused person who is arrested under section 46A for failing to attend at a police station to answer to live link bail, and who is brought to a police station in accordance with that section, is to be treated for the purposes of this Part—

(a)   as if he had been arrested for and charged with the offence in connection with which he was granted bail, and

(b)   as if he had been so charged at the time when he is brought to the station.

(6)   Nothing in subsection (4) or (5) affects the operation of section 47(6).]

NOTES

Amendment

Inserted by the Police and Justice Act 2006, s 46(1), (3) (date in force (in relation to the local justice area of Lambeth and Southwark): 1 April 2007: see SI 2007/709, art 3(n); (in relation to certain local justice areas): 14 November 2008: see SI 2008/2785, art 2; (in relation to certain local justice areas): 3 October 2011: see SI 2011/2144, art 2(1)(b), (2); (for remaining purposes): to be appointed: see the Police and Justice Act 2006, s 53(1)(a)).

Sub-s (3): para (a) repealed by the Coroners and Justice Act 2009, ss 107(1), (2)(a)(i), 178, Sch 23, Pt 3 (date in force (in relation to certain specified local justice areas): 14 December 2009: see SI 2009/3253, art 3(1)(b), (2); for transitional provisions see art 4(4)(a), (5) thereof; (in relation to certain specified relevant local justice areas): 3 October 2011: see SI 2011/2148, art 2(1)(b), (d), (e), (2); (for remaining purposes): to be appointed: see the Coroners and Justice Act 2009, s 182(5)).

Sub-s (3): in para (b) words 'at any such time,' in italics repealed and subsequent words in square brackets substituted by the Coroners and Justice Act 2009, s 107(1), (2)(a)(ii) (date in force (in relation to certain specified local justice areas): 14 December 2009: see SI 2009/3253, art 3(1)(b), (2); for transitional provisions see art 4(4)(a), (5) thereof; (in relation to certain specified relevant local justice areas): 3 October 2011: see SI 2011/2148, art 2(1)(b), (2); (for remaining purposes): to be appointed: see the Coroners and Justice Act 2009, s 182(5)); para (c) repealed by the Coroners and Justice Act 2009, ss 107(1), (2)(a)(iii), 178, Sch 23, Pt 3 (date in force (in relation to certain specified local justice areas): 14 December 2009: see SI 2009/3253, art 3(1)(b), (2); for transitional provisions see art 4(4)(a), (5) thereof; (in relation to certain specified relevant local justice areas): 3 October 2011: see SI 2011/2148, art 2(1)(b), (d), (e), (2); (for remaining purposes): to be appointed: see the Coroners and Justice Act 2009, s 182(5)); in para (d) words 'any other reason' in italics repealed and subsequent words in square brackets substituted by the Coroners and Justice Act 2009, s 107(1), (2)(a)(iv) (date in force (in relation to certain specified local justice areas): 14 December 2009: see SI 2009/3253, art 3(1)(b), (2); for transitional provisions see art 4(4)(a), (5) thereof; (for remaining purposes): to be appointed: see the Coroners and Justice Act 2009, s 182(5)).

Sub-s (4): words 'any of paragraphs (a) to (d) of subsection (3) apply' in italics repealed and subsequent words in square brackets substituted by the Coroners and Justice Act 2009, s 107(1), (2)(b) (date in force (in relation to certain specified local justice areas): 14 December 2009: see SI 2009/3253, art 3(1)(b), (2); for transitional provisions see art 4(4)(a), (5) thereof; (in relation to certain specified relevant local justice areas): 3 October 2011: see SI 2011/2148, art 2(1)(b), (2); (for remaining purposes): to be appointed: see the Coroners and Justice Act 2009, s 182(5)).

B.100

[46A   Power of arrest for failure to answer to police bail]

[(1)   A constable may arrest without a warrant any person who, having been released on bail under this Part of this Act subject to a duty to attend at a police station, fails to attend at that police station at the time appointed for him to do so.

[(1ZA)   The reference in subsection (1) to a person who fails to attend at a police station at the time appointed for him to do so includes a reference to a person who—

(a)   attends at a police station to answer to bail granted subject to the duty mentioned in section 47(3)(b), but

(b)   leaves the police station at any time before the beginning of proceedings in relation to a live link direction under section 57C of the Crime and Disorder Act 1998 in relation to him, *without informing a constable that he does not intend to give his consent to the direction.*]

[(1ZB)   The reference in subsection (1) to a person who fails to attend at a police station at the time appointed for the person to do so includes a reference to a person who—

(a)   attends at a police station to answer to bail granted subject to the duty mentioned in section 47(3)(b), but

(b)   refuses to be searched under section 54B.]

[(1A) A person who has been released on bail under section [37, 37C(2)(b) or 37CA(2)(b)] above may be arrested without warrant by a constable if the constable has reasonable grounds for suspecting that the person has broken any of the conditions of bail.]

(2) A person who is arrested under this section shall be taken to the police station appointed as the place at which he is to surrender to custody as soon as practicable after the arrest.

(3) For the purposes of—

(a) section 30 above (subject to the obligation in subsection (2) above), and

(b) section 31 above,

an arrest under this section shall be treated as an arrest for an offence.]

Amendment

Inserted by the Criminal Justice and Public Order Act 1994, s 29(2).

Sub-s (1ZA): inserted by the Police and Justice Act 2006, s 46(1), (4) (date in force (in relation to the local justice area of Lambeth and Southwark): 1 April 2007: see SI 2007/709, art 3(n); (in relation to certain local justice areas): 14 November 2008: see SI 2008/2785, art 2; (in relation to certain local justice areas): 3 October 2011: see SI 2011/2144, art 2(1)(b), (2); (for remaining purposes): to be appointed: see the Police and Justice Act 2006, s 53(1)(a)).

Sub-s (1ZA): in para (b) words ', without informing a constable that he does not intend to give his consent to the direction' in italics repealed by the Coroners and Justice Act 2009, ss 107(1), (3), 178, Sch 23, Pt 3 (date in force (in relation to certain specified local justice areas): 14 December 2009: see SI 2009/3253, art 3(1)(b), (2); for transitional provisions see art 4(4)(b), (5) thereof; (in relation to certain specified relevant local justice areas): 3 October 2011: see SI 2011/2148, art 2(1)(b), (d), (e), (2); (for remaining purposes): to be appointed: see the Coroners and Justice Act 2009, s 182(5)).

Sub-s (1ZB): inserted by the Coroners and Justice Act 2009, s 108(2) (date in force (in relation to certain specified local justice areas): 14 December 2009: see SI 2009/3253, art 3(1)(c), (2); (in relation to certain specified relevant local justice areas): 3 October 2011: see SI 2011/2148, art 2(1)(c), (2); (for remaining purposes): to be appointed: see the Coroners and Justice Act 2009, s 182(5).

Sub-s (1A): inserted by the Criminal Justice Act 2003, s 28, Sch 2, paras 1, 5 9 (date in force: 29 January 2004: see SI 2004/81, art 4(1), (2)(c); words '37, 37C(2)(b) or 37CA(2)(b)' in square brackets substituted by the Police and Justice Act 2006, s 10, Sch 6, Pt 1, para 1, Pt 3, para 7 (date in force: 1 April 2007: see SI 2007/709, art 3(i)).

B.101

47 Bail after arrest

(1) [Subject to the following provisions of this section], a release on bail of a person under this Part of this Act shall be a release on bail granted in accordance with [sections 3, 3A, 5 and 5A of the Bail Act 1976 as they apply to bail granted by a constable].

[(1A) The normal powers to impose conditions of bail shall be available to him where a custody officer releases a person on bail under section [[37] above or section] 38(1) above (including that subsection as applied by section 40(10) above) but not in any other cases.

In this subsection, 'the normal powers to impose conditions of bail' has the meaning given in section 3(6) of the Bail Act 1976.]

[(1B)   No application may be made under section 5B of the Bail Act 1976 if a person is released on bail under section [37, 37C(2)(b) or 37CA(2)(b)] above.

(1C)   Subsections (1D) to (1F) below apply where a person released on bail under section [37, 37C(2)(b) or 37CA(2)(b)] above is on bail subject to conditions.

(1D)   The person shall not be entitled to make an application under section 43B of the Magistrates' Courts Act 1980.

(1E)   A magistrates' court may, on an application by or on behalf of the person, vary the conditions of bail; and in this subsection 'vary' has the same meaning as in the Bail Act 1976.

(1F)   Where a magistrates' court varies the conditions of bail under subsection (1E) above, that bail shall not lapse but shall continue subject to the conditions as so varied.]

(2)   Nothing in the Bail Act 1976 shall prevent the re-arrest without warrant of a person released on bail subject to a duty to attend at a police station if new evidence justifying a further arrest has come to light since his release.

(3)   Subject to [subsections (3A) and (4)] below, in this Part of this Act references to 'bail' are references to bail subject to a duty—

    (*a*)   *to appear before a magistrates' court at such time and such place; or*

    (*b*)   *to attend at such police station at such time,*

as the custody officer may appoint

    [(a)   to appear before a magistrates' court at such time and such place as the custody officer may appoint;

    (b)   to attend at such police station as the custody officer may appoint at such time as he may appoint for the purposes of—

        (i)   proceedings in relation to a live link direction under section 57C of the Crime and Disorder Act 1998 (use of live link direction at preliminary hearings where accused is at police station); and

        (ii)   any preliminary hearing in relation to which such a direction is given; or

    (c)   to attend at such police station as the custody officer may appoint at such time as he may appoint for purposes other than those mentioned in paragraph (b)].

[(3A)   Where a custody officer grants bail to a person subject to a duty to appear before a magistrates' court, he shall appoint for the appearance—

(a)   a date which is not later than the first sitting of the court after the person is charged with the offence; or

(b)   where he is informed by the [designated officer for the relevant local justice] area that the appearance cannot be accommodated until a later date, that later date.]

(4)   Where a custody officer has granted bail to a person subject to a duty to appear at a police station, the custody officer may give notice in writing to that person that his attendance at the police station is not required.

(5)   ...

(6)   Where a person [who has been granted bail [under this Part] and either has attended at the police station in accordance with the grant of bail or has been arrested under section 46A above is detained at a police station], any time during which he was in police detention prior to being granted bail shall be included as part of any period which falls to be calculated under this Part of this Act [and any time during which he was on bail shall not be so included].

(7)   Where a person who was released on bail [under this Part] subject to a duty to attend at a police station is re-arrested, the provisions of this Part of this Act shall apply to him as they apply to a person arrested for the first time[; but this subsection does not apply to a person who is arrested under section 46A above or has attended a police station in accordance with the grant of bail (and who accordingly is deemed by section 34(7) above to have been arrested for an offence)] [or to a person to whom section 46ZA(4) or (5) applies].

(8)   ...

Amendment

Sub-s (1): words 'Subject to the following provisions of this section' in square brackets substituted by the Criminal Justice Act 2003, s 28, Sch 2, paras 1, 6(1), (2) (date in force: 29 January 2004: see SI 2004/81, art 4(1), (2)(c)); words 'sections 3, 3A, 5 and 5A of the Bail Act 1976 as they apply to bail granted by a constable' in square brackets substituted by the Criminal Justice and Public Order Act 1994, s 27(1)(a).

Sub-s (1A): inserted by the Criminal Justice and Public Order Act 1994, s 27(1)(b); words in square brackets ending with the words 'above or section' inserted by the Criminal Justice Act 2003, s 28, Sch 2, paras 1, 6(1), (3) (date in force: 29 January 2004: see SI 2004/81, art 4(1), (2)(c)); reference to '37' in square brackets substituted by the Police and Justice Act 2006, s 10, Sch 6, Pt 1, para 1, Pt 3, para 6 (date in force: 1 April 2007: see SI 2007/709, art 3(i)).

Sub-ss (1B)–(1F): inserted by the Criminal Justice Act 2003, s 28, Sch 2, paras 1, 6(1), (4) (date in force: 29 January 2004: see SI 2004/81, art 4(1), (2)(c)).

Sub-ss (1B), (1C): words '37, 37C(2)(b) or 37CA(2)(b)' in square brackets substituted by the Police and Justice Act 2006, s 10, Sch 6, Pt 1, para 1, Pt 3, para 11 (date in force: 1 April 2007: see SI 2007/709, art 3(i)).

Sub-s (3): words 'subsections (3A) and (4)' in square brackets substituted by the Crime and Disorder Act 1998, s 46(1) (date in force (in relation to certain specified areas): 30 September 1998: see SI 1998/2327, art 3(2), Sch 2; (for remaining purposes): 1 November 1999: see

SI 1999/2976, art 2); paras (a), (b) and words 'as the custody officer may appoint' immediately following them substituted, by subsequent paras (a)–(c), by the Police and Justice Act 2006, s 46(1), (5)(a) (date in force (in relation to the local justice area of Lambeth and Southwark): 1 April 2007: see SI 2007/709, art 3(n); (in relation to certain local justice areas): 14 November 2008: see SI 2008/2785, art 2; (in relation to certain local justice areas): 3 October 2011: see SI 2011/2144, art 2(1)(b), (2); (for remaining purposes): to be appointed: see the Police and Justice Act 2006, s 53(1)(a).

Sub-s (3A): inserted by the Crime and Disorder Act 1998, s 46(2) (date in force (in relation to certain specified areas): 30 September 1998: see SI 1998/2327, art 3(2), Sch 2; (for remaining purposes): 1 November 1999: see SI 1999/2976, art 2); in para (b) words 'designated officer for the relevant local justice' in square brackets substituted by the Courts Act 2003, s 109(1), Sch 8, para 283 (date in force: 1 April 2005: see SI 2005/910, art 3(y); for transitional provisions see SI 2005/911, arts 2–5).

Sub-s (5): repealed by the Criminal Justice and Public Order Act 1994, ss 29(4)(c), 168(3), Sch 11.

Sub-s (6): words from 'who has' to 'police station' in square brackets substituted by the Criminal Justice and Public Order Act 1994, s 29(4)(d); words 'under this Part' in square brackets inserted by the Criminal Justice Act 2003, s 12, Sch 1, paras 1, 10(a) (date in force: 20 January 2004: see SI 2004/81, art 2(1), (2)(a)); words from 'and any time' to 'be so included' in square brackets inserted by the Police (Detention and Bail) Act 2011, s 1(1) (date in force: 1 January 1986: see the Police (Detention and Bail) Act 2011, s 1(3)).

Sub-s (7): words 'under this Part' in square brackets inserted by the Criminal Justice Act 2003, s 12, Sch 1, paras 1, 10(b) (date in force: 20 January 2004: see SI 2004/81, art 2(1), (2)(a)); words from '; but this subsection' to 'for an offence)' in square brackets inserted by the Criminal Justice and Public Order Act 1994, s 29(4)(e); words 'or to a person to whom section 46ZA(4) or (5) applies' in square brackets inserted by the Police and Justice Act 2006, s 46(1), (5)(b) (date in force (in relation to the local justice area of Lambeth and Southwark): 1 April 2007: see SI 2007/709, art 3(n); (in relation to certain local justice areas): 14 November 2008: see SI 2008/2785, art 2; (in relation to certain local justice areas): 3 October 2011: see SI 2011/2144, art 2(1)(b), (2); (for remaining purposes): to be appointed: see the Police and Justice Act 2006, s 53(1)(a).

Sub-s (8): substitutes the Magistrates' Courts Act 1980, ss 43, 117(3).

B.102

[47A   Early administrative hearings conducted by justices' clerks]

[Where a person has been charged with an offence at a police station, any requirement imposed under this Part for the person to appear or be brought before a magistrates' court shall be taken to be satisfied if the person appears or is brought before [a justices' clerk] in order for the clerk to conduct a hearing under section 50 of the Crime and Disorder Act 1998 (early administrative hearings).]

Amendment
Inserted by the Crime and Disorder Act 1998, s 119, Sch 8, para 62 (date in force: 30 September 1998: see SI 1998/2327, art 2(1)(y), (2)(t)).
Words 'a justices' clerk' in square brackets substituted by the Courts Act 2003, s 109(1), Sch 8, para 284 (date in force: 1 April 2005: see SI 2005/910, art 3(y); for transitional provisions see SI 2005/911, arts 2–5).

B.103

50   Records of detention

(1)   Each police force shall keep written records showing on an annual basis—

(a)   the number of persons kept in police detention for more than 24 hours and subsequently released without charge;

(b)   the number of applications for warrants of further detention and the results of the applications; and

(c)   in relation to each warrant of further detention—

(i)   the period of further detention authorised by it;

(ii)   the period which the person named in it spent in police detention on its authority; and

(iii)   whether he was charged or released without charge.

(2)   Every annual report—

[(a)   under section 22 of the Police Act 1996; or]

(b)   made by the Commissioner of Police of the Metropolis,

shall contain information about the matters mentioned in subsection (1) above in respect of the period to which the report relates.

Amendment
Sub-s (2): para (a) substituted by the Police Act 1996, s 103, Sch 7, para 35.

Part V
Questioning and Treatment of Persons by Police

B.104

56   Right to have someone informed when arrested

(1)   Where a person has been arrested and is being held in custody in a police station or other premises, he shall be entitled, if he so requests, to have one friend or relative or other person who is known to him or who is likely to take an interest in his welfare told, as soon as is practicable except to the extent that delay is permitted by this section, that he has been arrested and is being detained there.

(2)   Delay is only permitted—

(a)   in the case of a person who is in police detention for [an indictable offence]; and

(b)   if an officer of at least the rank of [inspector] authorises it.

(3)   In any case the person in custody must be permitted to exercise the right conferred by subsection (1) above within 36 hours from the relevant time, as defined in section 41(2) above.

(4)   An officer may give an authorisation under subsection (2) above orally or in writing but, if he gives it orally, he shall confirm it in writing as soon as is practicable.

(5)   [Subject to subsection (5A) below] an officer may only authorise delay where he has reasonable grounds for believing that telling the named person of the arrest—

(a)   will lead to interference with or harm to evidence connected with [an indictable offence] or interference with or physical injury to other persons; or

(b)   will lead to the alerting of other persons suspected of having committed such an offence but not yet arrested for it; or

(c)   will hinder the recovery of any property obtained as a result of such an offence.

[(5A)   An officer may also authorise delay where he has reasonable grounds for believing that—

(a)   the person detained for [the indictable offence] has benefited from his criminal conduct, and

(b)   the recovery of the value of the property constituting the benefit will be hindered by telling the named person of the arrest.

(5B)   For the purposes of subsection (5A) above the question whether a person has benefited from his criminal conduct is to be decided in accordance with Part 2 of the Proceeds of Crime Act 2002.]

(6)   If a delay is authorised—

(a)   the detained person shall be told the reason for it; and

(b)   the reason shall be noted on his custody record.

(7)   The duties imposed by subsection (6) above shall be performed as soon as is practicable.

(8)   The rights conferred by this section on a person detained at a police station or other premises are exercisable whenever he is transferred from one place to another; and this section applies to each subsequent occasion on which they are exercisable as it applies to the first such occasion.

(9)   There may be no further delay in permitting the exercise of the right conferred by subsection (1) above once the reason for authorising delay ceases to subsist.

[(10)   Nothing in this section applies to a person arrested or detained under the terrorism provisions.]

Amendment

Sub-s (2): in para (a) words 'an indictable offence' in square brackets substituted by the Serious Organised Crime and Police Act 2005, s 111, Sch 7, Pt 3, para 43(1), (9)(a) (date in force: 1 January 2006: see SI 2005/3495, art 2(1)(m)); in para (b) word 'inspector' in square brackets substituted by the Criminal Justice and Police Act 2001, s 74 (date in force: 1 April 2003: see SI 2003/708, art 2(e)).

Sub-s (5): words in square brackets inserted by the Drug Trafficking Offences Act 1986, s 32(1); in para (a) words 'an indictable offence' in square brackets substituted by the Serious Organised Crime and Police Act 2005, s 111, Sch 7, Pt 3, para 43(1), (9)(a) (date in force: 1 January 2006: see SI 2005/3495, art 2(1)(m)).

Sub-ss (5A), (5B): substituted, for sub-s (5A) as inserted by the Drug Trafficking Offences Act 1986, s 32(1), by the Proceeds of Crime Act 2002, s 456, Sch 11, paras 1, 14(1), (2) (date in force: 24 March 2003: see SI 2003/333, art 2(1), Schedule); in para (a) words 'the indictable offence' in square brackets substituted by the Serious Organised Crime and Police Act 2005, s 111, Sch 7, Pt 3, para 43(1), (9)(b) (date in force: 1 January 2006: see SI 2005/3495, art 2(1)(m)).

Sub-s (10): substituted, for sub-ss (10), (11) as originally enacted, by the Terrorism Act 2000, s 125(1), Sch 15, para 5(1), (5)(date in force: 19 February 2001 (except in relation to a person detained prior to that date): see the Terrorism Act 2000, s 129(1)(b) and SI 2001/421, art 2).

B.105

57   Additional rights of children and young persons

The following subsections shall be substituted for section 34(2) of the Children and Young Persons Act 1933—

'(2)   Where a child or young person is in police detention, such steps as are practicable shall be taken to ascertain the identity of a person responsible for his welfare.

(3)   If it is practicable to ascertain the identity of a person responsible for the welfare of the child or young person, that person shall be informed, unless it is not practicable to do so—

    (a)   that the child or young person has been arrested;

    (b)   why he has been arrested; and

    (c)   where he is being detained.

(4)   Where information falls to be given under subsection (3) above, it shall be given as soon as it is practicable to do so.

(5)   For the purposes of this section the persons who may be responsible for the welfare of a child or young person are—

    (a)   his parent or guardian; or

    (b)   any other person who has for the time being assumed responsibility for his welfare.

(6)   If it is practicable to give a person responsible for the welfare of the child or young person the information required by subsection (3) above, that person shall be given it as soon as it is practicable to do so.

(7)   If it appears that at the time of his arrest a supervision order, as defined in section 11 of the Children and Young Persons Act 1969, is in force in respect of him, the person responsible for his supervision shall also be informed as described in subsection (3) above as soon it is reasonably practicable to do so.

(8)   The reference to a parent or guardian in subsection (5) above is—

   (a)   in the case of a child or young person in the care of a local authority, a reference to that authority; and

   (b)   in the case of a child or young person in the care of a voluntary organisation in which parental rights and duties with respect to him are vested by virtue of a resolution under section 64(1) of the Child Care Act 1980, a reference to that organisation.

(9)   The rights conferred on a child or young person by subsections (2) to (8) above are in addition to his rights under section 56 of the Police and Criminal Evidence Act 1984.

(10)   The reference in subsection (2) above to a child or young person who is in police detention includes a reference to a child or young person who has been detained under the terrorism provisions; and in subsection (3) above "arrest" includes such detention.

(11)   In subsection (10) above "the terrorism provisions" has the meaning assigned to it by section 65 of the Police and Criminal Evidence Act 1984'.

B.106

58   Access to legal advice

(1)   A person arrested and held in custody in a police station or other premises shall be entitled, if he so requests, to consult a solicitor privately at any time.

(2)   Subject to subsection (3) below, a request under subsection (1) above and the time at which it was made shall be recorded in the custody record.

(3)   Such a request need not be recorded in the custody record of a person who makes it at a time while he is at a court after being charged with an offence.

(4)   If a person makes such a request, he must be permitted to consult a solicitor as soon as is practicable except to the extent that delay is permitted by this section.

(5)   In any case he must be permitted to consult a solicitor within 36 hours from the relevant time, as defined in section 41(2) above.

(6)   Delay in compliance with a request is only permitted—

(a)   in the case of a person who is in police detention for [an indictable offence]; and

(b)   if an officer of at least the rank of superintendent authorises it.

(7)   An officer may give an authorisation under subsection (6) above orally or in writing but, if he gives it orally, he shall confirm it in writing as soon as is practicable.

(8)   [Subject to subsection (8A) below] an officer may only authorise delay where he has reasonable grounds for believing that the exercise of the right conferred by subsection (1) above at the time when the person detained desires to exercise it—

(a)   will lead to interference with or harm to evidence connected with [an indictable offence] or interference with or physical injury to other persons; or

(b)   will lead to the alerting of other persons suspected of having committed such an offence but not yet arrested for it; or

(c)   will hinder the recovery of any property obtained as a result of such an offence.

[(8A)   An officer may also authorise delay where he has reasonable grounds for believing that—

(a)   the person detained for [the indictable offence] has benefited from his criminal conduct, and

(b)   the recovery of the value of the property constituting the benefit will be hindered by the exercise of the right conferred by subsection (1) above.

(8B)   For the purposes of subsection (8A) above the question whether a person has benefited from his criminal conduct is to be decided in accordance with Part 2 of the Proceeds of Crime Act 2002.]

(9)   If delay is authorised—

(a)   the detained person shall be told the reason for it; and

(b)   the reason shall be noted on his custody record.

(10)   The duties imposed by subsection (9) above shall be performed as soon as is practicable.

(11)   There may be no further delay in permitting the exercise of the right conferred by subsection (1) above once the reason for authorising delay ceases to subsist.

[(12)   Nothing in this section applies to a person arrested or detained under the terrorism provisions.]

Amendment

Sub-s (6): in para (a) words 'an indictable offence' in square brackets substituted by the Serious Organised Crime and Police Act 2005, s 111, Sch 7, Pt 3, para 43(1), (10)(a) (date in force: 1 January 2006: see SI 2005/3495, art 2(1)(m)).

Sub-s (8): words 'Subject to subsection (8A) below' in square brackets inserted by the Drug Trafficking Offences Act 1986, s 32(2); in para (a) words 'an indictable offence' in square brackets substituted by the Serious Organised Crime and Police Act 2005, s 111, Sch 7, Pt 3, para 43(1), (10)(a) (date in force: 1 January 2006: see SI 2005/3495, art 2(1)(m)).

Sub-ss (8A), (8B): substituted, for sub-s (8A) as inserted by the Drug Trafficking Offences Act 1986, s 32(2), by the Proceeds of Crime Act 2002, s 456, Sch 11, paras 1, 14(1), (3) (date in force: 24 March 2003: see SI 2003/333, art 2(1), Schedule).

Sub-s (8A): in para (a) words 'the indictable offence' in square brackets substituted by the Serious Organised Crime and Police Act 2005, s 111, Sch 7, Pt 3, para 43(1), (10)(b) (date in force: 1 January 2006: see SI 2005/3495, art 2(1)(m)).

Sub-s (12): substituted, for sub-ss (12)–(18) as originally enacted, by the Terrorism Act 2000, s 125(1), Sch 15, para 5(1), (6) (date in force: 19 February 2001 (except in relation to a person detained prior to that date): see the Terrorism Act 2000, s 129(1)(b) and SI 2001/421, art 2).

B.107

60   Tape-recording of interviews

(1)   It shall be the duty of the Secretary of State—

(a)   to issue a code of practice in connection with the tape-recording of interviews of persons suspected of the commission of criminal offences which are held by police officers at police stations; and

(b)   to make an order requiring the tape-recording of interviews of persons suspected of the commission of criminal offences, or of such descriptions of criminal offences as may be specified in the order, which are so held, in accordance with the code as it has effect for the time being.

(2)   An order under subsection (1) above shall be made by statutory instrument and shall be subject to annulment in pursuance of a resolution of either House of Parliament.

Part VIII
Evidence in Criminal Proceedings—General

Miscellaneous

B.108

78   Exclusion of unfair evidence

(1)   In any proceedings the court may refuse to allow evidence on which the prosecution proposes to rely to be given if it appears to the court that, having

regard to all the circumstances, including the circumstances in which the evidence was obtained, the admission of the evidence would have such an adverse effect on the fairness of the proceedings that the court ought not to admit it.

(2)   Nothing in this section shall prejudice any rule of law requiring a court to exclude evidence.

[(3)   This section shall not apply in the case of proceedings before a magistrates' court inquiring into an offence as examining justices.]

Amendment
> Sub-s (3): inserted, in relation to alleged offences into which no criminal procedure has begun before 1 April 1997, by the Criminal Procedure and Investigations Act 1996, s 47, Sch 1, para 26 (see SI 1997/682 and SI 1997/683).

Standards of professional behaviour as set out in the Police (Conduct) Regulations 2008

C.1

Honesty and integrity

- Police officers are honest, act with integrity and do not compromise or abuse their position.

Authority, respect and courtesy

- Police officers act with self-control and tolerance, treating members of the public and colleagues with respect and courtesy.

- Police officers do not abuse their powers or authority and respect the rights of all individuals.

Equality and diversity

- Police officers act with fairness and impartiality. They do not discriminate unlawfully or unfairly.

Use of force

- Police officers only use force to the extent that it is necessary, proportionate and reasonable in all the circumstances.

Orders and instructions

- Police officers only give and carry out lawful orders and instructions.

- Police officers abide by police regulations, force policies and lawful orders.

Duties and responsibilities

- Police officers are diligent in the exercise of their duties and responsibilities.

Confidentiality

- Police officers treat information with respect and access or disclose it only in the proper course of police duties.

Fitness for duty

- Police officers when on duty or presenting themselves for duty are fit to carry out their duties and responsibilities.

Discreditable conduct

- Police officers behave in a manner which does not discredit the police service or undermine public confidence, whether on or off duty.

- Police officers report any action taken against them for a criminal offence, conditions imposed by a court or the receipt of any penalty notice.

Challenging and reporting improper conduct

- Police officers report, challenge or take action against the conduct of colleagues which has fallen below the standards of professional behaviour expected.

Annex D

Useful websites

D.1   Please note that the authors cannot be held responsible for the accuracy of these websites.

British and Irish Legal Information Institute

www.bailii.org

Free copies of British and Irish case law and legislation, European Union case law, Law Commission reports, and other law-related British and Irish material.

Legislation.gov.uk

www.legislation.gov.uk

Part of the National Archives, the website provides free access to original (as enacted) and revised versions of legislation.

Judiciary of England and Wales

www.judiciary.gov.uk

Website for the judiciary has links to high-profile recent judgments and basic information on the court process.

United Kingdom Supreme Court

www.supremecourt.gov.uk/

Website for the UK Supreme Court, contains judgments and video streaming of proceedings.

Joint Committee on Human Rights

www.parliament.uk/jchr

Website for joint select committee has links to reports on topical issues including written and oral evidence received.

DirectGov, *Your Rights and Responsibilities*

www.direct.gov.uk/en/Governmentcitizensandrights/ Yourrightsandresponsibilities

Government website rights and responsibilities, includes sections on the right to protest, human rights and how to complain.

European Court of Human Rights, HUDOC

www.echr.coe.int/ECHR/EN/hudoc

Database of decisions of the European Court of Human Rights.

Organization for Security and Cooperation in Europe and Office for Democratic Institutions and Human Rights

www.osce.org/what/human-rights and **www.osce.org/odihr**

The OSCE is an international security organisation with 56 member states including the UK. It has a comprehensive approach to security that encompasses human rights, democratisation and policing strategies. The ODHIR monitors the human rights situation in member states and publishes guidelines on the policing of protest.

Equality and Human Rights Commission

www.equalityhumanrights.com/human-rights-practical-guidance

A resource produced primarily for people working in the public sector, some of which will also be useful for advocacy organisations. It contains short, accessible summaries of a range of guidance documents, highlighting key human rights messages and other essential information.

Independent Police Complaints Commission

www.ipcc.gov.uk

Website for the IPCC which has information on bringing complaints against the police.

Citizens Advice Bureau

www.adviceguide.org.uk

A site which provides advice on a range of issues, including basic information regarding police powers and the legal system as well as advice on how to bring complaints.

Liberty, *Know Your Rights*

www.yourrights.org.uk/

An easily understood guide to help citizens understand what their rights are in different areas of law, including the right of peaceful protest and police powers.

Sheila McKechnie Foundation, *Campaign Central*

www.campaigncentral.org.uk/know-how/law-and-campaigning

A guide which takes activists through their rights, and the restrictions they may face, as a campaigner. Website also contains information on using the law to aid a campaign and general campaigning advice.

Activists Legal Project

www.activistslegalproject.org.uk/resources.html

A not for profit collective which provides information about the law to a wide range of grassroots social change activists. Has information sheets on legal issues relevant to direct activists.

Newham Monitoring Project

www.nmp.org.uk

An independent community-based anti-racist organisation based in the east London borough of Newham. NMP works with members of the black community suffering racial discrimination/violence, police misconduct and civil rights issues. Provides a 24/7 emergency service to give advice and assistance to those suffering racial harassment including at the hands of the police.

Campaign Against Criminalising Communities (CAMPACC)

www.campacc.org.uk/

CAMPACC brings together human rights activists, lawyers, journalists, and communities which find themselves targeted by so-called 'anti-terrorism' legislation. Website contains briefings on relevant legislation.

Advisory Service for Squatters

www.squatter.org.uk/

A volunteer service to support squatters. The website has useful information regarding civil and criminal aspects of trespass, including defending a possession claims.

Friends and Families of Travellers

www.gypsy-traveller.org

An organisation that seeks to end racism and discrimination against Gypsies and Travellers. Website provides legal information on evictions from unauthorised encampments which is relevant to occupations.

Statewatch

www.statewatch.org

A group comprised of lawyers, academics, journalists, researchers and community activists, Statewatch encourages the publication of investigative journalism and critical research on civil liberties in Europe. Published work is backed up by full-text documentation so that people can access primary sources for themselves.

European Civil Liberties Network

www.ecln.org

A platform for groups working on civil liberties issues across Europe. Contains links to national organisations and briefings on pan-European issues.

Key concepts

Actus reus

E.1   The 'act' that the prosecution must prove to have taken place to establish the defendant's guilt. For example, for an offence of criminal damage the prosecution have to prove that the defendant did in fact cause the damage.

Mens rea

E.2   The mental element that the prosecution has to prove for most (but not all) criminal offences. Also known as having to prove that the defendant had a 'guilty mind'. For example, for an offence of criminal damage the prosecution have to prove that the defendant caused damage (the act or the actus reus) and that he either intentionally or recklessly caused the damage (the mental element or mens rea). Only if both the act and the mental element are proved is the damage 'criminal' and the defendant guilty of an offence.

Criminal intent

E.3   A number of criminal offences (eg murder) require the prosecution to prove that the defendant intended to cause certain criminal consequences to follow from his actions. There is no presumption that a person intends or foresees the natural consequences of his acts, but a court must decide whether he has criminal intent based on all the evidence, drawing such inferences from the evidence as appears proper in the circumstances. If a defendant foresees such consequences will follow, it is evidence of intent but the question of whether the defendant intended the consequences must still be decided.

Recklessness

E.4   For a number of offences (eg criminal damage) the prosecution does not have to prove that the defendant intended to commit a criminal offence, only that he was reckless as to whether he would do so. In order to prove recklessness the prosecution must show that:

   (i)   the defendant was aware that a risk exists or will exist; and

   (ii)   he is aware that it is unreasonable in all the circumstances to take the risk.

The leading case on recklessness is the case of *R v G* [2004] 2 Cr App Rep 23.

Strict liability

E.5   There are a limited number of offences for which the prosecution does not need to prove that the defendant had a 'guilty mind'; proving the simple fact that he did the act is enough to convict him of a criminal offence. Examples of strict liability offences are contempt of court and outraging public decency.

Joint enterprise

E.6   Where two or more people set out on a joint enterprise each is equally responsible for the acts done in pursuit of that joint enterprise, which includes liability for unusual consequences if they arise out of that joint enterprise. However, if one person does something that goes beyond what was tacitly agreed as part of the joint enterprise, the other person will not be liable for the consequences of that further act.

Conspiracy

E.7   An agreement between two or more people for one or more of those persons to commit a criminal act is itself an offence contrary to the Criminal Law Act 1977, s 1. A person can be guilty of conspiracy even if the criminal act itself never takes place or is impossible. A party to the conspiracy does not have to intend to take part in the criminal act, but must intend to be a party to an agreement to do a criminal act.

Reasonableness

E.8   Where the court has to determine the question of reasonableness, for example in determining whether a person has a defence to an allegation under the POA 1986, s 5 (causing alarm, harassment or distress) then the question of what is reasonable must be assessed objectively in light of all the circumstances and take into consideration the defendant's rights under the European Convention on Human Rights.

Proportionality

E.9   Proportionality as a concept arises in the consideration of whether an individual's human rights, particularly those protected by the European Convention on Human Rights, Articles 8, 10 and 11 have been infringed. These rights are qualified, not absolute rights and can be interfered with as long as the interference is in accordance with the law and proportionate. Answering the question of what is proportionate involves a balancing exercise between competing rights and interests and will always depend on the circumstances of the case.

Precedent

E.10   Precedent is the common law principle that the decisions of higher courts will be binding on the lower courts. In England and Wales, the Supreme Court is the highest court, which binds the decisions of the Court of Appeal. Decisions of the Supreme Court and the Court of Appeal subsequently bind the decisions of all lower courts including the High Court, the Crown Court and the magistrates' court. Decisions of the High Court also bind the Crown Court and magistrates' court but do not hold as much weight as precedent as those of the Court of Appeal and Supreme Court. Decisions of the Crown Court do not bind the magistrates' court and do not form any sort of legal precedent. Only the decisions of the Supreme Court, the Court of Appeal and the High Court are usually reported in formal law reports.

Maximum sentence

E.11   The maximum sentence that can be imposed for any given offence is usually set out in the statute that creates the offence. If an offence can be dealt with either at the magistrates' court or the Crown Court then the maximum sentence will differ in each case, as the magistrates can only pass sentences of imprisonment of up to six months.

Sentencing guidelines

E.12   Sentencing guidelines come in a number of formats. The Sentencing Guidelines Council issues Guidelines in respect of certain offences, eg assault against the person, and these Guidelines should be the starting point for any sentencing judge or magistrates. The SGC also issues Magistrates' Court Sentencing Guidelines which set out starting points and sentencing ranges to assist magistrates in sentencing offenders for summary offences. Decisions of the Court of Appeal on appeals against sentence must also guide decisions of the lower courts.

Index

Index

Index